Political Map of the U S S R

ARCTIC OCEAN

NORWAY

SWEDEN

FINLAND

LITHUANIAN S S R

Tallinn

Riga

Leningrad

POLAND

Vilnius

LATVIAN S S R

ESTONIAN S S R

Minsk

WHITE RUSSIAN S S R

RUSSIAN SOVIET FEDER

Ob River

UKRAINIAN S S R

Kiev

Moscow

URAL MOUNTAINS

Kishinev

MOLDAVIAN S S R

Volga River

Tor

BLACK SEA

Omsk

Novosibirsk

GEORGIAN S S R

CASPIAN SEA

KAZAKH S S R

TURKEY

Tbilisi

Erevan

ARMENIAN S S R

AZERBAIDZHAN S S R

Baku

ARAL SEA

UZBEK S S R

Frunze

Alma Ata

IRAQ

TURKMEN S S R

Tashkent

KIRGHIZ S S R

Askhabad

Dushanbe

TADZHIK S S R

IRAN

AFGHANISTAN

INDIA

PERSIAN GULF

PAKISTAN

The Little, Brown Series

in Comparative Politics

Under the editorship of

GABRIEL A. ALMOND

JAMES S. COLEMAN

LUCIAN W. PYE

A COUNTRY STUDY

Politics in the
USSR

Frederick C. Barghoorn

Yale University

Boston
LITTLE, BROWN AND COMPANY

Published simultaneously in Canada
by Little, Brown & Company (Canada) Limited

PRINTED IN THE UNITED STATES OF AMERICA

Foreword

THE Little, Brown Series in Comparative Politics has three main objectives. First, it will meet the need of teachers to deal with both Western and non-Western countries in their introductory course offerings. Second, by following a common approach in analyzing individual political systems, it will make it possible for teachers to compare these countries systematically and cumulatively. And third, it will contribute toward re-establishing the classic relationship between comparative politics and political theory, a relationship which has been neglected in recent decades. In brief, the series seeks to be global in scope, genuinely introductory and comparative in character, and concerned with broadening and deepening our understanding of the nature and variety of political systems.

The series has two parts: the Country Studies and the Analytic Studies. The Country Studies deal with problems and processes deriving from a functional, as compared with a purely structural, approach to the study of political systems. We are gratified that the participants, all mature scholars with original insights, were willing to organize their discussions around a common set of functional topics in the interest of furthering comparisons. At the same time, each author has been urged to adapt the common framework to the special problems of the country he is discussing and to express his own theoretical point of view.

A forthcoming introductory book, *Comparative Politics: A Developmental Approach,* written by Gabriel A. Almond and G. Bingham Powell, provides an analytic supplement to the Country

Studies. It also opens our set of Analytic Studies, which will offer basic discussions of such topics as political change in the emerging nations, comparative analyses of interest groups, political social-ization, political communication, political culture, and the like. We hope these books will prove to be useful and stimulating sup-plements to the Country Studies as well as points of departure in more advanced courses.

Frederick Barghoorn's *Politics in the USSR,* the fourth volume in the Country Series, is a careful and penetrating analysis of one of the most important and problematic political systems of our time. It also represents the first full-length functional analysis of Soviet politics. Since he employs the same approach and analytical categories as those used in our other country studies, he takes a long step toward bringing Soviet political studies within the framework of comparative political analysis.

A number of significant themes not ordinarily treated in intro-ductory studies of Soviet politics are discussed here in detail. These include Soviet political culture and socialization, the form and content of interest group activity, and the policy-making process. Barghoorn's imaginative and prudent projection of the present and future of Soviet politics reflects the advantages of combining the knowledge of a lifetime spent in studying Russian history and Soviet society with the analytical insights and rigor of contemporary political sociology.

Gabriel A. Almond
James S. Coleman
Lucian W. Pye

Acknowledgments

BOOKS, it has been observed, are social as well as individual products. Partly for this reason it is difficult for any author to acknowledge adequately the help which he has received from other persons. I earnestly hope, nevertheless, that this volume appropriately reflects my debt to colleagues, friends, and in some cases casual acquaintances for information, insights, and impressions which helped to shape it. Many such persons are referred to in footnotes, but for reasons peculiar to this subject it is inappropriate to mention others to whom I owe appreciation and gratitude.

Certain individuals and institutions without whose encouragement and assistance this book would not have been what it is must be singled out. I am particularly grateful to Professor Gabriel A. Almond. Gabriel Almond is not only an innovative scholar and a cherished colleague but he has the rare gift of being able to share his insights generously and unobtrusively. If this study has achieved its purpose of approaching Soviet politics more from an inquiring than a polemical vantage point, much credit is due to Gabriel Almond.

I am also grateful to Lucian W. Pye and James S. Coleman for their part in creating the context in which this enterprise took shape. Although I began about 1959 to perceive the relevance to Soviet politics of the version of political culture and system analysis which I have sought to develop herein, my knowledge of and enthusiasm for these concepts was substantially reinforced by participation in the conference organized by the Social Science

Research Council Committee on Comparative Politics, under the leadership of Bryce Wood, along with Professors Almond, Pye, and Coleman, at the Center for Advanced Study of the Behavioral Sciences in Palo Alto, California in July, 1962.

I certainly could not have written this book without the precious freedom from routine pressures made available by sabbatical leave from Yale University in 1963–1964 and by a Ford Foundation Research Professorship in 1964–1965. I was also helped by a research grant from the American Philosophical Society in 1963–1964, for which I hereby express my appreciation. I should like also to declare my gratitude to my colleagues in political science and Russian studies at Yale University and to the many students at Yale, Columbia, and other universities who have stimulated my thinking in conversations and discussions. I enthusiastically thank all those at Yale and elsewhere who facilitated my work by their indispensable logistical support. In particular, I owe a special debt of gratitude to Miss Veronica O'Neill, secretary of the Yale Political Science Department, and to Mrs. Hazel O'Donnell, secretary of the Russian and East European Studies Council at Yale, both of whom, as in the past, rendered support far greater than I had a right to expect. I should like to express my deep appreciation to the editors at Little, Brown and Company, especially Donald R. Hammonds and David W. Lynch, whose cheerful expertise did so much to make the writing of this book less difficult and more delightful than it might otherwise have been. To Mr. Paul K. Cook I owe a very special acknowledgment for generosity with his time and for patient and expert assistance and guidance in identifying data. Among his many helpful acts was providing the organization charts of the Soviet Communist Party and government.

Frederick C. Barghoorn

Table of Contents

Politics in the
USSR

Introduction

POWER STRUGGLES AND IDEOLOGICAL DIFFERENCES among and within nations affect the prospects — indeed the survival possibilities — of us all in an era when both welfare potentials and destructive capabilities have increased to an almost incredible degree. In this context a detailed analysis of Soviet political structures and processes seems a useful undertaking. Among its possible contributions, such a study may help us to evaluate the Leninist belief that ours is an era of "proletarian" revolutions, inaugurated by the "great October revolution" of 1917, and destined to end only when Soviet-style "communism" has transformed the world.

In fact the political effects of the technological, social, and cultural revolutions of our era seem to have been profound and complex, varied and contradictory. Neither Marx nor Lenin proved fully successful as a political prophet. Stable, effective parliamentary democracies such as those of Britain or the United States successfully weathered the storms of change, although at times it appeared that their response to crisis was dangerously sluggish. Some fortunate countries have thus far demonstrated an ability to provide their citizens with more goods and services, more evenly distributed than before, and also with increasingly varied and exciting perspectives and opportunities. With this experience in mind it may seem that only pessimists can doubt that the growth of knowledge, skills, and productivity will over the long run benefit all men.

1

However, even potentially beneficial changes present difficult problems of adjustment. Where the pace of change outruns the capacity of governments and citizens for adaptation and response, revolutionary crises can develop. Of course such crises cannot mature, still less erupt, in the absence of certain preconditions, such as the alienation of a significant portion of the intellectual elite from the "establishment," economic crises, failure on the part of governments to resolve internal religious or ethnic conflicts, foreign policy fiascos, and the like. Perhaps the most crucial variable of all is the character, skill, and resolution of a country's political leadership during crises. Thus, in varied and in some ways unique circumstances nations surmount or succumb to the revolutionary challenges which confront them. There is of course also a wide range of attitudes among and within revolutionary movements and parties, reflecting differences of national political styles and of individual grievances and ambitions. To some of its members a revolutionary party may represent an instrumentality of human betterment — as well as a means of punishing those guilty of social injustice. To others, it can be a device for converting mass discontent into personal power for themselves.

The Russian bolsheviks long benefited from their claim to have replaced an exploitative, reactionary, obscurantist system by one dedicated to social justice, popular enlightenment, and the unrestricted application of science to human affairs. Ultimately, of course, the bolsheviks promised to free not only the peoples already under their control, but all of mankind, from poverty, ignorance, and the tyranny of restrictive customs and oppressive institutions.

It became apparent to Lenin soon after the bolshevik victory in Russia that the preservation of the revolutionary regime would require massive doses of coercion and the application, probably for a long period, of techniques of centralized administration and suppression of opposition. Lenin had long advocated and practiced such techniques as instruments of revolution, but he had talked and written as if he believed their relevance would diminish once his revolutionary party had taken power.

Lenin never shrank from coercion and guile, the use of which he justified by the doctrines and rules of "Marxism-Leninism" to which he was the principal contributor, for the avowed purpose of protecting the revolutionary regime against its enemies and for expanding its influence abroad. Lenin's practices reflected the Russian absolutist heritage from which he sprang, as well as his revolutionary passion and his keen appreciation of the potential power of modern techniques of organization and the manipulation of opinion.

To Lenin's objectives Stalin added that of making the Soviet Union so mighty an industrial and military power that it could serve as the all-powerful "base" of world revolution. The goal of universal social revolution was not abandoned. Judged by actions and policy commitments, it was transformed from the original Marxist vision of full and unfettered individual freedom to a systematic maximization of the party and state leadership's power over rank and file party members and, through the all-penetrating party organization, over the Soviet citizenry as a whole.

Perhaps even Stalin retained some faith in the possibility that the utopian, idealistic aspects of the bolshevik creed would one day be realized. However, his political practices, both domestic and foreign, were saturated with cynical expediency. Bolshevik veterans like Nikolai Bukharin, who continued to believe, even into the terrible early years of Stalin's ascendancy over the party machine, that Soviet policy should be guided by Marxist ideals, were made to confess in rigged trials to monstrous crimes against the revolution.

Marxism, as interpreted in Moscow, was converted from a set of revolutionary theories and convictions into the official creed of a powerful, autocratically governed state and its international network of propaganda, proselytizing, and espionage organizations. However, many naive and sincere people throughout the world continued to attribute to the Soviet Union the characteristics they regarded as appropriate to a professedly socialist society. Stalin encouraged such sentiments, especially during the years before World War II when he was skilfully mobilizing domestic and foreign opinion in order to exploit as best he could complex international power rivalries. In particular, he was able to win much support by associating the USSR with the defense of democracy and the freedom of nations against the threat of fascist enslavement.

It became especially clear after the war that Stalin's conception of internationalism involved subordinating as many nations as possible to Moscow's influence and imposing upon these nations Soviet economic, political, and cultural patterns.

On the basis of official Soviet statements and doctrines, it must be assumed that the Kremlin's over-all objective remains a world in which the Soviet political, social, and cultural models will be universally adopted. However, many factors in the contemporary international arena make it seem more unlikely than ever that this objective could be realized in any future which can now be envisaged. Indeed, it now seems not too wildly optimistic to hope that eventually the Soviet Union may be brought into a relationship with the major Western powers, if not of intimacy or alliance, at least of fruitful cooperation on many issues. Among the factors which might slowly bring such a relationship into being are the strategic implications of nuclear weapons, creating a balance of terror between the West and Russia, and thus providing both sides with time to build bridges of mutual understanding. Very important also are the modest and gradual improvements in the Soviet standard of living which have already been achieved and to the further development of which the present Soviet leaders seem dedicated, and their diminished reliance on coercion as an instrument of social control. These and other positive internal developments are conducive to greater Soviet ability to respond affirmatively to whatever overtures may emanate from the West regarding the settlement by peaceful means of disputed issues and the expansion of at least limited cooperation in cultural, educational, scientific, or other spheres. Contemplating such possibilities — and guarding against wishful thinking — the analyst may envisage the possibility that Russia may cease, perhaps sooner than now seems likely, to be a "cause" and may then become a country, like other members of the international community.

Today, it seems increasingly clear that the communists of China are determined to achieve not mere equality with the Soviet Union but supremacy, both in a world revolutionary movement in which they presently denounce Moscow's strategy as a continuation of Khrushchev's "revisionism," and on the world political stage. The study of Soviet politics takes on new interest. In time, Chinese and Russian attitudes toward both domestic and foreign policies might become so thoroughly incompatible that the Kremlin might feel compelled to turn to the

West for support against a militant and mighty China. We should not, of course, underestimate the psychological difficulties such a strategic reorientation poses for a Soviet power elite brought up to believe that Russian communism is destined to inherit world power. However, Sino-Soviet rivalry, whatever its ultimate issue may be, forces us to recognize the importance of the most careful study not only of the elements common to the different varieties of communism but of the deep and complex differences which divide the various communist regimes and parties.

From the point of view of noncommunist diversity within consensus, all forms of contemporary communist rule are frighteningly oppressive. Only a careful study of the structures and processes by which such systems perform the vital functions of politics and government can reveal the degree in which they have been able to attain their professed goals of reducing coercion and realizing maximum individual freedom of choice. It is clear, however, that the gulf between ideals and realities is vast. Why, after almost half of a century of communist rule, does Soviet Russia still employ such techniques of administrative control as the internal passport system, bitterly denounced by Lenin as a reactionary instrument of tsarist oppression?

Significant aspects of the Russian cultural heritage and of both the domestic and international environments in which the Soviet leaders have performed must be considered in attempting to answer such questions. The traditional Russian political culture was permeated with authoritarianism. Habits of give-and-take bargaining, tolerance, and relativistic skepticism painfully developed in centuries of Western experience had struck only shallow roots in Russia. Those who valued such practices and attitudes were not welcomed either by the tsarist bureaucracy or by its more militant opponents, especially Lenin's bolsheviks.

The bolsheviks, because of their hostility to "bourgeois" Western values, were in a poor position to learn, from the European and American patterns to which exile exposed Lenin, Trotski, Bukharin, and others, the traits which might have mitigated the absolutist, intolerant, and maximalist political culture which had so heavily influenced their thinking — even though they were dedicated to replacing it with a "democratic" socialist blueprint.

Moreover, and this point is perhaps crucial, the revolutionary leaders, being in a tiny minority in a vast, poor, hungry, back-ward, and politically immature country, were forced increasingly to present their policies in terms and images understandable to their subjects. Much of Stalin's apparent cynicism in assuming a role resembling that of Ivan the Terrible may be understood, though not necessarily condoned, as an effort to evoke the deep-est, most stirring historical memories of the Russian people. These memories favored a stern, harsh, astute ruler — provided he would safeguard state security.

The Russian revolutionary experience, like that of other countries, points not only to the possibility of rapid and drastic change but to the likelihood of stubborn persistence of deeply rooted ways of thought and action. Indeed, it reinforces the lesson that the excessive speed of attempted social change in a "revolution from above" may actually reinforce attitudes carried over from the past, to the elimination of which the revolutionary leaders apparently had been sincerely committed.

One might fall victim to an excessively pessimistic attitude toward the Soviet experience, however, if one failed to take into account the exceptionally unfavorable relationship which long prevailed between Soviet Russia and its non-Soviet external environment. In large part, of course, this relationship was the fault of the bolsheviks themselves, for they openly proclaimed their intention of subverting and destroying the noncommunist social order as quickly as possible. Kremlin expectations, in turn, were in part shaped by the defectiveness of Soviet information and analysis regarding the cohesion and stability of the Western industrial societies and particularly by their fatuous belief in the inevitability of "proletarian" uprisings in advanced industrial countries. The pattern of ideological orthodoxy of which such fallacies were a part is not yet dead. It still exerts a distorting effect on Soviet thinking, although it is now far less pernicious than it was in the 1920's and 1930's. It has always tended to spur Moscow to actions which could not fail to exacerbate its relations with countries desirous, on balance, of establishing normal economic and political relations with the USSR. Such a generalization about Western intentions is broad, of course; but with respect to the United States since 1933 and to the Western world generally since 1941 it seems to this writer to be un-doubtedly correct.

Faced by Western hostility, partly imagined and partly real, Moscow felt constrained to give the highest possible priority to strengthening its economic-military potential. The forced-draft industrialization and military preparation which logically resulted imposed grievous hardships on the population, especially the peasants, who during the 1920's had benefited from the revolution, since they had received most of the land seized by the bolsheviks from the tsar, the church, and the landlords. All classes and indeed all individuals, however, suffered the consequences of "socialism in one country." Those who suffered the most — but who in some ways benefited the most, too — were the backward non-Russian peoples of Turkic origin inhabiting such areas as Central Asia.

The draconian penalties, pressures, and threats by which Stalin whipped Russia toward greatness aroused bitter resentment. Soviet political doctrines were shaped accordingly. Stalin proclaimed the "Marxist" doctrine that the resistance of the "remnants" of the "exploiting" classes to the new social order became more frantic as their power decreased, and the equally remarkable proposition that Soviet Russia could become a "communist" society even if it retained a powerful, coercive police organization. The dread dictator's rationalizations of his totalitarian rule reflected the internal and external war which he regarded as normal under conditions of Soviet "encirclement" by the "imperialist" powers.

To win the support of party and police officials, factory managers, engineers, and other professionals for Soviet military-industrial development, Stalin instituted a policy of differentiated rewards for quality and quantity of services performed by citizens to the state. He thus laid the foundations of the Soviet social order denounced by Trotski and later and more fundamentally by the idealistic Yugoslav communist heretic Milovan Djilas.

The relaxation of terror and of pressure on the Soviet citizenry by Stalin's successors is a positive development and also a hopeful sign for possible future modifications, more fundamental than any which have as yet been effected. Such measures as increasing evocation of the "principle of material interest," as an incentive to improved labor performance, indicate that the Soviet leadership is capable of rational adaptation to changing circumstances and emerging challenges. Perhaps more fundamentally these adaptations, more humane than the policies and practices of Stalin — on the foundations of which, however, many of them are based — suggest the fallacies and basic defects of the utopian attempt of the bolsheviks to build the perfect society and create the perfect man. Historical experience and the findings of social science indicate that improvements in human relations and in the quality of life desired by men of good will are made possible, if they can be attained at all, only by patient experiment, trial and error, and by careful correction of previous mistakes, in a milieu of free, unfettered inquiry and discussion.

Is there any hope that the Soviet rulers will move toward the vision of the free society implicit in the foregoing? The record to date presents both discouraging and encouraging evidence. The Soviet "experiment," as the Russian pattern used to be called only a few years ago, has to its credit fundamental achievements in education, economic development, and scientific growth. These are indispensable prerequisites for social welfare. In some aspects of community policy, such as public health services and medical care for the citizenry, the Soviet record, considering the difficulties which had to be overcome before the present level could be achieved, is brilliant. The social welfare aspect of Soviet policy is, of course, regarded by Moscow as perhaps its most potent instrument of competition with the West for the good will, support, and eventual transformation of the less-developed lands, as underscored again in Prime Minister Kosygin's address on the occasion of the graduation of the first class of 228 students from the Patrice Lumumba Friendship University in June, 1965.

However, the rise of Soviet levels of welfare does more than attract foreign support. It also spurs the aspirations of Soviet citizens for further improvement in the quantity and quality of goods and services available to them, and for incentives and organizational forms capable of contributing thereto. Perhaps the dominant theme of Soviet politics in the year following the expulsion of Nikita Khrushchev was the search for ways of satisfying the needs of Soviet citizens for increased welfare and well being, without weakening the political system.

The West cannot realistically expect an early or easy end to its present fiercely competitive relationship with the USSR. Even in the unlikely event of the overthrow of the present system, dominated as it is by the oligarchy of the party apparatus, and its replacement by a military dictatorship, the West would in all probability still be confronted by a highly competitive, intensely nationalistic, and in many ways antagonistic Russian regime. Decades may be required before genuine — as distinguished from merely tactical — coexistence can be established between Moscow and the West. The capacity of the Soviet system to preserve its essential features while adapting to internal and external pressures has been proven by decades of experience. Still, the time may come when adaptation will pave the way to fundamental changes. As the generations of Russians with personal knowledge of the searing experiences which shaped and reinforced the bolshevik outlook pass from the scene, Leninism could lose its grip on Soviet political thinking.

The pull of the past is strong, though, and we should not expect rapid progress toward freedom (as we understand it) in Russia. The Twenty-third Congress of the CPSU, in fact, furnished evidence that Khrushchev's successors were determined to slow, even to reverse, Khrushchevian experimentation and improvisation, replacing them with a rededication to Leninist, even Stalinist orthodoxy. This conservative, if not regressive mood was made evident by Brezhnev's proposal (which was accepted) that the top party decision-making body be renamed "politburo," instead of the designation "presidium" that had been adopted in 1952. Another symptom of a flight to the past was the harsh criticism directed by congress speakers at new ideas in art and literature, whose principal champions, such as Alexander Tvardovski, lost the representation they had enjoyed in previous post-Stalin party congresses. It appeared that for the time being Russia's leaders did not feel secure and prosperous enough to encourage further indulgence in the luxury, dangerous for their kind of polity, of aspirations toward freedom, non-Marxist style. The proceedings and results of this first post-Khrushchev congress are discussed in more detail in the Postscript following Chapter X.

Doubtless the Soviet leadership could oscillate uneasily in the future between a flexibility which might pave the way to disintegration, and a rigidity which might threaten stagnation. The Kremlin's dilemmas are cruel and they will not become easier in the future. The Soviet ruling collective derives much of its legitimacy from a design for revolution which is of steadily diminishing relevance for an increasingly conservative Soviet society. The main instrument of Kremlin rule is a party apparatus already hard put to coordinate and control the efforts of the increasingly differentiated and sophisticated managerial-professional elements under its supervision. Moreover, as the USSR becomes ever more involved in a variety of cultural, scientific, and other relationships with "bourgeois" societies, control of access to information and the shaping of Soviet citizens' attitudes thereto becomes a more and more complex task. It becomes increasingly tempting to predict for Soviet citizens early and rapid movement toward freedom of choice in every sphere of social activity.

However, we must keep in mind not only the forces making for liberating change, but those fostering rigidity. The grip of tradition and the inertia of bureaucracy cannot be easily overcome. The proponents of orthodoxy are still dominant in Soviet educational institutions and in the communication media. The citizenry at all levels and ages is still dominated, for the most part, by beliefs and attitudes of fear and aversion toward Western "capitalism," about which Russians are abysmally ignorant. The weight of the past, both tsarist and Stalinist, hangs heavy over the Russia of today. Today's Soviet citizens are ruled, to a disturbing degree, by terrifying historical memories, which to the detached observer seem irrelevant, but which to the dedicated Soviet communist have the force of sacred dogma. Such memories and images, manipulated by party leaders, serve as weapons of political struggle, as props of the Soviet regime, and as impediments to critical thought.

Believers in modern Western welfare democracy must regret that the pattern of development chosen by modern Russia has been so distinctively coercive. They can, however, scarcely fail to be impressed by the energy and discipline generated by the Soviet experience and by the formidable challenges the Soviet system poses for the future world position of the relatively complacent, pluralistic societies of Western Europe and North America. One can, nevertheless, not unreasonably hope that the extremely coercive phase of the Russian transformation to industrial and scientific modernity is now beginning to end. Stalin may well have been a terrible, despotic, but unique ruler.

In assessing the possibilities for a less tense and strained, a more fruitful and mutually satisfactory Soviet-Western relationship, we cannot afford to be ignorant of the habits and perspectives inbred by centuries of backwardness, isolation, and despotism, or of the relatively brief but enormously intense period of pressures imposed by Soviet communism. The partial relaxation since Stalin, and the hypothesis that there may be further relaxation as internal and international tensions and instabilities diminish — if indeed they can be made to do so by sound policies in both Russia and the West — furnish some basis for projecting a less stormy future. It is to be hoped that this study, by describing and analyzing the perspectives, structures, and practices which drive and sustain the present-day Soviet pattern of organized, tightly coordinated power, may contribute to an informed, prudent, and yet not altogether unsympathetic understanding of a system which deals, often in ways repugnant to us, with the fundamental issues and problems by which all polities are beset.

CHAPTER I

The Dominant Political Culture

THE STYLE AND SUBSTANCE of Soviet political culture reflect its origins in a revolutionary movement and its development by a self-selected elite committed to achieving the titanic ambitions involved in transforming man and society, first in Russia and then throughout the world.

This is a political culture outwardly consistent but seething with hidden contradictions. It is rank-conscious but claims to be egalitarian. It practices coercion but promises the freedom symbolized by the Marxist premise that the state, under full communism, will wither away. It is oppressively orthodox and conformist but capable of great resourcefulness and adaptiveness. It is in many ways parochial and isolationist, yet it aspires to universality of application. Its fear of "alien" influences inspires an urge to control the world whence these disturbing forces spring.

STYLE OF MOBILIZATION

Despite its many tensions and contradictions, however, the political culture created by the elite, or "apparatus" of the ruling CPSU (Communist Party of the Soviet Union) possesses over-all coherence and formidable capabilities. Although it was imposed by force and coercion, it has adapted itself in many ways to the traditions of the peoples now reared in its values. It has enormous capacity for mobilization, derived from tight concentration of power in relatively few hands. Its capabilities for coordination and control are vast, because of the penetration of society by the polity. Perhaps most significant and characteristic of this hierarchic system of interlocking committees is the largely successful attempt of its leaders to monopolize the political functions of interest articulation and aggregation, of elite recruitment and political socialization, and the other dynamics of politics, leaving, insofar as possible, only the details of administration to carefully supervised party functionaries and state officials.

The party elite uses the official ideology of Marxism-Leninism to rationalize its monopoly of leadership roles. It seeks vigorously to inculcate homogeneity of beliefs, perspectives, and symbols among the citizenry and it asserts, with a nagging frequency that inspires skepticism, that "moral unity" has been achieved in the USSR.

The official ideology and the manner of its dissemination teach us much about Soviet political culture. Its pretension to universality reflects the enormous ambition and power drive of the CPSU leadership. The authority to interpret its major tenets is vested solely in the supreme political leadership, reflecting that concentration of authority to perform the most important political functions which is characteristic of this polity as well as its concomitant of an exceptionally high degree of penetration of society by the political system.

Nevertheless, the official ideology does not give a fully accurate picture of the political culture. Despite Khrushchev's efforts to revive the "Leninist style," Soviet Marxism bears the stamp of its transformation, by Lenin himself and especially by Stalin, from a body of revolutionary principles, openly debated in leadership circles at least, into an increasingly ritualistic system of dogmas manipulated by the elite to justify its powers and privileges. As such it only partially embodies the realities of political practice, which are obscured by a curtain of verbiage and by myriad devices of censorship and distortion. The tortuous techniques of Soviet secrecy are weapons of international political combat, as representatives of foreign governments have learned. They are also instruments of internal political control which hide the contradictions between promise and performance, ideals and realities, of political behavior. As a rule, Soviet sources successfully conceal the realities of the struggle for power raging in elite circles. Most of the hidden tensions of Soviet politics are the product of stresses and strains generated by the coercive planned modernization of a backward society. Although the manipulative and coercive operations involved in this kind of social change are abhorrent to those reared in the "civic cultures" of more fortunate lands, the process, it must be recognized, has generated not only disillusionment and deprivation but also a great deal of idealism, satisfaction, and pride.

Before we examine in detail the Soviet design for mankind's future, we must realize that, despite the frightening determination of its adherents to make it prevail, this elite political culture has not yet achieved the degree of support or even of acceptance desired by them. As we shall seek to demonstrate in Chapter II, the political culture of the USSR, despite the extreme centralization of the Russian political system, is not completely uniform. There are, even in this self-proclaimed "monolithic" polity, pluralistic tendencies, nurtured both by stubborn survivals of tradition and by the emergent differentiations of a developing industrial economy.

The dominant pattern might well be described as a participatory-subject culture. Ordinary citizens must be obedient to their rulers' demands and must also display both enthusiasm and initiative in complying with their leaders' instructions.

However, Khrushchev, and more especially his successors, perceived the harmful effects of "command" methods of leadership and administration. The post-Khrushchev leadership, to judge by a steady stream of articles in the press, sought to fashion a responsive, persuasive, support-inducing administrative style. Executives at all levels were urged to be attentive to the views and considerate of the dignity of colleagues and subordinates. Higher executives, in particular, were exhorted to pay heed to the opinions of the trained experts whose best efforts were needed to solve the economic problems facing the country, above all the thorny problem of agriculture. Local governments, especially in rural districts, and collective farm administrations were instructed to put an end to situations in which simple, necessary goods, such as spades, were not available in country stores, and farm widows' requests for needed housing repairs were denied because of lack of transport and materials.

More attention was being paid to letters of complaint addressed by citizens to newspapers. From these and other indications it appeared that both the responsiveness of the authorities and the demands of the citizenry were growing more active. It was still true that, for the most part, nonelite aspirations were translated, so to speak, and processed to conform to party criteria and requirements. One heard of them, as a rule, in statements tailored to fit the official propaganda line. Still, a few first steps had been taken to loosen and to melt the rigid, participatory-subject pattern which had so long prevailed.

Of course, the traditionally hypertrophied subject role of the Soviet citizen never legitimized passivity. On the contrary, the "masses" — and also all the party-guided, "voluntary" organizations in one or more of which almost all citizens are enrolled— have always been mobilized for active and continuous participation in political activity. The citizenry is swept up in successive "campaigns" to achieve whatever goals currently have priority. In this participatory-subject pattern, the party is incessantly acclaimed in official agitation and propaganda as the most "conscious" element, the "vanguard," and the "heart and brain" of society. The party demands that Soviet citizens display initiative and enthusiasm in the fulfilment of the tasks which it prescribes. It mobilizes them by means of directives and slogans, propaganda drives, demonstrations and pageantry; the image conveyed is one of an endless, victorious — though admittedly sometimes interrupted — onward and upward movement.

However, to a degree impossible to determine without field studies of a kind not permitted by the Kremlin, enforced participation is self-defeating. Frequent press criticism reveals that evasion or, more frequently, perfunctory compliance even by so-called activists, characterizes citizen responses to party prodding. Frequently, according to official accounts, only the overworked executives of party committees have a meaningful part in the activity of the "collective."

The leadership of the CPSU continues to assert, as it always has, that its goals are shared by all of "progressive mankind." The Soviet communists of today are the heirs to a successful revolutionary movement, who aspire to become the rulers of a world society and the shapers of a world culture.[1] In their efforts to realize this prophecy the Russian communists proclaim their identification with the teachings of Marx, Engels, and Lenin, and

[1] For massive documentation of this thesis see Elliot R. Goodman, *The Soviet Design for a World State* (New York, 1960).

also with whatever they regard as good and useful in the whole cultural heritage of mankind. They thus link their movement and policies with a vast range of aspirations and sentiments, choosing in any given phase of their activity the social, national, and cultural symbols they regard as appropriate for achieving their objectives.

However, in this broad and shifting stream of identifications and moods, certain patterns stand out. Persistent and conspicuous is the effort of the CPSU leadership to make certain that all communication within and from the USSR is consistent with its current policy. Soviet semantics presents a sharply patterned "two-value" orientation: everything identified with the party (by its leadership) is represented as virtuous, noble, progressive, and invincible, and all else is regarded as trivial, defective, transitory, or even as absolutely evil. Sometimes the party's pretension to infallibility involves its communicators in inconsistency, but this difficulty is dealt with by invoking authority, frequently in the form of a quotation from the writings of Lenin. Patriotism and pride in the cultural, scientific, and military achievements and traditions of prebolshevik Russia, once spurned by the Soviet leaders as "reactionary" and "bourgeois," have become significant aspects of Soviet ideology, but only in the form and usage prescribed by a Stalin, a Khrushchev, a Brezhnev-headed leadership, and who knows by whom in the future?

Similarly, the official image of Stalin, acclaimed until his death on March 5, 1953, as the great continuator of the work of Lenin and as the "genius of mankind," after Khrushchev's "secret" speech in 1956 was tarnished by association with the crimes committed during the period of the "cult of the personality of J. V. Stalin." After Khrushchev's removal, his very different "cult of personality" was criticized, but he was not mentioned by name, and indeed he became an unperson or, one might say, a quasi-person.

This is a pattern of prescribed, and in many ways, contrived identifications, and, to a striking degree, of loyalty by command. The Soviet communists, and indeed all attentive citizens, as well as men beyond the borders of the USSR who obey the discipline of Moscow-affiliated political movements, usually know whom they are expected to love and whom they are required to despise. The authoritative perspectives which we describe are known in Soviet political terminology as the "general line" of the party. Though it changes from time to time, it possesses in any given period the authority conferred by the power of those who proclaim it and an aura of sacredness, indeed almost of magic, derived from invocation of the name of V. I. Lenin and from an elaborate pattern of political rituals and ceremonials, such as those connected with the annual May Day and November 6 observances. It is often pointed out, with much justification, that communism is a kind of secular religion. It is well to keep in mind this pseudoreligious, pseudomystical aspect of what in Soviet terminology is designated as "ideology" or as "theory." It claims to constitute, in the hands of its trained and officially certified exponents, the sole reliable key to the "laws of social development," which ordain, so the ideology proclaims, the inevitable triumph of communism on a world scale.

A corollary of the semisacrosanct character of the Soviet political *mystique* is its intolerance of "deviations" from the "correct" ideological line. During the period of Stalin's rule the tendency, sometimes attaining almost hysterical intensity, to regard such "deviations" as threats to the Soviet "people," even, at times, as reflections of the sinister influence of the international bourgeoisie upon weak-willed Soviet citizens, was paralleled in the realm of political action by a virtual prohibition of all forms of political opposition.

Although these features of Soviet political behavior, since the death of Stalin, have assumed more moderate and "rational" forms, they still serve to reinforce the claims of the party leaders to the exercise of legitimate power, and also to inhibit freedom of intellectual inquiry and of artistic and even of personal aesthetic and emotional expression. If, unlike the Stalin regime, that of his successors has not usually imprisoned — or murdered — opponents, or imprisoned, exiled, or killed dissenting artists and scientists, its pretensions to infallibility too closely resemble those of Stalin's era to offer grounds for complacency about the future of personal security and opportunity for freedom of choice by Soviet citizens.

It is easy for noncommunists to perceive contradictions between the professed goals of the Soviet leaders and many of the means they employ in pursuit of these goals. However, one cannot simply dismiss as hypocritical demagogy or meaningless ritual phraseology the utopian side of Soviet communism. To the extent that they can convince themselves that their lives are dedicated to the ultimate creation of a world community of prosperity, justice, and happiness, communists can achieve a sense of purpose which facilitates effective leadership and the acceptance of leadership by those who must obey its commands. This sense of dedication is fostered by memories of past revolutionary victories. Soviet leaders have always devoted much attention to producing and disseminating documents elaborating their ultimate goals and proclaiming the uniqueness and superiority of their policies. The most elaborate, authoritative blueprints of the desired future, with numerous references also to the heroic past, appear in the official party programs, which were adopted, respectively, in 1903, 1919, and 1961. The 1903 program was a platform for making a revolution in Russia. The 1919 program looked toward the worldwide extension of the revolution successfully carried out in Russia by Lenin's party in 1917. It reflected the tensions and crises of the struggle for survival in which the bolsheviks were then engaged, but it also exuded optimism about the early achievement of world communism.

BLUEPRINT FOR THE FUTURE

The current party program, adopted by the Twenty-second CPSU Congress, is a much more realistic and even conservative document than that of 1919, being principally concerned with the means by which today's Soviet citizens within the foreseeable future may achieve a reasonable degree of material prosperity. It also professes confidence about the ultimate realization of the glorious vision of the classless society.[2] The party program, in its introduction, reiterates the intention of the CPSU to build a communist society, with the motto "From each according to his ability, to each according to his needs." [3] It asserts that the party proceeds according to the principle, "Everything in the name of man, for the benefit of man." It also asserts that the Soviet Union is already living under a system of socialism, first of the two stages

---

[2] The 1919 and 1961 party programs, as well as the 1952 and 1961 versions of the CPSU rules, are available in an excellent English translation, *Soviet Communism: Programs and Rules,* edited, with commentary, by Jan F. Triska (San Francisco, 1962).

[3] *Ibid.,* p. 25.

of development of the communist society. The principle of distribution under socialism is defined, according to Soviet tradition based upon a statement by Marx in his *Critique of the Gotha Program*, as "From each according to his abilities, to each according to his work." [4] Thus, prior to the attainment of the communist utopia, the distribution of rewards is to continue to be governed by what Khrushchev, and his successors too, have frequently referred to as the "principle of material interest." Also, Part II, section I, of the program declares that "the main economic task of the Party and the Soviet people is to create the material and technical basis of communism within two decades." [5] The program reflects a combination of practicality and of realization that achievement of the party's goals will require many years of hard work, implying that hard work and sacrifice are justifiable under Soviet conditions because they serve lofty purposes. The 1961 program expressed confidence that the "high road to socialism," along which, it stated, many peoples were already marching, would be taken "sooner or later by all peoples." [6] It heavily emphasized the pioneer role of Russia in blazing the path to revolution and the value of Soviet experience as a guide to the making and consolidation of socialist revolutions throughout the world. In numerous passages it reiterated the continued dedication of the CPSU to the worldwide overthrow of "capitalism."

The current program, though it emphasizes the devotion of the USSR to "peaceful co-existence," also asserts that the CPSU "considers it necessary to maintain the defensive power of the Soviet state and the combat preparedness of its armed forces at a level ensuring the decisive and complete defeat of any enemy who dares to encroach upon the Soviet Union." This military emphasis is justified by the doctrine that "as long as imperialism exists the threat of aggressive wars will remain." [7] Thus, the present party program remains within the "two-world" framework from which the Kremlin has traditionally viewed international relations. The party statutes adopted in 1961 contained a new section requiring that all party members "assist in the strengthening of the de-

[4] *Ibid.*, p. 32.
[5] *Ibid.*, p. 71.
[6] *Ibid.*, p. 35.
[7] *Ibid.*, pp. 105–109.

fensive might of the USSR in order that the USSR may lead the tireless struggle for peace and friendship among nations." [8]

One of the functions performed in Soviet society by the utopian vision described earlier is that of justifying a broad range of stern demands by the CPSU and the Soviet state upon the citizenry. The urgency, intensity, and comprehensiveness of these demands shape the style of Soviet politics. This style is innocent of the matter-of-fact descriptiveness and the customary separation of "fact" and "opinion" in at least the elite media of communication in the English-speaking countries, for example. Statements of "fact" and appeals for support in this mode of political discourse tend to take the form of commands. Characteristic of this pattern is the communist predilection for slogans. Such a political style is appropriate to a system in which, to an exceptional degree, the performance of political functions, such as the articulation of group and national interests and their aggregation into public policies, is the prerogative of a relatively small, self-selected elite.

The prior and central demand with which the Soviet citizen must comply, whether he is a member of the ruling CPSU or not, is enthusiastic and conscientious obedience to and support for the policy of the party leadership. The centrality of the doctrine of the party's leadership over society was not diminished following the death of Stalin. Indeed, it was reinforced, reflecting the replacement of Stalin's terroristic autocracy (symbolized by the dictator's retrospective glorification of Ivan the Terrible), by a new pattern of decision making and administration. In the new style, persuasion and guided but sometimes lively discussion and debate replaced the practice and threat of physical violence as an incentive to compliance with the commands of authority.

The statutes of the CPSU assert that the party is "the highest form of socio-political organization and is the leading and guiding force of Soviet society." They add that the party "directs the great creative activity of the Soviet people, and imparts an organized, planned, and scientifically-based character to their struggle to achieve the ultimate goal, the victory of communism." [9] The guiding and directing role of the party is also referred to in the

8 *Ibid.*, p. 159
9 *Ibid.*, p. 155.

constitution, or "fundamental law" of the USSR. Article 126 of the constitution characterizes the party as "the vanguard of the working people" and as "the leading core of all organizations of the working people, both public and state." Article 141 includes the CPSU in its list of the "public organizations" which nominate candidates for election.[10]

Many important speeches and articles in recent years have emphasized the view that as the complexity of Soviet society increases, particularly in the economic and cultural spheres, the CPSU, as the one force capable of channeling all social forces in accordance with the interests of society as a whole, must grow ever stronger.[11] Nowhere in any of these speeches and articles or in the 1961 party program is there any indication that the party will ever "wither away." From this and from many post-Khrushchev statements as well, it is clear that the communist leadership envisages the continuation far into the future of its policy initiating, coordinating, and controlling functions in Soviet society. Another traditional role of party executives, more than ever emphasized since Khrushchev's removal, is that of political-ideological training of their subordinates in party, state, and "cultural" organizations.

Although the party demands participation by both elite and masses in the fulfilment of party-assigned tasks, it usually prevents the articulation by either party members or ordinary Soviet citizens of unauthorized or otherwise inappropriate opinions or claims. The Lenin-Stalin doctrine of "democratic centralism" remains the basis of the CPSU's image of the proper relationship between leaders and led. This doctrine prescribes:

(A) election of all leading party bodies, from the lowest to the highest;

(B) periodic reports of party bodies to their party organizations and to higher bodies;

(C) strict party discipline and subordination of the minority to the majority;

10 The constitution referred to is translated in John N. Hazard, *The Soviet System of Government,* rev. ed. (Chicago, 1960), pp. 227, 229.

11 See, for example, Frol Romanovich Kozlov, in his speech entitled "Ob izmeneniyakh v ustave kommunisticheskoi partii sovetskogo soyuza," in *Materialy XXII sezda KPSS* (Moscow, 1962), pp. 266–96. See esp. pp. 267–68. See also E. I. Bugaev and B. M. Leibzon, *Besedyob ustave KPSS* (Moscow, 1964), p. 61.

(D) that the decisions of higher bodies are obligatory for lower bodies.[12]

Principles of organization such as these constitute a design for dictatorship and legitimize domination by the apparatus over the rank and file party membership. It is not surprising that the doctrine of "democratic centralism" has frequently been invoked to justify suppression of views regarded by the party leadership as "alien" to the principles of Marxism-Leninism. On the other hand, when suppression of criticism is employed by provincial officials to block implementation of Moscow directives, it is sharply attacked by *Pravda, Izvestiya,* and other central press organs.

THE DEMAND FOR OBEDIENCE

In particular, the doctrine of democratic centralism is employed to rationalize Lenin's demand, echoed by all his successors, that no "fractions" or "factions" should be permitted to conduct any kind of opposition activity against the policies and the authority of the party leadership. Acquaintance with Soviet attitudes toward opposition is so essential to comprehending the Soviet political process that a brief sketch of the development of these attitudes may be useful. Lenin's intolerance toward opposition or even of differences of opinion within his "bolshevik" faction of the Russian Social Democratic Labor Party can be traced at least as far back as his fundamental organizational treatise, *What Is to Be Done?* On the title page of this work Lenin quoted from a letter written by the German socialist Lassalle to Marx in which the former asserted that "a party becomes stronger by purging itself." Lenin went on to a furious attack on "revisionism," prefaced by scornful remarks on the dangers of "hypocritical" demands within the Russian Social Democratic movement for "freedom of criticism." [13] In 1921, intolerance toward political opposition acquired, in effect, the force of law. In that year, the Tenth Congress of the Communist Party adopted a crucial resolution entitled "Concerning the Unity of the Party." [14] This resolution forbade activity within the party by

[12] Triska, *op. cit.,* pp. 168–69.
[13] V. I. Lenin, *Polnoe sobranie sochinenii,* 5th ed., Vol. VI (Moscow, 1959), pp. 1–28.
[14] Until the Nineteenth Party Congress, in 1952, the party was officially designated as All-Union Communist Party (of bolsheviks), which was ab-

"factions," having "special platforms" and their own "group discipline." In a secret final section, not published until 1924, the resolution empowered the central committee of the party to take measures, including expulsion from the party, against those who engaged in such activity.[15] At the same time this resolution, which subsequently was often invoked against opposition groups within the party, promised that the party would exert every effort toward the "broadening of democratic principles and initiative." This resolution set a precedent for associating "democracy" with demands for conformity to leadership policies. Later, Stalin and Khrushchev, and those who ousted Khrushchev, also were to talk of democracy and of "collective leadership" in justifying their authority within the party.

At the Fifteenth Party Congress in 1927 Stalin asserted that "our Central Committee and Control Commission . . . are one of the most democratic and collectively functioning centers that our party has ever had." [16] This statement was made six weeks after a speech entitled "The Trotski Opposition Now and Then," in which Stalin reminded his opponents that Lenin had said at the Tenth Congress that the party could not tolerate further opposition — that it was time, in fact, to "put the lid" on opposition. Ten days earlier, Stalin had referred to the "anti-party game" of his critics.[17] Also typical of the way in which the 1921 unity resolution was applied during the Stalin era was the accusation in a Soviet encyclopedia article published in 1930 that Trotski, Kamenev, Zinovev, Bukharin, Rykov, and others who opposed Stalin had erred because they had not been guided by the resolution. This article implied, characteristically, that "opposition" within the party reflected the class interests of antiproletarian elements.[18] In equating opposition within the party to treason, Stalin's editors were carrying a step further a formula which Lenin had already applied in 1921 when the Soviet leadership denounced the uprising of formerly loyal sailors at the naval

---

breviated as VKP (b). Since the 1952 congress the party has been known as the Communist Party of the Soviet Union.

[15] The text of the resolution is contained in *KPSS v rezolyutsiyakh i resheniyakh sezdov, konferentsii i plenumov ts. k.*, 7th ed., Part I (Moscow, 1953), pp. 527–30.

[16] I. Stalin, *Sochineniya*, Vol. 10 (Moscow, 1949), p. 328.

[17] *Ibid.*, pp. 181–82, 263.

[18] *Malaya sovetskaya entsiklopediya*, 1st ed., Vol. VI (Moscow, 1930), cols. 97–100.

base of Kronstadt, near Leningrad, as a result of the instigation of foreign intelligence services. During and after the great purges of 1936–1938 it became standard Stalinist practice to assert that the followers of Trotski, Bukharin, and other "anti-party groups" had attempted to subvert the party by "factional activity." When such attempts failed, so ran the Stalin doctrine, opposition elements became agents of foreign intelligence services and "enemies of the people." [19]

Khrushchev's attitude toward political opposition was revealed in his struggle against and victory over what he, using familiar Stalinist language, called the antiparty group, centering mainly around Georgi M. Malenkov, Vyacheslav M. Molotov, and Lazar Kaganovich. In this, as in other significant details, Khrushchev's political terminology resembled that of Lenin, or of Stalin in the 1920's or early 1930's, before the period of the "cult of personality." However, the language used in the post-Stalin era to describe defeated competitors in the struggle for power — with the exception of Beria and his associates — has been considerably less abusive than that used by Stalin and his henchmen in the 1930's and 1940's. The defeated have been demoted, disgraced, and in some cases exiled. They have not, however, been denounced as "enemies of the people," or tried and executed as traitors.

Nevertheless, the post-Stalin leadership is firmly committed to what Kozlov in his speech on the party statutes at the 1961 congress referred to as "fundamental Leninist organizational principles." The current party statutes, adopted at the Twenty-second Congress, like those in force under Stalin, contain a prohibition against "attempts to form factional groupings destructive of Party unity," although they omit the warning contained in the statutes adopted in 1952 that such factions might shake the stability of the socialist system.[20] Also, like the 1952 statutes, those adopted in 1961 warn that although broad discussion of party policy is desirable it should not be conducted so as to lead to "attempts by an insignificant minority to impose their will upon the majority of

---

[19] *Malaya sovetskaya entsiklopediya,* 2nd ed., Vol. VII (Moscow, 1938), col. 743; see also *Politicheski slovar* (Moscow, 1940), cols. 388–89. According to the article in the second reference, Trotski began to work for the British in 1921 and for the Germans in 1926. This accusation is similar to the one made by *Pravda* for Dec. 17, 1953, according to which Lavrenti Beria, long Stalin's trusted police chief, had begun to work as an agent of foreign intelligence services in 1919.

[20] Triska, *op. cit.,* pp. 172–73.

the party." In his report on the statutes, Kozlov recalled that the report on the same subject had been delivered by Khrushchev at the last congress held during Stalin's lifetime. He thus emphasized a significant element of doctrinal continuity with the Stalin era. Continuity was indicated more obviously by the forcefulness with which Kozlov stressed the continued importance of centralism in the party. Discussion, he indicated, was a fine thing but the party could not permit "any small group of confused or immature people to undertake a fruitless discussion," nor could it allow "anti-party elements" to undertake activity which might lead to the disruption of its unity. He indicated that the question had been raised by some party members as to whether or not the "monolithic unity" enjoyed by the CPSU made it impossible for any further "splitting" activity to take place. Answering this question in the negative, Kozlov declared that although there was no longer any "social basis" for "opportunistic tendencies" in the party, individuals or even groups "might come under the influence of bourgeois propaganda from outside." Moreover, some party members, such as Molotov, might continue to defend "outmoded dogmas."

Khrushchev himself, in a section of his last major speech to the Twenty-second Party Congress, declared that in dealing with the problem of "various opinions" within the party, which he said might develop, particularly during "transitional stages," he stood for "Leninist methods of persuasion and explanation," rather than for "repression." As an example of such methods, Khrushchev cited Lenin's magnanimity toward Zinovev and Kamenev after the latter had admitted that they had been at fault in opposing Lenin's call for an armed uprising shortly before the bolsheviks seized power in 1917.[21] Such remarks imply that the party will display mercy toward defeated oppositionists if the latter, by their conduct, earn the right to be treated mercifully.

Against the background of the conception of unity surveyed above, the quasi-democratic reforms proclaimed by Khrushchev at the Twenty-first Party Congress in 1959 and set forth more systematically in the program and statutes adopted by the Twenty-second Congress seem modest. They were certainly not insignificant, however. In addition to spelling out in some detail the goal, set forth by Khrushchev at the Twenty-first Congress, of develop-

[21] *Materialy, op. cit.,* pp. 250–51.

ing "Soviet democracy" by gradually turning over to "public organizations," such as sports societies, trade unions, the Young Communist League (Komsomol), etc., certain functions previously performed by state agencies, the program declared that "the dictatorship of the working class will cease to be necessary before the state withers away." [22] The new program asserted, moreover, that the "dictatorship of the proletariat" had been replaced by a state "expressing the interests and will of the people as a whole." It added that the state "as an organization embracing the entire people" would survive until the complete victory of communism. Thus, the program took back much of what it gave in the form of increased emphasis upon the role of mass organizations. If those organizations must work under the supervision and within the framework set not only by the ruling CPSU but also by a state richly endowed with disciplinary and coercive powers, they could at best foster only such forms of "democracy" as rest upon increased — but supervised — participation in social and political life by rank and file citizens. They might even, under adverse circumstances, become agents of repression by increasing the interference of society in the life of the individual and also by undermining professional standards, for example, in the field of law enforcement.

Probably more significant in broadening meaningful participation in the political process than the expanded role of public organizations was Khrushchev's practice, abandoned by his successors during their first few months in power of inviting nonmembers of the CPSU central committee to take part in central committee plenary sessions. Indeed, so highly was this practice developed that, beginning with the November, 1962 plenum, no regular, properly restricted sessions were held.[23]

Lenin, Stalin, and Khrushchev all invoked similar doctrines against opposition, but differences of personality and especially in the situations impinging upon their actions rendered their behavior very dissimilar. Lenin put his moral authority, his "charisma," in Max Weber's terminology, behind his demand for unity.

---

[22] Triska, *op. cit.*, p. 98.
[23] This practice is mentioned and praised in A. I. Sidorov, *Verkhovnyi organ KPSS* (Moscow, 1964), p. 124; see also *Pravda*, June 19 and Dec. 10, 1963; Feb. 11, 1964.

Stalin transformed the demand for unity into a justification of despotism. In fact, it was not so much doctrine as terror that enabled him to maintain his autocracy.

Khrushchev, lacking both the legitimacy of Lenin and the capacity and taste for terror of Stalin, sought to base his regime on as broad a consensus as he considered compatible with maintenance of his leadership. By so doing he helped make possible the conspiracy which so smoothly and skilfully removed him in October, 1964. Disastrous though this implicit modification of the rules of the Soviet political game was for Khrushchev personally, it may have ushered in a new era, in which relatively orderly and peaceful political change becomes possible in the USSR. This would not preclude instability of leadership tenure or of presidium membership — these may well be intensified in conditions of collective leadership and broadened participation in top-level decision making, at least within the highest party bodies, with the possibility also of increased access to the decision-making process at levels just below the top. However, the smoothness of the Khrushchev expulsion and its apparent lack of violence suggested that a degree of constitutionality had been observed.

This of course did not involve any immediate overt challenge to the bedrock principles of the party's leadership over society and the hierarchic pattern of internal party structure.

Official comment following Khrushchev's fall implied that it resulted from failure of the former leader to obey Leninist principles. He was criticized for allegedly violating the provision of the statutes adopted in 1961 which condemned the "cult of personality." The new leaders implied that Khrushchev had developed delusions of his own infallibility. Also he had failed to consult his colleagues on important decisions, and had thus evaded "the control of the leading collective." [24]

The party program makes demands upon the citizenry relating to nearly every conceivable field of human endeavor, in the form of "tasks" which it "sets" in the spheres, to mention some, of nationality relations, ideology, education, industrial production and technology, and also "cultural development, literature and

---

[24] *Partiinaya zhizn,* No. 20, Oct., 1964, pp. 3–7, editorial entitled "Trebovatelnost-vazhnaya cherta partiinogo rukovodstva" ("Exactingness — Important Trait of Party Leadership").

art." Central to all of these "tasks" is the demand for "the education of the population as a whole in the spirit of scientific communism" in order that "all working people master the ideas of Marxism-Leninism, that they fully understand the course and perspectives of world development, take a correct view of international and domestic events and consciously build their life on communist lines." This last "task" constitutes, in effect, the demand that all Soviet citizens assist the party in its function of political socialization. It is worth noting that one of the ten duties that the party statutes require of each party member is that of mastering Marxist-Leninist theory and improving "his ideological knowledge" so as to "contribute to the moulding and education of the man of communist society." This item in the list of party duties further requires members to "combat all manifestations of bourgeois ideology," as well as "remnants of a private-property psychology." [25] Among numerous authoritative manifestations of the party's demand that Soviet citizens, and particularly CPSU members, participate actively in political indoctrination and propaganda work, especially significant was the central committee decree of January 9, 1960 entitled "Concerning the Tasks of Party Propaganda under Contemporary Conditions." The introduction to this document asserted that "in the period of the full-scale construction of a communist society in our country the ideological work of the party and especially its decisive sphere, party propaganda, takes on an especially important significance." Significantly, the decree concludes with the assertion that "peaceful co-existence of states with various social systems does not mean a slackening of the ideological struggle." [26] Similarly, a volume entitled *Lenin on Propaganda and Agitation* states that the party "directs all forms of ideational influence on the masses, including propaganda and agitation, toward the explanation of the decisions of the Twenty-second Congress, the program of the CPSU, the arming of the working people of Soviet society with a great plan of struggle for the victory of communism, and the mobilization of all of the workers for the realization of the new program of the party." [27]

[25] *Ibid.,* p. 157.
[26] *Voprosy ideologicheskoi raboty* (Moscow, 1961), p. 144. Full text of decree on pp. 144–64.
[27] *Lenin o propagande i agitatsii* (Moscow, 1962), p. 14.

PATRIOTISM AND INTERNATIONALISM

The character of the pattern of identifications, loyalties, and allegiances in which Soviet citizens are reared is reflected in such expressions as "proletarian internationalism," and "Soviet patriotism" (now increasingly described as "socialist patriotism"), especially in works intended for foreign communists. The primary loyalty of Soviet communists and other Soviet citizens is owed to the leadership of the CPSU, which in turn, as Khrushchev put it in his speech on the party program at the Twenty-second Party Congress, expresses its readiness to "fulfill its obligations to its foreign brothers." [28] Khrushchev, in the above address, went on to say that the party considered its principal "international obligation" to be the construction of communism inside the Soviet Union. He also declared that the USSR, and the "world socialist system" as a whole, were, by the force of their example, inspiring the working class and also all the working people generally of other countries to intensify their struggle against "the yoke of capitalism" and for their vital rights and interests, for social and national liberation and for a firm peace.[29] Although couched in relatively mild tones, Khrushchev's conception of the content of "internationalism" seemed rather similar to that set forth by Stalin in his well-known speech of February, 1931 "on the tasks of managers." In that speech Stalin demanded a rapid tempo of economic development because, as he said, "The backward are beaten" and also because the overcoming of Russian backwardness by rapid Soviet economic progress would constitute fulfilment of the Soviet Union's obligation to the world proletariat.[30] In the same speech, Stalin pointed out that the Soviet Union deserved the support of the "international proletariat" because it had been the first to enter into the struggle with capitalism and to begin the building of socialism. There are many indications that the self-imposed mission of the Russian communists to liberate mankind from "the yoke of capitalism" has many links with traditional Russian attitudes, such as belief in the moral superiority of Russia over the "decadent" West and the hope that the Russian people will one day become the most civilized in the world.

[28] *Materialy, op. cit.,* p. 136.
[29] *Ibid.,* p. 130.
[30] I. Stalin, *Voprosy leninizma,* 11th ed. (Moscow, 1945), pp. 328–29.

According to the party program, communists envisage the ultimate creation of "a single world-wide culture of communist society." [31] By implication this "world-wide culture" would be based primarily on the Soviet model, since the USSR considers that its experience and its power confer upon it the leading role in the transformation of world society. As Khrushchev put it in his speech on the party program at the Twenty-second Congress, the "world revolutionary process" is becoming ever broader. With the strengthening of the socialist system, and the full revelation of its superiority, more and more countries will enter upon the path of revolution and will become part of the socialist system. The CPSU regards it as its duty to "strengthen the unity and solidarity of the ranks of the great army of communists of all countries." [32] The twentieth century, Khrushchev indicated, is the century of communism, and mankind is close to the realization of the most glorious ideals. The pace of history will be enormously accelerated when a communist society has been constructed in the USSR.[33] In this and other important announcements, the Soviet leadership indicated that it considered as its right the encouragement of struggles for "national liberation" and the opposition or prevention of attempts by the "imperialist" powers to frustrate such efforts or to undo them after they had been successful, as in the case of Cuba. The use of force for such purposes by the United States and other noncommunist states has been branded in a number of official Soviet documents as "the export of counter-revolution."

The Soviet leaders came to the conclusion at an early stage in the development of the USSR that if they were to fulfill their worldwide mission they must inculcate in the population under their control sentiments of patriotic pride. The roots of the doctrine developed in response to this need can be traced to some of the writings of Lenin, and in a broad sense, as already indicated, to traditional Russian national sentiments. However, the systematic development of Soviet patriotism was mainly the work of Stalin; and Stalin's successors, though they propagated the doctrine less stridently than he did, have, in the main, followed in his footsteps.

[31] Triska, *op. cit.*, p. 109.
[32] *Materialy, op. cit.*, pp. 202–204.
[33] *Ibid.*, p. 231.

Soviet patriotism is the master symbol of the demands which the party poses to the Soviet citizenry. Shortly before the death of Stalin a Soviet philosopher defined Soviet patriotism as "the fusion of the progressive national traditions of the peoples with the common vital interests of all the toilers of the USSR. This marvelous fusion was created by the party of bolsheviks. The party of Lenin and Stalin is the inspirer and teacher of Soviet patriotism, the founder of the new patriotic traditions of the working people of the USSR." [34] Another typical definition, reflecting Stalin's years of effort to forge an integrated outlook for his subjects, read as follows: "Boundless love of the Soviet people for the socialist motherland, the unity of all the fraternal peoples around the party of Lenin and Stalin and the Soviet government." [35] It is interesting to compare the foregoing with a statement in a handbook for Soviet political workers published in 1960, according to which "one of the most important driving forces of Soviet society and at the same time one of the most important principles of communist morality is Soviet patriotism. Soviet patriotism is not simply a feeling of affection for the motherland. For the Soviet man love for the motherland is above all love for the socialist system, created by his own hands and the hands of his fathers, and embodying the aspirations of the working people for free labor, equal rights and social justice." [36] Similarly, it is stated by the most recent authoritative history of the communist party that history shows that the communist party is "a genuinely patriotic force," which defends the interests of the people and the motherland.[37] To the extent that the Soviet citizen shares these prescribed sentiments he feels an elementary affection for the society which has reared him and also a conscious attachment to a complex pattern of symbols and concepts. In other words, Soviet patriotism represents identification with a "way of life."

A conspicuous and probably appealing aspect of Soviet patriotism is the evocation of memories of heroic struggles of the Soviet

[34] N. I. Matyushkin, *Sovetski patriotizm-moguchaya dvizhushchaya sila sotsialisticheskogo obshchestva* (Moscow, 1952), p. 4.

[35] *Slovar inostrannykh slov* (Moscow, 1949), p. 482. For a more detailed discussion of the concept of Soviet patriotism, see Ch. I of Frederick C. Barghoorn, *Soviet Russian Nationalism* (New York, 1956).

[36] *Spravochnik agitatora* (Moscow, 1960), p. 131.

[37] *Istoriya kommunisticheskoi partii sovetskogo soyuza*, 2nd enlarged ed. (Moscow, 1962), pp. 770–71.

people and their ancestors against the tsar and his bureaucrats, against landlords and capitalists, and against foreign enemies. Closely related to these negative identifications is the concept of a ceaseless struggle against "survivals of capitalism" in the consciousness of Soviet citizens. The frequently mentioned "survivals" or, as they are sometimes called, the "remnants," include religious sentiments, an unconscientious attitude toward work and toward public property, and also "nationalistic" attitudes. The latter are often attributed to various members of the non-Russian minority nationalities of the USSR, but seldom to members of the dominant Great Russian nationality. A section of a handbook intended for the elementary political training of party members without higher education points out that although the working people of prebolshevik Russia were deprived of their rights, they nevertheless partiotically defended their fatherland against the foreign foe. According to this handbook, the patriotic devotion of the working people to their country was greatly intensified as a result of the bolshevik revolution and the turning over of political power to the people. Soviet patriotism, continues this source, developed on a socialist foundation. The handbook contrasts the altruism of Soviet patriotism with the "nationalistic and racial prejudices" which, it asserts, are disseminated by the bourgeoisie in capitalist society "under the guise of patriotism." The Soviet people, continues the text, are fully aware of the superiority of the social order under which they live to any other social system, but they respect the rights and the independence of all countries, both great and small. This text also contains many references to the successful efforts of the Soviet people to defend themselves against the machinations and actions of the capitalist countries.[38]

The pride of the party leaders in the achievements of the USSR, probably widely shared throughout the society, is indicated by expressions of satisfaction over the Soviet Union's improving international status and prestige. Khrushchev told a conference of leaders of the Soviet construction industry that "nowadays the whole world recognizes the might of the Soviet Union as a great world power and the imperialists are forced to reckon with this fact."[39] Like Lenin and Stalin before him Khru-

[38] *V pomoshch slushatelyam politshkol* (Moscow, 1955). See esp. pp. 167–69.
[39] *Pravda,* Dec. 28, 1954.

shchev was fond of quoting the well-known lines in which the nineteenth-century poet Nikolai Nekrasov described Russia as "poor and abundant, mighty but helpless." In his speech to the Twenty-second Party Congress on the party program, Khrushchev contrasted the Russia of Nekrasov's day, which, he said, was considered to be a country of "straw, wood and treebark," with the mighty Russia of today, which he likened to a three-stage rocket, lifting mankind from the depths of capitalism up to the orbit of communism, along a course marked out by the genius of Lenin.[40]

Insofar as the Soviet citizen responds positively to the officially approved beliefs, values, and sentiments surveyed thus far he becomes an appropriately motivated participant in the process of "building communism." How successful has the CPSU leadership been in molding the participatory subject, or, to use an expression coined by an American scholar, the "eager robot"? [41] Because of Soviet secrecy, censorship, and the propaganda-permeated communication output, the question can at best be only partially explored or answered. Some of the problems involved in attempting to deal with this and related questions will be examined in the next two chapters. The Soviet leadership, at least by implication and somewhat explicitly, admits that the creation of the "new Soviet man," equipped with the proper "communist" world outlook, is a tremendously difficult task. There is also much evidence that the Kremlin believes that although this effort has by no means been fully successful, it can succeed in the future if it is pursued with sufficient skill and energy. The most comprehensive of all available Western studies of Soviet attitudes came to the conclusion that the Soviet system, particularly after the death of Stalin, seemed "to enjoy the support of popular consensus." [42] Continued Soviet concern about excessive exposure of Soviet citizens to "bourgeois" influences (for example, in contacts with foreign tourists), and many other indicators of lack of confidence in the firmness of ideological convictions of Soviet people, may justify speculation about the effectiveness of the Soviet political socialization and communica-

[40] *Materialy, op. cit.*, pp. 125, 135.

[41] The phrase "eager robot" was used by Ralph T. Fisher, Jr., in his article in Cyril E. Black, ed., *The Transformation of Russian Society* (Cambridge, Mass., 1961), entitled "The Soviet Model of the Ideal Youth."

[42] Alex Inkeles and Raymond A. Bauer, *The Soviet Citizen* (Cambridge, Mass., 1959), p. 397. See also Chs. X, XI, and XII.

tion programs. But it would certainly be unrealistic to leave out of the equation the evidence of the vitality of Soviet communism offered by the Soviet record in World War II, the rapid recovery of the Soviet economy from the results of that war, and spectacular Soviet achievements in the exploration of outer space. The CPSU, with much justification and with even more plausibility, can claim to be the author of all of these achievements and victories. Its propaganda efforts and the gradually improving access of most Soviet citizens to a widening range of material and intellectual satisfactions facilitate the development of at least a passive acceptance of the political system by a majority of Soviet citizens and of the passionate conviction of some that they are indeed riding the wave of the future.

CHAPTER II

Social Structure
and Political Subcultures

WE SHALL EXAMINE in this chapter differences in the attitudes of major groups within Soviet society toward the dominant, elite political culture. We are interested here in the relationship between social and occupational factors and political attitudes. We must therefore begin with some vital statistics. The latest (1959) census indicated that the Soviet population was about evenly divided between urban and rural residents. Of the total population of almost 209,000,000, 38.8 per cent were engaged, according to official Soviet sources, in agriculture and 36.9 per cent in industry, construction, transport, and communication. Of the remainder, 14.6 per cent were employed in "nonproduction" jobs, including education, science, public health, and other services, and 5.2 per cent in trade and related work. Serving in the armed forces were 3.6 per cent.[1] Ethnically, Great Russians constituted 114,114,000 of the total Soviet population, leaving slightly under 100,000,000 divided among (approximately): 37,000,000 Ukrainians, 8,000,000 Belorussians, 6,000,000 Uzbeks, 5,000,000 Tatars, 3,622,000 Kazakhs, 3,000,000 Azerbaidzhanians,

---

[1] *SSSR v tsifrakh v 1960* (Moscow, 1961), pp. 27–35; see also P. Podyachikh, *Naselenie SSSR* (Moscow, 1961); Vernon V. Aspaturian, "The Soviet Union," in Roy C. Macridis and Robert E. Ward, eds., *Modern Political Systems* (New York, 1963), pp. 431–32; Demitri B. Shimkin, "Current Characteristics and Problems of the Soviet Rural Population," unpublished paper prepared for Conference on Soviet Agricultural and Peasant Affairs, held at Lawrence, Kansas, Sept. 20–22, 1962.

2,800,000 Armenians, and 2,700,000 Georgians. The other nationalities numbering more than 2,000,000 were the Lithuanians, the Jews, and the Moldavians.[2]

The number of Soviet citizens who had been graduated from institutions of higher education, or the equivalent, had increased from the 1939 figure of 1,177,000 to 3,778,000. Almost as many women as men had higher education. The urban sector had an overwhelming predominance in higher education: of those with complete higher education 3,170,000 were urban residents; 608,000 such persons resided in rural localities.[3] Almost 10,000,000 persons had completed secondary school (which prior to 1959 meant ten years of schooling), and of these about 7,400,000 were urban residents and about 2,500,000 lived in the rural districts. Almost the entire population was literate, in sharp contrast to the pre-revolutionary illiteracy rate of 76 per cent — and almost complete illiteracy among the non-Russian populations of Siberia and Central Asia.[4]

According to Soviet doctrine the fully communist society of the future will ultimately be "classless," but Soviet sources assert that at present two "friendly" classes exist in Soviet society: the workers and the collective farm peasants. Also, as in Article 126 of the USSR constitution, the doctrine postulates the existence of the crucially important and conveniently broad "stratum" or category of the "working intelligentsia." The intelligentsia, never defined precisely, in reality appears to include most of those whom Western social scientists would include in the leadership community or "elite" of Soviet society. The intelligentsia is that stratum of the Soviet population which receives a far larger share of such advantages and satisfactions as formal education, status and respect, income, and the more refined forms of leisure than it would if the good things of life were distributed equally. To it belong novelists, poets, and playwrights, as well as scholars, educators, engineers, and scientists. Often the Soviet intelligentsia is divided by Soviet sources into the "creative" (*tvorcheskaya*) intelligentsia and the "technical" intelligentsia, but although these terms are useful they do not cover the whole

2 *SSSR v tsifrakh, op. cit.*, p. 70.
3 *Ibid.*, p. 75.
4 Aspaturian, *op. cit.*, pp. 432–33.

range of professional and managerial groups and subgroups comprising this most dynamic and variegated upper crust of Soviet society.

It is tempting to equate intelligentsia and elite in the USSR, but such identification fails to account for the most significant division in Soviet society, which is not that between members and nonmembers of the intelligentsia but the political boundary between members and nonmembers of the CPSU, or, more precisely, between the "cadres," or responsible executives of the party and all other Soviet citizens, whether or not they belong to the CPSU. David Burg has perceptively noted that the Soviet elite is divided into two main sections, one of which consists of industrial executives and professionals whose members and significance have increased during the industrialization of the USSR. These strata, Burg notes, are less closely tied to the Soviet political system than are the members of the party bureaucracy, who devote most of their working hours to organizational or "ideological" activity within the party machine, and who direct and coordinate the activities of the economic, cultural, and other structures of society. It is in their hands that "real power" lies, Burg points out, whereas "The other members of the Soviet elite have neither political nor personal rights; they do not participate in decisions affecting their country's fate and, further, they do not even have command over their own lives." [5] Burg's interpretation, even if somewhat oversimplified, is useful. It highlights a social-political relationship which poses complex and difficult problems to the Soviet leadership and is pregnant with potential for dramatic changes in Soviet society. If the party apparatus is to maintain an appropriate pitch of militancy, confidence in its vocation of leadership, and psychological distance from those not subject to its stern discipline, it must not allow itself to be submerged in influences emanating from the society which it controls and which it has done much to shape. The problem confronting the Soviet leadership in dealing with emergent and in some ways disruptive social forces reflects unintended and un-

[5] David Burg, "Observations on Soviet University Students," in Richard Pipes, ed., *The Russian Intelligentsia* (New York, 1961), pp. 80–100. See p. 84. Aspaturian, *op. cit.*, derives from Soviet sources a figure of 4,600,000 for the Soviet "ruling elite" which he equates with those party members who also qualify for inclusion in the intelligentsia. See pp. 494–99.

predictable consequences of an increasingly successful program
of industrialization, urbanization, and modernization. This will
become clearer upon examination of relevant characteristics of
various social groups, but we shall first broadly outline the social
structure of the CPSU.

CATEGORIES OF PARTY MEMBERSHIP

Party members may be divided into three main categories,
each of which has a distinctive function in the Soviet political
process. The backbone of the system's structure consists of the
hierarchy of full-time paid professional party functionaries, including secretaries, deputy secretaries, department and section
chiefs, and instructors of party committees, at four descending
levels of status: central, regional, local, and primary. They are
vital in linking the committees with the network of party organizations and economic and cultural agencies which they control.
A vivid statement by Stalin in 1937 likened this hierarchy of
command to that of an army, with its generals, officer corps, and
noncoms. T. H. Rigby has estimated that the total body of party
executives numbered about a quarter of a million in 1954. These
professional rulers, often referred to as *apparatchiki* — men of
the apparatus — were augmented, Rigby estimated, by 300,000
secretaries of the lowest ranking, or primary party organizations,
who were for the most part not full-time party workers, but who
furnished valuable assistance to the cadres in fulfilling the party's
"central tasks" of "giving guiding directions, verifying their ful-
fillment, and selecting personnel." A more cautious estimate by
Merle Fainsod of the size of the apparatus, as of 1962, yielded a
figure ranging between 100,000 and 200,000. At present the apparatus may be even smaller than it was in 1962, despite the
growth of total party membership to 11,500,000 members in 1964
and its increase to 12,471,000 by March, 1966, as reported by
Brezhnev in his March 29 address to the Twenty-third CPSU
Congress. If so, this further contraction of the circle of effective
political participation was probably the result of the drive to
prune paid professional staffs, replacing them where necessary
and feasible with "volunteers." This drive has persisted throughout the post-Stalin period, perhaps with consequent widening of
social distances between apparatus members and nonapparatus
people, or even impairment of the former's influence over the

latter.[6] This streamlining, not merely an economy measure, also underscored the propaganda claim that in the construction of a communist society visible progress was at last being made.

The second category of political leadership embraces "all those party members who are distributed as leaders through the various levels of the administrative, productive, 'cultural' and 'voluntary' organizations of Soviet society." Unlike the apparatchiki, who are expected to relate their day-to-day activities to long-range national and international goals, members of this second group tend to be limited to "completing planned assignments in a limited field of activity with its own logic and sectional interests." Awareness of the differences between the first and second categories of party members helps us to appraise the potentialities and limitations for the development of pluralistic tendencies in the Soviet polity. Members of the second category, under pressure to give their primary loyalty to the party but also, by training and occupation, functional specialists in, say, industrial management or military science, sometimes develop perspectives divergent from those of the party professionals. On the other hand, the party apparatus acts as a "ministry of coordination," aggregating the interests of various functional agencies and occupational groups. To the extent that it is successful, it may appear to government bureaucrats (whose leaders, at the upper levels at least, are interchangeable with those of the apparatus) as well as to other successful and privileged members of the elite, that its work is beneficial to the society as a whole.[7] There does seem to be a kind of tacit alliance of the successful, whether the skills on which their status is based are political, administrative, or technical, although this alliance is not without its cleavages.

[6] T. H. Rigby, *The Selection of Leading Personnel in the Soviet State and Communist Party*, thesis submitted for the degree of Doctor of Philosophy to the University of London, 1954, p. 52; Merle Fainsod, *How Russia Is Ruled*, rev. ed. (Cambridge, Mass., 1963), pp. 205–207. The 1964 figure on total party membership given in the text is on p. 23 of an article by D. Chesnokov, in *Partiinaya zhizn*, No. 21, Nov., 1964. For 1965 figures, see *ibid.*, No. 10, July, 1965, and *Pravda* editorial of August 11, both reporting a swelling of party ranks by almost a million in 1964. George Fischer, in "The Number of Soviet Party Executives" (Cornell Soviet Studies Reprint No. 10, 1965), presents a careful analysis of available data on the apparatus. For party membership in 1966, see *Pravda*, March 30, 1966.

[7] On the party apparatus, and especially its middle-rank officials, as a coordinating body, see Jerry F. Hough, *The Role of the Local Party Organs in Soviet Industrial Decision-Making*, Ph.D. dissertation submitted to the faculty of Arts and Sciences of Harvard University (Cambridge, Mass., 1961).

At the bottom of the party pyramid but still privileged indeed in comparison with nonparty people, are the rank and file party members. They do not serve in positions of authority either in the apparatus or in state and "public" organizations. However, without these party "privates" the Soviet political army could not function. They furnish recruits for the upper levels, disseminate approved attitudes, communicate the party's policies to nonparty citizens, supply information to their local party organizations (thus acting as a political intelligence network), and are expected to set án example to the nonparty "masses" of superior performance in work and in the discharge of civic duties.

The party's structure is highly centralized, but it is also differentiated. Many party members are assigned to particular functions in highly specialized units. Units and agencies of the party are sealed off both vertically and horizontally from relationships and information which the party command considers unnecessary or dysfunctional for the effective performance of their assigned tasks. Political "messages" emanating from the "grass roots" are subject to screening at many levels. This elaborate and strict compartmentalization limits the political experience of most party members to what takes place in their local party organizations, at the bottom of the political ladder.[8] The party's penetration of the Soviet administrative and professional elites is the foundation of its control over Soviet society. Organizational control is reinforced by the practice of providing functionaries of the party apparatus with special training in the areas of specialization of those whose functions they are assigned to oversee so that they may understand the work they supervise and win the respect of those whose activity they guide. This practice, inaugurated by Stalin and further developed by his successors, is particularly important for leading party cadres engaged in super-

[8] T. H. Rigby, *Policy-Making in the U.S.S.R.* (Melbourne, 1962), p. 18. L. G. Churchward also contributed an essay to the above pamphlet. See also the contribution of Frederick C. Barghoorn to Sigmund Neumann, ed., *Modern Political Parties* (Chicago, 1956), esp. pp. 232–33. One might say that the threshold, or boundary, at which the lowest level "inputs" enter the political process is that between the rank and file members of primary party organizations and the leaders thereof. The instructions in *Spravochnik sekretarya pervichnoi partiinoi organizatsii* (Moscow, 1965), pp. 112–15, on how primary party organizations should process the demands and grievances of their members and of nonparty workers, peasants, etc., illuminate the structure of command and communication in this system and the relationship between the polity and its internal environment.

vision of and liaison with military, managerial, scientific, and other highly trained executives and professionals. It is probably also crucial in party supervision of police and intelligence work, but information on party-bureaucracy relationships in these sensitive spheres is extraordinarily limited. Politically active members of various professions, especially engineering, are increasingly brought into the party, apparently in the belief that such highly trained apparatchiki can contribute to both the political leadership and the economic-social control functions of the party.

In addition to professional training, party cadres are provided with formal political instruction. Dual-purpose training has been increasingly necessary since the 1930's because of the rise in the level of education of the party membership generally. In 1947 it was reported that more than 400,000 members of the CPSU had a higher education, representing 6.32 per cent of the total party membership; the 1939 percentage was 5.08. In 1947, 1,300,000 communists were listed as having completed secondary schooling, representing more than 20 per cent of the party members, as compared with slightly over 14 per cent in 1939 with the equivalent of an American high school education.[9] As of July 1, 1961, the number of "specialists" or professionals enrolled in the party who had a higher, or specialized secondary education, was reported as 3,076,237, more than 50 per cent above the 1956 figure of 1,877,773.[10] At the same date the CPSU had within its ranks more than 55,000 persons holding degrees of either Candidate or Doctor of Sciences, the two Soviet graduate degrees, roughly equivalent to the M.A. and the Ph.D. in the United States. The rapid rise in the educational qualifications of party functionaries is further indicated by the statement of Frol R. Kozlov, that although in 1956, 25.7 per cent of raion and city committee party secretaries had a higher education, this percentage was "now" — no date was given — 76.9.[11] It is also significant that a high proportion of the leadership cadres of the CPSU have an engineering education. In 1960, data indicated that the majority of members and alternate members of the presidium of the CPSU

9 Fainsod, *op. cit.*, p. 274.
10 *Ibid.*, p. 281.
11 The above data are developed from an article by Harry Schwartz in *The New York Times*, Feb, 18, 1962 and from Frol R. Kozlov, "KPSS — partiya vsego naroda," *Kommunist*, No. 8, May, 1962, pp. 10–21. Data cited on p. 15.

were graduates of engineering, agricultural, or other technical institutes.[12] John A. Armstrong points out that, "The party has placed enormous emphasis on increased education, not only because it directly improves the official's job performance but because it prepares him to cope with the problems of an increasingly complex society and to deal with the growing number of well-educated persons in the general population.[13]

PLURALISTIC TENDENCIES

Although the development of a pluralistic polity in the USSR will be impossible until the present system of controls by the CPSU over society as a whole is altered, certain characteristics of the Soviet social and political systems already are potentially or latently pluralistic. The problem of pluralism as confronted by the Soviet Communist Party has two main aspects. The party must cope with the survivals of attitudes and customs inherited from the prescientific, preindustrial political culture which it overthrew in 1917. Since 1917 it has been straining to reshape society by coercive modernization. Nationalism, religion, and other "survivals of capitalism" are among the elements of traditionalist pluralism against which, even today, the party is constrained to struggle. The party has gradually reduced to manageable proportions the ability of social groups imbued with prerevolutionary attitudes and customs to seriously or openly challenge its authority, except perhaps under stress of external or internal pressures which today are difficult to envisage. However, it is increasingly confronted by new challenges and problems, posed by the aspirations of social strata basically loyal to the "socialist" system which nurtured them, but critical of particular party policies and practices. Different attitudes toward certain arrangements and policies can engender dissatisfaction or discontent among members of important groups in the society. Irritation, frustration, or indignation so generated can cause individuals to become generally disaffected, or even alienated, from the political system. There is evidence that in the Soviet Union, as in other societies, the orientations of individuals and their families toward the political system are extensively shaped

---

[12] *Zapisnaya knizhka partiinogo aktivista* (Moscow, 1960), pp. 101–107.
[13] John A. Armstrong, *The Soviet Bureaucratic Elite* (New York, 1959), pp. 31–32.

by bureaucratic rivalries, professional interests, work experiences, traditions, and tastes reflecting occupational, class, ethnic, or "interest group" affiliations.

Both policy directives and Soviet social science writing in recent years have occasionally admitted that there are "groups," with varied attitudes and preferences, dependent upon such factors as occupation, education, income, etc. Those responsible for shaping opinion are sometimes instructed to carefully consider the interests of each of the groups — such as industrial workers, village dwellers, students, military personnel — with which they must deal.[14] Although group differentiation in Soviet society is given increasing, even if reluctant and insufficient, recognition, the party leadership still claims the right to forbid the expression of opinions or attitudes reflecting group interests if they clash with its criteria of what is permissible in a "socialist" society. More often than not, the official press still conceals or denies the existence of pluralistic trends in Soviet society. It is interesting, however, to see men with a vested interest in uniformity even grudgingly admit to the stubborn vitality of diversity. Although there are many gaps in the evidence available to outside observers on the structure of Soviet attitudes, there is enough to identify a number of group beliefs, grievances, aspirations, and demands, which furnish the basis for political subcultures within the ensemble of the Soviet political culture. There is some arbitariness in the selection of the groups and perspectives to be designated as political subcultures. We shall apply this concept to a few categories of the Soviet citizenry, namely, some subgroups of the intelligentsia, as well as the peasantry, the non-Russian ethnic groups, and the industrial workers. It is obvious that these categories are not exhaustive and that there would be a number of others if one were to attempt to break down the population into its various components. It is also clear that however the Soviet or any other society is classified, there will inevitably be much overlap among the various groups. One might treat all Ukrainians as members of a particular nationality group or some Ukrainians as members of subgroups of the intelligentsia, worker, or peasant groups with Ukrainian cultural traits. In other words, the same individual may enjoy a number of group affiliations and his attitudes and

14 See V. Shubkin, "O konkretnykh issledovaniyakh sotsialnykh protessov," *Kommunist*, No. 3, Feb., 1965, pp. 49–51; *Pravda* editorial, June 16, 1965.

values may be influenced by multiple and sometimes conflicting group memberships. Finally, the very large groups dealt with here embrace a variety of subgroups, especially as applied to the intelligentsia, which includes many professional groups, such as writers, painters, architects, composers, philosophers, journalists, etc. Apparently members of these specialized skill groups spend most of their work time and their leisure time with their colleagues and have little contact with counterparts from other professions. Such compartmentalization probably makes it easier for the centralized party apparatus to control them, than if there were more communication between professions. However, if this tendency for each profession to act as a world in itself militates against over-all solidarity of the intelligentsia, it presents problems as well as advantages to the controllers of society. In particular, it fosters what party officials sometimes criticize as "groupism" (*gruppovshchina*), interests and sentiments which interfere with the official goal of achieving ideological homogeneity.

PRIVILEGES AND PROBLEMS OF THE INTELLIGENTSIA

The successful members of the intelligentsia, especially outstanding scientists and artists, receive a share of the rewards available in Soviet society larger than that given any of their fellow citizens except for the upper-level party apparatchiki and state officials. In its access to knowledge, contacts with foreign colleagues, and the sense of self-enhancement derived from the acquisition and exercise of professional skills, the "creative" intelligentsia is the most privileged of all the Soviet social strata. The aspirations and state of mind of many of its members, particularly writers and artists, are obviously a source of deep concern to the Kremlin, as indicated by the Moscow All-Union Conference on Questions of Ideological Work in December, 1961 and especially by the June, 1963 plenum, devoted to "current tasks of the ideological work of the party." The tacit compromise between the "liberal" Soviet intelligentsia and the official controllers of culture was not fully satisfactory to either side. Whether it would long survive the fall of Khrushchev was a question much pondered as his successors cautiously sought to fashion policies of their own. It may be significant for the long-term development of Soviet society that since Stalin's death there have persisted at least rudiments of a "loyal opposition" among the Soviet intelligentsia. Despite the party's demands that they produce works fully conforming to its specifications, a respectable number of writers throughout the post-Stalin era stubbornly defended their claim to at least some creative independence. A frequent response to pressures consisted of partial retreats and outward gestures of conformity, combined with failure to retreat from criticized positions. Administrative measures were applied only against those intellectuals who appeared not merely to claim the right (even if the claim was only implicit) to interpret relevant aspects of official myths but who also rejected explicitly the party's interpretation of "the artist's duty to the people." It is possible that further development of various "within-system" aspirations in time will profoundly alter the temper and perhaps even the structure of Soviet politics. However, before we turn to a category-by-category survey of some attitudes of Soviet intellectuals and professionals, we must realize that recognition of diversity does not necessarily imply that we should be optimistic about the more "mellow" outlook in Soviet politics which George F. Kennan regarded as a possibility in his celebrated "X" article in *Foreign Affairs* in 1947. The power of the party apparatus to continue to control the society depends not only upon a formidable array of structures and techniques of organization but is reinforced by such widespread popular attitudes as ardent pride in Soviet achievements, which all elements, especially the elite, tend to share, and by officially nurtured suspicion of Western, especially American and German, "imperialists." Also, even discontented members of the intelligentsia are probably fearful of the threat to their privileged status resulting from a substantial lossening of state controls over the worker and peasant masses. Moreover, even if some Soviet intellectuals and professionals desire fundamental changes in the present political system, they seem still to lack the skills and especially the opportunities which would be needed to articulate and implement them.

The apparatus needs the loyal and efficient support and cooperation of Soviet intellectuals and professionals for at least two important reasons. First and most obvious, the members of the intelligentsia perform operations upon which the functioning of the society is dependent. In addition, creative intellectuals, especially those versed in communication and expression, are capable of articulating moods and attitudes which under certain circumstances could be dysfunctional if not downright subversive. Because it is far more likely that its members will have access to non-Marxist ideologies through printed matter and even through personal contact than will other social groups, the subversive potential of the intelligentsia is augmented. Official concern over the intelligentsia's susceptibility to "alien" ideas shows up in many forms, including frequent press articles. Knowledge of Western ways, wares, and ideas sometimes reinforces intelligentsia yearnings for professional autonomy or preserves such traditional values as scholarly objectivity, which the members of the Soviet learned professions share with their counterparts abroad.

Some access to such information on the part of Soviet scientists, engineers, industrial executives, and educators is necessary if the party is to increase economic productivity and administrative efficiency. However, there often appears to be tension between the interest of the party apparatus in relatively limited contacts with Western personnel and techniques and the desire of Soviet specialists and professionals for broader, freer, and more intimate relations with foreign colleagues.

The often-frustrated aspirations of Soviet intellectuals, especially writers and artists, are made partly visible by indirect references to them in official criticisms, as well as in such of their statements as the Soviet authorities approve for publication. Also, especially since the death of Stalin, these aspirations and frustrations have been reflected in perceptive reports by foreign visitors to the USSR. One of the most interesting indications of distinctive intelligentsia claims and sense of identity appeared in the criticism of Dmitri Shepilov after he was expelled from his high party posts following his denunciation for having "adhered" to the antiparty group in July, 1957. Shepilov was the only member of this group explicitly and in detail identified with a social stratum: the "liberal" intelligentsia. Shepilov was accused of making indiscreet public statements, especially at meetings of the Union of Soviet Writers and the Union of Soviet Artists. He was also accused of "flirting with demagogues," and even of seeking to develop a "platform" which was "broader" than that of the

CPSU.[15] The criticism of Shepilov was especially interesting in its implication that he had illegitimately exploited the frustrated aspirations of dissident Soviet intellectuals as an instrument of political opposition. This unusually explicit attack on a party leader inclined toward "revisionism" brought to the surface an old fear, probably shared by many members of the party leadership and the party apparatus, that some members of the creative intelligentsia possessed the dangerous ability of "softening up" susceptible members of the apparatus with whom they were in contact. Anxiety over such a potential may have been significant in the campaign begun by Khrushchev in mid-1957, and continued by his successors, to improve party control not only over writers and artists but also over all segments and levels of the Soviet intelligentsia. Particular attention was directed toward writers. Some members of that profession have demonstrated in their work and private behavior that at least one Russian tradition, that the writer is the conscience of society, still has a potentially liberalizing and even disturbing significance.[16]

Criticisms such as those directed at Shepilov and his friends among intellectuals in 1957, or the early post-Khrushchev demands that practices of "mutual amnesty" among writers and artists be rooted out, reflect one of the party leadership's traditional worries: the danger in collusion between controllers and those whom they are expected to control. Among the words used to describe this phenomenon, which, especially in material production, has great potential for corruption, are "familialness" (*semeistvennost*), "departmentism" (*vedomstvennost*), and "mutual protection" (*krugovaya poruka*).

A demand made by some Soviet intellectuals, especially by poets such as Evgeni Evtushenko, especially disturbs the political

[15] See article in *Kommunist*, No. 10, July, 1957, entitled "Za leninskuyu printsipial 'nost v voprosakh literatury i iskusstv," esp. pp. 16–21, and speech by N. M. Shvernik, reported in *Pravda*, July 7, 1957. Apparently Shepilov and possibly Malenkov, who is also briefly criticized in the above unsigned *Kommunist* editorial, favored more autonomy for creative intellectuals than Khrushchev and his supporters could tolerate.

[16] Among numerous valuable studies of the situation, aspirations, and frustrations of Soviet writers, see especially Harold Swayze, *Political Control of Literature in the U.S.S.R.* (Cambridge, Mass., 1962). See also Priscilla Johnson, *Khrushchev and the Arts* (Cambridge, Mass., 1964), for detailed information and astute interpretation of the 1962–1963 cultural "crackdown." Insightful, cautiously optimistic comment based on extensive personal contacts with Soviet literary "rebels" is contained in Peter Viereck's "The Mob within the Heart," *Tri-Quarterly* (Evanston, Ill.), Spring 1965, pp. 1–43.

leadership. It is that party administrative controls over the forms and content of aesthetic expression be diminished or in some cases eliminated. Poets such as Evtushenko or novelists such as Vladimir Dudintsev (whose *Not by Bread Alone* helped to fuel the ferment of 1956–1957) thought when they produced the works condemned by the party that they were furthering the cause of communism as they understood it. But, from the Kremlin's point of view, they were posing a dangerous challenge to political authority. In a statement published under his name in 1957 Khrushchev said there were even some writers and artists who went so far in advocating "creative freedom" as to oppose the guidance of literature and the arts by the party and the state. Khrushchev claimed that such people sometimes opposed this guidance openly but that more often they concealed their desires behind "talk of excessive tutelage, the fettering of initiative, etc." [17] It is of course difficult to gauge the truthfulness of such charges. Statements by Soviet literary figures tend to support the view that some of these charges were accurate. For example, in 1956 respected Soviet writer and critic Konstantin Paustovski, in a courageous speech only partly reported in the Soviet Union, attacked the new Soviet "bourgeoisie," as Paustovski called the bureaucrats. They were symbolized by Dudintsev's character, Drozdov, who, he declared, "dare to claim the right to represent the people — without the people's consent." [18] Because of the mood reflected in Paustovski's speech, it is not entirely surprising that in 1957 Khrushchev reminded Soviet intellectuals of the part played by their Hungarian counterparts in helping to bring about the uprising of October–November, 1956. Among at least a portion of the Soviet intelligentsia, particularly among students, moods of protest verged on vaguely formulated demands for political pluralism. Khrushchev himself had appeared to sanction such aspirations in his "secret" speech regarding the crimes of Stalin. *Pravda* for July 6, 1956 considered it necessary to publish an editorial entitled "The Communist Party is the Inspirer and Leader of the Soviet People," which accused "some people abroad" of wishing to see "created" in the USSR noncommunist parties financed

[17] N. S. Khrushchev, "Za tesnuyu svyaz literatury i iskusstva s zhiznyu naroda," *Kommunist*, No. 12, Aug., 1957, pp. 11–13. Quotation on p. 22.

[18] Hugh McLean and Walter N. Vickery, *The Year of Protest 1956* (New York, 1961), pp. 155–59.

by foreign capital and serving foreign interests. After the re-establishment in late 1956 and throughout 1957 of tighter ideological controls, an effort which was to continue, intermittently, into the post-Khrushchev era, the Soviet press did not find it necessary to issue such stern warnings against incipient aspirations for political pluralism as it did in 1956. However, from time to time voices were raised in requests for at least a limited cultural pluralism.

Evtushenko's "Letter to America," though anti-United States enough to temporarily satisfy the Kremlin, contained a quatrain referring to both "realist and abstractionist" Cuban artists rushing to the barricades together, which by implication proclaimed the legitimacy of cultural pluralism.[19]

It was suggested earlier that tension can develop between the party leadership and writers and artists over the question of foreign travel and other contacts between the "two worlds" of Soviet socialism and Western "capitalism." As with demands for creative autonomy, we are touching here upon a vast subject, which must be dealt with only sketchily.[20] The post-Stalin leadership of the CPSU, despite its broad relaxation of controls on international communications, was guided in this sphere by purposes and anxieties not fundamentally dissimilar to those of the Stalin regime. A characteristic episode concerned the well-known Soviet writer, Victor Nekrasov. In 1957 and in 1962 Nekrasov traveled in Italy. In 1961 he spent a month touring the United States as a member of a high-level Soviet delegation. Two long and interesting accounts of his experiences and impressions were published in the Soviet literary journal *Novy Mir* (*New World*) for November and December, 1962. *Novy Mir,* which had published Dudintsev's *Not by Bread Alone,* Alexander Solzhenitsyn's *One Day in the Life of Ivan Denisovich,* and many other literary "firsts," was perhaps even more venturesome than usual in publishing Nekrasov's two travel reports. During the period when Nekrasov's articles were published a new storm was brewing on the Soviet cultural front, which was to be shaken by ominous statements by Leonid Ilichev in December, 1962 and January,

---

19 *Pravda,* Oct. 25, 1962.

20 For extended treatment of some aspects of this problem, see Frederick C. Barghoorn, *The Soviet Cultural Offensive* (Princeton, N.J., 1960), esp. Chs. I–V.

1963 and by Khrushchev's angry tirade of March 8, 1963.[21] Nekrasov's reports appeared at an unpropitious moment but they would probably have aroused the severe displeasure of the highest authorities at any time.

To the party's cultural watchdogs it must have seemed that Nekrasov had flagrantly violated rules designed to make certain that the CPSU derived propaganda advantage from cultural exchange. Although many of his impressions of "bourgeois" Italian and United States culture and society were appropriately negative, Nekrasov also commented favorably on American architecture, and even found some good things to say about the Italian Catholic Church. However, it seems almost certain that his principal sin was that of being the first Soviet writer or journalist bold enough to criticize the Stalinist practice, continued by Khrushchev, of including in Soviet delegations sent abroad party or police functionaries, charged with surveillance and control over the activities and especially over the personal contacts of their members. Nekrasov did not mention the police in his ironical and comical description of the tour leader Ivan Ivanovich, whom he depicted as so zealous in guarding the welfare of the "Soviet collective" entrusted to his care in an alien environment that he was mortally afraid lest a member of his flock take an unauthorized walk along Broadway, but his readers must have recognized the type instantly.

Izvestiya for January 20, 1963, sharply attacked Nekrasov for his alleged "fifty-fifty" attitude toward the United States. In effect, Nekrasov was castigated for failing to produce standard anti-United States propaganda. Characteristically, the paper touched only lightly on what was undoubtedly the major cause of official anger. The *Izvestiya* blast made no mention of "Ivan Ivanovich" but it did contain a brief criticism of his alleged lack of "tact" in his relationship with his traveling companions. Although the Nekrasov affair did not mark a major turning point in Soviet cultural exchanges with the West, it was followed by events such as the cancellation of Evtushenko's expected visit to the United States in April, 1963 and by other indications, which continued after Khrushchev was removed, that Soviet intellectuals who

21 For the texts of Ilichev's and Khrushchev's pronouncements, see *Pravda*, Dec. 22, 1962; *Sovetskaya kultura*, Jan. 10, 1963; *Pravda*, March 10, 1963. For English translations, see Johnson, *op. cit.*

sought fuller freedom of communication and expression in cultural exchanges with "bourgeois" colleagues abroad than their supervisors thought wise, would be penalized.

In his harsh speech of March 8, 1963, to writers, artists, and party ideological specialists, Khrushchev once again reiterated the Stalin line, which had been proclaimed with exceptional fierceness by Andrei A. Zhdanov in his notorious address to the Leningrad writers in August, 1946. Like Zhdanov, Khrushchev asserted that literature, art, and music, together with the press and radio, are "an ideological instrument" of the party. In the threatening campaign which followed, the matter was put even more crudely at times. A major organ of the party central committee declared not only that there could be no such thing as nonpartisanship in the arts, or in society generally, but that "art is a form of ideology." [22] Thus once again the party press reaffirmed the Leninist demand that cultural expression play a "partisan" role. Also, Soviet intellectuals were reminded anew of the party's formula: although there can be "peaceful co-existence" between states with different social systems, the intellectuals must not succumb to the illusion that the relationship between "bourgeois" and "socialist" ideas can be other than one of irreconcilable struggle. Moreover, they were again warned in exceptionally sharp tones that to paint too black a picture of Soviet reality or violate in other ways the canons laid down by the party was to play into the hands of the class enemy.

On the other hand, though the Soviet press contained disturbing reports about the "voluntary" decisions of various young and hitherto dissident writers to go off to Siberia and other distant places for a taste of "production" work, the central committee "ideological plenum" in early June took a surprisingly mild tone. This stand may have reflected Khrushchev's unwillingness to yield to extreme demands made by "neo-Stalinist" elements in the party apparatus and by the "hard" faction of the writers. The latter, Vsevolod Kochetov, for example, insisted on reprisals against the Evtushenkos, the Voznesenskis, the Nekrasovs, and the Ehrenburgs. It may also reflect his sense of the difficulty or at least the inexpediency, at the time, of extreme harshness.

[22] *Partiinaya zhizn*, No. 6, March, 1963, editorial entitled "Iskusstvo prinadlezhit narodu," pp. 3–7. This editorial declared also that those who "sought to hide under the flag of nonpartisanship" often turned out to be servants of the bourgeoisie, opposed to the communist revolution.

Early post-Khrushchev policy toward creative intellectuals appeared to continue Khrushchev's position after the relatively mild crackdown of 1962–1963, and this generalization seemed applicable in 1965 to the specific question of contacts between Soviet intellectuals and foreign colleagues. The sending of "unofficial" Soviet delegations to the United States, such as the group of writers headed by Alexander Chakovski, editor of the *Literary Gazette,* to spend most of their time talking to American colleagues and visiting private homes, seemed to have interesting promise for freer communication. However, this may have been more than balanced by the selection of Chakovski, a major participant in the 1962–1963 campaign against "revisionist" writers, to lead the group, and by the deaf ear turned by the Soviet authorities to requests made by many American student groups to permit some of the more unorthodox, experimental writers to come to the United States. On the other hand, Voznesenski visited England in 1965 and Evtushenko journeyed to Italy — but the latter displayed a degree of caution indicating that he had been very carefully briefed. Voznesenski also behaved circumspectly on his visit to America in March, 1966.

In examining some attitudes and aspirations of the Soviet creative intelligentsia we have concentrated on the period since the death of Stalin because of limited space. However, it is well to bear in mind the sense of continuity with the past conveyed by Evtushenko's statement: "My poetry is only the expression of moods and ideas already present in Soviet society but which had not so far been expressed in verse." [23]

Especially since the death of Stalin, Soviet writers have given expression to a broad spectrum of findings, judgments, and demands. Any attempt to briefly discuss these runs a grave risk of oversimplification. However, three literary tendencies which, judging by official Soviet criticism thereof, have either indirect or direct political significance may be briefly summarized. These might be identified as the subjective, the objective, and the indirectly political.

Some Soviets, such as the late poetess Anna Akhmatova, condemned by Zhdanov in 1946 for "boudoir decadence" and "eroticism," express in their art their individual vision of the meaning of life. This tendency has most often been severely

[23] Evgeni Evtushenko, *A Precocious Autobiography* (New York, 1963), p. 14.

repressed, apparently because the controllers of culture considered that "lyricism," romanticism, and other "subjective" moods distract attention from official objectives and weaken morale by encouraging what the Kremlin regarded as "soft," escapist attitudes.

On the other hand, any kind of realism other than the officially approved "socialist realism," which is actually a form of didacticism, is usually frowned upon. The chief target of Zhdanov's savage criticism of the Leningrad writers in 1946 was the satirist Mikhail Zoshchenko, partly because this gifted writer dared to openly present the seamy side of Soviet reality. This was also one of the main targets for Khrushchev's criticism of Soviet writers in his statements of 1957, 1959, 1961, and 1963.

What has here been described as indirect political content in Soviet literature is the presenting in an unfavorable light of party officials, factory directors, and other characters symbolizing the Soviet elite, or even the total Soviet political and social order. Of course, even such unusually bold and candid Soviet writers as Dudintsev had made it clear that they were not attacking what they conceived to be the essential tenets of Marxism-Leninism. Only Boris Pasternak, among major Soviet writers, openly rejected the bolshevik revolution and its consequences, and that, undoubtedly, was the reason for the fury in the Kremlin when Pasternak was awarded the Nobel prize for literature in 1958.

However, in some ways, loyal communists such as Dudintsev or Evtushenko present more troublesome problems than a Pasternak. In a sense, what these authors did was to take at face value the promises made after Stalin's death that the Leninist gospel was to be applied. The utopianism inherent in such an approach to life appeals to idealistic Soviet readers, including many members of the party.

The persistence of unorthodox tendencies in the post-Stalin era attests to the survival of some elements of intellectual and emotional health in Soviet culture. Also, it points to a tacit alliance between some relatively tolerant, or perhaps merely pragmatic, elements in the CPSU, and writers who, though patriotic in the Soviet sense, seek to reconcile official norms with the demands of artistic integrity. From the point of view of orthodox elements in the party apparatus, especially among the professional shapers of opinion, even innocuous personalism or subjectivism are objectionable. The variety of perceptions they convey challenges official claims regarding the consistency and vitality of Marxism-Leninism.

The writer and artist in communist society have far greater potential political significance than those brought up in the American tradition might imagine. Khrushchev himself took cognizance of this fact after events in Hungary and Poland had called it forcefully to his attention. In Russia, as in other under-developed countries, literature was traditionally almost the only vehicle of free moral-political judgment. This tradition, though attenuated, survives in the USSR. One may well ask why, if the job of the writer is potentially so dangerous, writers have been favored as they have by a regime under which successful writers enjoy the highest available standard of living. Even Pasternak, after his condemnation, lived, until his death, in luxury in the literary "colony" of Peredelkino, near Moscow. One reason appears to be that the Soviet leaders have always understood that only the arts could breathe into the political socialization and communication effort the requisite emotional appeal. But if artists are to function, reasons the Kremlin, they must be rewarded not only materially, but also with as much freedom as is compatible with the ideological security of the community. And, encouraging to those who hope for what Peter Viereck calls "the revolt of the heart," the Kremlin apparently fears that Stalin-style repression of writers would be prohibitively counter-productive, even adjudged by its own values.

The post-Stalin literary ferment probably was politically significant in helping to articulate the interests not only of writers but of the Soviet intelligentsia as a whole. Unorthodox writing mitigated, somewhat, the fragmenting and isolative effects of Stalinist compartmentalization. It is one of the forces awakening the latent self-awareness of various social groups. Certainly the public or semipublic literary debates in Moscow, especially but not only in 1956, served as something of a bridge, linking students, writers, critics, and others. Other developments, not directly related, have contributed to a "shaking up" of society, and to stimulation of critical thinking. Among these were Khrushchev's denunciation of Stalinism, increased contact with "bourgeois" foreigners, and, perhaps, contact and interaction between secondary school graduates of intelligentsia background and genuine "proletarians" in the factories, the latter possibly an unintended consequence of the post-Stalin educational reforms. All may also have exerted a similar influence.

Literature, broadly speaking, still remains the handmaiden of propaganda in the USSR, but the solidarity displayed by writers in the face of pressures exerted by the highest political authorities may have much significance for the future. It is not impossible that the post-Stalin dialogue between Soviet writers and the party, whatever its future vicissitudes, may contribute to a liberalization of Soviet society as surprising as the present situation is, compared with the terroristic conformity which prevailed under Stalin.

We have less information on the situation and attitudes of Soviet painters, sculptors, architects, and composers than we have about writers. In general, creative artists suffered severe frustrations under Stalin, except for a minority of politically powerful individuals such as the late Alexander Gerasimov, a portraitist who specialized in heroic canvases of Stalin. These frustrations were especially intense during Stalin's last years, but artists have been able to function somewhat more freely since the dictator's death. Obviously, the details are intricate and the distribution of repressions uneven. The regime's continued disapproval of "abstract art" — a label apparently applied to anything even faintly nonrepresentational — violently expressed by Khrushchev after he visited an exhibition of contemporary Soviet art on December 1, 1962, renders the position of painters and sculptors very difficult. One hears, nevertheless, of bold spirits who hang their unorthodox works behind curtains or carpets, earning their living by poster art. Architects, on the other hand, seem to have been granted considerably increased freedom after Stalin's death.

The problems posed for the CPSU by attitudes prevalent in some circles of the creative intelligentsia have been discussed at length because material on these attitudes is relatively accessible and also because the attitudes of this segment of the intelligentsia are potentially so significant. Rebellious writers and artists are in many ways the most interesting and exciting element of the Soviet intelligentsia. But, lest we exaggerate their significance, it is well to bear in mind Fischer's generally sound judgment that the Soviet variety of modernization has "greatly accentuated the general modern preponderance of the elaborately organized and differentiated technical professions over the 'free' and humanistic professions." Fischer adds that in the Soviet case the recruitment and organization of "specialized and middle-range intellectuals," as against "general intellectuals," has been emphasized.[24] The post-Stalin ferment in the arts and the Kremlin's uneasiness regarding it may make it seem that Fischer has underestimated the importance of the "free" professions. But he usefully calls attention to the millions of Soviet engineers, administrators, and other salaried specialists who are far more conformist in their philosophical, cultural, and political outlook than the few score hundreds or perhaps thousands of nonconformist writers and artists whose intellectual restiveness has disturbed the party leaders. A rough indicator of the existence and relative importance of the various Soviet "skill groups" is furnished by representation of these groups in policy-making bodies of the CPSU and in the party membership as a whole. Although the party central committee usually contains a few leading scientists, writers, and high-ranking military and police officials, and, indeed, representatives of the most diverse occupations, it has always been overwhelmingly dominated by the most successful leaders of the party apparatus, and the party presidium has shown an even greater predominance of them. A similar pattern prevails in the party organizations of the fifteen constituent republics of the USSR.[25]

Top party apparatus officials — first secretaries of republic and other territorial party organizations, particularly those of Moscow, Leningrad, Kharkov, and other major cities, and high-ranking functionaries of important central committee departments — are the group most heavily represented in the central committee, its secretariat, and the CPSU presidium, as well as in other policy-making party bodies. Next in strength is the top leadership of the Soviet state bureaucracy. Although at the highest levels most of the party and state bureaucracies are interchangeable and indeed for most purposes are aspects of a single party-state complex, the party leadership has always been concerned lest the specialization, conservatism, and routinism of bureaucracy de-

[24] George Fischer, "The Intelligentsia and Russia," in Cyril E. Black, ed., *The Transformation of Russian Society* (Cambridge, Mass., 1960), p. 267.

[25] Robert Conquest, *Power and Policy in the U.S.S.R.* (New York, 1961), p. 35; John A. Armstrong, *The Soviet Bureaucratic Elite* (New York, 1959), pp. 66–68, 144–45.

stroy its revolutionary élan. The achievement of eminence in the Soviet state machine would be unthinkable without the approval of the party apparatus. Indeed, this relationship is safeguarded by the system of "nomenclatures," by which the party secretarial apparatus supervises appointments to executive positions in all fields of activity.[26] Strikingly symbolizing the party-state fusion, Lenin, Stalin, and Khrushchev all eventually added the highest executive office in the Soviet state to their incumbency of the top party post. Most specialists on Soviet affairs were doubtful after Khrushchev's fall that the division of party and state leadership between two individuals, Leonid Brezhnev and Aleksei Kosygin, would endure very long.

PARTY-BUREAUCRACY RELATIONSHIPS

The party has always devoted much effort to safeguarding its control over the state bureaucracy, and thus implicitly has indicated that it recognizes a certain lack of "fit" between its primary mission as an agency for the revolutionary transformation of society and the somewhat different interests generated by the requirements of administrative efficiency, particularly in its industrial sphere.[27] The party apparatus at all times has had at its disposal a panoply of specialized agencies for the supervision and control of the state bureaucracy.[28] Stalin, after the great purges of 1936–1938, built up the state machine at the expense of the party apparatus, but he kept both instruments of rule under the control of his political police. It appeared for a time after Stalin's death that this pattern would be still further strengthened, under the leadership of Georgi Malenkov, at the head of an amalgam of elite elements, the bulk of which was formed by state bureaucrats and industrial administrators. However, one of the main thrusts of Nikita Khrushchev's successful bid for power was in the direction of a "Leninist" revival of control of all policy and decision-making organs by men clearly identifiable as party apparatchiki. Once he had consolidated his power, Khrushchev

[26] On this point, see Fainsod, *op. cit.*, pp. 224, 515, 518. See also the sections of Chapter VI in which we deal in some detail with the "nomenclature" system.

[27] Armstrong, *op. cit.*, esp. Chs. IV, V, and X, and Barrington Moore, Jr., *Terror and Progress* (Cambridge, Mass., 1954) have analyzed various aspects of the problems posed by the efforts of a revolutionary party to develop and operate an efficient and stable administrative mechanism.

[28] For the history of these control agencies, see Fainsod, *op. cit.*, Ch. XXI.

reversed this trend, but he did not return to the bureaucratic rule characteristic of the late Stalin and early post-Stalin periods.[29]

Perhaps the most conspicuous feature of the first year of rule by Khrushchev's successors was their reversal of the extremely intimate involvement of the party apparatus — and of himself personally — in the details of everyday administration, especially of industry and agriculture, and their efforts to restore a more traditional division of labor between party apparatus and government in the execution of public policy. Presumably, both economic administrators, especially planners often dismayed by Khrushchev's interventions in their sphere of competence, and ideological specialists, whose prestige sank during the era of Khrushchevian "empiricism," were comforted by these moves to return to patterns which Khrushchev had upset, without, however, success in demonstrating the superiority of his alternatives to them. ("Empiricism," traditionally a term of abuse in Soviet political discourse, was unleashed against Khrushchev after his fall.)

In some ways, party leaders such as V. M. Molotov, N. A. Bulganin, or A. N. Kosygin, whose careers have been made primarily in the Soviet governmental bureaucracy, may be regarded as links between the party apparatus on the one hand and the intelligentsia on the other. The largest segment of the intelligentsia, heavily represented in the membership of the CPSU and also, as a rule, in its highest organs, might be described generally as the economic intelligentsia. Robert Conquest has estimated that about a third of the party membership are "members of the Party who have directed the main branches of Soviet industry, the planning centres, and that large section of the State apparatus devoted to economic matters (in effect practically the whole State machinery except for the administrative machinery, foreign affairs and the armed forces)." [30] If to executive, engineering, planning, and various categories of economic supervisory personnel, we add party members engaged in manual labor or in agriculture, there emerges an organization overwhelmingly dominated numerically by persons engaged either directly or indi-

[29] For an attempt to apply a kind of "interest group" analysis to the Khrushchev-Malenkov struggle for power, see Roger Pethybridge, *A Key to Soviet Politics* (New York, 1962).

[30] Conquest, *op. cit.*, pp. 46–47.

rectly in production. This of course is not remarkable in a society straining every effort toward industrialization and modernization. But it is perhaps worth noting that in 1954 and 1955 Khrushchev began to push a vigorous policy of including more and more factory workers and collective farm peasants among new recruits to the party. However, despite a partial reversal of the late Stalinist trend toward managerial and intelligentsia domination in party recruitment, the percentage of party membership of managerial, professional, and intellectual elements is still far greater than would be indicated by their representation in the population as a whole.[31]

Stresses and strains appear to be at a relatively low level between the party and physicists, chemists, mathematicians, and exponents of other disciplines less affected than are writers and artists by ideological constraints. However, some, perhaps many, leading Soviet natural scientists opposed basic features of changes in Soviet educational policy introduced in recent years, especially in the educational reforms of 1958. These scientists apparently felt that requiring graduates of secondary schools to work for two years before entering higher educational institutions, lessened dependence upon entrance examinations and other academic criteria, and increased emphasis upon political criteria would lead to a lowering of the quality of Soviet scientific training.[32]

Scientists and educators were able to soften the reforms by persuading Khrushchev to make them less drastic than he had originally intended and by finding loopholes in the regulations actually put into effect. Social scientists, historians, legal scholars, biologists, and psychologists, though less favored than their colleagues in the "hard" sciences, today enjoy far more than the bare minimum of freedom necessary for performing their functions, including greatly increased access to foreign publications, than the Stalin regime grudgingly accorded them. Indeed, within still pretty narrowly defined, ideologically determined limits, the social sciences, especially in the last two or three years, have entered upon what by comparison with the Stalin era seems like

[31] For details see Fainsod, *op. cit.,* pp. 275–78. See also *Pravda,* March 30, 1966.

[32] Some indication, in veiled form, of such sentiments is given in the article by a high-level Soviet educational administrator, V. Stoletov, in *Kommunist,* No. 16, Nov., 1958.

an efflorescence. Vast areas of methodology and subject matter
are still tabu — for example Freudian approaches in psychology.
But it would appear that social scientists who can make a good
case for the applicability of their projects to the improvement of
labor productivity, teaching methods in the schools, economic
planning and management, the use of computers in legal research, and a host of other "practical" outputs find it increasingly
easy to obtain the support necessary for the pursuit of their re-
searches. These trends reflect the lively interest of Soviet social
scientists in improving their methodological equipment and cannot fail to be gratifying to many of them. Some examples are the
addition, beginning with the September, 1964 issue, of a department dealing with administrative science to the leading Soviet
legal journal, *Soviet State and Law,* the growing output of labor
and leisure time studies produced by an increasing number of
research centers, or the plea made by the chief of the legal statistics department of the USSR Supreme Court for systematic
gathering and analysis of such statistics in order to discover the
causes and develop methods for prevention of crime.[33]

Criticism by the post-Khrushchev administration of previous
failures to pay sufficient attention to the contributions which
scientific knowledge could have made to national policy, together
with other straws in the wind, warranted the tentative conclusion that the improved situation of the Soviet scientific and
scholarly community begun under Khrushchev would be accelerated by his successors. This impression was confirmed by
well-informed reports from Moscow that Soviet intellectuals
seemed pleased by the fall of Khrushchev. It seemed likely that
researchers might be under less intense pressure than that exerted
by the shrewd, resourceful, but poorly educated Khrushchev
to achieve immediate "practical" results — or, as in the case of
Khrushchev's friend, T. D. Lysenko — the appearance thereof.
Interestingly, Khrushchev complained in 1957 that among Soviet
economists and philosophers there were "people removed from
life, from the practice of communist construction." [34] In his address to the Twenty-first Extraordinary Party Congress, Khrushchev said that it was "the duty of our economists, philosophers
and historians to study deeply the laws governing the transition

[33] *Isvestiya,* Nov. 12, 1964.
[34] *Kommunist,* No. 12, Aug., 1957, p. 17.

from socialism to communism, to study the experience of economic and cultural development, to help train the working people in a communist spirit." [35] There is no reason to doubt that his successors would endorse this view but the younger and better educated among them may be more discriminating in their exploitation of scientific cadres for power purposes.

In appraising the "frustration level" of Soviet natural and social scientists, one must weigh, against the continued pressures for at least a measure of ideological conformity with which they must cope, certain compensatory factors. High-ranking scientists, especially mathematicians and natural scientists, are rewarded for successful endeavor by (1) comfortable standards of living, including, often, domestic servants and chauffeurs, (2) a social status far above that enjoyed by their American counterparts, (3) much freedom of contact with foreign colleagues, albeit of a rather stiff and formal character, both in the USSR and at scientific and professional meetings abroad, and (4) a relative abundance of equipment and the best working conditions that the regime can arrange. In all probability, they have achieved a reasonably satisfactory *modus vivendi* with the regime. Indeed, some competent foreign observers believe that the improved conditions of the post-Stalin period have brought optimism and self-confidence to Soviet natural scientists.[36] Eugene Rabinowitch expressed the view that natural science was the freest sector of Soviet society.[37] Compared to historians, economists, sociologists, and writers, natural scientists, in the opinion of Rabinowitch, were much more "their own masters." For this reason, science has great attractiveness as a career for bright young people.

Soviet scientists belong to what Soviet people sometimes refer to as the "learned world" (*ucheny mir*). As this expression implies, theirs is indeed a highly esteemed world, remote from that of the workers and peasants, and also from the more sensual world of the arts, and from other segments of the intelligentsia subsociety. As far as this writer has been able to learn, the style of life of Soviet scientists — probably also that of historians and

---

[35] *Vneocherednoi XXI sezd Kommunisticheskoi partii sovetskogo soyuza*, Vol. I (Moscow, 1951), p. 61.

[36] Such was the conclusion of R. F. Marshak, in his article "Nature of the Soviet Scientific Challenge," in *Bulletin of the Atomic Scientists* (Jan., 1958).

[37] "Soviet Science — A Survey," *Problems of Communism* (March–April, 1958).

social scientists — might be described as genteel, dedicated to their own work, but respectful also of "higher culture" in general, and somewhat ascetic. In a way, it is "Victorian" and also somewhat escapist, at least in politics. Nevertheless, one cannot help speculating as to whether or not scientists, particularly "military scientists" in the future will indirectly influence increasingly Soviet politics simply because of the vital functions they perform. The pinnacle of the Soviet "learned world" is of course the party-controlled, but immensely respected, membership of the Academy of Sciences of the USSR. This is often colloquially referred to by Soviet scientists and scholars as the "big academy." Below it in the prestige and power hierarchy, but nonetheless very important, are such bodies as the Academy of Pedagogical Sciences, which controls most Soviet psychological research, the USSR Academy of Medical Sciences, the All-Union Lenin Agricultural Academy, etc.

PARTY-MANAGEMENT RELATIONSHIPS

Foreign observers of the Soviet political scene have expressed the view that the industrial managers and their allies in the party leadership might wrest control of Soviet society from the main body of the party apparatus; they have thus far been proved in error. During Malenkov's ascendancy it did appear that the "technocrats" might gain the preponderance of power in the party and state. Even under Khrushchev, despite his emphasis on apparatus supremacy, a partial "technocratization" of the apparatus itself seemed to be occurring, as the apparatchiki were pressed into economic administration. However, the party apparatus thus far has successfully demonstrated its ability to (1) partly satisfy the professional interests of the managerial elite while maintaining party control over this group, and (2) coordinate its activities with goals and policies formulated by the party leadership. The regime succeeding Khrushchev, with veteran party apparatchik Brezhnev at its head and skilled economic administrator Kosygin as chief of government, symbolized this combination of command-subordination and cooperative relationships.

Since the first post-Stalin years the communications media have reasserted the doctrine of party supremacy, which was of course a major theme of the party program adopted in 1961. Persons whose careers had been made primarily in the party apparatus elbowed out of the presidium, the central committee, and other decision-making bodies of the CPSU at least some of the members whose lives had been spent in the ministerial bureaucracy, particularly in its economic chains of command. Concurrently, in the party organizations of the constituent republics, party secretaries were moved into state posts, such as chairmen of the republic councils of ministers.[38]

In 1957, most of the economic ministries were abolished and the councils of national economy were set up. Although this move struck a heavy blow at top-level economic administrators allied with Malenkov,˙ such as Saburov and Pervukhin, and brought dislocation into the lives of many officials who had to give up posts in Moscow for jobs in provincial cities, it may have pleased the rank and file of Soviet factory managers, by relieving them of the necessity for clearing many decisions with superiors in Moscow. On the other hand, this reform, and particularly the division of most *oblast* party organizations at the November, 1962 plenum into separate agricultural and industrial chains of command, created extraordinarily difficulties of coordination and gave rise to chaos and confusion which apparently irritated and frustrated many executives of both the party and the economic bureaucracies. Appraising the results of the party bifurcation retrospectively, *Partiinaya zhizn* declared editorially that "there were doubts" about the wisdom of this measure which, it said, violated the basic principle of party organization: in any given territory there must be a single unified command center to coordinate all party, economic, and other activities and to bear full responsibility for all aspects of political, economic, and cultural life.[39]

Long before the fall of Khrushchev there were signs that his various major economic reorganization measures were creating more problems than they were solving. The floundering of the Khrushchev regime in attempting to deal with these matters clarifies relationships and differences of attitudes between the party apparatus and the managerial-administrative elements that it seeks both to spur and to check. For example, the 1957

[38] See, for example, Radio Free Europe, *Background Information USSR,* April 13, 1959.
[39] No. 23, Nov., 1964.

economic decentralization measures had the disadvantage of encouraging economic regionalism, which the Kremlin was clearly not prepared to tolerate. On April 24, 1958, the presidium of the Supreme Soviet of the USSR issued a decree, "Concerning Responsibility for the Non-fulfillment of Plans and Tasks in the Supplying of Products," the first paragraph of which reads as follows:

> It is established that the non-fulfillment by directors and other leading personnel of enterprises, economic organizations, councils of national economy, ministries and departments, of plans and tasks in the supplying of products to other economic-administrative regions, or union republics, and also for the needs of the country as a whole, is a crude violation of state discipline and entails disciplinary, material or criminal responsibility.[40]

When exhortation proved insufficient, organizational measures were taken to curb "localism" (*mestnichestvo*). In 1960 and 1961 various coordination and integration measures were instituted to combat continued tendencies criticized in the decree cited above. And at the November, 1962 CPSU plenum, along with the agricultural-industrial division, further drastic impetus was given to the economic-administrative "recentralization" begun in 1958–1961. The number of the economic councils was reduced to about forty, new control agencies were established, and renewed, sharp attacks were made on familialism and nepotism, especially in Central Asia.[41]

Whatever the merits of the sweeping reorganization of November, 1962 may have been, they aroused misgivings in party ranks, because of inconveniences and the lowering of the status of some party secretaries involved in the reshuffling of posts connected with the division of the party hierarchy into industrial and agricultural chains of command. It is interesting that, perhaps as a conciliatory gesture to the economic elite, Khrushchev put forward as justifying his proposals for party reorganization the somewhat specious claim that Lenin had asserted of mankind that it had entered an era when economic values had achieved primacy over political ones.

---

[40] *Vedomosti verkhovnogo soveta,* May 28, 1958, p. 499.

[41] Fainsod, *op. cit.,* pp. 396–98, 512–13; Khrushchev's major speech in *Pravda,* Nov. 20, 1962; speech by S. P. Pavlov, First Secretary of Komsomol Central Committee, *Pravda,* Nov. 23, 1962; *Kazakhstanskaya Pravda,* Dec. 26, 1962.

Khrushchev's successors sought a new relationship between the party apparatus and the managerial and state bureaucracies which would, it was hoped, please and energize all these groups. Indirectly, statements demanding vigorous but tactful party guidance of industrial executives, engineers, and other "specialists" gave some information on the relatively subordinate role of the latter. Numerous articles and editorials urged that party organizations see to it that capable executives, especially those with a feel for new technological developments, were encouraged and promoted. They were enjoined, however, to curb factory directors and other economic leaders, who either failed to adjust to the prescribed requirement for leadership by persuasion instead of by "command" or, worse yet, who took advantage of their positions to cheat the state by shady transactions. Particularly stressed was the duty of economic executives to participate in the political education of rank and file workers — a party demand which simultaneously underscored the leadership status and the subordination to the party apparatus of the *Khozyaistvenniki* (bosses).

The vastly important role of the Khozyaistvenniki, however, probably second only to that of the party apparatchiki in the total scheme of things, was indicated in numerous ways, including heavy representation in the CPSU central committee and the frequent appearance in the press of policy suggestions by factory and state farm directors, planning officials, economists, and others primarily involved with the realm of production.

Moreover, as the first secretary of the party in the city of Lipetsk pointed out, the long-deplored tendency for party secretaries to become "dependent" on industrial executives had not been overcome.[42]

THE STATUS OF WORKERS AND PEASANTS

Although in the official myth the industrial worker is the leading class of Soviet society, the gulf between myth and reality is wide — not only as perceived by noncommunist foreigners, but also because the ruling CPSU is so very far from being a "proletarian" party. In 1960, according to official sources, 43.1 per cent of new party members were manual workers and 21.7 per cent were collective farmers, compared with 30.4 per

42 *Pravda*, May 25, 1965.

cent workers and 21.3 per cent farmers in 1955. As Harry Schwartz noted, 48 per cent of party members, as of 1960, were still "white-collar employees." [43] However, *Partiinaya zhizn* reported with satisfaction in early 1965 that "in the last three years" 931,800 new "workers" and 225,700 collective farmers had been brought into the party — and the percentage of those strata in total party membership had increased by one and one-half.[44]

In his report to the Twenty-third CPSU Congress on March 29, 1966, Brezhnev asserted that, since 1961, the proportion of workers among new party members had substantially increased. Both wage-earning workers and salaried employees are organized in the All-Union Central Council of Trade Unions (VTSPS), a mammoth system of industrial unions. However, there are elaborately differentiated provisions for vacations, etc., for the various occupational groups and income levels. As is well known, neither the VTSPS nor its affiliates are permitted to engage in what in "capitalist" countries would be regarded as free collective bargaining. The Soviet doctrine that in the USSR there are no class conflicts implies that labor strikes are unnecessary. However, in recent years there have been a number of sporadic, *ad hoc* manifestations of labor unrest. Minor work stoppages caused by administrative inefficiency but also possibly reflecting labor-management tensions are now occasionally and cautiously reported in *Trud,* the official trade union newspaper. Formal representation of the interests of labor is entrusted to the party-controlled VTSPS, still headed in 1966 by V. V. Grishin, since 1961 an alternate *(kandidat)* member of the CPSU presidium.

Unions, as well as the organizations of the elite professions, such as artists, seek to organize the leisure-time activities of their members, in clubs, "palaces of culture," etc. The spirit in which the directors of those facilities are expected to approach their task was suggested in an article on a VTSPS conference on workers' clubs. It pointed out that the mere "killing of time" had nothing in common with "the communist way of life," in which leisure was "not a passive but an active factor in the upbringing of the new man." [45]

[43] *The New York Times,* Feb. 2, 1961.
[44] No. 10, March, 1965.
[45] *Komsomolskaya Pravda,* Dec. 2, 1960, p. 2.

It would probably be a serious error to imagine that the Soviet factory, railroad, or construction worker is seething with discontent. The Soviet factory and trade union have achieved some success in their prescribed function as "schools of communism." Certainly the worker in the Soviet Union feels a sense of superiority to the farmer, and derives some satisfaction therefrom. Also, particularly in the highest-paid, skilled categories, he is better off materially than lower-level members of the intelligentsia, not to mention clerical workers. Soviet wages are highly differentiated. They are based on a complicated piece-rate system, increasingly replaced in recent years by hourly rates, probably as a concession to labor dissatisfaction. The distribution of relative material values does resemble that in other industrial countries, and it is perhaps not idle speculation to assume a certain similarity also of attitudes, stratum by stratum.

However, many burdens and frustrations, unknown since the early, deprivational stages of industrialization in the West, have long beset the Soviet worker. He is not allowed to strike. When this writer raised the question of the rights of labor in conversing with a *Pravda* editor in 1956, the latter shouted angrily, "Are you advocating that workers strike against the state?" His housing is cheap but of wretched quality, despite the improvement effected in recent years. In a very short time Soviet-built housing often looks years older than it actually is. His general standard of living, unless he belongs to the minority of the highly skilled, remains low. Maurice Hindus, writing in 1961, reported that the average Soviet worker could not support his family without the assistance of a working wife. This is still true today. Despite the myth of the proletariat, the workers' social status is far lower than that of "educated" people, as Soviet workers themselves often refer to professionals, civil servants, etc. For scientists the Soviet man in the street has deep respect; toward writers and especially toward entertainers he often feels envy, even contempt. It is striking that few ordinary factory workers are included among Soviet "delegations" sent abroad, or even among the parties of Soviet tourists who travel now in large groups to Europe and Asia, and in smaller numbers in the United States. This policy of selection symbolizes the modest status of the worker in the workers' state.

Khrushchev took measures to elevate the status and improve the material situation of Soviet workers, and his successors appear to be committed to furthering this improvement. The apathy apparently displayed by Soviet workers toward the ouster of Khrushchev seems to indicate that they did not respond to his efforts on their behalf. Sincere though these efforts may have been, they were mostly nullified by continued shortages of goods, especially by the agricultural failure of 1963, which forced the Soviet Union to purchase large quantities of grain from the United States, Canada, and Australia. In Moscow, Leningrad, Tashkent, and other Soviet cities in October of that year this writer saw long queues in front of bakery shops and signs notifying customers of restaurants and lunch rooms that the practice — announced with fanfare a few years earlier — of providing free bread with meals, had been canceled. There were many other indications of shortages of staple foodstuffs. We gained the impression in conversations with Soviet workers that some of them felt that material conditions had actually been better under Stalin. Not only workers, of course, but probably all strata of the population were depressed and disturbed by the aggravation in 1963 of what for years had been at best a mediocre food situation. Toward the end of October, 1963, in a long conversation with two Soviet citizens, it became clear that, despite the sharp disagreements between them on some subjects, they could not understand why a nation which, as one of them put it, could "conquer the cosmos," was unable to properly feed its citizens. A few weeks earlier we had listened in Leningrad to what seemed despair or at least extreme frustration expressed by a highly paid writer. He spoke of failures of the Soviet economy — for example, the lack of a rational system for pricing goods — and particularly about the catastrophic agricultural situation, which, interestingly enough, this man blamed not only on the mistakes of Stalin (did he also mean Khrushchev?) but even more on the laziness, stubbornness, and conservatism of the Russian peasant.

The Soviet system makes no formal provision for workers or other citizens, in their capacity as consumers, to articulate their interests or to lobby in support of such interests. It has long been clear that consumer discontent is a factor in Soviet politics, not only domestically but also in international relations. Fear of its stimulation by unfettered communication with the outside world is probably a major factor in impelling the party to maintain the so-called Iron Curtain. Even Stalin realized that if levels of consumption were pushed too low not only would the health and the morale of consumers suffer, but discontent might rise dangerously. Knowledgeable foreign observers of Soviet attitudes agree that there is still, despite post-Stalin reforms, much discontent regarding living standards. When in June, 1962 prices charged in government stores for meat and butter (the latter, incidentally, often unobtainable) were raised, respectively, 30 per cent and 25 per cent, the official announcement of this unwelcome news by implication blamed the increases on the necessity for the USSR to hold its own in the international arms race.[46] This decree, besides thus seeking to deflect discontent outward, in its disclosure that prices paid to collective farmers for meat were to be substantially increased, revealed concern about peasant attitudes.

Lest we create the impression that the Soviet version of "consumerism" signifies the likelihood of early development of the mature mass consumption economy, we must point out that in Soviet policy statements heavy emphasis is placed on communal or collective rather than individual use of major appliances, and that even in regard to clothing and footwear, frills are frowned upon. Unlike Japan, where the automobile industry is beginning to boom, Soviet policy thus far excludes production of passenger cars for mass consumption. The Soviet government seems to be acutely aware of the potentially unsettling consequences, for the present still rather austere Soviet style of life, of a substantial increase in production of the more elaborate consumer goods.

An increased supply of consumer goods permits a certain freedom of choice to purchasers. It whets appetites. It makes it more difficult to rule by coercion, for the idea develops that superior effort is to be rewarded materially, whereas under Stalin emphasis was more upon punishment for failure than reward for success. Also, increasing the supplies of consumer goods creates marketing problems by putting an increasing premium upon managerial-administrative skills and, perhaps, reinforces a bit the general

[46] This action was commented on by Victor Zorza, in *Manchester Guardian Weekly*, June 7, 1962. For the decree announcing it, see *Kommunist*, No. 8, May, 1962, pp. 3–9.

tendency in Soviet society to elevate the functional autonomy of economic administrators. Perhaps it was with such considerations in mind that the post-Khrushchev regime, while pledging efforts to produce more and better consumer goods and to provide the people with sorely needed services, also stressed the vast amount of difficult "unfinished business" and the hard work needed to bring a substantial improvement in the Soviet standard of living. Perhaps more frankly than ever before, the new leadership set about its business, as indicated by Brezhnev's statement in his November 6, 1964, speech: "We know that the quality of many of our manufactured articles is inferior to the best models," and his invocation of Lenin's authority in support of an injunction to party and nonparty citizens alike to face up to difficulties and "see life in all its complexity." One of the objectives of the new collective leaders may have been to assure the population that they understood and sympathized with dissatisfactions regarding both quantity and quality of goods and services, but that, unlike Khrushchev, they realized the uselessness of flamboyant promises in dealing with the problems posed by these deficiencies. The new sobriety of tone, symbolized by failure for the first time in several years to hold a Kremlin New Year's Eve party, also warned the citizenry not to expect too much too soon.

The largest segment of the population, the farmers who live and work on collective farms (*kolkhozy*) is also the most poorly represented in the party and government, has the least access to channels by which its grievances and aspirations may be brought to the attention of the party leaders, and of course is least able to obtain goods and services. Collective farmers do not belong to trade unions, although some persons who work on or supply services to collective farms are union members, as are the workers and executive and clerical personnel of the state farms (*sovkhozy*). Soviet farmers have no organizations, and probably even no knowledge of those through which farmers in the United States can bring pressure to bear upon legislators. The moods of the collective farmers are kept under close observation through the rural party organizations and a network of informers operated by the police agencies. In spite of the poverty of its organizational resources, exceptional even by Soviet standards, the collective farm peasantry has proven to be one of the most difficult social forces for the party to control. Indeed, it could be argued that the collective farm peasants and the creative writers are the two social groups which have offered the most effective resistance to the party's efforts at coordination and control.[47]

Soviet industrialization, the penetration of the village by motion pictures, radio, and television, and, of course, the school-teacher as the link between the industrializing city and the changing village, have already wrought a transformation of peasant ways of life and thought. In his book, *House without a Roof*, Maurice Hindus quotes a peasant girl, who asked "Why should we workers on the land be different from girls who work in factories?" But Hindus also pointed out that what Khrushchev referred to in a 1959 speech as "kulak psychology," the desire for individual enrichment, remained a source of worry to the Kremlin.

His successors professed to feel less fearful than did Khrushchev of peasant acquisitiveness. Indeed, the attentive reader of the Soviet press of the year after his fall gets the impression that their major interest, at least in domestic affairs, was to gratify it and other peasant aspirations as fully as the over-all security of the system permitted. The record of Kremlin-peasant relations justifies the suspicion that Brezhnev and his colleagues were guided by expediency rather than by a new-found affinity for agrarian interests in making concessions to the Soviet farmer.

Concessions they did make, and on a large scale. Set forth in Brezhnev's speech and other materials of the March, 1965 party plenum, and in the usual fulsome subsequent glosses thereon, these included higher prices for farm products and a promise that prices would remain stable. They also included a pledge of more and better machinery and other needed aids to farming and, perhaps most important, lightening of what were denounced as "senseless" restrictions on freedom of the collective farmers to operate and dispose of the produce of their small but precious "private" plots. An article entitled "The Personal and the Public in the Collective Farm" was very revealing both of the motives for these measures and of the peasant attitudes to which they presumably responded.[48]

Cautiously but unmistakably this article admitted that for the

[47] On this point, see Conquest, *Power and Policy, op. cit.*, pp. 18, 22–24, 82–83, and Ch. VI.

[48] *Partiinaya zhizn*, No. 10, May, 1965.

majority of collective farmers the private plots were the most important stimulus to productivity. Stressing the hope that more appropriate "socialist" incentives would be found by skilful management — as had already been done on a minority of "advanced" farms — the article concluded by asserting that where party organs made "one-sided" and "poorly thought out" decisions, the results were farmer dissatisfaction and great harm to productivity.

The initial results of the 1965 reforms were apparently beneficial, for Theodore Shabad reported that there was a "boom" in peasant sales of foodstuffs in Moscow.[49] Alarm was evident, however, in press coverage of agriculture during the summer, and by fall new large purchases of wheat abroad indicated that the new leaders might be no more successful than Khrushchev in coping with the stubborn physical, social, and psychological problems of agriculture.

Available evidence indicates that in the USSR the peasant aspirations and frustrations, especially in such important areas where strongly distinctive non-Russian patterns of culture survived as the Moslem republics of the Caucasus, Transcaucasia, and Central Asia, are rather contradictory. There is resentment over economic policies which favor the cities over the countryside, standards of material life and services, access to education, and availability of services and recreational facilities. At the same time, there is resistance, especially among non-Russians, to party ideological and organizational pressures. Relations between collective farmers and the party-state machine are apparently sometimes exacerbated by the arrogance, even the contempt, displayed by the city trained or bred party workers, agronomists, engineers, and other personnel increasingly sent to the rural areas since World War II, and especially since the death of Stalin. There seems no reason to believe that peasant apathy or discontent, impediment though it is to the productive efficiency sought by the party, is a potent threat to political stability. But it is possible that these attitudes became more troublesome to the Kremlin after Stalin's death, because Khrushchev faced up to the USSR's serious agricultural problem more honestly than Stalin did, and also because some of his measures for dealing with it aggravated tensions. One of these was the despatching to the countryside of urban cadres, including retired military officers, and the accom-

[49] *The New York Times*, March 14, 1965.

panying numerical buildup of the party in collective and state farms. In 1961 there were 1,100,000 party members on collective farms and 557,000 on state farms.[50]

About peasant attitudes in Central Asia, Shimkin wrote in 1962 that ". . . while the juridical authority of Islam, the mosque and public celebrations have been eliminated, the essential patterns of behavior remain Islamic and Turco-Iranian in content, and deeply familial in orientation." Also, he found, "genuinely acculturated individuals" were "limited essentially to the well-educated elite." [51]

Both Hindus and, more emphatically, Nicholas Vakar, in a perceptive study point to the surviving rusticity in Russian peasant culture.[52] In Vakar's opinion that heritage exercised a preponderant influence on the development of Soviet culture as a whole, and even today, he feels, it is being only gradually overcome. Despite the powerful effect of industrialization, peasants in the USSR clearly differ culturally from city workers, and in particular from city bureaucrats, administrators, and professionals, far more than American farmers differ from the urban population of the United States.

Rural-urban differences are compounded by ethnic factors. The Uzbek or Kazakh peasant — the latter not long removed from a pastoral economy — are likely to speak limited Russian, with a strong accent. Like Armenia, Georgia's links with Russia have been much closer than those of the Moslem peoples of Central Asia or the Caucasus because of a common Christian heritage and joint struggles with the Turks and Persians. During four visits from 1946 to 1963 the writer found it startling how many Georgian customs and attitudes differed from those of the Slavic peoples of the USSR.

Particularly noticeable are distinctive, strict customs regarding the behavior of women. They are not normally seen in the restaurants, where groups of males sit for hours drinking wine, without feminine companionship. Conspicuous, too, is the beautiful, ancient Georgian script. Georgia also has its special local cuisine and its local architectural styles. Its culture has many other dis-

---

[50] Cited by Shimkin, *op. cit.,* p. 17, from *Partiinaya zhizn,* No. 1, Jan., 1962. Some of the interpretations in the foregoing paragraph are based in part on Shimkin's study.

[51] *Ibid.,* p. 30.

[52] *The Taproot of Soviet Society* (New York, 1962).

tinctive features, such as an extraordinarily highly developed sense of hospitality, in which elaborate, traditional toasts in wine play a major role. Also, despite their long association with the Russians, Georgians, at least in the countryside, usually speak Russian badly. It is also noticeable that they seem invariably to speak their native language, rather than Russian, when in the company of other Georgians.

POLITICAL IMPLICATIONS OF NATIONAL DIFFERENCES

Problems of nationality and of national sentiments assume complex and unusual forms in the USSR because of the multi-national composition of the Soviet population. Of a total population of almost 209,000,000 reported by the 1959 official all-union census, 114,500,000 were listed as Great Russians.[53] The cultural counterpart of Soviet political centralism is an assimilationist nationality policy with strong Russifying tendencies. Particularly since the early 1930's, linguistic Russification, exalting the cultural heritage of the Great Russians, and glorifying Russian history regarded as appropriate by the Kremlin have reduced Stalin's formula according to which Soviet culture was "national in form, socialist in content." Its successor grants non-Russians the right to say, in their native languages if they wish, the same things and to think the same thoughts as the members of the Russian nation, which was described by Stalin in his widely publicized Kremlin toast to the marshals of the Red Army in May, 1945 as the "leading nation" of the USSR. The doctrine of Russian cultural leadership has been applied since Stalin's death in a more tactful and and skilful manner. Restitution has been made for some of the worst excesses committed by Stalin in relations among the peoples of the USSR. With the exception of the Volga Germans and the Crimean Tatars, the seven peoples deported entire by Stalin during World War II for alleged collaboration with the Nazis by early 1957 had been restored to their former status insofar as it was still possible.[54] In 1964, after Khrushchev's fall, a decree legally restored the civil and cultural rights of the

[53] *Spravochnik agitatora* (Moscow, 1960), pp. 228–30; Vernon V. Aspaturian's contribution to Roy C. Macridis and Robert E. Ward, eds., *Modern Political Systems* (Englewood Cliffs, N.J., 1963), contains a good brief description of the ethnic composition of the Soviet Union.

[54] On this point see Robert Conquest, *The Soviet Deportation of Nationalities* (New York, 1960).

Volga Germans, but they were not given permission to return to their former home area.

Post-Stalin Soviet nationality policy appears to be a judicious blend of concessions to national sentiments, indicated in such gestures as the transfer of jurisdiction over the Crimea from the Russian Republic of the Soviet Federation to the Ukrainian Republic in 1954, and continuation of the Stalin policy of assimilation. Khrushchev admitted as much in his speech of October 18, 1961, to the Twenty-second Party Congress, when he said that two tendencies were at work in nationality policy. He asserted that each nation of the USSR was undergoing further development, with the expansion of the rights of the union and autonomous republics, and at the same time the various Soviet nations were drawing closer to one another with increasing mutual influence and enrichment of one another's cultures. Post-Stalin policy toward the non-Russian nationalities fosters national-cultural development so as to strengthen economic and cultural links among the nations of the Soviet federation. It also seeks, as in the Stalin era, to encourage development of what literary critic Mikhail Shkerin called a "Soviet character" in a book published in 1963.[55]

The Soviet system of course has always provided for limited, formal pluralism in nationality relationships. Thus, the Soviet government is federal in form. The USSR is divided into fifteen union republics, nineteen autonomous republics, five autonomous oblasts, and ten national *okrugs,* or territories. Each of these classes of units has, respectively, twenty-five, ten, five, and one vote in the Soviet of Nationalities, one of the two chambers of the bicameral Soviet parliament. In addition to such constitutional provisions, there have existed since the first RSFSR constitution (1919) and the first USSR constitution (ratified January, 1924), complex legal, administrative, educational, and cultural arrangements designed to guarantee and even facilitate expressions of national and ethnic values felt by the CPSU leadership to be compatible with its over-all objectives.

Limited decentralization of public administration in the post-Stalin period, particularly in industrial management, has somewhat increased the administrative functions of the constituent republics. It was clearly intended, though, to increase the efficiency of the national economy, rather than as a concession to

---

[55] *Sovetski kharakter,* or *The Soviet Character* was actually the title.

the political aspirations of the non-Russian nationalities. Of course, Soviet federalism, along with the political rights of the non-Russian nationalities of the USSR, is and always has been severely limited. The ruling communist party is described as and functions primarily as an "international" organization, directed from Moscow and shifting its functionaries, especially those of high rank, from one part of the country to another in accordance with Moscow's requirements. Similarly, the economy of the USSR is and always has been administered according to national rather than federal principles. The contemporary interpretation of federalism expresses satisfaction about "the constant exchange of qualified cadres among the nations." Without that, said Khrushchev at the November, 1962 party plenum, it would be impossible "to correctly combine the interests of the state with the interests of the individual republics." [56]

Similarly, Sh. Rashidov, leader of the Uzbek party organization and alternate member of the CPSU presidium since 1961, wrote in an article on nationality problems that, because representatives of so many nationalities worked in Uzbekistan at the common tasks of building communism, it was a model of the "unification of the peoples." [57] Rashidov's article typifies the Soviet practice of turning over to non-Russian party leaders most of the work of celebrating the virtues of the official nationality policy, including the benefits to non-Russians of friendship with "the elder brother, the Great Russian people." Thus Rashidov referred to the dominant nationality, in accordance with a custom established under Stalin. Also typical of many such articles were the copious criticisms directed by Rashidov against survivals of "feudal" customs among his countrymen, such as forcing their women to wear the veil, child marriages, etc. Typical again was Rashidov's warning that wherever "internationalist teaching" is neglected, such "nationalistic survivals" as the advocacy of national parochialness, idealization of the past, praise for "reactionary traditions and customs," etc., invariably manifest themselves.

Although less stridently than during Stalin's lifetime, official statements continue to emphasize the Russian language as the

[56] For example in his important speech to the November, 1962 party plenum, reported in *Pravda*, Nov. 20, 1962.
[57] *Kommunist*, No. 10, June, 1964.

medium of intercourse and cooperation, of brotherhood and friendship among the peoples of the USSR. The 1961 party program proclaimed that the Russian language facilitated "mutual exchange of experience and the access of each nation and nationality to the cultural achievements of the other peoples of the USSR and to world culture." [58] The program also made it clear that the party regarded as the ultimate solution for the problems of ethnic pluralism the establishment of "a single world-wide culture of communist society."

Khrushchev asserted in his speech on the party program to the Twenty-second Congress that although the party would continue in the future to foster the free development of the various languages of the USSR, the development of these languages must not lead "to the strengthening of national barriers, but to the bringing of nations closer together." Similarly, he inveighed against the use of "archaic" national forms of architecture. He also observed, however, that although "the complete unity of nations" would be achieved in the course of the full-scale construction of communism, it would be premature to speak of the "fusion" of nations even after communism had "in the main" been built. He reminded his listeners of Lenin's view that state and national differences would continue to exist even after the victory of socialism in all countries. But, he went on to say, communists would not work to preserve national distinctions. They would support, instead, "the objective process of ever-increasing intimacy" among nations.[59] In Khrushchev's application of the concept of Soviet patriotism to nationality and cultural problems within the USSR there seemed to be an implicit intention of pressing for as rapid and complete Russification of the non-Russian peoples of the Soviet Union as possible.

Illustrating the systematic, though selective and relatively tactful, Russification policy of the post-Stalin era was a feature of the education reform laws of 1958–1959. It granted to parents of non-Russian children the right to decide whether or not their children should be sent to schools in which Russian was the primary language of instruction, or in which all classes were conducted in the Russian language, or, on the other hand, to schools teach-

---

[58] Triska, *op. cit.*, p. 109.
[59] *Materialy XXII sezda KPSS* (Moscow, 1962), pp. 191–92.

ing mainly in a non-Russian language, but with Russian as a required additional language.[60] This provision is significant because one form of "bourgeois nationalism" which has been criticized in the Soviet press is the alleged insistence of some non-Russian parents that their children study in native language schools — an insistence which, it is often charged, is associated with other "nationalist" attitudes.[61] Soviet data indicate that in spite of some parents' resistance to Russification, as early as 1955–56 about two-thirds of Soviet pupils attended primary and secondary schools in which all subjects were taught exclusively in the Russian language.[62] The apparent liberalism of the linguistic choice granted by the educational reform law may have masked an intention to pressure non-Russian parents, formerly required by law to send their children to schools teaching in non-Russian languages, to send them instead to Russian-language schools. Such are the intricacies and subtleties of cultural-subcultural interactions and tensions in Soviet society.

From the Kremlin's vantage point, organized religion and indeed all forms of religious sentiment and practice share with the other attitudes discussed above the objectionable characteristics of "survivals of capitalism." The Soviet leaders see the problems of coping with both religion and "bourgeois" nationalism as aspects of the relationship between the "socialist" state and a not fully reconstructed peasantry. Among Stalin's most successful wartime measures (regarded with less than enthusiasm, however, by the present leadership) were concessions to the Russian Orthodox Church and to other organized religious bodies, obviously meant to secure maximum support from the peasantry. Two control and liaison agencies, the Council for the Affairs of the Russian Orthodox Church and the Council for the Affairs of Religious Cults, were established. Although these bodies remained in existence after the war, and indeed are still functioning, the traditional antireligious propaganda of the Soviet press and

[60] A good analysis of the linguistic implications of the 1958 educational reform is contained in Yaroslav Bilinsky, "The Soviet Education Laws of 1958–9 and Soviet Nationality Policy," *Soviet Studies*, XIV, No. 2 (Oct., 1962), pp. 238–57.

[61] See articles by N. Dzhandildin in *Kommunist*, No. 13, July, 1959; by A. Azizian, in *Kommunist*, No. 15, 1961; and by N. Gadzhiev, in the same magazine, No. 1, Jan., 1962, and V. Mzhavanadze, in No. 2, Jan., 1966.

[62] Nicholas DeWitt, *Education and Professional Employment in the U.S.S.R.* (Washington, D.C., U.S. Government Printing Office, 1961), p. 112.

other media of communication, suspended to foster unity in the struggle against the Nazis, was resumed. Striking evidence of the party leadership's uneasiness at the continued influence of religion, and in particular that of groups such as Jehovah's Witnesses and Baptists, appeared in an important resolution of the central committee of the CPSU.[63] One statement in this decree held that many rural party organizations had neglected their duty of energetically conducting atheistic propaganda, and that as a result "the church and various religious sects have significantly increased their activity, have strengthened their cadres and, flexibly adapting themselves to present conditions, are energetically disseminating religious ideology among the backward strata of the population." The decree went on to charge that churches were devoting particular attention to women and the youths and that they were utilizing choruses and orchestras to increase their attractiveness. At the same time, the resolution charged, they were engaging in the dissemination of religious literature and conducting missionary activities.

The 1954 resolution inaugurated a policy which has been pressed energetically ever since. Reviewing its results as of the end of 1963, Leonid Ilichev expressed some satisfaction and at the same time much chagrin and urged a still more energetic and skilful campaign of "scientific atheism" to eliminate religion.[64] Significantly, he thought it necessary to warn those in charge of antireligious propaganda that they had to deal with people who did not trust them and who would skilfully exploit any mistakes they might make. Similar warnings appeared in 1966.

Puzzling questions are raised by this very limited sample of expressions of concern over the persistence of customs, beliefs, and attitudes that the party felt were inimical to its efforts at mobilization and homogenization. How long will religious and national groups be able to resist the party's pressures for cultural assimilation? How long will even latent political subcultures persist? It is impossible to answer such questions because Soviet authorities refuse to permit outside observers to conduct systematic field studies. This circumstance itself gives rise to speculation as to the phenomena the leadership may wish to conceal. Cer-

---

[63] "Concerning Serious Errors in Scientific-Atheistic Propaganda and Measures for Its Improvement" (July 7, 1954) *Voprosy ideologicheskoi raboty* (Moscow, 1961), p. 144.

[64] *Kommunist,* No. 1, Jan., 1964.

tainly the persistence of national and cultural difficulties so
troublesome as to require continuous and massive propaganda
and administrative countermeasures almost fifty years after the
establishment of Soviet power attests impressively to their
tenacity.

Few scholars would argue that nationality problems could lead
to disintegration of the Soviet system or even that those or other
difficulties stemming from the pre-Soviet heritage present major
obstacles to the regime's ability to achieve its goals. The consensus of informed opinion is reflected in the carefully qualified
finding of Inkeles and Bauer that the nationality composition of
the Soviet Union is unlikely, ". . . under normal conditions," to
be decisive in determining the system's long-range stability. Some
highly competent specialists, however, offer impressive arguments
and evidence contradictory to the view of most experts that the
significance of nationality and related factors is diminishing with
the progress of Soviet modernization and industrialization.
Richard Pipes and Alexandre Bennigsen argue that non-Russian
nationalism is a force of growing intensity precisely because
modernization strengthens the consciousness of kind, the cultural distinctiveness of groups such as the Turkic peoples of the
Soviet Union. Only a generation or two ago they were mostly
illiterate, peasant or even pastoral by occupation, socially and
culturally dominated by patriarchal family traditions, and unable
to perceive and articulate their own sense of identity. According
to this view, which certainly deserves a hearing, the chiefly Russian Soviet communist movement has created, together with the
multinational Soviet state, an increasingly difficult nationality
problem.[65]

Obviously, the continued ability of the CPSU to effectively
perform its work of coordination and mobilization, and indeed
to maintain its very existence, depends upon the loyalty and
enthusiasm of a large segment of Soviet youths. As with almost
every problem of interpreting the situation of the USSR, the

[65] *The Soviet Citizen, op. cit.*, pp. 372–73. Pipes' recent views are briefly
summarized and his earlier studies are cited in "The Forces of Nationalism,"
Problems of Communism, XIII, No. 1 (Jan.–Feb., 1964), pp. 1–6. For Bennigsen's position, see "La famille musulmane en Union Soviétique," in
Cahiers du Monde Russe et Soviétique, No. 1, Jan., 1959, pp. 83–108. For a
strong but scholarly, voluminously documented argument that nationalism in
the Ukraine has great political potential, see Yaroslav Bilinsky, *The Second
Soviet Republic* (New Brunswick, N.J., 1964).

opinions of foreign observers, including participants in the United States-Soviet exchange of graduate students and young scholars which began in the fall of 1958, differ concerning the attitudes of Soviet students and other youths toward the regime. Some observers stress the patriotism of Soviet youths and their at least passive acceptance of official doctrine. Others, such as David Burg, himself a former Soviet student, discern sharp resentment and conscious opposition to the Soviet system among many of the students. There is certainly evidence of disquiet regarding the mood of Soviet youths, particularly student youths, in the minds of Khrushchev and other ranking party leaders, although it is difficult to estimate the intensity of this concern. Numerous statements by the leaders of the Komsomol have pointed to the dangers to Soviet youths inherent in excessively free contests with foreign students and other young people. Khrushchev's most striking statement on this subject was his indication, at the Twenty-first Extraordinary Congress in 1959, of the belief that Soviet youths were more susceptible than their elders to corruption by alien influences, just because they had never lived under a "capitalist" system. Khrushchev said that "we cannot overlook the possibility of bourgeois influence, and we are obligated to conduct a struggle against it," and especially, he added, against the penetration of "alien views and customs" among the youths.[66] Khrushchev indicated that because of this situation it was particularly important that the youths know well the "heroic history of the communist party," and the "revolutionary traditions" of the working class.

A number of important policy decisions of the Khrushchev regime, including the educational reform and the intensification of internal party propaganda following the central committee's decree of January 9, 1960, were apparently motivated principally by the state of mind of Soviet youths. Khrushchev's successors, too, early displayed anxiety over the attitudes of young people. At the end of January, 1965, the Moscow party organization held a plenum devoted to "measures for the further improvement of the work of the Moscow city party organization in the communist upbringing of the youth" — according to Soviet newspapers for January 30. N. G. Egorychev, head of the Moscow party com-

[66] *Vneocherednoi XXI sezd Kommunisticheskoi partii sovetskogo soyuza,* Vol. I (Moscow, 1951), p. 58.

mittee, shortly thereafter published an article on the same subject.[67] Egorychev expressed concern over the "disorienting" effect on youth's morale of Alexander Solzhenitsyn's depiction of the Stalin era in his novel, *One Day in the Life of Ivan Denisovich*. In subsequent months, there were published many other criticisms of literary works whose "nihilistic," or "negative," content, it was held, could sap the faith of youths in communist ideals. Brezhnev, in his March 29, 1966 speech to the Twenty-third Congress, expressed a similar concern.

DIVERSITY VS. UNITY

We have been examining a pattern of contained diversity. It took shape in the Stalin era but has changed much in the years since the death of that despotic ruler. If to Stalin diversity was an evil to be eliminated, to his successors it became increasingly a group of problems to be acknowledged and coped with. There was a significant shift of emphasis from command to persuasion, from hierarchy to bargaining, from punishment to reward, from control to guidance.

The picture remains one of preponderant concentration in a single, relatively highly unified organization — or system of organizations, namely, the party apparatus — of political legitimacy and intelligence, of initiative and over-all supervision over community problems. Despite the diversity of perspectives surveyed, Soviet society in 1966 remained under effective apparatus domination, which seems likely to persist as long as the apparatus can respond with vigor to foreign and domestic challenges by effectively harnessing the resources it commands to well-coordinated policies. To enumerate these prerequisites for continued success seems almost to remind oneself of the abundance in which the Soviet polity seems still to be endowed with them.

However, the durability of this pattern of contained diversity depends on the Kremlin's capacity to incorporate into society and secure the allegiance of the upcoming generation. It depends also upon skill in selecting from this generation leaders capable of maintaining and adapting the system in the difficult years ahead. Failure to perform all the necessary functions adequately could lead to rigidity and stagnation on the one hand, or to disintegra-

---

[67] *Kommunist*, No. 2, March, 1965. See also A. Chakovski in *ibid.*, No. 4, March, 1966.

tion. Another possibility, in a severe succession crisis or a major economic or foreign policy failure, is the appearance of an anti-apparatus coalition, capable of articulating grievances and demands that are at present only diffuse and mutually antagonistic.

It seems likely that the political system will develop increased responsiveness to a widening range of public aspirations, generated by economic growth and development. It also seems probable that for a long time to come the party apparatus will remain by far the most powerful element in the polity, but that it will gradually adapt its control methods in the direction of greater sophistication and will perhaps also slowly relinquish some of its supervisory powers in spheres regarded in the Western democracies as nonpolitical.

Survival or collapse, rigidity or responsiveness, evolution or revolution, will be determined by the style and content of programs of socialization, political communication, and elite recruitment. In the next four chapters we shall survey past developments and emerging trends in the performance of these functions.

CHAPTER III

The Socialization Process

THE PROMETHEAN THRUST of the Soviet political culture, reflected in the bolsheviks' fierce determination to transform a backward society into the model for mankind's future, has been a vital source of Soviet communism's vitality. At the heart of the leadership's attempt to transform society and its individual members has been perhaps the most systematic effort ever attempted to shape and control a people's political outlook. This cradle-to-grave process is so vast and complex that we have devoted two chapters to it, dealing first with the distinctive Soviet methods of inducting children and youths into the political system, and in Chapter IV with the unique Soviet program of adult political socialization.

The Soviet leaders seek to shape communication and personal relationships in school, family, and other attitude-forming institutions so as to inculcate the maximum possible devotion to the polity. At the same time parents and teachers are expected to instill in the rising generation the beliefs and skills that will keep the political system flourishing. The party directs all those who shape the character of the new generation to cooperate in producing citizens most of whom will, it is hoped, become responsible and productive participants in the political life of the country. The party expects a selected fraction to become resolute and farsighted leaders. Such auxiliary organizations as the Young Pioneers, the Komsomol, and school officials and teachers enable the party to discover and develop potential leaders, especially during the adolescent years. Those who survive this early, tentative screening will eventually become party members, and if they meet the rigorous standards for party leadership, they will receive training in the elite institutions which train party functionaries. Others will be sent to special, secret schools for police and intelligence cadres.

Authoritative Soviet statements of goals and methods for the upbringing of youth reflect both short-range operational and long-run ideological factors. A Soviet educational psychologist quotes with approval a statement by A. S. Makarenko, an educator of the 1930's who more than any other formulated the principles of pedagogy still in force. He said that in bringing up children the aim is "the formation of behavior, character, and traits of personality necessary to the Soviet state." [1] Official statements on the aims and spirit of political socialization continue to emphasize the more distant goal of creating the "new Soviet man." In this superior type of human being, as the central committee said in its revealing "theses" on the educational reform of 1958–1959, "Spiritual wealth, moral purity, and physical perfection will be harmoniously combined." [2] The 1961 CPSU program contains numerous references to the "new man" and the means by which he may be "molded."

There can be no doubt that the Soviet leaders are sincere in their determination to rid their citizens of "bourgeois" attitudes, and replace them by a new outlook appropriate to the new society that they believe they are building. Logically, the new society requires "new" people. However, if one examines the content and the historical sources of Soviet moral training, one cannot fail to see how conservative and even traditional it is. Many Soviet pedagogical concepts and techniques are derived from conservative, patriotic figures such as the nineteenth-century educator K. D. Ushinski, who is praised in educational encyclopedias and in an extensive biographical literature.[3]

Whether seeking efficiency and discipline or more fundamental changes in human character, Soviet policy in education and

[1] N. A. Lyalin, ed., *Kollektiv i razvitie lichnosti shkolnika* (Leningrad, 1962), p. 28. Lyalin's work was published by the Leningrad State Pedagogical Institute, perhaps the second most important institution for teacher training in the Soviet Union. The best training center is probably the corresponding Moscow institution, the V. I. Lenin State Pedagogical Institute.

[2] George S. Counts, *Khrushchev and the Central Committee Speak on Education* (Pittsburgh, 1959), p. 33.

[3] See the article on Ushinski in *Pedagogicheski slovar,* Vol. II (Moscow, 1960), pp. 549–53, praising his stress on inculcating patriotism, discipline, and firmness of will in children.

character formation is obviously based upon the assumption that the communist party can shape human consciousness to desired specifications through a centrally planned program of indoctrination and supervised group activity. This faith is clearly tempered by awareness of the immense difficulty in achieving the party's ambitious educational objectives.

EDUCATIONAL INSTITUTIONS AND SOCIALIZATION

A tightly woven network of formal educational institutions has always been the most important instrument of political socialization in the Soviet Union. We shall therefore seek some acquaintance with the main stages in the development of party and governmental organization of education. The party has initiated and announced all major community decisions in the field of education. Pronouncements by Lenin, Stalin, or Khrushchev and joint decrees of the party central committee and the highest governmental agencies are among the vehicles that have been chosen by the leadership to proclaim new departures in educational policy. Execution of party educational policies has been entrusted to functional departments of the central committee of the CPSU and of republic party organizations, and to members of the highest ranking party bodies assigned to positions of central importance for educational administration. These include the minister of education of the Russian Soviet Republic and the president of the Academy of Pedagogical Sciences, the two agencies principally responsible for policy and methods in primary and secondary education. At a higher level is the minister of higher and specialized secondary education, the top-ranking professional in the administration of higher education. Within educational institutions Young Pioneer, Komsomol, and party organizations perform prescribed control, indoctrinational, and other functions. The territorial party and Komsomol organizations exercise some of their political supervision through a panoply of agencies specialized in selecting school and university administrators, financing educational programs, and disseminating propaganda and education materials to educational personnel and students. In controlling the educational system, the party and party auxiliary networks are joined by the appropriate echelons of the All-Union Central Council of Trade Unions, the mammoth network of industrial unions embracing most industrial workers and government employees in the USSR. Party and trade union organizations share responsibility with educational officials in screening applicants for admission to institutions of higher education.[4]

STAGES IN EDUCATIONAL POLICY

After the consolidation of communist power in Russia about 1921 and especially since rapid industrialization and collectivization of agriculture began in 1928, Soviet educational institutions embarked on an immense, continuing, and increasingly complex effort to impart necessary industrial skills and orderliness, punctuality, etc., to a population which was and distressingly still is preindustrial in its outlook, especially in some of its more backward non-Russian segments. Concurrently, Soviet educators have had to equip millions with the rudiments of political "consciousness" and to provide the relatively small number who finish secondary school or go on to higher education with a "scientific" Marxist-Leninist training in party history, philosophy, and political economy. The style, scope, and tempo of this effort have undergone many vicissitudes as the Kremlin responded to the severe domestic and the international pressures.

The historical development of political socialization in the Soviet school system may be divided into three main phases. During the confused, hopeful, and groping early postrevolutionary years some Soviet teachers experimented with American-style "progressive" educational methods and there was even talk of eventual "withering away" of the school, along with such other "bourgeois" institutions as government and law. It is striking that John Dewey was favorably impressed by the pragmatic, industry-oriented aspects of Soviet education which he observed on a visit in 1928. However, Dewey noted that, to the communist leaders, "propaganda is education and education is propaganda." Another American educator observed at the time that although

4 George Z. F. Bereday and Jaan Pennar, eds., *The Politics of Soviet Education* (New York, 1960), pp. 45–56; Nicholas DeWitt, *Education and Professional Employment in the U.S.S.R.* (Washington, D.C., U.S. Government Printing Office, 1961), pp. 246–56. Prescriptions for and interesting descriptive detail on party control of all operations of institutions of higher education are contained in A. Svinarenko, "Partorganizatsiya vuza," in *Partiinaya zhizn*, No. 4, Feb., 1965, pp. 29–36. Svinarenko stresses the need for party organizations to strengthen "public control" over research, instruction, and student life.

the Russian "system of experimental schools is admirable," the Soviet attempt to thrust "communism and materialism down the throats of her children" seemed "criminal." [5]

The second phase of Soviet educational policy extended from about 1931 until 1956–1959. As before, the inculcation of loyalty and support for the polity, its leaders, and their policies were the central tasks of education. The methods of pursuing these objectives changed drastically under Stalin, however. The spirit of Soviet education became a projection of Joseph Stalin's pessimistic estimate of an increasingly threatening international situation and of the dictator's drive for personal and world power. Soviet children continued to be reared in the belief that they were the beneficiaries of a morally superior social order, destined to inherit the earth. Increasingly, however, it was emphasized that the very survival of Soviet Russia, not to mention its economic development, its defense against external enemies, and the longed-for world revolution, required that the operation of historical "laws" be helped along by informed and purposeful action, using all available trained intelligence, scientific knowledge, unremitting toil, and stern discipline. Teachers were called upon to proclaim an implacable struggle not only against the class enemy abroad and his "spies" in the Soviet Union, but also against harmful prejudices and personal weaknesses, which Soviet leaders and ideological experts described as "survivals of capitalism in the minds of the people." [6]

A question often debated by specialists on the Soviet Union is whether the educational, ideological, and cultural departures of the 1930's represented not just highly significant shifts in emphasis and adaptations to changing circumstances but a fundamental transformation of Soviet culture. Perhaps only time will tell whether Stalin engaged in what Professor Nicholas Timasheff described as a "great retreat" and Leon Trotski denounced as the "betrayal" of the revolution in favor of a new elite of party, state, and economic "bureaucrats." It does seem clear that fundamental parts of Stalin's neoconservative educational and cultural

[5] George Z. F. Bereday, William W. Brickman, and Gerald H. Read, eds., *The Changing Soviet School* (Boston, 1960), pp. 64–67.

[6] Perhaps the most penetrating study of the educational changes of the 1930's is Raymond A. Bauer's *The New Man in Soviet Psychology* (Cambridge, Mass., 1952), but these changes have been discussed by many other students of Soviet education and politics.

policy, including selective and controlled revival of Russian national traditions and exalting of the virtues of obedience and discipline, have become central and seemingly permanent in the official Soviet culture. There is, in addition, strong continuity of administrative structure between Stalin and post-Stalin education. However, the modifications introduced into this system after the death of Stalin were sufficiently important to justify the labeling of educational policy since about 1958 as a third period in its development.

Two of the "Khrushchev school reforms" were very significant politically. One was the establishment of a system of boarding schools, called *internaty,* in which as of 1961–1962 about 700,000 students were enrolled. The other was the reintroduction throughout the entire elementary and secondary school system of a modified version of "polytechnical" education, which had been experimented with in the 1920's, but had been eliminated by Stalin and replaced by a principally conventional curriculum. In the Khrushchev system, the polytechnical element of vocational training was added to the academic workload in the lower school grades and in the upper secondary school grades one-third of students' time was devoted to work in agriculture or industry. Probably the most important feature of the revival of the polytechnical principle was the requirement that most secondary school graduates (the exceptions were mostly gifted students in mathematics and the physical sciences) were required to engage in "productive" work for two or more years because 80 per cent of places in institutions of higher education were reserved for youths with at least two years of work experience.[7]

The educational reform, adumbrated by Khrushchev at the Thirteenth Congress of the Komsomol in April, 1958, was set forth in CPSU central committee "theses" in September, 1958, and enacted into law in general form by the USSR Supreme Soviet in December of that year and into specific laws, with some minor variations, by the Supreme Soviets of the constituent republics in 1959. It had important economic, technological, and pedagogical implications. With these we are not primarily concerned, although the reforms did help to overcome the shortage

[7] Jeremy R. Azrael, "Soviet Union," Ch. 8 of James S. Coleman, ed., *Education and Political Development* (Princeton, N.J., 1965), p. 259. This excellent study is an important contribution to understanding of the political socialization process in the Soviet Union.

of trained industrial and agricultural manpower caused by heavy
losses in World War II and a sharp decline in the Soviet rate of
birth during the war. Politically, the reform and the concurrent
program for establishing boarding schools, may be viewed as an
effort to heighten the ideological commitment of Soviet students
by overcoming major defects of the Stalinist educational system.
The positive goals of production training and compulsory work
experience for secondary school graduates expecting to enter
institutions of higher education include generating enthusiastic
commitment to the economic objectives of the Soviet regime,
inculcating respect for labor, and endowing traits of "collectivism," discipline, and organization.[8] One major purpose of
both the 1958–1959 reform and the establishment of boarding
schools was eliminating the disrespect for manual labor apparently engendered by Soviet schools, because of the "classical"
content of their academic curriculum, and also because graduates
of secondary schools had been permitted to assume that they
were automatically entitled to a higher education which in turn
would assure their entering the ranks of the professional or
managerial elite. The major post-Stalin measures were also designed, in part, to correct a situation incompatible with the
egalitarianism of Marxism-Leninism: in 1958, of the students in
institutions of higher education, 60 to 70 per cent were children
of "officials" and "members of the intelligentsia." [9] Another important remedial feature of the changes in educational policy,
and particularly in the boarding school movement, was a
strengthening of the state's hand in the upbringing of children,
as against that of the family, especially in cases involving de-
linquent parents, broken homes, etc. Many authoritative figures
proclaimed that "the boarding schools will become the new
schools of communist society," and that they would come to dominate or eventually even to monopolize the entire educational
system.[10]

An additional factor in post-Stalin educational policy was
clearly the failure of the political indoctrination program in the
schools to produce desired results. In spite of its impressive
achievements the Stalin system of education had not prevented,

8 *Ibid.*, pp. 260–61.
9 *Ibid.*, p. 22.
10 *Ibid.*, p. 27.

and had perhaps even indirectly contributed to the development of undesirable attitudes among Soviet youths. These included selfish, narrow careerism, a growing psychological gulf between intelligentsia and nonintelligentsia, political apathy, and even disaffection.[11] It is ironic, as a number of Western students of Soviet education have pointed out, that the authorities undertook drastic measures to correct serious defects in their educational program at the very time when respect for Soviet education, inspired by spectacular Soviet achievements in space science, was reaching its height. It is perhaps equally ironic that, as pointed out with particular cogency by Jeremy Azrael, one motive for the post-1956 educational innovations was the rulers' realization that they had "gotten away with" de-Stalinization partly because the program of political indoctrination during the Stalin era had not inspired the kind of deep conviction among Soviet youth which might have led to violent revulsion against the dethronement of the formerly revered leader, "teacher," and "genius of humanity."

After Khrushchev's ejection his educational reforms were subjected to fundamental criticism by Soviet educators and educational administrators, although news reports from Moscow, including an extensive survey by Theodore Shabad, indicated that the reformers of earlier reforms were taking a cautiously experimental approach.[12] Long before Khrushchev's fall, however, it was apparent that his attempt to infuse a heavy dose of "labor training" into secondary school education was adversely affecting the quality of Soviet education and thereby was causing concern and dissatisfaction.

As RSFSR Minister of Education Afanasenko pointed out in a speech reported in the Soviet press on July 16, 1964, the extension of time devoted to production training had not justified itself and the learning of subjects such as mathematics, physics, and chemistry was suffering. Beginning with the school year 1964–1965, the length of time required for a complete secondary education was reduced from eleven years to the pre-Khrushchev reform period of ten years. This measure reduced significantly the time spent by students on nonacademic activity. It was among many indications of a reaction against the radically dis-

[11] *Ibid.*, pp. 255–57.
[12] *The New York Times,* Jan. 13, 1965.

turbing features of Khrushchev's educational policies. Other examples were criticism of the Khrushchev innovation of boarding schools and the increased stress in discussions of education on the family's importance in the moral upbringing of children, seen in editorials.[13] There was no reason to believe, however, that there would be a return to Stalinist policies. Rather, in the early post-Khrushchev period an educational pattern appeared in which it seemed that the extremes of narrow specialization and other features common to both the Stalin and Khrushchev policies would gradually be eliminated and that while, borrowing from Western — especially American — educational methods, an attempt would be made to improve the specifically Soviet, ideological style of instruction. For example, a comparative, "sociological," element would be introduced into political indoctrination courses to facilitate the acquisition by students of an integrated, "scientific" world outlook.

There were even indications in the fall and winter of 1964 that perhaps those directing the political indoctrination machine were trying to revive and apply the elements of genuine social science inherent in Marxism, which in their very different ways both Stalin and Khrushchev had neglected. It may be significant that in 1964 a three-month school for training more than five hundred "young workers, teachers, students and graduate students" in problems of social psychology, labor psychology, etc., and staffed by leading philosophers, psychologists, and economists opened in Moscow.[14]

Khrushchev's successors apparently were striving to infuse into Soviet school-level social science a relevancy and a convincingness which it still lacked. The available evidence regarding their efforts suggested the difficulty, though not necessarily the impossibility, of achieving this objective without abandoning Leninist "dialectics."

INCULCATING COMMUNIST MORALITY

The changes made by Khrushchev in all areas of Soviet education and those already begun by his successors are important. However, common to Stalin and post-Stalin periods alike is the basically manipulative conception of education as "the definite,

13 *Izvestiya,* Nov. 24, 1964; *Pravda,* Dec. 16, 1964.
14 *Komsomolskaya Pravda,* Nov. 27, 1964.

the purposeful, and systematic influencing of the mind of the person being educated in order to imbue him with the qualities desired by the educator." [15] Thus far, continuity overshadows change in the evolution of Soviet education, including its political socialization effort. A major thread linking all periods in the history of this effort is the view that its overriding purpose is the inculcation of "communist morality."

In a speech to the Third Congress of the Komsomol in 1920, Lenin set forth a conception of communist morality which is still frequently lauded in Soviet statements on education. According to him, "our morality is completely subordinated to the interests of the class struggle of the proletariat." [16] The politically subordinated morality preached by Lenin in this and other major statements (its theoretical underpinnings were set forth most fully in Lenin's *State and Revolution,* published in 1918) has much in common with the great traditional moral systems. Still, it differs from them in its avowed subordination of moral norms to the shifting interests of the leadership of a particular political movement. Soviet moral philosophy was shaped in large part by Lenin's experience of revolutionary conspiracy, political combat, and propaganda manipulation. It has a humanistic side, to be sure, and it promises as the reward for discipline and sacrifice splendid vistas of future fulfilment, but it also fully and openly justifies cunning and ruthlessness in the political struggle. Soviet communist morality, as shaped by the requirements of ideological combat, has tended to judge the virtue of men and their actions more by the assumed interests and motives of the groups to which they belong than by universal moral norms.

There was sufficient ambiguity in Lenin's attitude toward ethical norms, however, to give rise to widely different interpretations by his successors in the Soviet leadership of this, as of other items in his legacy. Especially after 1934, Stalin emphasized the coercive side of Leninist morality. Stalin's successors denounced his "Talmudistic" preachment of unquestioning acceptance of authority and advocated for both teachers and students a limited amount of individual initiative.

During the Stalin and post-Stalin periods alike the most promi-

[15] From a speech by M. A. Kalinin, who for many years, in his post as chairman of the presidium of the Supreme Soviet, was chief of the formal Soviet state machinery, in Azrael, *op. cit.,* p. 264.
[16] V. I. Lenin, *Izbrannye proizvedeniya,* Vol. II (Moscow, 1943), p. 608.

nent feature of the teaching of "communist morality" has been
the inculcation of "patriotism." During the Stalin era it was
usually described as "Soviet," but since Stalin's death it has more
frequently been described as "socialist." [17] The first principle in
the "moral code of the builder of communism," incorporated
into the 1961 party program, is "devotion to the communist
cause, love of the socialist motherland and of the other socialist
countries." Idolatry of Stalin has been replaced by identification
of youth with "the people" and above all, the party.[18] To preserve the emotional appeal of what one might describe as the
"Stalin-Lenin cult" the symbol of "the great Lenin" was in-
tensively evoked. More than ever, Lenin is the supreme Soviet
father symbol; his idealized image is the model for the "Soviet
super-ego." He is constantly referred to as the inspirer of Soviet
educational — and all other — policies. His portrait hangs in the
offices of all Soviet school directors; and young children, under
the direction of specially trained adults, organize "Lenin corners"
in schools and Pioneer palaces.[19]

In the inculcation of patriotism and of political perspectives
generally, the humanities and the social sciences are most influential. But the presentation of all other subjects taught in Soviet
educational institutions, beginning at the preschool level, is also
permeated with a strong political flavor.[20] In the teaching of
history, probably the most important school discipline for fostering patriotism, emphasis shifted, especially after 1958, from the
individual to the "masses" and from the prerevolutionary to the
Soviet era. This change was accompanied by great confusion. Apparently it proved difficult to retrain history teachers brought
up in the Stalin school of historiography. In December, 1962,
three years after a central committee decree on the revision of
history teaching, it was necessary to hold a national conference
on improving the training of history teachers and historical

17 See N. I. Gubanov, *Otechestvo i patriotizm* (Moscow, 1960), Ch. 4.
18 Azrael, *op. cit.*, p. 263.
19 At a Pioneer palace in Alma-Ata in October, 1963, the writer was told
that the children working in the "Lenin corner" of this institution were engaged in teaching all the schoolchildren of the city how to organize "Lenin
corners."
20 See A. M. Arsenev, *Stroitelstvo kommunizma i shkola* (Moscow, 1962),
p. 7, for a brief discussion of the ideological function of each major school
discipline.

scholars.[21] The systematic teaching of history begins in the fourth grade of Soviet schools, with a course on "Highlights of History of the USSR," and continues with ancient history in grade five, medieval history in grade six, and history of the USSR and modern history of other countries in grades seven and eight. It concludes with a course on the history of the USSR and current events in the USSR and abroad in grades nine through eleven, for the minority of students who complete the full, eleven-year secondary school program. According to Soviet sources, the program in history is designed to develop a "conscious acceptance of the scientific law of the inevitability of the downfall of capitalism and the victory of communism." [22]

The political teachings of the history studied in Soviet schools, it is apparently hoped, will be reinforced and heightened by the study of Soviet-style political science. A leading Soviet educator wrote in 1962 that the course on "Fundamentals of Political Knowledge," which had shortly before been added to the final year of the secondary school curriculum, would "complete the formation of the social outlook of the students of the secondary school." [23] Even before the post-Stalin reform in the teaching of history was implemented, the life and activities of Lenin and of the Soviet period generally were overwhelmingly emphasized. In 1958 the final examination in history for secondary school students, at the end of their total period of instruction, was devoted entirely to Soviet history, with no questions whatever on either ancient or medieval history or on the history of countries other than Russia during the modern period.[24]

Presumably, one purpose of the narrow focusing of historical study is to prevent invasion of the student's mind by "harmful" ideas. The negative aspect of "Soviet patriotism" is strikingly exemplified by the demand that children be taught hatred for "the enemies of communist society." [25] The "moral code of the builder of communism" puts this demand in somewhat milder

21 DeWitt, *op. cit.*, p. 110; *Ezhegodnik bolshoi sovetskoi entsiklopedii*, 7th ed. (Moscow, 1963), p. 496.
22 DeWitt, *loc. cit.*
23 Arsenev, *loc. cit.*
24 Bereday and Pennar, *op. cit.*, pp. 111–12.
25 George S. Counts, *The Challenge of Soviet Education* (New York, 1957), p. 122.

language. It calls for "an uncompromising attitude to the enemies of communism, peace and the freedom of nations." Reflecting the concern evident during a central committee plenum on
ideological matters called mainly in the hope of whipping rebellious writers into line, Khrushchev asserted on June 21, 1963,
"Hatred of class enemies is necessary, because it is not possible
to become a good fighter for your people or for communism if
one does not know how to hate enemies." [26]

Together with patriotism, teachers are expected to inculcate in
their pupils such attitudes and concepts as "a scientific world
outlook" and "a communist attitude toward labor." [27] Among
the principles included in the "moral code of the builder of communism" are "conscientious labor for the good of society — he
who does not work, neither shall he eat; concern on the part of
everyone for the preservation and growth of public wealth; a
high sense of public duty; intolerance of actions harmful to the
public interest." [28] In addition, teachers are called upon to assist
in satisfying "the cultural requirements of children and youth." [29]
This demand is closely related to the section of the 1961 party
program calling for the "all-round and harmonious development
of the individual." This, the program states, includes access for
all citizens to the arts and sciences and sports, "equal opportunities for education and creative labor," and respect for the personal dignity of individuals. These goals of Soviet education are
often grouped together as inculcation of "socialist humanism." [30]

The acquisition of habits of disciplined endeavor, always a
salient feature of Soviet education, has been particularly emphasized in recent years as of prime importance for citizenship
training. As one authority puts it, "Preparation for labor activity,
labor tempering, the inculcation of love and respect for labor as
a first requirement constitute the essence and the heart of the
entire system of communist training." [31] Apparently it is hoped
that Soviet citizens at an early age will acquire respect for manual
labor, all kinds of hard work, and sound work habits, which will

---

26 Quoted by John Beaufort, in "Cold-War Survey," *Christian Science
Monitor,* Jan. 22, 1964.
27 Arsenev, *op. cit.,* p. 8.
28 Triska, *op. cit.,* p. 112.
29 *Ibid.,* p. 27.
30 Counts, *Challenge, op. cit.,* pp. 123–29.
31 Arsenev, *op. cit.,* p. 9

contribute greatly to the development of homogeneity of outlook and ideological cohesiveness.

PEDAGOGICAL TECHNIQUES

In Soviet schools dedication to desired goals and attitudes is sought not merely by controlling the content of instruction but also by creating an appropriate "atmosphere and spirit" of school life.[32] Pedagogical techniques employed in the schools are meant to foster discipline, respect for duly constituted authority, and the mastering of prescribed patterns. Classroom drill and memorization of course content for testing in examinations are heavily emphasized. In the upper grades of secondary school, lectures are the predominant mode of instruction.

Pupils in the first grade of elementary school are required to memorize and obey "Rules for Schoolchildren," to assist them in acquiring orderliness, politeness, discipline, and respect for teachers, parents, and their elders generally. The hierarchic structure of the school system, with its elaborate scheme of grades and examinations, together with what they learn from teachers, parents, and classmates, impresses upon pupils as they ascend the educational ladder the connection between their performance in school and their after-school career prospects. The importance of obtaining the top grade of "5" in conduct is everywhere stressed. Such devices as reproof by the teacher in front of the entire class, public announcement in an assembly and, for severe and continued misbehavior, expulsion and placement in a detention home are among the broad gamut of instruments available to Soviet teachers and school principals for the inculcation of desired traits of character.[33]

Judging by frequent statements both in pedagogical literature and in the general political press, the Soviet leadership has always set great store by the "collective" (*kollektiv*), the study or work group to which an individual normally belongs, as an instrument of socialization and organized social pressure. Throughout life, a Soviet person is held accountable and responsible to the collective or collectives to which he belongs and to the success or failure, good name or disgrace of which his own behavior contributes. Soviet writing emphasizes that a collective is not

[32] Azrael, *op. cit.*, pp. 243–47, 264–65.
[33] Bereday, Brickman, and Read, *op. cit.*, pp. 440–49.

merely a group of individuals associated more or less spontaneously for this or that purpose but that it has specific characteristics such as organization for particular work or tasks, organs of administration and coordination, and relationships of subordination, responsibility, and mutuality.[34] Citing the famous Russian physiologist-psychologist I. P. Pavlov and the highly authoritative educator Makarenko as theoretical mentors, contemporary Soviet educators assert that personality and behavior are produced, not by the "whims" of a "free spirit," but by the influence of demands upon the individual by society and the state.[35] The agencies for conveying social demands to the child are identified as teacher, parents, and the peer-group. The powerful emotional pressure of group approval or disapproval is used to foster a "communist conscience," which will experience feelings of guilt if party-approved norms are violated.

In addition to control and mobilization — the latter exemplified in nationwide collections of scrap metal, waste paper, etc. — the school collective functions as an early channel of political recruitment, especially in the upper grades of secondary school. The collective is considered useful in enabling teachers to identify "children of initiative," and to develop in such potential leaders the desired combination of obedience and initiative.[36] Opportunities for developing leadership qualities include service as "class monitors," assisting the teacher in distributing supplies and maintaining order in the classroom, performing special "social obligations" (ranging from aiding backward classmates with their schoolwork to writing articles for local children's newspapers), or assuming leadership of a Pioneer detachment in the school or participating in various agitational campaigns, etc.[37] And, as Azrael further notes, students who fulfill "social obligations" satisfactorily are "singled out, in turn, for further and more intensive initiation into the rites of responsibility." For such students, there are bright prospects of entrance into the

34 Lyalin, *op. cit.*, pp. 25–29. *Pedagogicheski slovar*, Vol. II, *op. cit.*, p. 100, refers to the "children's collective" as the "foundation of the system of communist education, through which the teacher should exercise his leadership role." The collective is here defined as both object and subject of education; its usefulness is enhanced, it is asserted, when it is drawn into practical activity, directed toward the attainment of goals which are clearly defined and attractive to its members.

35 N. A. Lyalin, *op. cit.*, p. 30.
36 Azrael, *op. cit.*, pp. 246–47.
37 *Ibid.*, p. 16.

Komsomol apparatus, early membership in the CPSU, and enrollment in the "cadres reserve" maintained by local party committees. Ultimately, such students can hope for membership in the Soviet "power elite."

Both in the primary and secondary schools and the institutions of higher education reinforcement of political indoctrination and acquisition of political skills is a function of classroom and study groups and also of Pioneer and Komsomol collectives.[38] Almost all Soviet schoolchildren belong to the Pioneers and most students in higher education are members of the Komsomol. In school groups, as well as in Pioneer "houses" and "palaces" the Pioneers engage in activities designed to heighten children's sense of comradeship and participation in achieving socially acceptable goals. Some activities of the Pioneers, such as hiking and camping trips, resemble parallel activities of the Boy Scouts of America. But Pioneer organization's broad coverage, its subordination to the CPSU, and particularly the political militancy which pervades the messages it conveys to its membership (in supervising it selected members of the Komsomol play an important role), as well as the characteristic Soviet emphasis upon collectivism as opposed to "bourgeois" individualism, distinguish it sharply from the Boy Scouts. The Pioneers supplement the indoctrinational and character-building work of the schools by mobilizing schoolchildren for revolutionary holidays, assisting in patriotic "drives," organizing "Lenin corners" in Pioneer palaces (major urban centers for conducting educational and propaganda work among school children), conducting correspondence with children's organizations in foreign countries, etc. Perhaps even more important, though not overtly political, are the recreational and vocational activities of the Pioneers. Many Soviet schoolchildren, especially in the larger cities, spend several weeks each summer in Pioneer camps. Also, the Pioneers, under the guidance of teachers and Komsomol workers, both paid and volunteer, operate a wide range of impressive and attractive hobby groups and study circles, especially in the Pioneer palaces of important cities. In

[38] On the structure and activities of these organizations see Fainsod, *How Russia Is Ruled,* Ch. 9; Ralph T. Fisher, Jr., *Pattern for Soviet Youth* (New York, 1959), and also Fisher's contribution to Cyril E. Black, ed., *The Transformation of Russian Society* (Cambridge, Mass., 1960). See also Counts, *Challenge, op. cit.,* pp. 104–108. The socialization functions of the Komsomol are analyzed in Allen Kassoff's important study, *The Soviet Youth Program* (Cambridge, Mass., 1965).

Moscow or Leningrad, they offer opportunities to acquire and exercise dozens of skills. These range from relatively simple, practical activities, such as auto mechanics, to music, foreign languages, the arts, natural sciences, and chess. Participating in and, at the Komsomol level, assisting in the guidance of such activities strengthens a sense of identification with the political system and also provides training in leadership.

The finest Pioneer palaces are housed in the former residences of leading families of the prerevolutionary aristocracy. This architectural symbolism probably still impresses upon the few Soviet children who have access to these, the best of the Pioneer facilities, the national leadership's justice and solicitude for the popular welfare.

The facets of political socialization described thus far are directed more at the emotions and the will than at the intellect. They focus primarily on cultivating political loyalty, developing desired habits, and acquiring rudimentary political skills. We now turn to the means by which political education, building upon the foundations described here, seeks to equip Soviet students with a "scientific," Marxist-Leninist understanding of social dynamics, social relations, domestic and international politics, and the rights, duties, and obligations of citizenship. The most systematic program of instruction in the official system of beliefs and ideas begins in the last year of secondary school and is developed most fully in institutions of higher education. It should not be forgotten that the Komsomol, for the majority of Soviet youths who do not go on to higher education, and also the trade unions and the local party organizations for the adult working population, continuously provide appropriate political instruction. Also, at all levels of the educational system and indeed throughout Soviet life, the party attempts to elevate the individual's political "consciousness," particularly by manipulating the work and other groups to which he belongs. Not merely educational institutions but also trade unions, factories, courts, and many other institutions are often described as "schools of communism," which tempts one to the extreme but not entirely false conclusion that Soviet society is permeated with the atmosphere of the "asylums" brilliantly studied by Erving Goffman.[39]

39 Erving Goffman, *Asylums* (Chicago, 1962).

POLITICAL STUDIES

Until a few years ago a course on the USSR constitution was the only systematic instruction in political matters offered in Soviet secondary schools. It dealt with the origin of state and law, the functions and types of "exploiting" states, and the nature of "the Soviet socialist state — a state of a new higher type." It also presented, in the same order as in the constitution itself, the following topics: the social structure of the USSR, the state structure of the USSR, the state organs of the USSR, and the rights and obligations of Soviet citizens.[40]

A secondary school course on "Fundamentals of Political Knowledge" (*Osnovy politicheskikh znanii*) was introduced in the early 1960's, as previously mentioned. Before that, systematic knowledge about the political system was presented to secondary school students by the course on the Soviet constitution. A central committee resolution dated March 5, 1958, called for the addition to this course of information on civil, labor, collective farm, family, and criminal law, to better prepare pupils finishing school for "active participation in the social and political life of the country."[41]

It was apparently felt that even the strengthened course on the constitution was not adequate, for a resolution of April 25, 1960, ordered its replacement by the more overtly ideological course, designed to present an overview of Marxist-Leninist philosophy and to make clear the ". . . increasing significance of the activity of the party in the building of communism," etc.[42] The textbook for this course was also designed to be used at the lower levels of the adult political education program, as indicated by the preface to the fourth edition, published in 1963, under the direction of a group of top-level theoreticians headed by Leonid F. Ilichev.

At about the same time as the above course was being developed, a similar one on "Social Studies" (*obshchestvovedenie*) was

[40] A good brief account of the "political courses" at the university level, based mainly on material gathered in the USSR, was contained in *Yale Russian Seminar Report* (New Haven, Conn., July, 1963), pp. 4–5. Some of the material that follows on the teaching of social and political studies in Soviet secondary schools and institutions of higher education was obtained from the above report and from a study entitled "The Teaching of the 'Social Sciences' in Soviet Higher Educational Institutions," prepared by Guy Miller Struve for a graduate seminar at Yale University in May, 1963.

[41] *Voprosy ideologicheskoi raboty* (Moscow, 1961), pp. 198–99.

[42] *Ibid.*, pp. 230–33.

being introduced in the same secondary schools. Its purpose:
"to systematize and generalize the whole work of the school in
forming the communist world outlook of the school pupils."
Khrushchev stated that it was introduced because "We want
youth to acquaint itself more deeply with the most important
tasks of communist construction, with the doctrine of Marx,
Engels and Lenin on communism." [43]

It is not clear from available Soviet sources what the relationship between the above two courses was, since references to both
continued to appear throughout the 1960–1964 period, yet their
content, judging by these references, was similar. The ferment
in secondary school political indoctrination indicated both the
significance attached to it by the party leadership and the somewhat unsatisfactory results it was producing. Most of the confusion in this, as in so many areas of Soviet political behavior,
resulted from de-Stalinization. That process deprived the party
of much of its aura of infallibility and forced it to seek a consensus based less on fear and blind obedience and more on a
reasoned and relevant explication of its decisions and their
doctrinal context than had been necessary in the Stalin era. In
teaching the new courses it was recommended that seminars and
conferences be used, on the ground that in preparing for them
students would take examples from "actuality" and connect the
problems discussed with life in their "collective." This recommendation was in line with the evident desire of the leadership
to overcome the dull, "abstract" teaching of ideological subjects,
which was often, and still is, criticized in the Soviet press. A
desire to link up the new secondary school social science courses
with work in the same subjects in institutions of higher education was indicated by the recommendation that teachers at the
university level furnish assistance and guidance to teachers of social science in the secondary schools. [44]

Formal study of political subjects in higher education consists
mainly of required courses in the history of the communist party
of the Soviet Union, dialectical and historical materialism, and

[43] On the purpose of the above course, see F. I. Monoszon, "Formirovanie
kommunisticheskogo mirovozveniya," in *V. I. Lenin i problemy narodnogo
obrozovaniya* (Moscow, 1961), pp. 92–93. Khrushchev was quoted regarding it
in an article entitled "Kurs obshchestvovedeniya-novoe vashnoe snedstvo
vospitaniya uchashcheisya molodezhi," in *Sovetskaya Pedagogika*, Feb. 1963,
p. 3.
[44] *Ibid.*, pp. 8, 9.

political economy. In addition, beginning in 1959, courses in "scientific atheism" and in ethics and esthetics were introduced. Minister of Higher Education Elyutin deplored the fact that these new, additional courses were still not generally taught and declared that "lack of concern for atheistic, ethical and esthetic education leaves loopholes for the penetration of alien sentiments and tastes into student circles." [45] These words were a sign of some confusion, or perhaps merely that a qualified faculty was lacking, and so too was the motivation for introducing these courses.

The significance attributed to political education courses is indicated in many ways. For example, approximately 10 per cent of the heavy workload of 4,800 to 5,000 hours carried by a Soviet university student during his five-year or five-and-a-half-year course is devoted to these subjects. [46] Instruction is given by party members, using syllabuses and other materials prepared under the direction of the Administration of Instruction in Social Sciences, an agency of the Ministry of Higher and Specialized Secondary Education. The Administration publishes a program for each basic course, specifying in detail lecture themes, topics, and required and supplementary reading assignments for each topic. According to the regulations for institutions of higher education of the USSR published in 1961, the councils, highest administrative bodies of institutions of higher education, must include in their membership the heads of the social science departments. This provision is one of a number of administrative reactions to the assertion in the educational law of December, 1958 that "knowledge of the fundamentals of Marxism-Leninism is necessary for specialists in all fields." [47]

The programs of the political courses underwent extensive change after 1953. It was demanded that they, along with the rest of the educational program, be brought toward "closer ties with life," and a systematic effort was made to rid these courses, especially those in party history, of "remnants of the cult of personality." The content of political instruction was revised in a way

[45] Cited by Struve, *op. cit.,* from speech by Elyutin reported in *Pravda,* July 5, 1961.

[46] DeWitt, *op. cit.,* p. 312, says "at least 8 per cent" of the total number of hours of study in institutions of higher education, but Struve presents data indicating that the number, for example in the physics faculty of Kharkov State University in 1955, can be as high as 12.4 per cent.

[47] Bereday, Brickman, and Read, *op. cit.,* p. 97.

that might be called "Leninization." Even greater emphasis was placed on Lenin's contribution to "the theory of the socialist revolution." In the political courses it was attempted to establish connections between ideological "fundamentals," embodied in the "classics of Marxism-Leninism," with "life," as reflected in speeches, resolutions, and directives dealing with urgent, "concrete" matters of public policy.[48] A quick glance at the 1958 and the 1962 programs in party history will give some indication of the content and tone of post-Stalin university-level political education in the USSR. In the 1958 version was a section entitled "Death of J. V. Stalin," which expressed satisfaction about the "confounding of those enemies of socialism who counted on the weakening of the communist party with the death of J. V. Stalin." This item was omitted in 1962, but a new topic on the beginning of the revolutionary activity of V. I. Lenin was added. Similarly, though the 1959 edition of the official history of the CPSU, used as a textbook in institutions of higher education, blamed "certain party organizations" for haste in collectivizing agriculture in 1930, the 1963 edition of the same work blamed Stalin for allegedly "scorning" warnings by Engels and Lenin against "excessive haste." It is too early to know what effect the fall of Khrushchev will have on the teaching of party history and other political subjects, although the elaborate rationalizations and intricate revisions required will almost certainly further weaken the authority of the official doctrine. But, judging from the tone to date of the criticisms of the still unnamed leader, "haste" will be attributed to him also.

Despite post-Stalin revision, available study plans and readings used in the political courses continued to reveal to a noncommunist a content which seemed dogmatic, rigid, and schematic in the extreme. In particular the attitude toward "capitalism" and "imperialism" and all of their ways and works, as well as toward "bourgeois and revisionist" scholarship, remained as uncompromising as ever.

Soviet sources frequently criticize both the lecture and "seminar" portions of the political courses. On the basis of what can be learned about the "seminars," which have been required

[48] The basic outlines of the political courses for the higher educational level as of about 1957 are available in English translation in *Administration of Teaching in Social Sciences in the USSR* (Ann Arbor, Mich., 1960); new syllabuses are issued annually for these courses under the title "Programmy."

since 1938, it can safely be said that they certainly do not foster "independent" or "creative" thinking, at least as these words are understood in the West. However, they may, in a fashion appropriate to Soviet conditions, "make possible a deep understanding of the Marxist-Leninist theory" and "develop a quality necessary to the future specialist and director of socialist production, the ability to speak independently." [49] It is apparently standard practice to distribute seminar plans two weeks in advance of the seminar meeting and to assign each of several listed topics to one or more students for preparation of a report. Students have at their disposal, in addition to the required reading, official guides entitled "Consultations," as well as oral consultations with instructors. The reports must be written out in a notebook, ready to be checked by the instructor.

THE KOMSOMOL'S ACTIVITIES

As in his other subjects, a Soviet student must pass examinations in the political courses.[50] If he wishes to go on to graduate work, he must bear in mind that one of the requirements for becoming an *aspirant,* as the Soviet graduate student is called, is passage of a competitive examination in the history of the CPSU.[51] The effect of specifically political courses is reinforced by including in all other courses an ideological component, a particularly heavy one in the humanities, and in many other ways. One of the major Komsomol activities at the university level is participation in "circles" for further study and discussion of Marxism-Leninism; moreover, students as well as professors are encouraged to participate in mass educational work. Then too, there are special lectures on political subjects, such as the "international situation." Other channels for ideologically saturating students include radio broadcasts; the posting of newspapers such as the Komsomol paper, *Komsomolskaya Pravda,* on bulletin boards in university buildings and dormitories; special newspapers published jointly by the administrative staffs of

[49] These claims were made for the seminars in an article published in *Vestnik vysshei shkoly* for October, 1948. Quotation on p. 9.

[50] According to Counts, *Challenge, op. cit.,* p. 167, in a five-year program of training a Soviet student must take approximately fifty examinations.

[51] See *Aspirantura, spravochnik dlya postupayushchikh v aspiranturu i soiskatelei uchenykh stepenei* (Moscow, 1960), p. 15; see also Counts, *Challenge, loc. cit.,* where it is noted that completion of graduate work required passage of an examination in "The Principles of Marxism-Leninism."

universities and the university trade union, party, and Komsomol organizations; and, too, such peculiarly Soviet institutions as "wall newspapers," or "lower press" organs published jointly by students, faculty, and party and Komsomol organizations of university departments, for intramural reading.[52]

As at the primary and secondary school levels, classroom political indoctrination in institutions of higher education is supplemented by organized extracurricular activity. Most Soviet students belong to the Komsomol — estimates range as high as 95 per cent.[53] The indoctrinational work of the Komsomol at the college level appears to be essentially similar to that which it performs in the upper grades of secondary school and in industry. For each institution there is a Komsomol unit with an elected secretary and governing board, its activities guided by directives from regional Komsomol and party organizations. The Komsomol is officially designated as the "reserve" and "helper" of the party. In schools, technical institutes, and universities one of its main assigned functions is to reinforce other agencies engaged in "moral" education, as well as to aid in improving scholarship and maintaining discipline.

The Komsomol also assists the authorities, in educational institutions and elsewhere, in conducting physical culture, sports, and military training programs. It is an important auxiliary agency of social mobilization and social control. It has played an important part in persuading, or pressuring Soviet youths to "volunteer" for such campaigns as that which began in 1954 for settling the virgin lands of Kazakhstan and Siberia, or for labor on vast Siberian hydroelectric and other construction projects, or for many, many others. "Personal sacrifices for the sake of social welfare" rank high on the regime's scale of values.[54] In conducting its agitational and propaganda activities the Komsomol operates an extensive system of political schools and study circles

52 The wall newspaper of the Law Department of Leningrad University when this author visited there in October, 1963, was devoted mainly to an exceptionally dismal picture of conditions in the United States, written by a professor of law who had been in the United States, ostensibly to study the application of "cybernetics" to law, in the spring of 1963.

53 Burg, in Pipes, *op. cit.*, p. 84, says "more than 90 percent"; DeWitt indicates that it may reach 95 per cent.

54 Komsomol activities are systematically described in the works of Burg, DeWitt, and Fainsod, already cited, and on pp. 271–75 of Herbert McClosky and John E. Turner, *The Soviet Dictatorship* (New York, 1960).

and publishes more than a hundred newspapers, some forty magazines, and thousands of books and pamphlets.

Perhaps the most important function of the Komsomol, especially in higher education, is its contribution to the early stages of recruitment into the Soviet political elite. The Komsomol assists the party in identifying and training "activists." These are persons who distinguish themselves in community activity, such as propaganda and assistance in welfare and recreational programs, and often also exercising surveillance over fellow students and submitting reports on their attitudes and behavior to Komsomol and party organizations. As Burg puts it, "The fundamental assignment of every Komsomol worker is to repress 'nonconformity' in everyday life." [55] Foreign visitors to Soviet institutions of higher education are likely to meet members of Komsomol organizations, who, because their propaganda and administrative duties in the Komsomol occupy so much of their time, are permitted to study part-time and are allowed extra time to complete their studies. Frequently philosophy majors who are also Komsomol activists go on to careers as professional propagandists or as teachers of political courses in higher education. Activists who are students of journalism can hope some day to become editors of the leading Soviet newspapers such as *Pravda, Izvestiya,* or *Komsomolskaya Pravda.*

Other Komsomol activists, whether in universities or in industrial establishments, if the Soviet past is an accurate guide to the future, can hope to occupy paid positions in the Komsomol organization. A few achieve this status while still in the university, and eventually rise to the highest posts in the party apparatus. Such leaders as Leonid F. Ilichev, Boris Ponomarev, or the late Frol Romanovich Kozlov served as leaders in the Komsomol apparatus early in careers which led to membership in the secretariat of the CPSU central committee. Some of the social control work of Komsomol activists makes it interesting that after Stalin's death the Komsomol apparatus became a major source of top personnel for the political police forces. In 1958, Alexander Shelepin was transferred from his post as First Secretary of the central committee of the Komsomol, which he had held since 1952, to the

[55] Pipes, *op. cit.,* p. 185. See also Peter H. Juviler, "Communist Morality and Soviet Youth," *Problems of Communism,* X, No. 3 (May–June, 1961), pp. 16–24. See esp. pp. 16–17.

chairmanship of the Committee of State Security. After Shelepin's transfer in 1961 to lead the Party-State Control Committee, he was replaced by Vladimir Semichastny. Semichastny had been a professional Komsomol apparatus worker since 1941. Both men rose still higher after the fall of Khrushchev, Shelepin to full membership in the party presidium, skipping the alternate stage, and Semichastny from alternate to full membership in the central committee.

THE FAMILY AND OTHER FACTORS

In examining political socialization in the Soviet Union, we have concentrated primarily on formal instruction in schools and institutions of higher education. We have neglected important parts of the educational system such as preschool education or the new system of boarding schools. Space and other problems make it impossible here to deal adequately with many of the activities and institutions involved in the making of Soviet man. Among these perhaps the most important is the family's part in transmitting attitudes, values, and systems of belief.

Much of the spadework necessary to analyze systematically how the family assists socialization in the Soviet Union has not been done. It is certain that the party assigns to the family an important job as an auxiliary to the school in the socialization process. A good example of the official image of the family-school relationship is furnished by the following sentences: "Of course the school is responsible for the behavior of each of its pupils. But full responsibility is also borne by the parents. Upbringing begins long before school, in the family. The personal example of fathers and mothers, their views and mutual relations and the home atmosphere exert a great influence on children." [56]

It appears that the role allotted to the family, though potentially threatened by Khrushchev's plan for an expanding program of boarding school education (and this is highly conjectural), has been relatively stable throughout most of the regime's history. Apparently the compromise represented by the relatively loose control of an important part of the social environment has not proved to be seriously detrimental from the party's point of view.

A very careful scholarly study of the relationship between regime pressures and family resistance led to the conclusion that

[56] *Pravda,* editorial for Dec. 16, 1964.

"The family has on the whole not been a significant force in resisting the ideological indoctrination of Soviet young persons. While there is some evidence that politically tinged parent-youth conflict was a prominent feature in the prewar Soviet family, of equal or greater importance is the fact that Soviet parents so frequently minimized such conflict by their adaptive-conforming responses to the regime's ideology." [57]

It seems clear that the family does act as an impediment to full and enthusiastic acceptance of the official system of beliefs, especially of those which stress militancy, total conformity, and instant adaptation to shifting official demands. Not infrequently, the Soviet press criticizes parents for allegedly coddling their offspring, thus failing to instill in them the ability to cope with the challenges and difficulties of "life."

Serving, therefore, as an emotion-saturated insulator against regime's pressure for developing a cold, impersonal, instrumental ethos, the family reinforces pluralistic tendencies generated by status or economic functions, or shaped by tradition. Such variations impede the party's drive for uniformity and are not conducive to identification with officially approved patterns.

Among the most significant family influences at variance with ideological tenets, so deeply rooted that they are never openly and systematically discussed, are the proclivities of intelligentsia parents to assure for their children the advantages of status which they themselves have achieved by succeeding in the vigorous Soviet competitive struggle. David Granick has assembled impressive evidence of the advantages enjoyed, as a result, by Soviet "white-collar" children over their working-class and peasant competitors in seeking to become members of the managerial elite.[58]

Among non-Russians, especially peasants of Moslem religious background, many parents, partly consciously, partly unwittingly, interfere with the regime's efforts to eliminate "bourgeois nationalist" survival — a kind of resistance to pressure highly synonymous with resistance to the wholehearted adoption of the dominant urban, industrial Russian communist culture. As indicated in Chapter II, the survival of religious beliefs is closely associated with the phenomena referred to above, and here again

[57] Alex Inkeles and Kent Geiger, *Soviet Society* (Boston, 1961), p. 557. See also Chs. VIII and IX of Alex Inkeles and Raymond A. Bauer, *The Soviet Citizen* (Cambridge, Mass., 1959).
[58] David Granick, *The Red Executive* (New York, 1960), Ch. 3.

the family is a major, and from the point of view of those direct-ing the organized socialization effort, a very negative agent. A recent study on the so far unsuccessful campaign against various religious sects expresses the view that their survival results, ulti-mately, from the inability or unwillingness of the party to abolish the family.[59]

RESULTS OF THE SOCIALIZATION EFFORT

Even more difficult than assessing the Soviet family's ability to influence, in many subtle ways, the total program of political socialization, is evaluating the over-all success of this gigantic effort. Certainly it has not been fully successful. If it had been, neither the continued, frequent criticism of indoctrinational work nor the complaints of so many persisting "survivals of capitalism" in the people's thinking at so many social strata would be as prominent as they still are in the Soviet press. Neither would it have been necessary to undertake such a massive reorganization of education as the "Khrushchev school reform." It would be un-wise to dismiss as mere wishful thinking frequent statements of the Soviet leadership that although "ideological work" has by no means fully achieved its objectives, it can do so in the future if it is properly organized and pursues them with sufficient dedication and energy. As Azrael notes, the "ultimate goal of creating a 'new Soviet man' has never been abandoned, and in fact has recently been reaffirmed with renewed vigor." [60] Despite its numerous and serious shortcomings and often criticized defects, political social-ization in the USSR has many formidable achievements to its credit. There seems to be general agreement among objective Western scholars that if it has not created "the sort of all-inclusive, monolithic, and homogeneous political culture" desired by the Soviet rulers, it has created a fairly high level of "popular con-sensus." [61] Qualified Western observers agree that although only a few even among "activist" Soviet youths have a profound knowl-edge of Marxist-Leninist doctrine, the youths shaped by the agencies described here, and especially the student activists who are the future leaders of the society, are imbued with the peculiar

59 Ethel and Stephen P. Dunn, "Religion as an Instrument of Culture Change: The Problem of the Sects in the Soviet Union," *Slavic Review* (Sept., 1964), pp. 476–78.

60 Azrael, *op. cit.*, pp. 270–71.

61 *Ibid.*, p. 17; see also Inkeles and Bauer, *op. cit.*, p. 397.

mixture of anticapitalism and nationalism known as Soviet patriotism. Many, perhaps most, are convinced not only that "socialism" is morally superior to capitalism, but that it is destined to replace it throughout the world both by the unfolding of the "dialectic," and by the determined application of Soviet power.

If presently observable trends persist, future Soviet educators will face increasingly complex and subtle problems in shaping the outlook of the emerging generations. Their major dilemma, it seems, will be that of offering a satisfactory and convincing blend of idealism and pragmatism, of metaphysic and analysis. Can Marxism-Leninism incorporate enough empiricism and pragmatism to satisfy a rising generation that will be increasingly inclined to judge the validity of ideas by their productiveness in action without losing, gradually — or possibly faster than now seems likely — the vitality it still derives from its pseudochiliastic character? The official creed is likely to be attentuated also by increasing preoccupation with computer technology, consumer goods, and numerous other aspects of the mature economy developing now in Soviet Russia. Preoccupation with the contemporary cannot fail to make an ideology seem increasingly irrelevant that is heavily oriented toward such particular past events, problems, and realities as those to which Marx and Lenin reacted so passionately, even if reverence for it persists. Of course, continued dilution and modification, or even gradual disintegration of ideological orthodoxy would not deprive the Soviet elite of its arsenal of unifying myths and sentiments. Patriotism and nationalism, especially Great Russian nationalism, would doubtless continue to flourish, especially if domestic and foreign policies enjoyed success; but in a multinational society a patriotism that appeals mainly to the dominant people can be divisive. The tenacity of Soviet ideology and the survival of other community myths far longer than external critics would have thought possible should caution us against expecting early and rapid alienation of Soviet youth from the political system, but it seems most probable that in the future the Soviet leaders will have to employ more sophisticated methods and greater finesse than they have if they are to maintain even the present level of support among youths, particularly at the higher levels of education.

CHAPTER IV

Adult Political Indoctrination
and Training

FROM ITS BEGINNING, the CPSU has conducted a large-scale, systematic program of adult, after-work political instruction and training. This vast program, performed mainly by unpaid activists who thus fulfill a part of their expected duty to the community, has several objectives. It has reinforced, elaborated, and at times modified the beliefs and attitudes already imparted by schools and other institutions. In concert with the mass media of communication, it has also sought, in carefully organized settings, to promote receptivity to and support for current party policies by associating them with officially approved Marxist-Leninist doctrine. Under Stalin, especially after 1938, the program of "political enlightenment" (*politicheskoe prosveshchenie*), also often referred to as "party propaganda," became increasingly scholastic and ritualistic, and its clientele came to be restricted to members of the party apparatus and other elite elements. The elitist exclusiveness of the adult indoctrination program was one of many facets of Stalin's rule considered obsolete by his successors, especially the extroverted, popularity-craving Khrushchev. Khrushchev moved vigorously to expand it, hoping by this and other measures to close the gap between party propaganda and "life."

Once Khrushchev had grasped the levers of power he launched a revival of mass oral instruction in a vulgarized version of Marxism-Leninism. It involved bringing to the training system for party cadres a practicality and vocational relevance somewhat similar (in its nondoctrinal aspects) to the American style of business administration training. It also involved rapidly expanding and opening up to nonparty persons the intermediate- and lower-level programs previously offered mainly to middle and lower ranking party members. It was announced that the ultimate objective of this part of Khrushchev's "democratic" policy was to provide a Marxist political education for all Soviet citizens.

As will be shown in this chapter, there were startling departures from the adult political socialization practices applied by Stalin. There were also fundamental continuities in objectives and in terminology. Perhaps Khrushchev thought he was pursuing Stalinist goals but that his methods were more appropriate than those employed by the hated autocrat. Lacking Stalin's power, his successors sought to achieve by persuasive communication the ends he had pursued by command and decree. Like Stalin, they failed to create a voluntary consensus between rulers and ruled, but they experimented more freely than did Stalin and since Khrushchev's fall they have continued to express the hope that increased effort and new methods will lead to more effective political communication. More than under Stalin, they recommended a "differential" approach to the occupational, ethnic, educational, and other peculiarities of the varied groups enrolled in the institutions of political indoctrination. Increasingly, this prescription provided complex and variegated political education and a corresponding sequence of textbooks on party history and other subjects. On the other hand, the leaders tried to provide programs of political instruction including common elements for all audiences, presumably in keeping with post-Stalin attempts to counteract cleavage that had flourished in the late days of Stalin between elite and nonelite. By the beginning of the 1964–1965 school year, on the eve of Khrushchev's fall, a "unified study plan" for all levels of the system had been adopted and promulgated. In this area, much is obscure to the outside observer. Also, perhaps partly for this reason, there appears to be much contradiction. Still, it is certain that after Stalin the adult political socialization program entered a period of unprecedentedly stormy growth and flux.

FUNCTIONS OF ADULT POLITICAL SOCIALIZATION

The Soviet adult political training system not only is an agency of socialization and of elite recruitment, but is also one of the major networks of political communication. It will be easier to understand its function in the Soviet political system if we examine briefly the Leninist conception of the political objectives of various kinds of communication; we must also gain some acquaintance with the terminology used in the USSR to describe them.

The Soviet approach to political communication was formulated and heavily influenced by some of V. I. Lenin's major works. Fundamental is Lenin's statement that it is the duty of all party members to act as "theoreticians, propagandists, agitators and organizers." [1]

In Leninist usage, "propaganda" signifies communication activities which convey a complex, "intellectual" content, which is often so difficult to comprehend as to presuppose for its understanding relatively advanced education and superior intelligence. Politically, the general object of propaganda is to consolidate predispositions, gain adherents to programs, win converts, and mobilize individuals and groups to support the demands of the propagandist.

In contrast, "agitation" conveys a simpler message than "propaganda," and is often intended for relatively unsophisticated persons. Its end usually is to spur action. As a rule, the language of agitation is simple, direct, and to the point, although its effectiveness must be limited by repetition of outmoded clichés. In its purest form, agitation is couched in hard-hitting, action-oriented slogans. Its message is often conveyed by posters and placards. The distinction between the spheres and techniques of propaganda and agitation is still preserved in the contemporary Soviet lexicon. However, the lines between these concepts have become increasingly blurred. Khrushchev, who was even less sophisticated theoretically than Stalin, contributed to this confusion. In the section of his report to the Twentieth CPSU Congress in 1956

---

[1] V. I. Lenin, *Chto delat*, in *Izbranniye proizvedeniya* (Moscow, 1943), Vol. I, pp. 157, 176, 186. Originally published in 1902, this work is available in many languages. A good English edition was published in 1929 in New York by International Publishers.

which dealt with "Problems of Ideological Work," he used the word "propaganda" almost in the sense traditionally reserved for "agitation." Khrushchev's careless pragmatism in such matters was echoed in 1960 by Leonid F. Ilichev, at the time head of the central committee department of agitation and propaganda for the union republics. In 1961 he became a member of the party secretariat and retained his eminence as the top USSR communication leader for a time after Khrushchev's fall. Ilichev wrote: "In our era the boundaries between propaganda and agitation become more and more relative and conditional." He explained that the intermingling of the two modes of communication resulted from the expanded sphere of propaganda — because of advances in communication technology — and from the heightened intellectual level of political agitation resulting from education.[2]

Despite the tendency since Stalin's demise to amplify the agitational element in propaganda and political training by linking them more closely with "life" and "practical" goals, such as productivity of labor, the word "propaganda" still primarily refers to the inculcation of basic beliefs and attitudes. "Agitation," in turn, continues to mean primarily the stream of day-to-day commands intended to hold public attention and to elicit prompt and appropriate responses. "Propaganda" is often regarded as roughly equivalent to "political enlightenment," whereas "agitation," under Soviet conditions, bears some resemblance to "news" in a noncommunist society. The Soviet conception of information's political function was stated succinctly a few years ago by a former director of the TASS news agency, when he wrote that "news" was "agitation by means of facts."[3]

GROWTH OF THE POLITICAL EDUCATION PROGRAM

There have been three main stages in the development of Soviet adult political socialization. The first included the years of revolutionary struggle before Soviet power was established, the Lenin period of Soviet leadership, and that portion of Stalin's rule which culminated in 1938 with *History of the All-Union Communist Party (of Bolsheviks)*, usually referred to as the "Short

[2] See *Kommunist*, No. 13, Sept., 1960, p. 35.
[3] N. G. Palgunov, *Osnovy informatsii v gazete* (Moscow, 1955), p. 35.

Course" (*Kratki Kurs*). Except for a few of Lenin's major works this book undoubtedly influenced the minds of Soviet citizens more than any other.

The second period began in 1938 and ended with Stalin's death. This was the time of rigidity, when all political and social thought and teaching were gripped by the passions and prejudices conveyed in the Short Course. Above all, every kind of thought was constrained by fear of offending the jealous, suspicious master of the Kremlin.

The third, post-Stalin, era, has been one of ferment and experiment, confined, at least in formal prescription, within the authoritarian framework of "Leninism." In contrast to the late Stalin era, the post-Stalin one has been characterized by a measure of diversity. At least, the pronouncements of several living party leaders, rather than those of only one, have been studied — but it still remains unthinkable in this closed system to include in the official courses of political instruction the speeches or writings of "bourgeois" statesmen or scholars.

In each of the three periods the Kremlin set a pattern of political indoctrination appropriate for that phase. Organization, teaching methods, and curricula at all times have been highly standardized. Since Stalin's death, however, the Kremlin has taken care to suit the content of instruction to the students' backgrounds. Always, it has vigorously attempted to exclude from the political training program "incorrect," "harmful" views.

As early as 1911, Lenin had established in Paris a school for training party propagandists, partly to counteract the influence of a similar program for underground party workers set up by rival Russian Marxist exiles on the island of Capri.[4] A comprehensive system of political instruction was first established in Soviet Russia in the early 1920's. Because of the low level of general education then prevalent in Russia, the party educational system overlapped extensively with the educational network as a whole. For the most part, however, this duplication was eliminated by the late 1930's. Since both the party and the general educational structures are controlled from one center, changes in their practices and curricula are closely coordinated. The basic system of political education established in the 1920's still per-

4 Robert V. Daniels, *The Conscience of the Revolution* (Cambridge, Mass., 1960), p. 21.

sists, but it is subject to constant tinkering. In its early form, it operated at four levels: schools of "political literacy"; lower-level Soviet and party schools (*sovpartshkoly*); higher-level Soviet and party schools; and, finally, communist universities, of which the most famous was the Sverdlov University, founded in 1918.[5] The level of education offered by these early party institutions corresponded roughly to that given in regular Soviet schools of elementary, secondary, and higher education respectively. At all levels, these institutions were expected to instill enthusiastic support for the Marxist-Leninist creed and aversion to "bourgeois" concepts. The Soviet and party schools trained lower-level party functionaries. They were oriented particularly to the training of propagandists and agitators. The communist universities specialized in training high-level editors, educators, and other cadres of the "cultural apparatus."

Rapid growth of party membership in the 1930's was accompanied by expansion of the adult political education system. Thus, the number of party schools and study circles grew from 52,000 in 1930 to 210,000 in 1933. Student enrollment increased during the same period from 1,000,000 to 4,500,000. Almost half of these students were not party members at all. They fell into the category of "non-party bolsheviks," persons who actively supported the party and many of whom eventually became party members. By 1934, 130,000 trained party propagandists were teaching in the above school system, more than five times the number enrolled in 1928.[6]

Joseph Stalin altered the political indoctrination program described above in 1937 and in 1938. He imposed on it an elitist direction, intended to strengthen party control over the new technical, scientific, and administrative cadres rapidly being created to staff the fast-growing Soviet industrial and military bureaucracies. The new approach toward adult political education, which was to persist throughout the years 1938–1953, was set forth systematically in a very important committee resolution dated November 14, 1938. This resolution, "Concerning the Structure of Party Propaganda in Connection with the Publication of the

[5] George S. Counts, *The Challenge of Soviet Education* (New York, 1957), pp. 275–79; Nicholas DeWitt, *Soviet Professional Manpower* (Washington, D.C., U.S. Government Printing Office, 1955), p. 15.
[6] Alex Inkeles, *Public Opinion in Soviet Russia* (Cambridge, Mass., 1951), pp. 36–37.

'Short Course in the History of the All-Union Communist Party (of Bolsheviks),' " [7] described the new textbook on the history of the party as "an encyclopedia of fundamental knowledge in the sphere of Marxism-Leninism." The textbook, it further stated, would arm members of the party with "a knowledge of the laws of social development and political struggle," and would intensify the "political vigilance of party and non-party bolsheviks." [8] It was necessary, continued the resolution, to provide the party with a single guide to party history, which would allow for no "arbitrary" interpretations. The introductory section of the resolution also sharply criticized "vulgarization" of the party history by earlier texts, one result of which had been a depreciation of the "Soviet socialist state." However, its main point was that the principal defect of political education had been failure to achieve Marxist-Leninist training of the Soviet Union's "leading cadres." The resolution condemned previous reliance on study circles as the main instrument of propaganda, declaring that this method had characterized the "illegal" period of party history but that now it was time to base party propaganda primarily upon the press and upon "independent study." It was made clear, however, that independent study was to be guided by "centralized" advice to be given by highly qualified persons. [9] The resolution also severely criticized the directing of propaganda mainly at bench workers, neglecting "higher Soviet, party and non-party intelligentsia, consisting of yesterday's workers and peasants." [10] It quoted Stalin as saying that nine-tenths of the party's problems could be solved if the Soviet "cadres" could be trained as "mature Leninists." The intelligentsia, it went on, were the cadres of the state apparatus, with whose aid the working class conducted its domestic and foreign policy. [11] Failure to properly "temper" the intelligentsia politically, according to the document, had enabled foreign intelligence services and their "Trotski-Bukharin and bourgeois-nationalist accomplices" to recruit for their spy networks some members of the Soviet intelligentsia. [12]

---

[7] *O postanovke partiinoi propagandy v svyazi s vypuskom "kratkogo kursa istorii VKP (b)"* (Moscow, 1944), issued in 200,000 copies, by the Pravda Publishing House. This was one of several reissues of this document.

[8] *Ibid.*, p. 1.

[9] *Ibid.*, p. 6.

[10] *Ibid.*, p. 10.

[11] *Ibid.*, p. 11.

[12] *Ibid.*, p. 12.

The resolution set forth twenty-six directives for reorganizing and improving party political training. It prescribed "differentiated study" of the new party history textbook. The "lower level cadres," including many "poorly prepared comrades," were to study an abbreviated version of the Short Course. For the "middle level cadres," with somewhat better preparation, the Short Course was to be studied in full. Finally, for the "higher level" party members, the Short Course was to be supplemented by appropriate works of Marx, Engels, Lenin, and Stalin in the original.[13]

One of the resolution's most important provisions pertained to improvement in the system for training party propagandists. It was ordered that one-year courses for propagandists and newspaper workers be established in Moscow, Leningrad, Kiev, and seven other major cities. The resolution also ordered establishment of a higher school of Marxism-Leninism, attached to the central committee, with a three-year course for training highly qualified theoretical cadres for the party. It also contained important directives on teaching political subjects in institutions of higher education.[14] Moreover, the Marx-Engels-Lenin Institute was instructed to improve the translation of the works of Marx and Engels into the Russian language, while correcting "crude political mistakes" allegedly committed in translations. Finally, it set forth provisions for the over-all structure of both oral and published propaganda and agitation. The most important was consolidation into one system of the previously separate publications section of the central committee and the section for propaganda and agitation, thus creating new departments for propaganda and agitation, which were made responsible for all printed and oral propaganda. To improve the propaganda of Marxism-Leninism, it was ordered that those engaged in such work should be cadres freed from any other work. This emphasis on employing professionals in propaganda work was a part of Stalin's policy which was to be most drastically modified after his death.[15]

The November 14 resolution systematized the structure and methods of political propaganda. Post-Stalin changes, despite their significance, should be regarded more as adaptations of the

13 *Ibid.*, p. 13.
14 *Ibid.*, pp. 18–21.
15 *Ibid.*, pp. 21–24.

system established by Stalin to new challenges than as fundamental reforms.

The shattering and distracting effects of World War II made necessary another major program to revitalize adult political instruction. Indoctrination had been badly neglected during the struggle for survival against the Nazis. During the same years, the party's ranks were swelled by millions of new members, some of whose decisions to join the party had reflected wartime relaxation of stringent entrance requirements and such emotions as patriotism, often of a traditional character. Many of the new members were deficient in the attitudes and traits which the Kremlin had previously regarded as necessary for properly "tempered" bolsheviks. Perhaps even more dubious, from the leadership's point of view, many rank and file party members, influenced by the wartime propaganda of national unity and international cooperation with the Western allies, and by their yearning for a return to "normalcy," had come to hope that a less militant world outlook would, after the war, guide Soviet domestic and foreign policy.

It soon became apparent that these hopes would be long deferred. Above all in party control over the arts, sciences, and education but also in internal party indoctrination, Stalin in 1945 and 1946 restored the control relaxed by the war and by contacts with the West. On August 2, 1946, the central committee adopted a resolution, "On the Training and Retraining of Leading Party and Soviet Workers," the preamble to which complained that many party and Soviet workers had ceased to work systematically at enhancing their intellectual and theoretical development. The resolution declared that in the next three or four years the "main leading cadres" of the apparatus, both party and governmental, must be enrolled in party schools and courses. It contained detailed directives for achieving this objective. It provided for reopening the central committee Higher Party School which had been closed during the war, and ordered that the lower-ranking party schools be reorganized and that there be established an academy of social sciences to train theoretical workers for the party under the administration of propaganda and agitation of the central committee.[16]

16 *O partiinoi i sovetskoi pechati* (Moscow, 1954), pp. 556–64.

Although some significant modifications in political education occurred from 1953–1956 (in 1954 a new textbook on political economy was published and the Short Course, at first extolled,
gradually ceased to be mentioned), it was not until Khrushchev's
report to the central committee at the Twentieth Party Congress
that a major new phase in the Kremlin's approach to political
indoctrination began. A systematic attempt to improve and expand ideological indoctrination has indeed been one of the major
preoccupations of the party leadership since 1956. The demand
for livelier, more "practical," and broader political education
found expression in Khrushchev's main speeches, in a number
of central committee documents, and in a profusion of handbooks and pamphlets intended for party functionaries and propagandists.[17]

POST-STALIN CHANGES IN POLITICAL TRAINING

The renewed emphasis upon mass indoctrination was a response to major difficulties confronted by the post-Stalin political
leadership. It was, formally, a logical result of the party's proclaimed intention to proceed with the full-scale building of a
communist society. One requirement of that program, according
to both Leninist theory and political reality, would seem to be
broad public understanding of the leadership's objectives and
policies. More fundamentally for political reality, it reflected the
Kremlin's anxiety about the political apathy of some Soviet
young people and also some among the industrial working class
and the peasantry. Perhaps the most important motive for the
new course was uneasiness about the moods and attitudes of
Soviet intellectuals and students when the requirements of national policy and of Soviet standing within the international communist movement seemed to necessitate increased contact between
Soviet citizens and representatives of the "bourgeois" world.
The party sought to make certain that the Soviet citizens would
effectively present the Soviet policy line and also would be able

[17] See key statements by Khrushchev in *XX sezd KPSS*, Vol. I, pp. 111–18;
XXI sezd, op. cit., Vol. I, pp. 55–62; *Materialy XXII sezda KPSS* (Moscow,
1961), pp. 109–117; "O zadachakh partiinoi propagandy v sovremennykh
usloviyakh," in *Voprosy ideologicheskoi raboty, op. cit.*, pp. 144–64; V. I.
Evdokimov, *Politicheskoe prosveshchenie-reshayushchee zveno propagandist-
skoi raboty* (Moscow, 1962); *Partiinaya propaganda i sovremennost* (Moscow,
1961).

to resist the ideological and cultural blandishments of their capitalist colleagues.

Perhaps the most urgent task posed by the new course in party propaganda was systematically eradicating Stalin's influence, which was begun by Khrushchev at the Twentieth Congress, and requiring reinforcement and explanation if it was to revitalize a political culture paralyzed by years of ritualistic scholasticism, sterile exegesis, and despotic tutelage. Khrushchev demanded in his statements on "ideological work" at the Twentieth, Twenty-first, and Twenty-second CPSU congresses that indoctrination serve as a stimulus to action. It must assist the party in laying the "material and technical foundations for communism." Above all, it must stimulate Soviet workers, engineers, and industrial executives to increase their productivity. Khrushchev sought to justify his pragmatic approach with quotations from Lenin. He summed up his position in his report to the central committee at the Twenty-second Congress: "The ideological work of party organizations heightens the communist consciousness and the labor and political activity of the masses and serves as a very important, constantly active factor in the building of communism." [18] Although Khrushchev took the position that propaganda which did not produce tangible results was useless, he did not urge that communists should be satisfied with production alone. At least he paid lip service to an old tenet of Marxism-Leninism: the unity of theory and practice. As he also said at the Twenty-second Congress, the party's strength lay in its ability to "fuse in its revolutionary, transforming activity the theory and the practice of scientific communism." Khrushchev here asserted that the "world-historical victories" of the party and the Soviet state were an expression of theory in action, adding that the answers to the kinds of theoretical questions which would confront Soviet society increasingly in the future must be sought "not only in books but above all in the life-creating practice of communist construction itself." [19] Although he attacked "revisionism" in this and other key speeches, Khrushchev in effect seemed to be propagating a version of revisionism, for he implied that in the relationship between theory and practice the latter was to

18 *Materialy, op. cit.*, p. 109.
19 Ibid., p. 113.

be given unquestioned priority. In the theoretical conception set forth by Khrushchev — and even more clearly in his actual behavior — theory came to be reduced to pure terminology and decoration. Khrushchev thus seemed to dissolve theory in the muddy stream of "life." Some colleagues rejected his apparent lack of interest in ideological "purity," as indicated by a number of statements following his removal, and by a certain shift of propaganda emphasis away from Khrushchevian preoccupation with short-run, practical goals and back to involvement with traditional ideological topics such as party history and dialectical and historical materialism.

It is important to keep in mind, however, that even Khrushchev's pragmatism was of the piecemeal, unconscious variety, permitting him to continue to perceive himself as a true "Marxist-Leninist" revolutionary, capable of indignantly demanding that all "alien" ideas be excluded from Soviet intellectual life.

The most comprehensive and systematic party propaganda directive since the 1938 central committee resolution was the corresponding one dated January 9, 1960. The 1960 resolution began by observing that, in the full-scale building of a communist society, ideological work and, in particular, its "decisive aspect," party propaganda, took on exceptional significance. A communist world outlook had now become "a vital necessity" for every Soviet citizen. The resolution advanced four reasons for this change. In the first place, successfully realizing the program for building communism, laying down its material and technical foundations, and achieving an abundance of material goods, all depended directly on enhancing the consciousness of the working people.

Second, with the further development of socialist democracy and the gradual transformation of the socialist state into communist public self-government, persuasion and the education of the masses more and more would become the chief method of regulating the Soviet society.

Third, shaping the new man with communist traits of character and eliminating the survivals of capitalism in human consciousness was becoming a more and more important, practical task.

Peaceful coexistence with states having different social systems, according to the resolution, could not lead to a relaxation of the

ideological struggle. On the contrary, the party would carry on
an irreconcilable struggle for communist ideology.[20] The 1960
resolution repeated Khrushchev's favorite demand, that party
propaganda be closely linked with "life" and with the building
of communism. It stressed the need for a proper "communist"
attitude toward labor. The principle "He who does not work,
neither shall he eat," was to be stressed in propaganda work.[21]
One demand expressed in the critical preamble of this resolution
was that propaganda inculcate in Soviet citizens more effectively
than in the past "a spirit of Soviet patriotism and national pride."
However, the resolution also demanded that this be done without
any tolerance for survivals of "bourgeois nationalism," or other
harmful traditions or reactionary customs.

The second major defect of party propaganda singled out for
criticism by the preamble was the "narrowness of its sphere of
influence," its lack of "massiveness," and the weakness of its presentation. Local party organizations, as well as research institutes
of the Academy of Sciences of the USSR, the Institute of Marxism-
Leninism, the Higher Party School, and other organizations and
institutions were severely criticized because, according to the
resolution, they had failed to give sufficient attention to the
"bringing up of the workers in a communist spirit." [22]

The resolution presented sixteen sets of instructions and demands for the improved conduct of party propaganda. The tenor
of these instructions is displayed in the following paragraph:

> The chief task of party propaganda consists in a deep and many-
> sided explanation of the ideas of Marxism-Leninism, in the indica-
> tion as to how they may be successfully applied to life in the course
> of the struggle of the party for the victory of socialism and commu-
> nism in our country, study of their utilization in the practical
> activity and creative development of the theoretical values accumu-
> lated by the party, the raising of the workers in the struggle for the
> realization of the policy of the party in life, and the training of
> active and firm fighters for communism.[23]

It was prescribed that desired attitudes be inculcated by studying
and explaining "the classics of Marxism-Leninism" and party

20 "O zadachakh partiinoi propagandy . . . ," *op. cit.,* p. 144.
21 *Ibid.,* p. 147.
22 *Ibid.,* pp. 147–49.
23 *Ibid.,* p. 150.

speeches and documents, as well as by studying the history of the CPSU, political economy, and Marxist philosophy. It emphasized that the results of party propaganda were proportional to the relating of propaganda to "the life and the activity of the people, and to the practice of the building of communism." [24]

The resolution demanded that outstanding agricultural and industrial work be popularized and that propagandists and agitators be adequately informed about production work. Third, the resolution demanded that propaganda work be expanded and brought "to every Soviet person." To achieve this objective, "abstractness" in propaganda was to be ended and every possible form of the mass media was to be utilized. Moreover, the document demanded more active "utilization of the intellectual and emotional influence of the best productions of literature and art" to increase the effectiveness of propaganda. Also, conferences of leaders and viewers were to be called regularly to discuss literature, films, etc.[25] Point four of the decree stipulated that a "differentiated" approach be taken to propaganda, making suggestions with respect to such groups as workers and collective farmers, intellectuals, young people, women, and minority nationalities.[26]

Operationally, the most significant section of the resolution was its directive that party organizations achieve an orderly sequence in propaganda work, so that "each communist from year to year would systematically and purposefully raise his ideological and political level and master Marxism-Leninism as an integrated teaching." [27] The following sequence of programs of political instruction was recommended: (1) the political school (*politshkola*), as the first rung of Marxist-Leninist training; (2) circles and theoretical seminars for studying the history of the CPSU; (3) circles and theoretical seminars for studying the fundamentals of Marxism-Leninism; (4) theoretical seminars and circles for studying Marxist-Leninist philosophy, political economy, concrete economics, problems of atheism, current politics, the international situation, the international communist movement, and economic schools; (5) universities of Marxism-Leninism, independent study according to individual plans, and also theoretical seminars for studying particular classic works of Marxism-Leninism or par-

[24] *Ibid.*, p. 152.
[25] *Ibid.*, p. 153.
[26] *Ibid.*, pp. 154–55.
[27] *Ibid.*, p. 157.

ticular problems in the history of the Communist Party of the Soviet Union, political economy, dialectical and historical materialism, ethics, esthetics, atheism, the world communist, labor, democratic, and national movements, and others.

The resolution pointed out that the success of party propaganda depended upon the quality of the propagandist cadres engaged therein. It issued instructions to party organizations to improve the recruiting and training of propagandists. This was followed by instructions regarding the establishment of "houses" and "cabinets" for political enlightenment, which were to assist propagandists in their training and in their work. Other sections of the resolution were devoted to such methods of propaganda work as lectures, the press, radio, and television. A rather long section stressed the importance of the social sciences in communist indoctrination and propaganda work and called for appropriate works on such subjects as the history of the CPSU, philosophy, economics, history in general, and also for works on the world communist movement, with proper attention to "the collapse of the colonial system of imperialism and the development of a national-liberation struggle of the peoples of Asia, Africa and Latin America." [28]

SCOPE AND ORGANIZATION OF POLITICAL EDUCATION

The 1960 resolution presented a comprehensive program for moulding the political outlook of all categories of the Soviet citizenry, except for party functionaries. Data available in Soviet sources indicate that this program, already in its early stages of development when the January, 1960 resolution was promulgated, was implemented on a very large scale. Leonid Ilichev stated in a speech that "more than twenty million people are engaged in organized study of the history, theory and policy of the party in the political enlightenment system." [29] According to another authoritative Soviet source 22,553,000 persons were enrolled, as of the academic year 1961–1962, in the system of political enlightenment. Of these, slightly more than 7,000,000 were party members; the remainder were nonparty persons.[30] The total number then enrolled was more than 26,000,000.[31] These figures

28 *Ibid.*, p. 162.
29 *Pravda*, June 19, 1963.
30 Evdokimov, *op. cit.*, p. 20.
31 *Pravda*, Jan. 16, 1965.

are surprising not so much because 70 per cent of the members of the CPSU were engaged in organized political studies but because of the very large number of nonparty people so engaged.[32] Evdokimov stated that in 1958–1959 the combined figure for party and nonparty students in the political instruction network had been 6,700,000, of whom 4,500,000 had been members of the party.

It is not unlikely that figures in Soviet sources regarding numbers of students enrolled in the adult political indoctrination program are somewhat inflated. Some inflation would conform to the Soviet tradition of exuberant, confidence-boosting reporting on the results of important party "campaigns." It is clear that an educational effort of such vastness and rapidity of growth must present many problems to those in charge of it.

In Moscow oblast alone, including the city of Moscow, it was reported that during the academic year 1961–1962, 2,300,000 persons, of whom 65 per cent were not members of the party, were enrolled in the "political enlightenment network." [33] This was two and one-half times as many as in the preceding year. Of the more than 2,000,000 persons enrolled in political study programs in Moscow oblast, 450,000 were at the highest levels, in theoretical seminars or in "individual plans."

The training of instructors — known as "propagandists" — for the schools, study circles, seminars, and other elements of this vast network had to be expanded. As of 1961, there were 95,000 propagandists in Moscow oblast alone, an increase of 12,000 over the previous year. Propagandists were assisted in improving their qualifications (80 per cent of them already had either been graduated from institutions of higher education or had some higher education) by leaders of propaganda seminars, located in the raions and in enterprises. These leaders, in turn, received instruction and assistance in 477 "cabinets of political enlightenment" and from 740 "methodological councils." The summit of these guidance agencies was the "House of Political Enlightenment" (*Dom politicheskogo prosveshcheniya*) of Moscow city and oblast.[34] For the top leadership of the Moscow city and oblast politi-

[32] According to V. Zasorin, in an article in *Partiinaya zhizn*, No. 8, April, 1963, as of Jan. 1, 1963, total party membership had been 10,387,196, of whom 806,047 were candidates.

[33] F. L. Tsipkina, ed., *Metodicheski tsentr moskovskikh propagandistov i agitatorov* (Moscow, 1961), p. 4.

[34] *Ibid.*, pp. 4–7.

cal instruction system, and also for heads of factory and collective farm "agitation collectives," the House of Political Enlightenment provided and organized special programs of lectures, advice on teaching methods, seminars, and meetings with representatives of foreign communist parties and with Soviet "production leaders," outstanding scientists, and other distinguished citizens.[35] It also arranged exhibitions, prepared bibliographies, etc.[36]

One adult political socialization problem is providing a focus of subject matter and a depth of content suited to the varied backgrounds of the students. Although the 1960 resolution indicated that the political school was to be the lower rung of the political education ladder, Evdokimov stated that the ladder started with "elementary economics schools and circles." [37] It appears that the political schools and the economic schools, and also the more elementary types of study circles and theoretical seminars, were designed to meet the needs of party and nonparty students who had not been graduated from secondary schools or institutions of higher education. After first obtaining, in these programs, an introductory acquaintance with information on "the laws of social development," history of the CPSU, elementary economics, and related topics, and then studying "the fundamentals of Marxism-Leninism," Soviet citizens could go on to study particular aspects of Marxism-Leninism, such as party history, dialectical and historical materialism, etc. These subjects are studied separately, in courses or advanced seminars, by persons who have already taken general training of the kind given in the politshkola or other elementary, mixed programs. Finally, the communist or nonparty activist embarks on a program of individual "independent study." This independent study is supplemented by group discussions once or twice a month, by lectures and conferences, and by "consultations" for clarifying difficulties and correcting mistakes. Thus the student's ideological development and his progress — or lack of progress — are kept constantly under expert, authoritative supervision. During the 1961–1962 school year about five and a half million persons were enrolled in supervised study programs of this kind.[38]

A brochure by V. Volodin contains much valuable informa-

35 *Ibid.*, pp. 7–18.
36 *Ibid.*, pp. 63–78.
37 *Ibid.*, pp. 30–31.
38 *Ibid.*, p. 37.

tion on the style, structure, and pedagogical methods characteristic of the elementary rungs of the political education ladder.[39] Indirectly, it illuminates the objectives, methods, and problems of the political socialization process as a whole. In the preface to his booklet, Volodin notes that the politshkola imparts to its pupils a "taste for revolutionary theory" and teaches them to work "independently" with books.[40] Its seven sections instruct propagandists working at the politshkola level in preparing annual or semiannual study plans, preparing and conducting lessons, using "local material" to render instruction "concrete and purposeful," planning excursions to museums, art galleries, and places of historical interest, and ways of instilling in students approved habits, such as regular, systematic reading of the Soviet press, visual aids, and other substantive and methodological topics.[41] The tone of the booklet is one of practical pedagogy, combined with devout preachment of the Marxist-Leninist message. In exhorting that propaganda be "not primitive but popular," since the propagandist deals with living people, not with "objects of propaganda," it displays a feel for the psychological problems in political indoctrination.[42]

A model plan for the first year of instruction in a politshkola is presented by Volodin. After a preliminary organization meeting and selecting a *starosta,* or monitor, the first topic, entitled "What One Must Know about the Development of Society," is dealt with in three meetings in October. This topic is followed by "The Construction of Socialism in the USSR," and four others, the last defined as "The Communist Party — the Leader of the Soviet People." A total of twenty sessions, normally lasting about two hours each, but in exceptional cases as long as six, is listed. Discussion is the mode of instruction, since the attention span of politshkola students is considered too limited for them to cope with lectures.[43]

One of the propagandists' tasks in preparing the study plan is to find appropriate places in it for showing films, playing phonograph records of speeches by Lenin, or inviting veterans of the

[39] *The Politshkola and the Organization of Its Work (Politshkola i organizatsiya ee raboty)* (Moscow, 1961).
[40] *Ibid.,* p. 7.
[41] *Ibid.,* pp. 26–31, 40–42.
[42] It is one of fifteen published by 1961 in the "Little Library of the Propagandist."
[43] *Ibid.,* pp. 5–8.

revolutionary movement, Supreme Soviet deputies, scientists, or other distinguished persons to attend meetings when their presence is appropriate.[44]

A basic textbook is used by the propagandist in preparing for the sessions, but he is warned that he must go far beyond the text and must spend up to eight to ten hours in preparing for a single meeting if he is to achieve full effectiveness.[45]

Only if the sessions are prepared and conducted in a conscientious, thorough, and skilled manner will such objectives be realized as helping the students to become better, more productive workers, to acquire firm personal convictions based on the "principles of communist morality," and to develop intolerance of "manifestations of bourgeois ideology."[46] Volodin's text is liberally sprinkled with examples showing how to render political instruction attractive and convincing. Some, comparing Soviet and United States economic conditions, elucidate problems run into by official attempts to deflate popular impressions of American prosperity and are interesting examples of propaganda technique.

It is noted that frequently the leaders of political schools compare the levels of consumption of various products in the United States and in the USSR and that often they fall into the error of uncritically accepting average figures for the United States, forgetting that "it is impossible to compare two families in American society: the millionaire and the unemployed."[47] Propagandists sometimes naively accept the picture of American life contained in the official United States Russian language publication *Amerika*. Volodin presents an imaginary conversation between a propagandist and one of his politshkola students, in which the latter remarks that there are a great many automobiles in America. The reply is given that it is true that there are many automobiles but they are very unevenly distributed among the wealthy and among ordinary workers and their working class owners live under the constant threat of unemployment. Furthermore, it is argued, because the automobile industry is much older in the United States than in the Soviet Union, the former has an

44 *Ibid.*, pp. 6, 50, 53.
45 *Ibid.*, pp. 10–11, listing nine operations in proper preparation for a session.
46 *Ibid.*, pp. 4, 12.
47 *Ibid.*, pp. 29–30.

advantage and, finally, Soviet progress in this industry was severely handicapped by the first and second world wars.[48]

Although the teaching methods which Volodin recommends might strike American readers as heavy-handed, with their frequent references to Lenin, Kalinin, and Khrushchev as models to be emulated in teaching the fundamentals of politics, still his book contained many signs of an effort to rid political indoctrination of the oppressiveness and woodenness which had characterized it during the Stalin era. In dealing with the "summing up" sessions which conclude the two-year program in the politshkola, Volodin noted: "Long gone is the time when the summing up sessions became stern examinations and the propagandists played the role of incorruptible examiners." He asserts that the final sessions today are conducted in "a comradely atmosphere." That old traditions die hard, however, is shown by an example, which is criticized, when all seven members of the bureau of a party organization took part in the final session of the study year in a politshkola and each asked questions. In another case the propagandist in charge at the final session made notes, which created an atmosphere of anxiety. Volodin noted that grades are not given in the politshkola but asserted that it was useful for the propagandist in charge to sum up the results of a year's work and to give appropriate advice to his students so that they might be better prepared for the work of the following year.[49]

Upon completing the work in the politshkola, the students are expected to proceed to more advanced study, in which they will be required to do "independent work with books." Consequently, even at the politshkola stage it is necessary to require some preparation of talks and other exercises so that students may begin to acquire habits of independent study.[50] Toward the end, Volodin quoted a passage from the January, 1960 Central Committee resolution on propaganda enjoining participants in the party study process to conduct agitational and propaganda work among the masses. He notes that this requirement applies not only to persons studying the history of the party or philosophy in higher-level study circles but also to students in the political schools. Although the latter cannot be expected to lead political circles

48 *Ibid.*, p. 34.
49 *Ibid.*, pp. 54–55.
50 *Ibid.*, pp. 56–57.

or present theoretical reports, "the best prepared students of the political schools successfully work as agitators." The objective is to turn as many students of the politshkola as possible into agitators who can carry the party's word to the workers of factory and farm. Thus the politshkola seems to be a recruiting agency for the lower levels of the Soviet propaganda machine. There is no indication, however, that persons recruited by it are likely to rise to higher levels. From all the information available it appears that neither the instructors nor the auditors of the political schools, as a rule, can expect to become members of the Soviet elite.

Persons engaged in work other than manual or clerical, usually equipped with secondary or higher education, or, in Soviet terminology, the *intelligentsiya,* receive their political indoctrination in programs more advanced than those previously described. They may attend an institution known as the evening university of Marxism-Leninism, more frequently referred to simply as the University of Marxism-Leninism. At this second level of the adult socialization system the evening university of Marxism-Leninism corresponds to the politshkola at the first level. Like the politshkola, it provides a two-year program of instruction, but uses lectures and "seminars" rather than the guided discussion of the primary level, and a much heavier workload. As at the lower level, upon completing the basic course of instruction students are expected to continue their political self-improvement in "independent" — but guided — study. However, these levels are separate; Soviet citizens apparently remain indefinitely at the level for which their educational and other capabilities fit them, in the judgment of the local party authorities charged with recruitment to these graduated rungs of the enlightenment ladder.

Prior to 1956 the universities of Marxism-Leninism provided industrial executives, engineers, scientists, educators, artists, and other professionals, and also some members of the party apparatus, with intensive training in such theoretical subjects as dialectical and historical materialism. However, subsequent to the central committee resolution on the political instruction system dated August 21 of that year, there were significant shifts, apparently responding to the need for rapid expansion of teaching staffs for political training institutions and to Khrushchev's pressure for propaganda with a "practical" content.[51] Khrushchev's demand that indoctrination be directed toward the tasks of the day, especially in production, was expressed in the resolution's directive that time spent in the study of "political economy and the economics of industry" be increased at the expense of other disciplines. Also, the course in the universities of Marxism-Leninism was reduced from three years to two years.

Perhaps as important as the shift of curricular emphasis was that which transformed these institutions from advanced theoretical study agencies into training centers for propagandists charged with carrying the party's current ideological interpretations to the "masses." Although this demand was not contained in the 1956 resolution it was to be included in that of January, 1960 on propaganda matters. However, the evening universities, while concentrating their efforts on the training of propagandists, continued also to offer advanced study of theory to members of the artistic, scientific, and managerial elite. There is clear evidence that the attempt to combine these different and somewhat incompatible functions in the same institution led, after 1956, to confusion, frustration, and dissatisfaction among instructors and students alike.[52] In addition to the already mentioned need to train a rapidly expanding corps of instructors, there is another possible reason for the shift in function of the evening universities after 1956. That was a belief on the part of the party authorities that rank and file members of the better educated strata of the population no longer needed — and indeed might be irked by — the tightly controlled course and seminar work in party history, Marxist-Leninist philosophy, etc., which they had received in the Stalin era. It was apparently believed that better results would be achieved by providing, for the continued indoctrination of the intellectuals, improved forms of individual study and also by providing such persons with a broader variety of opportunities for participating in public enlightenment work, as lecturers and consultants, for example.

Upon completing his study in the university of Marxism-

[51] Text of resolution in *Spravochnik partiinogo rabotnika* (Moscow, 1957), pp. 346–53. On the universities of Marxism-Leninism, see pp. 350–51.

[52] The above conclusion was reached by Mrs. Ellen Mickiewicz in material developed by her in preparing her Ph.D. dissertation, based on a wide range of Soviet sources, including, in particular, the important brochure by M. Ya. Tsibulki, *Universitet Marksizma-Leninizma* (Kharkov, 1957), and other material covering the period from 1956 through 1964.

Leninism, a highly educated citizen continues his political training
in a theoretical seminar or a planned individual study program. He may also continue his studies for a time in the evening
university, for this institution has a number of departments and
courses. At all levels and in all branches of the system, the principle of sequence is combined with study of such basic materials
as the party program and "the most important documents of the
CPSU and the international communist movement, where all the
constituent parts and aspects of the Marxist-Leninist teaching
are represented in their organic unity." [53] The inclusion of such
materials throughout the system ensures uniformity of perspective. It also imparts to the program timeliness and relevance to
everyday matters. The striving for timeliness in the political
study program, far from being new, is actually traditional. Just
as the Stalinist 1938 resolution criticized the remoteness from
reality of much of the teaching in the political education system,
so also did the Khrushchevian directives criticize, on the same
grounds, the Stalin program. In both periods criticism of previous practice was correct, yet it was also somewhat disingenuous.
Throughout the history of the USSR, especially during the Stalin
era, it appears that propagandists who teach in the political
study program avoid touchy topics, which is probably why one
finds so much criticism that students in study circles and seminars are permitted to go on year after year, repeating topics
already covered. In both the Stalin and post-Stalin periods one
finds criticism of a "mechanical" or an "abstract" approach, which
ignores the policy implications of political indoctrination.[54]

To facilitate the work of persons pursuing "independent"
political study, the central committee in 1957 established the
magazine, *In Aid of Political Self-Training* (*V pomoshch politi-
cheskomu samoobrazovaniyu*). It has had a significant part in this
field of indoctrination ever since.[55]

At the third and highest level of adult political socialization

53 "O zadachakh . . . ," *op. cit.,* p. 33.
54 The editorial in *Partiinaya zhizn,* No. 18, Sept., 1964, discussing the
1964–1965 political training program, again criticized such practices. It noted
that in the past, circles and seminars set up to study philosophy, political
economy, and history had sometimes devoted years to "problems remote from
the urgent questions of the day" and expressed the hope that the transfer of
the central focus of the whole system to "current problems of the theory and
policy of the CPSU" would raise the intellectual level of political training.
55 *Spravochnik partiinogo rabotnika, op. cit.,* p. 352.

the outlook and skills of the party functionaries are shaped. They are the driving force, the movers and shapers of Soviet society. The students of the special schools for party function- aries and executives are a rather select group. As with the far more numerous students of the programs already described, little is known about the intellectual atmosphere of the classrooms of the elite political training institutions.

It is not difficult to describe generally the instruction program in the schools for party functionaries. Like the lower-ranking political education institutions, these schools were affected by the pragmatic post-Stalin emphasis. In his report to the Twentieth Congress Khrushchev, though he expressed satisfaction over the results of the party cadre training program since 1946, also severely criticized the failure of the party training schools to pre- pare their students adequately in the fundamentals of agricul- tural and industrial administration. He indicated that lack of knowledge of the fundamentals of applied economics adversely affected the performance of party workers in directing the Soviet national economy. In 1956 and 1957 the system of training for party cadres was reorganized. The main links in the new struc- ture, which seems still to be functioning relatively unchanged, were four-year inter-oblast party schools in Moscow, Leningrad, Alma-Ata, Tashkent, Baku, Minsk, and some twenty other major cities, and at the summit of party education, the Higher Party School in Moscow, attached to the CPSU central committee. The term of instruction of the latter was changed from three to two years. The June, 1956 resolution which instituted this reorgani- zation also stipulated that the party schools of Moscow, Lenin- grad, Kiev, Minsk, Khabarovsk, Alma-Ata, and Tashkent should have special faculties and courses for training journalists. The resolution also provided that the four-year inter-oblast party schools would be included in the category of institutions of higher education, together with the Moscow Higher Party School. Presumably, this step was designed to increase the prestige of "party intellectuals" in the eyes of their nonapparatus colleagues. Also, the Higher Party School was to continue to maintain a division for journalistic personnel.[56] To adjust the party training

---

[56] The text of the resolution is in *ibid.*, pp. 410–15. See the 1964 edition of the same reference work, pp. 257–63, for curricula of party training institutions established by the 1963 resolution.

system to the 1962 reorganization of party and state structures, a central committee resolution dated March 9, 1963, divided the party school programs into industrial and agricultural sections, with appropriate differences of subject matter. Also, the 1963 resolution provided for some differences in training for high-level communicators, depending on whether their specialization lay in press work or in the radio-television field. This 1963 resolution indicated that two-year as well as four-year schools were to be provided both for party and state leaders and for communication officials.

According to the 1956 resolution, in the ten years prior to its promulgation more than 55,000 persons had been graduated from party schools outside Moscow. During the same period, the Higher Party School in Moscow had graduated 2,833, and its correspondence division had graduated more than 6,000. Most graduates of the party schools were engaged in party or Soviet work — in other words, in executive functions in either the party or the Soviet governmental apparatus. Perhaps the most interesting information in the 1956 and 1963 resolutions applied to curricula for the two-year and four-year party schools. These were divided into regular curricula and curricula for the journalistic divisions. Each curriculum listed about twenty subjects, of which most were required; only a very few were elective. The curricula established by the 1956 and 1963 resolutions required a heavy load of more than 3,000 hours of instruction, for all the four-year party school programs. For two-year schools, however, the required number of classroom hours was fixed in 1963 at 1,500 or 1,600, depending on the program.

All programs include such basic political subjects as history of the CPSU, dialectical and historical materialism (renamed "Marxist-Leninist philosophy" by the 1963 resolution), political economy, and the history of the international "labor and national-liberation movement," as well as history of the USSR and "party and Soviet construction." In addition, all require a wide range of technical and specialized as well as "practical" subjects, ranging from law, economics, and "planning of the national economy" through bookkeeping, statistics, and, for regular school curricula, "production practice." For the journalistic division, photography and stenography are among the required special courses. The over-all topical breakdown in the four-year program is about one-third political and ideological subjects and the remainder general educational and technical and practical subjects. It is interesting that the 1963 resolution included in the curricula of two-year programs an optional forty hours of instruction in civil defense, which is a required subject in the four-year programs. Foreign language, Russian language (presumably for foreign students), and "problems of art and literature" are optional subjects in all two-year and four-year programs.

Members of the CPSU with a secondary education are admitted up to the age of thirty-five to the four-year party schools. They must pass entrance examinations on the history of the USSR, Russian language, geography, and "fundamentals of Marxism-Leninism." Admission to the Higher Party School requires a higher education and "adequate experience" in leadership work.

Admission to the Moscow Higher Party School is open to persons not more than forty years of age. Among the interesting admission procedures for the Higher Party School is one providing for admission of "workers, commissioned for study by communist and workers parties of foreign countries." [57] According to both the 1956 and 1963 resolutions, passage of "state examinations" in four subjects (party history, dialectical and historical materialism, political economy, and either agricultural or industrial economics) is required for graduation from the party schools. In the journalism programs an examination in that subject is substituted for the one in economics.

So far as can be determined, the differences among the levels of adult political education in the USSR consist mainly in the quantity, complexity, and intensity of instruction, rather than in content or point of view. The noncommunist observer is inevitably restricted, in appraising the adult political socialization program, to an incomplete sample even of published sources, and has no opportunity to scrutinize its operation at first hand. To him it appears to present, particularly during a given year, basically standardized topics, terminology, and tone, but is not completely devoid of flexibility.[58]

[57] *Ibid.,* 1957 ed., pp. 411–13.
[58] These generalizations are based on examination of the "model study

It is clear that since 1956 the Soviet leadership has sought to infuse into the elite "cadre" institutions the same "practical," vocational element it has attempted to put into the mass indoctrination programs described earlier. While maintaining and indeed intensifying its demand that all "leading workers" be "politically developed," with broad horizons and a lofty sense of dedication to the building of communism, the party has also demanded that political and economic "cadres" equip themselves with modern administrative and managerial skills. Apparently at least the nonideological side of this campaign as yet is far from fully successful in the eyes of the leadership. At least this conclusion could be drawn from an article which severely criticized Soviet efforts in training the "directing cadres of the national economy," and pointed out that the science of management was not merely one aspect of this or that branch of knowledge but a special field in itself.[59] It would certainly be superficial to conclude from this and other recent Soviet statements that introducing a "business administration" element into the adult socialization program has not produced useful results. Such expressions of concern, however, point to an important dilemma facing the Soviet leaders in many fields — the conflict between ideological orthodoxy and economic productivity. Certainly, if far less time were devoted to "ideology," superior training could be given in economic planning and administration!

THE CONTENT OF POLITICAL INSTRUCTION

What is the political and ideological content of instruction in these various schools? Generally speaking, the ideological matter which they offer may be divided into four sections: (1) the philosophy of "dialectical materialism"; (2) the historical-sociological teaching of "historical materialism"; (3) political economy; and (4) political doctrine, or, by its American name, political science. The latter is categorized under such titles as "theory and tactics of the international communist movement" and "the doctrine of socialism and communism."[60] We must confine our presentation

plans" for the political schools, published in 1960 and 1962, and on the "unified study plan" for the entire political training system for 1964–65, which is discussed subsequently, as well as on an article in *Partiinaya zhizn*, No. 16, Aug., 1956, and on the other works referred to in this chapter.

59 *Izvestiya*, Aug. 23, 1964.

60 Wolfgang Leonhard, *Sowjet-ideologie heute* (Frankfort am Main and

of the content of Soviet political, economic, and social doctrine to a brief sampling of a few representative texts. The range of textbooks and other reading material for the political courses is now much wider than it was during the Stalin era. Although the basic theme of all this literature remains the Lenin-Stalin thesis of a struggle between "socialism" and "capitalism," the official perception of this struggle and the style of the language used to describe it have changed. These periodic shifts of emphasis may be illustrated by comparing key passages of the Short Course with some of the basic post-Stalin political textbooks.[61]

The introduction to the Short Course asserted that the history of the party was "the history of the overthrow of tsarism, the overthrow of the power of the landlords and capitalists, a history of the smashing of foreign military intervention during the civil war, the history of the building of the Soviet state and the socialist society in our country." The introduction also asserted that the study of party history strengthened faith in "the final victory of the great cause of the party of Lenin-Stalin, the victory of communism in the whole world." The Short Course was essentially a chronicle — extremely biased and full of calculated distortion — of Lenin's contributions to communism as interpreted by Stalin and, above all, of Stalin's struggles against and victories over his enemies. Apart from praise of Lenin and of Stalin, what stands out most clearly in the Short Course is its invective against the "spies," "monsters," and "dregs of humanity" — Trotski, Bukharin, Kamenev, Zinovev, *et al.* — who are presented as the agents of foreign intelligence services, dedicated to the subversion of the Soviet state but destroyed by Stalin, loyal follower of Lenin and loyal servant of the Soviet people.[62] The elementary textbook *Foundations of Political Knowledge,* though highly oversimplified in structure, seems to be a rather rational, sober, and well-balanced work in comparison with the primitive and hysterical Short Course. It is organized more topically than

Hamburg, 1962), introduction. Leonhard's study presents an excellent, clear outline of Soviet political and social doctrine.

[61] *Istoriya vsesoyuznoi kommunisticheskoi partii (bolshevikov) Kratki Kurs* (Moscow, 1938); *Osnovy politicheskikh znanii,* 4th ed. (Moscow, 1963); *Osnovy Marksizma-Leninizma* (Moscow, 1959); *Istoriya kommunisticheskoi partii sovetskogo soyuza,* 2nd ed. (Moscow, 1963).

[62] See esp. Ch. XII, Section 4, the heading of which begins as follows: "Liquidation of the Remnants of the Bukharin-Trotski Spies, Wreckers and Traitors of the Motherland."

chronologically, beginning with a chapter entitled "What It Is Necessary to Know about the Development of Society," treating of the class struggle, the socialist revolution, and "the problem of power — the chief problem of the revolution." There follow chapters on "socialism — the first phase of communism"; the victory of socialism in the USSR, etc. The third section of the book begins with a chapter entitled "Communism — the Future of Mankind," which is followed by chapters on "the international liberation movement," "peaceful co-existence and the struggle for peace," and the final chapter, "The Communist Party — the Leader of the Soviet People." Stalin is ignored in this work, and the book gives to Lenin all credit for the ideas upon which the Soviet state and party are built. It emphasizes heavily the international communist movement and the struggle of the "liberation movement" of Asia, Africa, and Latin America against United States "monopoly capitalism." This theme is dramatized by numerous derisive cartoons, such as one entitled "Aid à l'Américaine," showing a smoking Uncle Sam, armed with a revolver, holding in his hands a large metal dollar sign with a chair attached.[63] Although the 1963 edition of this text did not criticize the Chinese communist leadership, it did emphasize the necessity for international communist unity and contained the significant statement that "V. I. Lenin wrote that bolshevism is suitable as a model of tactics for all." [64] Typical of the calculated oversimplification in which this volume abounds is its account of the Cuban crisis of the fall of 1962. There is no mention of Soviet rockets or the measures taken by President Kennedy to assure their removal but it asserts that the "ruling circles of the United States of America" were planning an invasion of Cuba, using American troops, and that "as a result of the efforts of the Cuban people, and the efforts of the Soviet Union and other countries of socialism, as well as of other democratic, anti-imperialist forces this fully prepared invasion was prevented." [65] The concluding section expresses confidence that if capitalism was mankind's "yesterday," socialism and communism are "the today of many peoples and the future of all of mankind." [66] A large part of the text is devoted to attempts to

---

[63] *Osnovy politicheskikh znanii, op. cit.,* p. 415.
[64] *Ibid.,* p. 527.
[65] *Ibid.,* p. 419.
[66] *Ibid.,* p. 533.

demonstrate that the victory of socialism throughout the world will be assured by the Soviet Union's success in economic competition with capitalism. At the same time, the work contains numerous warnings that "bourgeois ideology" still possesses a dangerous power "to poison the consciousness" of Soviet people.[67] In general, the tone of this text is less grim than that of the Short Course, and it stresses more strongly the benefits attributed to the party's leadership and less strongly the dangers threatening from the outside world. But the book does contain numerous warnings of the dangers inherent in the international situation. The text asserts that if the "imperialistic maniacs" of the West seek to unleash an aggressive war the rebuff they will receive will mark "the end of the existence of the anti-people's imperialist system." [68]

In addition to this textbook, students of the political schools also read selected writings of Lenin, the 1961 CPSU program, and a number of speeches by Soviet leaders.[69] Beginning in about 1960 the writings of Stalin and also of Mao Tse-tung were no longer included in the curriculum of the Soviet adult political training program. Following the removal of Stalin's body from the mausoleum on Red Square during the Twenty-second Congress, textbooks used at the higher levels of the political education program devoted much attention to denouncing Stalin's violation of the "Leninist principles and norms of party life." [70]

[67] *Ibid.*, p. 331.

[68] *Ibid.*, p. 467.

[69] The 1960 version of the Study Plan for the political schools included, besides numerous selections from writings and speeches of Khrushchev, speeches by M. A. Suslov, N. M. Shvernik, N. G. Ignatov, L. I. Brezhnev, E. A. Furtseva, A. B. Aristov, O. V. Kuusinen, and A. I. Mikoyan. The reading list for the 1962 version consisted mainly of the above textbook, selections from Lenin, and selections from Khrushchev, principally his speeches to the Twenty-second Party Congress in 1961. The only other party leader any of whose writings were included in the required reading was F. R. Kozlov, whose report on changes in the statutes of the communist party, delivered at the Twenty-second Congress, was listed.

[70] 1962 edition of *Istoriya kommunisticheskoi partii sovetskogo soyuza*, p. 486. On the same page it is stated that at the Seventeenth Congress, in 1934, many delegates, especially those acquainted with Lenin's testament, considered that the time had come to remove Stalin from the post of General Secretary of the party "to other work." Also referred to is Khrushchev's statement at the Twenty-second Congress regarding the suspicious circumstances of the assassination in Dec., 1934 of S. M. Kirov and of Stalin's using this event as a pretext for "mass repressions and crude violations of socialist legality." As recently as 1960 three works by Mao and seven by Stalin were included in a reading list for those preparing to take the entrance examination in the history of the CPSU required for admission to graduate work at

Thus, as in the past, current political developments continued to influence powerfully the current agenda of the political training program — although they did not produce any noticeable basic alteration. The concepts, categories, and terminology of the materials studied in the program continued to seem, to the non-Soviet, noncommunist analyst, dogmatic, ritualistic, and not very relevant to the social, economic, and international problems of the 1960's.

The names assigned to persons, or states, in the Soviet and world political dramas changed, but the motivations and roles assigned to these actors and "forces" continued to conform to traditional Marxist-Leninist scripts. From time to time, however, old categories were associated with new metaphors. Articles and commentaries heralding the 1964–1965 program referred to Marxism-Leninism as the "compass" of the Soviet people's advance toward communism.[71]

The 1964–1965 study plan for the political training program was described as a "new" approach, featuring current political issues and the most relevant problems of theory. As for topicality, this claim was correct. Of the plan's twelve "themes," beginning with "The Characteristics of Our Epoch and the General Line of the World Communist Movement" and ending with "Marxism-Leninism or the International Unity and Solidarity of the Communist Parties," at least eight seem to have been directed at urgent problems of international politics. The novelty of this prospectus was that it, and especially the comments heralding it, for the first time placed at the center of the vital adult political socialization program the frustrating problems posed by Sino-Soviet rivalry in international communism. Editorials in *Pravda* and *Partiinaya zhizn* on the 1964–1965 plan listed as one of its six main foci "the need for the resolute exposure of the personality cult in the ideology and practice of the Chinese leaders."

Soviet institutions of higher education. See *Aspirantura, spravochnik dlya postupayushchikh v aspiranturu i soiskatelei uchenykh stepenei* (Moscow, 1960), pp. 76–85. Later editions of this work did not list works by Stalin or Mao. The 1963 edition of *Obshchestvovedenie,* the social science text for the senior year of secondary schools, criticized the Stalin personality cult, as was to be expected, and the 1964 edition criticized "left opportunism," obviously with Peking in mind, as a grave danger to the world communist movement.

71 See editorials in *Pravda,* Sept. 12, 1964, and in *Partiinaya zhizn,* No. 18, Sept., 1964. This issue and the next one contain the "model study plan for the system of political enlightenment 1964–65."

It is impossible for the non-Soviet observer to know what vicissitudes affected the fulfilment of the 1964–1965 study plan as a result of the fall of Khrushchev. In the readings originally assigned for that plan his writings were heavily represented, and we can be sure that they must have been dropped from it. Presumably also, at least from the evidence available in the official, published statements of the post-Khrushchev leadership and in the Soviet press generally, the sharpness of tone originally planned for discussing the activities of the "Chinese leaders" was substantially softened. It is difficult to believe, though, that the basic perspective on international communism presented by the propagandists in the political schools, study circles, and seminars could have been much altered — the plan was intended to serve all levels of the system, with the usual provisos for its proper adaptation to each level.

The textbook *Foundations of Marxism-Leninism,* published by the State Publishing House for Political Literature in 1959, is a fair sample of the content of intermediate and higher level Soviet political training. This major work of almost 800 pages was prepared by a group headed by the late Otto Kuusinen, at the time an alternate member of the party presidium. Kuusinen was assisted by leading Soviet scholars and also by "responsible party and Soviet workers." It was divided into five sections, headed respectively, "The Philosophical Foundations of the Marxist-Leninist World Outlook"; "The Materialistic Conception of History"; "The Political Economy of Capitalism"; "The Theory and Tactics of the International Communist Movement"; and "The Doctrine of Socialism and Communism." The Russian edition of this text appeared in 600,000 copies and, according to Leonhard, 500,000 copies were published in Soviet-controlled East Germany.[72] More than half of this work was devoted to problems connected with the international communist movement and the transition within the Soviet Union from socialism to a communist society. The work represents a well-organized, systematic application of Leninism to contemporary conditions. It reiterates firmly and in detail the Leninist doctrine of the necessity for the "dictatorship of the Proletariat" as the first stage of the socialist revolution, a concept repeated in

72 Leonhard, *op. cit.,* p. 11.

the 1961 party program.[73] The last chapter attempts to set forth an outline of communist society, which is described as one of "general plenty and abundance" and in which true equality and freedom will prevail. The description warns against anarchistic illusions that this future society will be one of "individuals who do not recognize any social bonds." In order that production shall function and develop "normally" and that culture and civilization may flourish, a form of social organization will be necessary. Consequently, the state will be replaced by a "public self-administration." [74] This formulation appears to be consistent with the positions taken at the Twenty-first and Twenty-second CPSU congresses regarding the organization of society and the relationship between society and the individual. These positions, incidentally, remained valid following the ejection of Khrushchev, as indicated by frequent press statements. Of international relations, the textbook notes that nations, as well as national cultures and languages, will exist "for a very long time after the victory of communism," but that all conflicts and differences among human groups will gradually disappear.[75] Like other major post-Stalin doctrinal products, this text saw that the "successes of the building of communism in the Soviet Union" would significantly influence the political development of "that portion of toiling mankind, condemned by capitalism to the most grievous burdens of involuntary labor, poverty, hunger and national humiliation." In addition the text viewed as a "mission of salvation" of the "camp of socialism" the possibility of banishing world war from the life of mankind.[76]

EFFECTIVENESS OF ADULT POLITICAL INDOCTRINATION

How effective is the program described in this chapter? Only a partial and somewhat speculative answer can be given to this multifaceted question. The Soviet authorities' unwillingness to permit outside observers to study systematically the political enlightenment system constitutes both an obstacle to its investigation and a source of skepticism as to how well it achieves the

[73] *Osnovy Marxizma-Leninizma, op. cit.*, pp. 535–44. On p. 534 it is stated that the problem of the dictatorship of the proletariat is central to the ideological differences between Marxist-Leninists and "reformists."
[74] *Ibid.*, pp. 747–48.
[75] *Ibid.*, pp. 748–50.
[76] *Ibid.*, pp. 732–33.

goals set for it by the Kremlin. That Soviet social scientists and journalists were reluctant to discuss political education with this writer in October, 1963 may be a sign of this practice. A prominent legal scholar interested in "cybernetic" methods of inquiry told the writer that the questionnaire on group attitudes which he was attempting to use was unsuitable, because Soviet society, unlike that of the United States, lacked "caste" features. A high-ranking journalist in Alma-Ata said that if the writer were to try the same questionnaire on an ordinary Soviet citizen he would be told to "Go away!" Answers to the questionnaire, in Leningrad and in Alma-Ata, several thousand miles distant, were almost, but not quite, uniform in content and in their extraordinary evasiveness.

Nothing approaching a thorough study of the published sources has yet been undertaken that would make possible a partial answer regarding the effectiveness of the adult political socialization agencies. From the material on which this chapter is based, however, certain pertinent inferences may be drawn.

It seems clear that the program inherited from the Stalin era was badly out of date and inadequate to deal with the requirements of a citizenry better educated and better informed than the terrified, relatively primitive population for which Stalin had designed the earlier political catechism. The somewhat paranoid Short Course was obsolete. The Khrushchev reforms, in this as in other fields, were reactions to urgent pressures.

On the other hand, Stalin's approach to indoctrination, and to political communication generally, may have possessed certain strengths lacking in that of his successors. According to Harold D. Lasswell's criteria for propaganda effectiveness, the Stalinist program, though increasingly irrelevant to emergent realities, nevertheless was strong in "distinctiveness." It was, however, weak in "adaptiveness." [77] Stalin's methods of indoctrination had the strengths inherent in sharpness of tone, intensity of mood, and simplicity of presentation. To be sure, the consistency of Stalin's message was achieved by rejecting alternative views and in general by suppression and distortion. Nevertheless, it at least achieved a certain plausibility, especially since the penalty for failure to heed it could be so impressive.

[77] Harold D. Lasswell and Dorothy Blumenstock, *World Revolutionary Propaganda* (New York, 1939), esp. pp. 247–358.

In contrast, Stalin's successors sought relevance, timeliness, and concreteness for their propaganda and ideological programs, but they did not wish to sacrifice ideological orthodoxy. Perhaps unwittingly, they furthered a "secularization" of Marxism-Leninism. Their blend of orthodoxy and adaptability, however, may have helped to set in motion processes which may lead to the disintegration of the official ideology.

The vast expansion of the adult socialization program must have brought with it badly deteriorated administration and presentation, all the more because increasingly teachers at all levels of the program and even many of those who supervised and assisted them were nonprofessional, "volunteer" personnel. The nonprofessionalization of the system may have had the advantage of bringing in fresh points of view and, perhaps, new enthusiasm. But it also must have sapped the authority of a program still, to be sure, closely supervised by the party, but nevertheless rendered flabby by expansion, loss of the authority of the old professional propaganda cadres, administrative complexity, and diffuseness. One wonders how much of an impression even a university professor serving as a volunteer propagandist can make on such different members of his audience as a leading scientist or a successful engineer.

The adult socialization campaign was also weakened by the increasing heterogeneity, of both the teaching staff and the student body, which undoubtedly accompanied quantitative expansion, in its early stages at least. The crucial development was the recruiting of thousands of nonprofessional teachers from diverse categories of the intelligentsia. It appears to have been difficult for members of the party apparatus, factory managers, writers, and physicists to achieve homogeneity of perspective whether as propagandists or as students, and yet such homogeneity was required to make the post-Stalin program of adult indoctrination succeed.

Finally, Stalin's successors' attempt to adapt the whole program to the varied occupational and local interests of its clientele may have been dysfunctional in several ways. Subordinating ideology to the requirements of production could conceivably rob it of the "sacred" quality which has always been a major source of its authority. Despite central controls, uniform teaching methods, and other safeguards, it could also have caused a certain fragmenting.

Now the potentially disintegrative changes made in this gigantic try at adult education after Stalin's death should not be exaggerated. Without more conclusive evidence than is presently available of weaknesses in the system it would be prudent to assume that it functions with respectable effectiveness.

For one thing, its ritualistic flavor is less repugnant to Russians, with their authoritarian traditions, reinforced by generations of Soviet rule, than it would be to people with a livelier tradition of criticizing the political powers that be. The systematic teaching of Marxism-Leninism probably enhances greatly the cohesiveness of Soviet society. The main appeals of the doctrine, presumably, are its comprehensiveness and apparent consistency — achieved by suppressing information and opinions deemed inappropriate by the party authorities — and its moralistic aspects. Also, the strongly emphasized inevitability of mankind's progress from "feudalism," through "capitalism," up to "socialism," and, finally, "communism" probably still has appeal. This prophecy is of course supported by selected data on the political history of the world since the emergence of Leninism, especially since the bolshevik revolution of 1917, and by abundant data on the economic, technological, and scientific progress of the USSR, which, in the absence of competing points of view, can create an impression of irresistible power.

It should be borne in mind that the organized program of formal instruction described above is supplemented by many agencies, in fashions so varied as to preclude even mentioning most of them. The Soviet trade union network, with its millions of members, carries on a huge program of "ideological work," by means of lectures, factory libraries and clubs, theatrical and other recreational activity with ideological overtones, "scientific-atheistic propaganda," the popularization of "advanced technology," "people's universities of culture," assistance to parent-teacher's organizations, "organization of cultured leisure for the workers," and the like.[78] In the Soviet Union, the line between political indoctrination and current information often is not clear. Both are subordinated to the CPSU "general line." The process de-

[78] *Kniga predsedatelya komiteta profsoyuza* (Moscow, 1962), pp. 277–309.

scribed in this chapter and the mass communication activities discussed in the next interact with and reinforce one another.

One major technique, applied to all ages and occupations, and common to the political processes examined in the last two chapters and in the one to follow, should again be mentioned here. In Chapter III we brought up the "collective" as an agency for indoctrinating schoolchildren. In factory shop and mine shaft, in office and scientific laboratory, in city apartment house and farm community, the collective, under party and trade union leadership, is called upon to reinforce and check on the effectiveness of current agitation and propaganda programs. The collective (the word is used very imprecisely and can denote the thousands of workers of a big factory like the Ural Machine Building Works, or the pupils and teachers of a village school) is expected to make each and every one of its members conscious of his responsibilities to the community. The collective, in fact, is assigned many functions, including those of conscience-prodder and public watchdog. Judging by a flood of official statements, however, its direction remains firmly lodged in the hands of party executives.[79]

The emphasis on collective responsibility in all of this presumably heightens the individual's sense of the pressure constantly exerted on him by the authorities. It is difficult for the outsider to balance the reinforcement and probably the support of such mobilized social pressure against the anxieties and resentments to which it may give rise.

It is obvious that Stalin's successors attribute enormous importance to the indoctrinational and socializing uses of the collective. Probably its effectiveness in the future, like that of the formal instruction program discussed herein, will depend on the degree of flexibility, adaptiveness, and sophistication mustered by administrators in direct contact with the "masses," and this in turn depends on many other factors, especially upon informed guidance from above.

Fundamentally, the problem for the long run will be that of the Kremlin's continued ability to accommodate diversity of interests among the clientele of propaganda programs without causing disintegration of a centrally managed consensus.

[79] See, for example, V. Zirmin, party secretary of the pattern shop of the Ural Machine Building Plant, in *Pravda*, Oct. 28, 1964.

CHAPTER V

The Shaping and Direction
of Public Opinion

IN THE last two chapters we described the methods by which the CPSU seeks to instill in Soviet citizens sentiments and beliefs which nurture and sustain the political culture. Now, we shall look into the day-to-day mobilization of public opinion. We shall examine the organizations which seek to orient and stimulate the citizenry as a whole, and, using appropriate strategies, its occupational, professional, ethnic, and other segments to respond enthusiastically and actively to the party's demands. Thus we turn to agitation, in contrast to the propaganda functions discussed earlier, especially in Chapter IV. Though the primary function of the press, radio, television, and other mass media is agitation, they carry on propaganda activities as well.

To perform the orientation and information operations vital to the successful functioning of the political system, the CPSU uses an interconnected communication network, centrally guided but administratively decentralized, and able to tailor its messages to its differing audiences. We cannot understand how this net operates without knowing something of the techniques by which the Kremlin seeks to protect its monopoly. These include an array of communication-preventing activities, which minimize Soviet citizens' access to dissonant, distracting, or disorienting messages, especially those originating in the United States. It is typical of the regime's tight control over information of non-Soviet origin that in Moscow, even in 1966, no "bourgeois" foreign newspapers or periodicals were to be found in newsstands, bookstores, or other public outlets. To be sure, the Kremlin's allergy to communication from outside subsided somewhat after Stalin's death and persons who needed foreign books and other materials for their work, or who for whatever purpose somehow succeeded in obtaining them, were permitted to have them, partly because the authorities realized the disadvantages of isolation, and partly in response to the intelligentsia's growing demand for fuller information. Party leaders were still warning at the Twenty-third CPSU Congress in 1966 that "immature" young people were "swallowing the bait" of hostile propaganda. The Kremlin seemed as determined as ever to combat "harmful" influences. In the last few years, however, it has increasingly substituted refutation and rebuttal of dissonant messages for its former silent suppression and prohibition. Other techniques used to combat "alien" ideas and their alleged disseminators include publishing in the press citizens' letters denouncing unorthodox literary works and, occasionally, court trials, in which an incidental or principal charge is ideologically subversive activity. A prime example was the trial and severe sentence for "subversive anti-Soviet activity" imposed on the British tourist Gerald Brooke in July, 1965.[1] In recent years Soviet information control strategy has shifted, probably because an increasingly educated, information-hungry public can no longer be denied knowledge of events in the outside world

[1] N. V. Podgorny, one of the most powerful members of the party presidium, was reported in *Pravda Ukrainy*, April 10, 1963, to have bitterly denounced the "imperialists" for spending "billions of dollars" on sending into the USSR books and music, and using exhibitions, radio broadcasts, etc., in the hope of animating pessimistic, unpatriotic attitudes among Soviet young people. I am indebted to Mrs. Ellen Mickiewicz for this information. For careful, well-documented analyses of pivotal aspects of recent Soviet practices in controlling access to information about, and especially information originating in non-communist societies, see the articles by Mary Jane Moody, Leon M. Herman, and Maurice Friedberg in *Problems of Communism* (Nov.–Dec., 1964). Miss Moody's article, entitled "Tourists in Russia and Russians Abroad," is much broader in content than its title implies and is particularly pertinent. Ch. 9 of Antony Buzek, *How the Communist Press Works* (New York, 1964) contains a useful discussion of communist "self-censorship" exercised by the heavily indoctrinated communication personnel, as well as of communist use of more conventional forms of censorship. This book is useful, generally, in supplementing and updating Inkeles' fundamental study, *Public Opinion in Soviet Russia*.

On the above-mentioned shift from mere suppression to refutation, see Theodore Shabad, *The New York Times*, July 12, 1965, and *Pravda*, Aug. 18, 1965, in which Leningrad propaganda official Zagorski complained that propagandists' effectiveness was hampered because they were not briefed on foreign radio broadcasts. On the Brooke case see *Izvestiya*, July 24 and 25, 1965.

and the party's attitude toward significant developments of all kinds must be plausibly explained to them.

The party, then, is still conducting a "struggle," more sophisticated than in the past, against the corruption of Soviet minds by "alien" ideas; it also seeks to increase its communication network's coverage and make it more effective. Thus, the press frequently admits that the communication system fails to catch the attention of some segments of the population. Worse yet, go the complaints, it sometimes does not exert the desired influence on those it does reach. Studies by non-Soviet scholars confirm that there are conditions disturbing to the Soviet authorities, though they are not necessarily dangerous, and may be correctable. Facilities for attracting and holding the attention of the less-educated among the population, especially in the countryside, are inadequate, and at various social levels unofficial sources of information such as rumors are relied upon.[2] Being aware of such problems, we can avoid the mistake of regarding Soviet public opinion as a mere carbon copy of Kremlin perceptions and moods. Of course we must also avoid the false view that Soviet mass communication is a total failure.

Another assumption regarding Soviet public information which should be shunned is that there is complete uniformity of opinion and interpretation, even in the official media. Those who shape the day-to-day reporting and interpretation of events share a common perspective instilled by school, university, and adult political socialization programs. Also, there are numerous devices that bring about, from the noncommunist point of view, an amazing amount of conformity. The editors of newspapers are affiliated with the party, those of provincial level belonging to oblast or republic committees — the *Pravda* and *Izvestiya* editors even belong to the all-union central committee. There are other institutional arrangements: "party life" departments are placed in the editorial boards of newspapers; press organs and agencies are supervised by appropriate party bodies; and a stream of regulatory directives is issued to the press. Since Stalin's death, however, Soviet listeners and readers (illiteracy is almost nonexistent) have had increasing access to a widening range of both official and unofficial information and opinion. Discerning and knowledge-

[2] For details, see Alex Inkeles and Raymond A. Bauer, *The Soviet Citizen* (Cambridge, Mass., 1959), Ch. VII.

able readers have been able to perceive evidence of policy differences and even to sense the existence of power rivalries among high-level political leaders and groupings by picking up shadings, nuances, and subtle differences in the handling of particular events by different publications. To use a favorite expression of Lenin and of Khrushchev, "life itself" provides powerful stimuli to thought. De-Stalinization, the struggle with "revisionism" in some Eastern European countries, and the Sino-Soviet rivalry were among the problems which, however obliquely reflected in the Soviet press, were difficult to fit into the official framework, and stimulated a questioning mood. Even the carefully tailored interpretation of such events in the official media could not wholly contain their profoundly disturbing effect. Knowledge of such events, like knowledge during World War II of aid given by the British and American "imperialists" to the Soviet Union, inevitably complicated the party's task of manipulating Soviet public opinion. The difficulty was increased by Western and also Chinese communist information agencies, which tried to reach the Soviet public. These troubles must have been enhanced by perhaps unintended consequences of measures designed to prove both to the noncommunist world and to Soviet intellectuals that the leadership was interested in doing away with the cruder aspects of Stalin's Iron Curtain. It is more difficult to discourage access to foreign books when the top leaders are preaching the virtues of international "contacts," than when they take the firm and simple position that all noncommunist foreigners are enemies. To achieve some interaction between party and community in shaping the Soviet consensus, Stalin's successors took the fundamental step of ruling more by persuasion and less by terror than had the dread party chief (*vozhd*). To make this effort successful, communication practices had to be made more flexible. Professional communicators had to be given some small measure of freedom of interpretation and style, if their messages were to have any liveliness and interest. One conspicuous development in Soviet journalism after Stalin's death was Khrushchev's demand that the news be presented more interestingly. The Leninist practice of backstopping professional staffs of newspapers and magazines by nonprofessional auxiliaries was revived, also contributing somewhat to fresher presentation.

The bolder, more venturesome among Soviet poets, novelists,

and dramatists benefited, indirectly, from the party's effort to reduce the dullness of the printed page. Under cover of faithfully executing the party's commands, especially its de-Stalinization campaign, they were able during the 1956 and 1962 "thaws" to smuggle into their writing unconventional ideas and experimental styles. The controllers of literature were chagrined to find that the experimentalist writers attracted and held a substantial following, especially among the youths. This was important because poetry and other types of imaginative literature form a far bigger share in the daily reading of Soviet citizens than they do in Western Europe or the United States.

The somewhat more variegated content of Soviet communication media after Stalin's passing reflected the emergence, restricted and spasmodic still, of pluralist tendencies in political life. Top-level participants in the succession crisis during the crucial years 1954–1957, and also afterward, utilized their access to channels of communication, both public and restricted, to articulate cautiously and attempt to muster support for their policies. Differences of opinion became more conspicuous, though obscure and muffled by Western standards, even after Khrushchev had seen (1) his power consolidated, (2) his administration of the economy losing momentum after 1958, (3) party apparatchiki, specialists, and economic administrators confused and irritated by his drastic reorganizations and innovations in industrial administration and planning, agriculture, and other spheres.

Differences in top policy councils were strikingly, though indirectly shown by Khrushchev's failure to stage any public discussion of his November, 1962 party reorganization. For earlier Khrushchev domestic policy initiatives, broad campaigns had been organized to send letters to newspapers, advocating numerous proposals, which were discussed in articles by public figures and at party, Komsomol, and trade union meetings. Foreign policy remained unaffected by post-Stalin "openness," e.g., the resumption of large-scale nuclear weapons testing in August, 1961, which was not even reported on until the test series was over.[3]

That the lack of advance publicity for the 1962 reorganization

[3] Herbert Ritvo commented on these discussions in *The New Soviet Society* (New York, 1962), p. 248, note 350. In his article in *Survey* (Oct., 1963), he pointed to the secrecy and speed with which the 1962 party reorganization was prepared and carried through as possible evidence of discord in the presidium.

indeed indicated a weakening of leadership consensus was confirmed within a few months after Khrushchev's fall. Confirmation appeared particularly in an editorial retrospectively sneering at the allegedly specious arguments defending the reorganization at the time of its adoption.[4] Party executives suppressed their doubts regarding its soundness — doubts which, according to the editorial, deepened into convictions after two years of conscientious but vain efforts to implement the new administrative line.[5]

During the months just before Khrushchev's fall attentive readers, of whom there are many who are exceptionally adept at reading between the lines, found startling, though highly ambiguous evidence of opposition to his handling of economic problems. Khrushchev criticized "some comrades," who, he asserted, opposed his "Leninist" sharing with the citizenry generally, in advance, information about the agenda for the plenary session of the party central committee scheduled for November. The perceptive readers must have recognized that he was trying to mobilize support for this policy line and perhaps for his continuing as party leader, against a determined opposition.[6] One reason for the apparently general indifference to Khrushchev's fall was that hints in the press, supplemented by rumors circulating in elite circles, had prepared many, if not to expect the conspiracy by which he was overthrown, at least to be less than astonished when his time came.

HOW GROUP INTERESTS ARE
REFLECTED IN COMMUNICATION

In post-Stalin USSR, influential members of bureaucratic or occupational interest groups have gotten into the habit of injecting their claims and preferences into the channels of communication to which they have access. We cannot cover in detail the Soviet version of "lobbying," but we can say that in recent years military leaders, industrial executives, scientists, educators, and

---

[4] *Partiinaya zhizn*, No. 23, Dec., 1964.

[5] It is interesting to compare the above-mentioned editorial with the completely positive, if perhaps not enthusiastic, appraisal of the measures adopted at the November — and also the March, 1962 plenums in A. I. Sidorenko, *Verkhovnyi organ KPSS* (Moscow, 1964), pp. 96–97. Released to the press in April, 1964, this lengthy pamphlet was published by the Higher Party School of the CPSU Central Committee.

[6] See *Pravda*, Aug. 10 and 11 and Oct. 2, 1964.

others have felt free to express opinions and to advance proposals which, though they supported party goals, also reflected particular bureaucratic and professional interests. The press continued to reflect clashes of interest and opinion after Khrushchev's fall. Indeed, even in the weeks just before the Twenty-third Congress, a sharp debate between advocates of economic reform and their conservative opponents was conducted in *Pravda* and *Izvestiya;* the former served as the channel for reformist views and the latter championed more dogmatic positions. This confrontation conformed to the reversed roles of these major organs after Khrushchev's son-in-law, Aleksei Adzhubei, lost his position as editor of *Izvestiya.* An earlier, equally dramatic manifestation of *Pravda*'s relative liberalism compared with *Izvestiya*'s dogmatism appeared in September, 1965, when A. M. Rumyantsev, then editor of the former, criticized *Izvestiya*'s publication of attacks on the liberal writer Vasili Aksenov.

Journalists themselves, in recent years, seem to have become a latent interest group. Judging by official criticism of tendencies unacceptable to the central party leadership, they have sometimes used the newspapers which they edit to express opinions at variance with those of the party committees to which, according to the party statutes, their newspapers are subordinated.[7]

In spite of incipient appearances of a pluralistic pattern in Soviet communication media, those who legitimately articulate the demands of their interest groups are still keenly aware of, and on the whole probably approve of, the Kremlin's restrictions upon the public expression of group interests and personal preferences. Those limitations are necessary because the Kremlin continues to apply the traditional doctrines of "partisanship" (*partiinost*) and "democratic centralism." Perhaps even more important is the power still wielded by the Moscow authorities over the lives and fortunes of communicators themselves. If substantial and continued violation of orthodox practices of communication were to be permitted — if, in other words, it were no longer to be claimed that "socialist" and "bourgeois" approaches to art, education, or social science are incompatible, and the practice of "ideological coexistence" were begun on the pages of *Pravda* — we

[7] A discussion of problems associated with this alleged tendency is in A. V. Romanov, *Stroitelstvo kommunizma i pechat* (Moscow, 1963, published by Higher Party School), pp. 32–34.

might be witnessing the beginning of the Soviet political system's end as we have known it. For reasons such as this, presumably, the party, while condemning Stalinist conservatism, routinism, and abuse of authority, has continued to warn against "anarchistic" attitudes toward authority and their expression in the media of public communication. The party's conception of its right to limit free expression, which is decisive for Soviet communication behavior, was forcefully summed up in a statement by L. F. Ilichev in December, 1961. He said that it was inadmissible to permit a blow to be struck at Marxist-Leninist theory under the guise of conducting a struggle against the remnants of the cult of personality. He also inveighed against criticisms of old abuses which would allow "anti-Leninist views and tendencies" to "penetrate into our press." [8] He thus upheld the orthodox practice of party leaders, who decide at any time how the word "Leninist" is to be interpreted. Similar views found frequent expression subsequently.

Doctrinal surveillance over Soviet communication is supplemented by more conventional administrative and legal controls. Formal censorship is exercised by Glavlit (Chief Administration for the Affairs of Literature and Publishing Houses), an agency established in 1922. Besides the safeguarding of military and economic secrets, its duties include prohibiting the publication of materials which "agitate" against the Soviet authorities.[9] A control over communications far more important than that exercised by Glavlit is the indirect censorship effected by party organizations at various levels in their day-to-day operations, through party members selected to act as editors and journalists. Also, the party issues directives in a steady stream governing the content of the media of communication.[10] That Khrushchev's "secret speech" of 1956 was never published in the USSR, although it was front-page news in most of the other countries of the world, proves that these controls are effective. Finally, a number of harsh Soviet laws govern such "especially dangerous crimes against the state" as

[8] *XXII sezd KPSS i voprosy ideologicheskoi raboty* (Moscow, 1962), p. 44. See also Frederick C. Barghoorn, "Soviet Political Doctrine and the Problem of Opposition," *Bucknell Review*, XII, No. 2, (May, 1964), esp. pp. 9–11, 25–28.

[9] Inkeles, *Public Opinion in Soviet Russia, op. cit.,* pp. 184–88.

[10] See numerous items in *Voprosy ideologicheskoi raboty* and also in *XXII sezd KPSS i voprosy ideologicheskoi raboty.*

"anti-Soviet agitation and propaganda," including such vaguely worded acts as "spreading slanderous fabrications" or "defaming the Soviet political and social system" orally or in writing.[11] An additional link was added to the chain of communication control agencies by the central committee resolution of August 10, 1963, establishing the State Committee of the Council of Ministers for Publications, or State Press Committee, apparently intended to tighten control over book publication and distribution.

AGENCIES OF COMMUNICATION

Before we discuss in detail the Soviet communication network's political functions it will be helpful if we describe briefly its structure. Public information is disseminated by a number of party agencies and organizations as well as by governmental and public organizations supervised by party officials of appropriate rank. The top party political communication agency is the section for propaganda and agitation within the CPSU central committee. From November, 1962 until shortly after Khrushchev's fall it was replaced by the ideological section for the union republics and that for the RSFSR. The party plenum held in that month additionally established the Ideological Commission, headed by Leonid F. Ilichev, then a member of the powerful central committee secretariat. The Ideological Commission, abolished in the post-Khrushchev days, functioned through counterpart commissions at lower levels, including some very large primary organizations. At the lowest levels (little is known about the upper ones) such commissions seem to have been part of Khrushchev's network of auxiliary, "public," or non-staff, backstopping, and helper agencies. The p.p.o. level of these commissions was still included in an authoritative instructional handbook for party cadres, published in 1965.[12]

For a time the ideological sections of republic central commit-

---

[11] English and Russian texts of these laws are available in *Law in Eastern Europe, III, The Federal Criminal Law of the Soviet Union* (Leyden, 1959), pp. 74–76.

[12] *Spravochnik sekretarya pervichnoi partiinoi organizatsii* (Moscow, 1965), pp. 120–23. This handbook devotes pp. 65–123 to "ideological work." It contains extremely interesting sections on party guidance of the "lower press" (factory newspapers, etc.) on clubs, and on libraries, etc. Regarding local public libraries, party secretaries are urged to prevent wide reading of foreign books which make the "bourgeois way of life" seem "picturesque."

tees absorbed the staffs of both the previously existing republic agitation and propaganda sections and the old science, school, and culture sections, but in 1964 separate science and culture sections again appeared. In the meantime, the republic ideological commissions, in conformance with the general party reorganization, were divided into industrial and agricultural subsections, only to undergo new reorganizations after Khrushchev's fall. These details are mentioned because they demonstrate how important the Kremlin feels it is to gear communication controls tightly into over-all national policy — and also because they give us some inkling of the ponderous but penetrating structure of the administration in whose grip Soviet practitioners of verbal skills still must work.

The close links between the party power structure and the communication hierarchy are apparent also in the men who are executives of major organs and agencies of information. Until Khrushchev's fall his son-in-law, Aleksei Adzhubei, and the veteran journalist, Pavel Satyukov, for several years had been editors, respectively, of *Izvestiya* and *Pravda* — and also of the CPSU Central Committee and of the Ideological Commission. Interestingly enough, Adzhubei's *Izvestiya* delayed, for a day, publication of the *Pravda* announcement of Khrushchev's "resignation." Adzhubei and Satyukov, together with Mikhail Kharlamov, head of the press department of the Ministry of Foreign Affairs since 1958, were often referred to by knowledgeable foreigners as Khrushchev's "press group," reflecting their joint function in advising him on public relations matters during his 1959 tour of the United States. Adzhubei, Satyukov, and Kharlamov were all dismissed from their high positions shortly after Khrushchev himself "resigned." They were replaced, respectively, by Aleksei M. Rumyantsev, experienced journalist and party central committee member, Vladimir Ilich Stepakov, formerly head of the RSFSR agitation and propaganda section, who in August, 1965 left *Izvestiya* to become head of all Agitprop work, and Nikolai N. Mesyatsev, Komsomol official and journalist. Thus, although seemingly of lesser stature than the men whom they replaced, all three were of the same general apparatchik, professional communicator background, as were Mikhail Zimyanin, who replaced Rumyantsev as *Pravda* editor in September, 1965, and the dogmatic L. N. Tolkunov, who at about the same time replaced Stepakov at *Izvestiya.* Of similar background was Dmitri Goryunov, who in August, 1960, succeeded Nikolai Palgunov as director of TASS, the telegraphic agency which dominates the foreign news reporting to the Soviet press and also does much of the gathering and distributing of domestic news. When he was appointed he was a member of the central committee.[13] Dropped entirely therefrom in 1961, he reappeared as an alternate in 1966.

Similar overlapping and interpenetration prevails at lower levels of the communication system. As one would expect, *Pravda,* the most important Soviet newspaper, is published by the central committee of the CPSU. The very important daily *Sovetskaya Rossiya* since 1956 was published by the bureau of the Russian Republic party organization, which was, however, abolished by the Twenty-third Congress. Each of the fifteen republics of the USSR has a republic newspaper that is published jointly by the republic party central committee and the council of ministers of the republican government. The republic newspapers are published both in Russian-language editions and in the local languages. The central committee as well as lower organs of the party frequently intervene in communication matters, as in September, 1958, when the central committee passed a resolution condemning "serious defects" in the content of the popular magazine *Ogonek.*[14] How closely the party apparatus supervises communication activity was suggested by the "seminar" called in Baku, capital of the republic of Azerbaidzhan, in March, 1964. The chief of the Transcaucasus Bureau of the CPSU central committee, Bochkarev, opened the seminar, the theme of which was "The Press, Radio and Television in the Struggle to Realize the Decisions of the Twenty-second Congress of the CPSU." [15]

In 1962 the CPSU central committee ordered that more than three thousand local (*raion*) newspapers be "liquidated," in connection with the changes in the party and government administration which took effect at that time, and also for economy. They

---

[13] *The New York Times,* Aug. 16, 1960. The best available account of the structure and work of TASS still appears to be Palgunov's brochure, *Osnovy informatsii v gasete.* See also Buzek, *op. cit.,* pp. 184–98 and 205–209.

[14] This and similar cases are discussed by Romanov, *op. cit.*

[15] *Pravda,* March 21, 1964.

were replaced by about a thousand inter-raion papers, supervised by oblast committees of the party.[16] After Khrushchev's removal, however, the raion newspapers, and the raions as administrative units, were re-established.

At the base of the party pyramid, the primary party organizations engage in varied communication activities. One of the most important is organizing groups of agitators, known in Soviet political jargon as "agitation collectives." Participating in an agitation group is perhaps the most usual after-hours chore by means of which rank and file party members perform their share of the unpaid service to the community required of all members of the CPSU. Primary party organizations also publish newspapers, even if only the sheets posted on factory or office bulletin boards, which are called "wall newspapers." Some party members serve as unpaid voluntary "worker and village correspondents" (*rabselkory*). Not all the rabselkory, of course, are party members — many are non-party "activists." According to a central committee resolution of June 28, 1960, more than 5,000,000 Soviet "workers, collective farmers and representatives of the intelligentsia" were voluntarily participating in the work of newspapers, magazines, and also in radio and television broadcasting.

This auxiliary mass participation in communication activities is directed by the local party organizations.[17] It takes numerous forms. Nonprofessional correspondents of small-town and rural newspapers, or in big-city factories and offices, serve as two-way communicators, backstopping major opinion mobilization drives of the big newspapers in factories and collective farms, and also bringing to the newspapers and radio and television stations information about the workers' job performance and morale. One of the most dramatic rabselkory activities is participating in "raids," to verify whether or not factories, farms, or organizations are satisfactorily fulfilling party directives. These raids are usually directed by a professional journalist supervised by the appropriate party committee.[18]

The rabselkory also send in a stream of reports and letters to

16 Romanov, *op. cit.*, pp. 29–30.
17 *Ibid.*, pp. 48–54.
18 On this and other aspects of the "mass work" of newspapers, etc., see I. Teteruk, *Ruka ob ruku s rabselkorami* (Moscow, 1962); N. Bogdanov, V. Lapin, V. Pronina, *Raionnaya gazeta* (Leningrad, 1957), Ch. VI; and Romanov, *op. cit.*, pp. 52–54.

the newspapers to which they are attached, and some are published. Such letters, both those written by rabselkory and those of rank and file readers, serve important purposes. They supplement the information obtained by the press and hence by the party about popular moods and lend to the organs of mass communication a "democratic" aura.

Among the many kinds of nonprofessional participation in public communication one which deserves mention is unpaid assistance to the party and government agencies responsible for disseminating reading matter. The government agency involved in this function is *soyuzpechat* (All-Union News Agency), an organ of the Ministry of Communications. In Moscow it has nine offices, each with "instructor-organizers" on its staff, who direct the placing of subscriptions to periodical publications by factory and office workers and students aided by "public disseminators of the press." In 1963 there were 60,000 of these public disseminators, immediately supervised by unpaid organizers, in turn supervised by deputies to the party secretaries in charge of propaganda and agitation. Each was responsible for serving about fifty persons, keeping them informed about the publications available, regulations about subscribing, etc. Public disseminators who fulfill their tasks exceptionally well are honored by governmental awards and publicity.[19]

In addition to such newspapers and magazines as *Pravda* and *Izvestiya*, others are so important that they must be listed here. The most important newspaper of the Soviet armed forces is *Krasnaya Zvezda* (*Red Star*); of the trade unions, *Trud* (*Labor*); of the Komsomol, *Komsomolskaya Pravda*. Soviet central newspapers, other than *Pravda*, are published only six times a week. Important national magazines published in Moscow include the central committee theoretical journal *Kommunist* and its organizational journal *Partiinaya zhizn* (*Party Life*), both of which appear twice a month, the satirical magazine *Krokodil*, published by the Pravda Publishing House, the illustrated magazine *Ogonek*, and a number of periodicals with specialized interests but large circulations in such fields as literature, economics, history, philosophy, the natural sciences, etc. Important magazines are also published in such cities as Leningrad, which is very strong in

[19] L. Narimanov, *Partiinye organizatsii i rasprostranenie pechati* (Moscow, 1963), pp. 3–7.

literary periodicals; in the most important republic capitals, such as Kiev, which is rich in publications with a strong local orientation; in Tbilisi, and in others.

The State Committee on Radio and Television is responsible for administering these vital fields.[20] Control of the Soviet film industry is exercised by the State Committee for Cinematography. The Znanie (Knowledge) Society, before 1963 known as the All-Union Society for the Dissemination of Political and Scientific Knowledge, is most important in organizing public lectures. According to the 1964 edition of the *Annual* (*Ezhegodnik*) published by the Great Soviet Encyclopedia, this society had 89,000 groups and 1,299,000 members in January, 1964. From October, 1961 through the end of July, 1962 its members reportedly delivered more than 1,000,000 lectures.[21] The chairman of Znanie, according to the above-cited *Annual,* is Academician V. A. Kirillin, a scientist extensively experienced as a party functionary. N. N. Mesyatsev, until his elevation to head the foreign office press department, was Kirillin's deputy in Znanie. These facts, incidentally, enlighten us indirectly as to how political professionals direct some activities of Soviet scientists and scholars. Important agitational and public information activities are also conducted by such professional organizations as the Union of Soviet Writers, the Union of Soviet Composers, and the Union of Soviet Journalists. Finally, the Ministry of Culture, which administers theaters, libraries, and other cultural institutions, is somewhat involved in shaping public attitudes.

All these agencies and their executives, employees, and unpaid collaborators are engaged in mobilizing opinion or, in Soviet words, they assist the party in establishing and maintaining "links with the masses." The party has always feared that a loss of contact with the population might diminish its orienting, influencing, and mobilizing capabilities. Stalin compared the party to the legendary Greek hero Antaeus, who lost his invincibility and

[20] In an article in *Esquire* (March, 1964), former Senator William Benton commented interestingly on this agency's activities and on Mikhail Kharlamov, its chief at that time.

[21] *Pravda,* Oct. 16, 1962. One difficulty confronting the party in using the mass media for moral uplift shone through a resolution dated Aug. 27, 1959, which stated that although most members of this society — learned men, party and Soviet workers, representatives of the "village intelligentsia," etc. — were guided by "patriotic" motives, some had attempted to turn their participation in the society's activities into "a source of regular income." See *Voprosy ideologicheskoi raboty, op. cit.,* pp. 138–39.

perished at the hands of Hercules only when he lost contact with his mother, the earth.[22] Stalin meant that the party must be ever visible to the masses, must command their attention and shape their thoughts. Its communicators must see to it that Soviet citizens, whether party members or not, share the party's perspectives and opinions and actively support its policies.

More prosaically but also in accordance with the Lenin-Stalin tradition, Khrushchev said in 1960 that Soviet journalists were the "loyal helpers" and the "right hand men" of the party. They deserved to be so called, he continued, because "As soon as some decision has to be explained and carried out, we call on you, and you make the most loyal kind of conveyor belt, take the decision of the party and carry it to the very midst of our people." [23] In the present era the over-all frame of reference for all communication activity in the Soviet Union is officially defined as "the deep explanation of the program of the party." [24]

One of the chief duties of party organizations, from the central executive staffs in Moscow down to the humblest primary party organization in the provinces, is to make certain that all patterns and instruments of communication are coordinated and attuned to current party policy. Members of the executive bureaus of local party organizations are expected to organize voluntary lecture groups, composed perhaps of physicians, teachers, agronomists, etc. They also select party and nonparty workers in factories and plants to serve as editors of wall newspapers, "radio newspapers," and the like. From time to time, the party bureaus invite editors of wall newspapers and worker and village correspondents to confer and discuss their work. The local party organizations see to it (or are supposed to) that lectures are well attended, that local clubs and other "cultural-enlightenment" institutions are functioning properly, and, generally, that both the propaganda and the mass media agitation activities on which we are concentrating our attention in this chapter are reaching their targets.[25]

[22] *Istoriya vsesoyuznoi kommunisticheskoi partii* (*bolshevikov*) (Moscow, 1943), p. 346. This work is often referred to as the "Short Course."

[23] *Agitator,* No. 8, April, 1960, as quoted in *Current Digest of the Soviet Press,* XII, No. 15 (April, 1960), pp. 32–33.

[24] *XXII sezd KPSS i voprosy ideologicheskoi raboty, op. cit.,* pp. 16–20.

[25] The local party organizations check regularly on, and coordinate the activities of, communication agencies. See A. Abramenkov and V. Tolstov, *Byuro pervichnoi partorganizatsii,* Bibliotechka sekretarya p.p.o. (Moscow, 1962), pp. 43–49, and *Spravochnik sekretarya, op. cit.,* Ch. II.

ORAL AGITATION

Personal oral agitation and the daily press are perhaps the two most potent instruments used by the party for mass orientation and mobilization of popular opinion. As Alex Inkeles was the first to demonstrate systematically, the Russian communists pioneered in using oral communication to shape public opinion. Inkeles pointed out that "The greatest importance of this type of agitation lies in the fact that it provides a direct channel of communication between the masses and the otherwise distant party leaders." [26] In various ways oral agitation enhances and reinforces other modes of communication. Unlike the journalist, the agitator operates in face-to-face contact with his audience. The personal quality of his message, combined with the opportunities that a group setting affords for some interchange of attitudes and opinions, confers upon oral agitation coverage, flexibility, and adaptability that newspapers and other mass media do not have. Like the "worker and village correspondents," agitators, in direct contact with ordinary people, are able to observe and report to their superiors on public attitudes and moods.[27] What might be described as the agitator's scapegoat role serves various needs of both the political elite and the population as a whole. Like lower-ranking representatives of the regime generally, the agitators may serve on occasion as targets for resentment which might otherwise be directed against the party. This function of the millions of Soviet citizens who act as a "safety valve," daily popularizing and explaining party policies, is somewhat analogous to "self-criticism," in the public expression of which the chief role is that of the press.

For the agitator's audience, usually a group of workers to whom a particular agitator is assigned, organized oral communication supplies information in a form far more accessible and easier to assimilate than if it were conveyed by the press, and provides a line of communication between ordinary people and the local political authorities.

The recruitment of agitators has a complex history, but in the post-Stalin era, apparently, they have been trained mainly in the adult socialization program described in the preceding chapter.

26 Inkeles, *Public Opinion, op. cit.*, p. 70.
27 *Ibid.*, pp. 121–28.

The politshkola and the political study circles, according to Volodin, send their students out to work among the masses, although only the best politshkola graduates are now considered capable of performing the agitation function.[28]

Agitators are organized in groups, each headed by a qualified party "activist." The groups receive instructions from their party organization leader. One wartime account of such a group, or *agitkollektiv*, in a rural area reported that it consisted of twenty members, including agitators and the editors of collective farm wall newspapers and "fighting leaflets." [29]

Party organizations periodically hold meetings to check on the performance of tasks assigned to members in agitation activity or lecturing, etc. They also operate agitation "schools." [30] The supervision and guidance furnished to agitators by the party organizations to which they belong is supplemented by publications, such as various pamphlets and handbooks and the magazine *Agitator*, established by a 1956 central committee resolution.[31] They also receive assistance in special conferences and seminars organized by houses and cabinets of political education.[32]

One of oral communication's most important uses is "production agitation." Some major elements in production agitation are clearly identified in the following statement:

> Agitators, working in industry, must assist each collective in enterprises, shops, sections and brigades, to fulfill and overfulfill each day the production plans for all technical-economic indices and steadfastly obtain an increase in the quality and a decrease in the cost of the products they put out. Rural agitators are called upon to mobilize the toilers of collective and state farms in a struggle for the improvement of agricultural production, for the most rational use of land, an increase in the livestock production, efficient preparation for the spring sowing, and successful winter care for cattle.[33]

28 V. Volodin, *Politshkola i organizatsiya ee raboty* (Moscow, 1961), pp. 58–63.
29 Ya. Yakovlev, *Agitkollektiv v kolkhoze* (Moscow, 1944), p. 3. See *Spravochnik sekretarya pervichnoi partiinoi organizatsii*, pp. 100–102.
30 A. Svinarenko, *Planirovanie partiinoi raboty v kolkhoze* (Moscow, 1960), pp. 53–60.
31 *Spravochnik partiinogo rabotnika* (Moscow, 1957), pp. 355–56.
32 *Ibid.*, p. 354.
33 *Partiinaya zhizn*, No. 3, Feb., 1963, p. 6. My attention was called to this quotation by Mr. David Powell. The saliency of production agitation in the daily activities of the party apparatus in industry was impressed upon this writer by a party organizer of a Riga textile factory, whom he met in Tbilisi in 1958, and who told him that the main function of party organizations in factories was "to make the workers produce more."

Production agitation combines appeals to altruism and to self-interest with other methods, such as the popularizing of advanced technology and organization. In addition, agitators are called upon to set a worthy personal example both in their own work and by assisting the party and the trade unions in "socialist competition" for higher labor productivity and increased total output. Underlying the Soviet belief in production agitation's efficacy is the notion that each worker has an untapped "reserve" of creative energy which agitation can translate into production. Khrushchev suggested that:

> . . . each worker has his own reserve. . . . But . . . it is necessary to go to the worker, not like some administrator-bureaucrat, but as a comrade of this worker; then the worker will open his heart and demonstrate his capabilities for increasing labor productivity and lowering costs.[34]

The Soviet leadership systematically endeavors to associate production agitation with political goals, such as success in economic competition with the United States. It is claimed that "innovators," as workers with superior records are called, outproduce American workers.[35] Agitators are told, and they in turn tell the workers, that by working harder and more efficiently they will help themselves through increased wages (the piece-rate system of payment is a major element in the Soviet economy). They are also told that they will help the nation and the "international working class" by contributing to the best of their ability to achieving the party's objective: laying down the material and technical foundations of communism. In the factory, and indeed at all levels of Soviet life, daily tasks are imbued with moral significance. As Leonid Ilichev said in 1961, "The man of the communist future" will be formed not by labor alone but only when every worker, collective farmer, and student understands the social significance of his work.[36]

How well production agitation and, indeed, other kinds of agitation fulfill the hopes which the party professes to repose in them it is impossible to determine. As in other mass persuasion

[34] Quoted by David Powell in an unpublished paper, "Agitation and Political Communication in the Soviet Union," from *Agitator*, No. 5, March, 1963, pp. 32–33.

[35] See I. I. Changli, *Sotsialisticheskoe sorevnovanie i novye formy kommunisticheskogo truda* (Moscow, 1959), p. 105.

[36] *XXII sezd KPSS i voprosy ideologicheskoi raboty, op. cit.,* pp. 32–33.

fields the party leadership admits defects and failures but expresses determination to correct them. In the speech just referred to, Ilichev expressed satisfaction that in the five years since the Twentieth Party Congress millions had been brought under the influence of mass agitational work. As a result, farm and factory work had improved and the Soviet people's "communist consciousness" had grown.[37] And yet, complained Ilichev, on many enterprises and collective farms agitational work still existed "only on paper." Unlike foreign students of the Soviet system Ilichev did not refer to some possible negative consequences of agitation, such as workers resenting incessant pressure.

In addition to spurring the citizen as producer to be aware of his duties and opportunities, agitation orients him to the political system and alerts him to the threats and challenges emanating from the international environment. During World War II, it was the principal task of agitators, and, on a higher intellectual plane, of lecturers, to enlist every citizen's full emotional energies in defending the nation. Personal oral agitation reaches its most massive proportions in peacetime during elections to the village, town, republic, oblast, and USSR Supreme Soviets. These periodic campaigns combine mobilization for action with efforts to achieve maximum citizen identification with the political system. The huge army of more than 2,000,000 agitators is swollen during election campaigns to more than 3,000,000.[38] Of course, from the point of view of Western constitutional democracy the one-party, one-candidate Soviet elections are not elections at all since they do not involve open, competitive articulation of different interests and programs. But from the point of view of Soviet doctrine, the absence of an opposition party or other overt ideological or political pluralism is a virtue. The unity between society and the party indicated by nonexistent opposition and by the nearly 100 per cent vote by which the officially approved slate of candidates is elected is one of the numerous themes that agitators disseminate at election time. Elections give the party an opportunity to dramatize its ideology and its domestic and foreign policy. They involve a prodigious effort in mass persuasion, which is conducted in special "agitation points" (*agitpunkti*), at places of work and

37 *Ibid.*, p. 62.
38 Alex Inkeles and Kent Geiger, *Soviet Society: A Book of Readings* (Boston, 1961).

residence, and even on trains and boats. During these campaigns the agitators' work is supplemented by lectures given by scholars and scientists and by musical and theatrical performances. Election campaigns, somewhat like the May Day and November 6 national holidays, combine solemnity with stage-managed mass emotion, and orchestrated ideological solidarity with individual holiday exuberance.

We have examined its positive functions, but agitation also has an important negative and even coercive side. Agitators assist the party in its generations-long struggle against "survivals of capitalism." Apparently, new types of moral coercion were added to Soviet agitation and other forms of social pressure after the rise of Khrushchev. One function of the Brigades of Communist Labor, launched late in 1958, is to "diffuse the communist ethos amongst the population," as a British student of Soviet affairs has pointed out.[39] The same author notes that groups competing for this title "must not only set themselves high production norms but must undertake a programme of collective self-improvement, and watch over each other's everyday behavior, outside as well as within working hours."

During recent years a conspicuous negative function of agitation has been conducting atheistic propaganda. In the "struggle against religious prejudice" some methods are establishing councils on atheistic work in factories, lectures, question-and-answer evenings, person-to-person talks with believers, and libraries on atheism. This serious, systematic campaign is described by a statement in a Soviet periodical for agitators: "The success of atheistic work will be guaranteed only when it is studied seriously, with neither strength nor time wasted, when party organizations exercise care in the selection of agitators and their studies, and when agitators know the believers well." [40]

The Soviet program of oral agitation, briefly sketched above, is in some ways more flexible and perhaps even more effective than the Soviet press, but of course it could not work without the press. The press is important in training agitators as well as propagandists, and supplies them with much material that they use in their work. Indeed, one traditional form of agitation work is

---

[39] H. T. Willetts, "Dynamic Conformity: The Public Image of the CPSU," *Soviet Survey* (Jan.–Mar., 1961), p. 74.

[40] *Agitator*, No. 6, March 1963, p. 15.

reading from or summarizing newspapers. Such practices are, however, condemned as "formal" and "mechanical." The Soviet press might be described as the largest journalistic operation in the world under one management. The exceptionally uniform perspective and approach that party control assures is reinforced by the special place that the major Moscow newspapers, especially *Pravda*, occupy in the total press system. The predominance of the "central" newspapers is made obvious by their circulation, vast compared with those of other press organs. The official Soviet press handbook listed *Pravda*'s 1957 circulation as 5,500,000, *Komsomolskaya Pravda*'s as 1,809,000, and *Izvestiya*'s as 1,550,000. According to information supplied by United States official sources, by May, 1962 *Pravda*'s circulation was 6.3 million and *Izvestiya*'s 4.1 million. By early 1965, however, *Izvestiya* had increased its circulation to more than six million copies.[41] *Pravda*, *Izvestiya*, and some other central newspapers are printed in major Soviet cities from plates flown daily from Moscow. Most editorials in republic and other important provincial newspapers are reprinted from those of *Pravda*, received by radio at dictation speed. In 1957 the Moscow newspapers formed almost a third of Soviet newspaper circulation.[42] Another reason for uniformity of content in the Soviet press is that so much of the information published in all newspapers, except for strictly local news, is obtained from TASS. According to the official Soviet view there is no "provincial" press in the Soviet Union but only a "peripheral" press. The doctrine holds that since all Soviet citizens are active builders of communism bound together by common goals, they view the life of their communities not "through the prism of local interests but through the prism of general state interests, the interests of the whole of Soviet society and the interests of all of progressive mankind." Consequently, the peripheral press must supply to its readers the same information regarding national and international events as is given readers of the central press.[43] Although local Soviet newspapers, especially in the countryside, carry far less national and international news than do the big metropolitan dailies, the readers of even the low-ranking Soviet

[41] According to a study reported in *The Times* of London, Feb. 24, 1965.
[42] See *Pechat SSSR* (Moscow, 1958) for these and additional figures. Buzek, *op. cit.*, pp. 270–73, lists major Soviet newspapers and magazines and gives figures on their circulation.
[43] Palgunov, *Osnovy, op. cit.*, p. 53.

newspapers, as a rule, are kept systematically informed regarding the national political leadership's interests and goals. How does the party expect the press to fulfill its functions of orientation and mobilization? The author of an article in the main central committee ideological journal gave this typical answer:

> Daily to seek out and find the most important problems in the life of socialist society, problems of the development of the economy and culture of the daily life of the workers and at the same time to display an irreconcilable attitude toward defects, to subject to annihilating criticism survivals of capitalism in the consciousness of the people and to sharply expose ideas alien to Soviet policy — those are the demands which the party now presents to the press.[44]

These demands obviously require correct analysis by the party leadership and loyal and skilful support by the communicators it directs. Journalists are spurred to effective performance by a steady flow of party resolutions as well as by articles emanating from high-ranking communication officials, members of university journalism faculties and especially that of Moscow University, professors in the Higher Party School, etc. In a word, the press applies to its own work the traditional bolshevik corrective device, self-criticism.

The former director of TASS whose instructive brochure was referred to above has written that in addition to being timely and truthful, newspaper "information" (*informatsiya*) must be "organized," "instructive," and "didactic," as well as "purposeful." Particularly interesting was the word "purposeful." Information, he stated, must pursue a definite aim, must assist in solving the problems facing Soviet society. Then he defined information as "agitation by means of facts," and went on to say that not all facts or events have to be reported but that those facts should be selected which "contribute to the solution by the Soviet people of the tasks of building communism by which it is confronted." [45]

Priorities in selecting themes for journalistic articles and editorials vary from time to time in accordance with changes in party policy. During the Khrushchev period of party leadership, especially after party direction of the national economy was re-

44 M. Chepikov, "Pechat-udarnaya ideologicheskaya sila partii," *Kommunist*, No. 7, May, 1964, p. 128.
45 Palgunov, *op. cit.*, pp. 31–37, esp. p. 35.

organized at the November, 1962 party plenum, journalists and teachers of journalism were urgently reminded that "the building of communism and communist upbringing" required emphasis and, in particular, that priority must be given "to the economic theme as against the general political theme." [46]

After Khrushchev's fall both newspaper editorials and news items continued to stress economic development, but with a new twist. An editorial stated that, the most urgent theme of the press now had become "the active struggle for improving the quality of industrial production." [47] In January, 1965 the press turned its attention to a new version of "socialist competition." Factories all over the country pledged their efforts to attain in the next few years the "level of the best world standards" in the most important production fields.

Probably the most significant difference in press content between the early post-Khrushchev months and the Khrushchev era's last years was the complete disappearance from the pages of Soviet magazines and newspapers, for five months, of the bitter attacks on the Chinese communist leadership which they had been featuring so prominently. Open polemics were replaced by the esoteric language of hints and innuendo, with Moscow stressing that it was the central force and pioneer of the world communist movement and pleading for "unity." When the Chinese charged Soviet brutality against Chinese citizens in curbing an anti-American demonstration in Moscow early in March, 1964, there was a flareup in the press. Whether such occasional, significant outbursts would become more frequent and thus lead back to the incessant recrimination of Khrushchev's time, only the future would tell.

TRAINING COMMUNICATORS

Increasingly in recent years, and especially since Stalin's death, the recruitment of Soviet journalists has included professional training in the journalism departments of institutions of higher education, supplemented for some exceptionally successful and promising men by study in the journalistic department of the Higher Party School. In addition to a very intensive ideological

[46] Romanov, *op. cit.,* pp. 10–11.
[47] "The Great Tasks of the Soviet Press," *Pravda,* Dec. 22, 1964.

indoctrination, Soviet students of journalism receive training in journalistic writing, as well as philological-literary instruction. Departments of journalism are, in fact, included in university philological faculties.

The Moscow State University journalism faculty is divided into newspaper, editorial and publishing, and radio-television studies. Its six chairs, roughly equivalent to departments of American universities, include one on "the party-soviet press," and one on "the foreign communist press," as well as those teaching journalistic techniques, and one specializing in the history of Russian literature and journalism.[48]

The course in journalism in the Higher Party School is divided into five sections, requiring three-hundred forty hours of classroom work. The first three sections are historical; the fourth is concerned with the "theory and practice of the party-soviet press," and offers material on the structure of the Soviet press, radio, television, etc., and on how to prepare articles, editorials, "party life" items, reporting on international, economic, military matters, etc., articles on the "propaganda of Marxism-Leninism," and the like. The final section devotes thirty hours to "the contemporary foreign press" and, in addition, has sections on "topics" for classes and seminars.[49]

The preface to the prospectus on the Higher Party School journalism course describes journalism as "the sharpest weapon of the class struggle." This approach presumably is applied systematically in all Soviet journalistic training and is certainly evident in the many handbooks, instructional aids, and collections of the writings of Lenin on journalism, propaganda, etc., which are published to assist journalists in preparing for their careers and in further perfecting their skills on the job.[50]

CONTENT OF THE PRESS

Understanding and evaluating the performance of the Soviet press is very difficult for the non-Soviet observer. One reason is that content analyses of particular themes and periods and the other specific studies necessary for such an appraisal are almost

48 *Spravochnik dlya postupayushchikh v moskovski universitet* (Moscow, 1961), pp. 85–87.
49 *Programma po kursu zhurnalistiki* (Moscow, Higher Party School, 1958).
50 See B. Yakovlev, *Lenin-publitsist* (Moscow, 1960); *Voprosy zhurnalistiki* (Moscow, 1962).

nonexistent. To undertake such studies is beyond the scope of this chapter. However, it may be instructive to briefly survey here the contents of a few issues of *Pravda,* selected more or less at random.

We shall begin with and devote most of our attention to the issue of *Pravda* published on Friday, November 2, 1956. It was this issue which was included in the unique comparative study by Wilbur Schramm of fourteen major world newspapers which appeared on that day — the day when *The New York Times* hailed developments in Eastern Europe under the headline "Victory in Hungary." [51] One unusual feature for that day must be mentioned first: *Pravda* appeared in an edition of six pages. It usually has only four, but when there is a great deal of news, as during meetings of the USSR Supreme Soviet or CPSU congresses, it expands to six, eight, or even ten or twelve pages. Since advertising in the American sense does not exist in the Soviet Union the relative lack of space available to Soviet journalists is not as serious a problem as it might appear and it may have the advantage of forcing them to carefully organize their material.

Four of the six columns of *Pravda*'s front page on the date in question were devoted almost entirely to an editorial attack and to negative, highly editorialized reporting on military operations of Israel, the United Kingdom, and France against Egypt. The editorial, placed as usual in the two left-hand columns of the page, was entitled "Hands Off Egypt!" and the two right-hand columns were headed "Stop at Once Armed Aggression Against Egypt!" The two middle columns and two photographs at the bottom of the page were devoted to the visit to Moscow of the President of the Syrian Republic. As it had since its founding in 1912 and as it does still, *Pravda* carried on its masthead the slogan "Proletarians of the World, Unite!" and also at the extreme left a picture of a medallion of Lenin.

As Schramm pointed out in his commentary, the news of the British and French action overshadowed everything else in this issue of *Pravda.* The issue carried official statements of indignation from various Soviet republics and used almost a page to carry statements from other countries. The approach taken toward the Anglo-French Israeli operation was typified by a paragraph in the editorial which began with the statement that "the Israeli

[51] Wilbur Schramm, ed., *One Day in the World's Press* (Stanford, Cal., 1959).

attack on Egypt was but the first step in carrying out the coloniz-ers' carefully elaborated conspiracy."

The other main theme of this issue was Hungary. However, this subject was not treated directly except in a brief TASS item from Budapest reporting "instances of bandit raids." However, items from Warsaw, Oslo, and (it seems ironic) Peking, under the heading "Friendship and Unity of Socialist States," reported sup-port for a declaration issued by the USSR government regarding relations among "socialist" countries. Approximately 20 per cent of the issue was given over to historical material on events lead-ing up to the bolshevik revolution in 1917. This material and several slogans printed at the top of page one were part of the traditional propaganda buildup for the November 6 holiday, only four days off. There were many brief, miscellaneous domestic and foreign news items. One of these, from TASS, which would have been prominently featured in a newspaper of another type, was a short summary with brief quotations and also with quotation marks supplied by the editors, of President Eisenhower's radio address commenting on the Anglo-French military operations. Another event reported was the award of the Nobel Prize for chemistry to a Soviet scientist. That the prize was shared with a British chemist was not mentioned except in the Soviet chemist's own remarks and it was not mentioned that at the same time three American physicists won Nobel prizes.

Of the ten issues of *Pravda* covering the period from May 26 through June 4, 1964, nine had the usual front-page editorials. On May 28 most of the space usually devoted to an editorial was occupied by the text of a radio and television speech delivered on the previous day in which Khrushchev reported on his "visit of friendship" to Egypt. This speech went over onto page two and took up about a quarter of the space in this issue. In the same issue news of the death of Prime Minister Nehru of India and related items, including official messages of condolence and a warmly sympathetic obituary article, were overshadowed by Khru-shchev's speech. Continuing with our inventory of the editorials published during this period we find that the one of May 26 was devoted to Khrushchev's visit to Egypt; that of May 27, to the work of party organizations in agricultural administration; that of May 29, to Soviet-East German relations (on that date Walter Ulbricht, First Secretary of the ruling Socialist Unity Party of

Germany, arrived in the Soviet Union and an article on him and a photograph of him dominated the front page); also, *Pravda* carried a streamer headline in Russian and German greeting the "dear German friends." On May 30, the editorial was devoted to the one hundred and fiftieth anniversary of Azerbaidzhan's entry into the Russian state, which was made the occasion for a typical article on Soviet nationality policy and the "friendship of peoples." However, Ulbricht's visit was played up, with a front-page photograph of Khrushchev, Leonid Brezhnev, Ulbricht, and the Ambassador of the German Democratic Republic prominently displayed at the top of page one. For the remaining four days the editorials dealt, respectively, with applying electric welding and other scientific and technological developments to industry; with the party's efforts to raise the level of education of its cadres engaged in agriculture; with the work of the All-Union Knowledge Society, especially in popularizing and applying the natural sciences; with the problems of cement production and other aspects of the construction industry; and finally, on June 4, with the mobilizing and propaganda work of party groups in factories and plants.

An example of an expanded issue of *Pravda,* reflecting the increasingly sharp Sino-Soviet dispute, was that for April 3, 1964. The dominant item in this issue was the text of a very important speech given on February 14, 1964, at a central committee plenum by M. A. Suslov, entitled "Concerning the struggle of the CPSU for the Solidarity of the International Communist Movement." This speech and also the editorial, entitled "Loyalty to the Principles of Marxism-Leninism," defended the Soviet position and criticized the Chinese communist position in the dispute. In addition, Suslov's speech systematically covered Soviet expectations regarding relations with the United States, Britain, France, Japan, West Germany, and other "imperialist" powers. With the appearance of this issue, it became crystal clear to all politically conscious Soviet citizens that the Soviet Union was engaged in a two-front cold war. The long delay in publishing this vital speech was typical of the careful preparation and timing of news disclosure in Soviet political communication, in contrast to the commitment of the commercial, competitive Western press to promptness in reporting. It may also have reflected differences of opinion in the leadership on policy toward China.

POST-STALIN COMMUNICATION CHANGES

One gets the "feel" of the Soviet press only by extensive contact with it, but the foregoing examples convey some indication of its character. It is a highly political instrument, with the strengths and weaknesses inherent in systematic subordination to official policy and saturation with official doctrine.

Since the death of Stalin the network of communication has continued to be primarily an instrument of pressure applied by the political authorities to the citizenry. In a number of ways, however, it has become more responsive and adaptive than it had been. The most important adaptations of post-Stalin communication behavior appeared to be, first, providing increased opportunities for the citizens to articulate their frustrations as consumers — and other group attitudes — and, second, a more sophisticated awareness of the variegated characteristics of Soviet public opinion.

It appears that what the party sought was a deeper and broader consensus than that which prevailed under Stalin. Values were to be more widely shared but their definition and shaping was to remain the party's monopoly. The vision of the communist future, which all communication is ultimately dedicated to realizing, remained coercionless conformity — but nevertheless one of conformity.[52] If the party's system of communication were to encourage, even to reflect, increasingly diverse tastes and aspirations in the future, it would be in spite of rather than because of those who directed it. Despite their operational pragmatism, Khrushchev's reforms in public communication, as in other fields, were heavily fundamentalist and traditionalist. It seems that they were inspired more by nostalgia for the golden age of early bolshevist fervor than by accommodation to the aspirations of new social forces. Perhaps it would be more accurate to say that they reflected a hope that Leninism, freed from Stalinist aberrations, could galvanize the energies and fuse the efforts of all decent Soviet citizens.

The new policies' orthodoxy was made clear by the conspicuous

<hr />

[52] On the need, even under full communism, for a "form of organization" to assure normal social production, etc., and "assist" the population in governing itself and also in "bringing to reason" individuals who "might not wish to follow communist customs and rules of community living," see *Osnovy Marxizma-Leninizma, op. cit.*, p. 747.

place given the symbol of Lenin. During the Stalin era the day of Lenin's death, January 21, was celebrated as an occasion of homage. Khrushchev considered it more appropriate to institute as a national holiday Lenin's birthday, April 22. Like Stalin, Khrushchev associated all his policies with Lenin's name. In 1957 it was proclaimed that the antiparty group had been defeated by the "Leninist kernel" of the party. The efflorescence of the Lenin cult's new version notwithstanding, Soviet leaders continued to urge writers and artists to produce still more and better works "on the immortal man and his immortal deeds." [53]

More significant, perhaps, was the continuity with the Lenin-Stalin organizational attempts to make the press "fulfill the Leninist principles" of "popularity" and "mass character." [54] Certainly, "links with the masses" were much larger and more impressive than they had ever been. In addition to the millions of agitators and "worker and village correspondents," it was claimed that 1,300,000 "scientists, engineering-technical workers, leaders of culture and art" were engaged in lecturing and other activities of the All-Union Knowledge Society. [55] Even the most important newspapers, *Pravda* and *Izvestiya,* devoted much effort to large-scale "raids" by their nonprofessional staffs of worker correspondents. In February, 1960, cooperating with a newspaper in the city of Lvov, *Pravda* conducted a "raid" on furniture factories. One result was a series of articles in *Pravda* under the heading "Where is good furniture available?" [56] On a larger scale than ever before the press exercised its traditional public control and self-criticism. [57] Also, the post-Stalin years saw extensive application of the traditional Soviet technique: public "discussion" of policies, the main outlines of which the party had already formulated but regarding which it desired to elicit informed expert opinion and for which it sought to mobilize all possible public support. Among such discussions the carefully controlled but nevertheless lively debate of 1958–1959 on educational reform was particularly interesting. As DeWitt observes, during the months following Khrushchev's indictment of Soviet education at the

[53] Ilichev, in *XXII sezd KPSS, op. cit.,* p. 77.
[54] *Kommunist,* No, 7, May, 1964, p. 127.
[55] *Pravda,* June 2, 1964.
[56] S. Gorovich, *et al., Voprosy zhurnalistiki* (Moscow, 1962), pp. 34–36.
[57] On the organization and history of these functions see Inkeles, *Public Opinion, op. cit.,* Ch. XIV.

Thirteenth Komsomol Congress in the spring of 1958, "both the central and local Soviet press as well as periodicals published hundreds of statements and articles by officials, educators and others, all bearing on the problem of educational reform and most of them deprecating grossly the past educational practices." [58] Other issues were similarly discussed, including, as George Fischer noted in 1963, "the culture issue, the peace issue, and the consumer issue." As Fischer also pointed out, however, "first-hand evidence on post-Stalin public opinion suggests amorphousness and a good deal of ambivalence. In particular, the *status quo* at present benefits from strong patriotism and an equally intense sense of feebleness and inexperience beyond the ken of the state." [59]

After Khrushchev's fall, organized public discussion seemed to shift to productivity and such character traits as "initiative" and "responsibility," which were extolled by hundreds of factory and collective farm directors, economists, party secretaries, and others over whose names the leading newspapers published articles and letters. Various opinions, proposals, and emphases were represented in the post-Khrushchev economic discussion. The respective roles of monetary and psychological incentives in facilitating individual productivity elicited materially different views.

Obviously, the Soviet leadership was as determined in the 1960's as Stalin had been in the 1930's and 1940's to contain developing Soviet public opinion. To maintain its tutelage it had at its disposal an enormous mechanism of organization and mobilization; as the secret trial but public vilification, in early 1966, of the unorthodox writers Andrei Sinyavski and Yuli Daniel reminded Soviet intellectuals. The threat of force was always in the background if other instruments failed. Also, for the first time since the 1920's, it was now attempting to adapt for its purposes opinion polls, surveys, and other modern, empirical social science techniques in order to analyze group attitudes and shape a satisfactory consensus.

How successful will this effort be? No certain answer can be given under present Soviet secrecy. It is true of course that the analytical methods of social science can be useful in manipulating public opinion. Ralph K. White has suggested, though, that if

---

58 Nicholas DeWitt, *Education and Professional Employment in the U.S.S.R.* (Washington, D.C., 1961), p. 13.

59 George Fischer, "The Role of Public Opinion in Soviet Politics," *Public Opinion Quarterly* (Winter, 1963), pp. 621–22.

these techniques and the concepts associated were increasingly disseminated, they might bring about an "evidence oriented" mentality incompatible with Marxist-Leninist dogmatism and authoritarianism.[60] The growing, if still not triumphant, trend toward freedom of inquiry in Soviet social science seems to justify White's qualified optimism.

As was to be expected, orthodox theoreticians and communicators confidently asserted that Leninist "historical materialism" already constituted a genuine science of society, which could subsume and transcend the "bourgeois" social science's achievements. "Some Marxists" were accused of "imitating" American sociology, though their error was partially excused as a justifiable but exaggerated reaction to earlier dominant dogmatism.[61] Such a position might satisfy some elite elements, especially the ideological apparatchiki, but it was less likely to appeal to young legal scholars, psychologists, economists, natural scientists (or writers, for that matter) who were increasingly knowledgeable about what their foreign colleagues were thinking and accomplishing.

The problems raised by the apparatus' attempt to incorporate selected elements of Western empiricism into Leninist orthodoxy were connected with emergent changes in the relationship between the Soviet polity and both its internal and external environments. Internally, as the harsh trials of the heroic past faded from memory, the possibility loomed that youths might become bored by Leninism. Would not a creed born in struggle and dedicated to ascetic self-sacrifice be undermined by the increasingly hedonistic, skeptical, and relativistic ethos of a maturing industrial society? If a widespread sense of the irrelevance and obsolescence of Leninist doctrines were ever to develop, the Kremlin's ability to shape and impose a national consensus could be gravely weakened.

Replacing the Stalin cult by an intensified and much more

[60] Ralph K. White, "Social Science Research in the Soviet Bloc," *Public Opinion Quarterly* (Spring, 1964), pp. 20–26. See also the articles by Paul Hollander and Michael Cole on sociology and psychology in *Problems of Communism*, XIV, No. 6 (Nov.–Dec., 1965).

[61] See the article by F. Konstantinov and V. Kelle in *Kommunist*, No. 1, Jan., 1965, in which they attempt to define the proper sphere of sociology — and social science generally — within the framework of "Marxism-Leninism." Particularly interesting is the criticism on p. 14 of "some Marxists" who, allegedly influenced by American sociology, seek to create a "new sociology, separate from historical materialism." One sign of the party's interest in harnessing social science for its purposes is that the central committee's Academy of Social Sciences, beginning with the academic year 1966–1967, offered courses in the "criticism" of "bourgeois" sociology.

broadly disseminated cult of Lenin might, then, prove to have been a source not of strength, but of weakness, for it encouraged critically minded and better and better informed Soviet citizens to examine more closely the relevance of the ideological legacy upon which the political leadership bases its claim to legitimacy.

At the same time the effects of increasing, if still severely limited contacts with and knowledge about modern Western industrial societies (Soviet acquaintance with empirical social science is one important facet), posed excruciating dilemmas for Soviet opinion-shapers. To compete with the West, to convince Soviet intellectuals that Soviet civilization was not only as advanced as, but was indeed superior to that of the "imperialist" world, Soviet communicators and theoreticians were challenged to demonstrate that Marxism-Leninism could incorporate the proceeding stream of Western achievements and could also transform and transcend these achievements.

Finally, Soviet Marxist-Leninist leaders and their ideological high priests were challenged by Peking to prove their doctrinal purity and the militancy of their deeds. The pressure applied by the orthodox, "sectarian" wing of communism of course heightened the Kremlin's difficulties — and also compounded those of Soviet "liberals," whose freedom to maneuver was automatically reduced by Moscow's need to present a stern mien to the "imperialist" West. Even the casual newspaper reader can gain some impression of the torture to which the Sino-Soviet rivalry subjected the Soviet presidium. The newspapers devote fuller and more enthusiastic coverage to noncommunist political systems such as those of India, Ghana, Guinea — or the Brazzaville Congo regime — than to that of mainland China.

To the "bourgeois" analyst of Soviet communication behavior in increasingly complicated circumstances it seems likely in 1966 that it will oscillate for a long time between harshness and leniency, between rigidity and responsiveness. Probably it will continue, at any given time, to seem contradictory or even confused. Those who controlled it were in all probability not united in such matters as the proper attitude toward Soviet "contacts" with the West, or how much access Soviet intellectuals should have to "bourgeois" books, films, etc. Presumably, the policemen and the propagandists, for the most part, were at one end of the "liberal-conservative" continuum on such matters, and scientists, social scientists, and writers were at the other (with sundry members of all groups at various points in between), and even at extremes opposite to those which neat, schematic pigeonholing might suggest.

At all events, no major concessions to unfettered variety and fullness of expression seem likely in the foreseeable future, unless their proponents define their goals with greater clarity and acquire far more power to articulate them than they seem to possess. After all, the power, privileges, and perhaps the very survival of the apparatchiki depend upon preserving at least the passive allegiance of the citizenry's rank and file to official policy and ideology. Still, it might not be easy to keep the man in the street docile if intellectuals continue to learn more and more about Western ideas capable of undermining or drastically transforming the traditional Marxist-Leninist dogmas. Tsarism perished partly because of such a gulf between elite and mass thinking. Whether the CPSU's still strong ideological dynamism and its skill at mobilization would save it from a similar fate remained to be seen as the new phase of Soviet history ushered in by the Twenty-third Congress began. The first major pronouncement of the leadership confirmed by the congress, its May Day slogans, were published in the newspapers for April 17, 1966. They contained a hint that this leadership trusted the Soviet people less than Khrushchev had. The slogan hailing the Soviet state no longer used the Khrushchev wording, "the state of the entire people," but reverted to the more conventional "socialist state." It remained impossible to predict whether or not this change signified more repressive relations between government and citizenry. If it did, Soviet propagandists were in for painful problems in the future.

CHAPTER VI

Elite Recruitment and Organization

IN ALL MODERN SOCIETIES, including Soviet Russia, power, prestige, and other values are unequally distributed. A few people share disproportionately what the society produces, whether distribution of the social product is regulated by "merit," "achievement," or other criteria, such as birth, kinship, or "ascription." Governmental policy and other factors can mitigate and cushion inequality's effects, but whether or not unequal endowment with talents and energy at birth, only one of a host of relevant "social justice" problems, can ever be fully counterbalanced remains one of mankind's great unsettled questions.

The presence of an elite is indicated by unequal distribution and particularly by a clearly defined minority of the citizenry whose access to channels of political communication, honorific publicity, and especially the arenas where momentous matters are confidentially discussed and important decisions are made, is far greater than that of their fellows. If we accept these criteria, then we may be as certain that there is a Soviet elite as we are that there is an American, a British, or a Japanese elite. To be sure, biographical and other data regarding Soviet people of distinction are exceedingly difficult to obtain and, when obtainable, are scanty, but the difficulty confronting one who seeks such knowledge has been much reduced in recent years.[1]

[1] *Deputaty sovetskogo soyuza i soveta natsionalnostei* (Moscow, 1962) contains extensive data on Supreme Soviet deputies, which category includes many leaders in politics and other fields of Soviet life. Other useful Soviet sources include encyclopedias, especially the *Ezhegodnik* (*Yearbook*) published

By painstakingly analyzing Soviet sources Western scholars have put together a very useful body of knowledge regarding the composition, characteristics, and selection of the Soviet elite and leadership.[2] The Soviet elite's special characteristics are shaped by the society which it dominates, and by the socialization and recruitment processes that shape and sift it. Its experience and training are unusually homogeneous. In its training formal instruction is exceptionally significant. It is subjected to very strongly centralized, hierarchic control and discipline. The Soviet elite, in effect, is the upper echelons of a society organized as interlocking bureaucracies, composed of persons whose performance over long periods of time has conformed outstandingly to the criteria of operation — partly overt and partly covert or informal — of the dominant political culture.

Since this system of organizations is controlled by the CPSU, or, to be more accurate, by its top leadership, elite recruitment is principally planned and supervised by the party's central organs. The party, and especially its personnel agencies, are particularly concerned with the selecting, assigning, and training "leading workers," who staff the full-time paid "apparatus" of party officials. Broadly defined, the Soviet elite consists of the party apparatus and at least two other elements. The first includes government officials, industrial managers, and leaders of the professions. Although many are members, they usually are not full-time executives of upper-level party organs, and have achieved their leading positions in Soviet society not primarily as party bureaucrats, but as managers, high-ranking army or police officers, engineers, scientists, writers, artists, etc. Finally, and least important but still

annually since 1957 by the publishers of the Great Soviet Encyclopedia, the published stenographic reports of party congresses, the reports of party plenary sessions, the *khronika* items in the daily press (on major party-government appointments), and other scattered sources. Non-Soviet reference works containing biographical and personnel data include H. Schulz and S. Taylor, eds., *Who's Who in the U.S.S.R. 1961/1962* (Intercontinental Book and Publishing Co., New York, etc., 1962); Hans Koch, *5,000 Sowjetköpfe* (Köln, 1959); and a variety of other reference works, such as *The International Who's Who.*

[2] The most significant available contributions to knowledge of the Soviet elite structure and recruitment, and particularly its political characteristics, include the cited major studies of John A. Armstrong and T. H. Rigby. See also Rigby and L. G. Churchward, *Policy-Making in the U.S.S.R.* (Melbourne, 1962); Sidney Harcave, *Structure and Functioning of the Lower Party Organizations in the Soviet Union* (Maxwell Air Force Base, Alabama, 1954); Inkeles and Bauer, *The Soviet Citizen, op. cit.;* and Fainsod, *How Russia Is Ruled, op. cit.* The major elite studies now being prepared by Severyn Bialer and George Fischer will add significantly to our knowledge of the Soviet elite.

worth mentioning are those among the intelligentsia, who, though not party members, have achieved such outstanding distinction as scholars, scientists, or artists that they must be regarded as members of the Soviet elite. Most Soviet citizens who occupy positions of distinction, responsibility, and, at the highest levels, of leadership, have achieved these positions because the party has facilitated their rise, stage by stage, to the top of the social pyramid. Even those whose eminence comes from exceptional scientific or artistic talent cannot do so without the approval or encouragement of powerful party leaders who control access to nearly all the positions to which ambitious Soviet citizens may aspire. Even more than in other more or less highly developed societies, advancement depends on ability but also on acquaintance — although not, as a rule, on kinship or other inherited advantages.

In effect, the methods of elite recruitment in the USSR constitute an exceptionally centralized but also an extremely political civil service system. It operates through what is known as the "nomenclature" (*nomenklatura*), a comprehensive set of job categories and descriptions, which is defined in Soviet texts as a list of posts confirmed by superior organizations. It is administered, in accordance with their status, by party and government chiefs and is supposed to assure standardized, rational selection, tenure of office, and promotion, on the basis of merit. (The requirements most frequently referred to in the "Party Life" section of *Pravda* are proper "businesslike and political" characteristics.) [3] As we shall see, this Soviet "merit system," like those of other polities, does not always achieve its professed objectives.

Frequent articles in *Pravda, Partiinaya zhizn,* and other Soviet press organs complain of abuses in its application. Only too often, we read, considerations other than "businesslike and political"

[3] See *Kratki politicheski slovar* (Moscow, 1964), p. 199, and the discussion of party direction of appointments of factory directors, directors of scientific laboratories, etc., by Moscow party secretary N. G. Egorychev, in *Partiinaya zhizn,* No. 8, April, 1962, pp. 18–24. See also A. Lebed, *Podgotovka i raspredelenie rukovodyashchikh kadrov SSSR,* and K. A. Krylov, *Nekotorye osobennosti nomenklaturnoi sistemy* (Institute for the Study of the USSR, Munich, 1965). The last two items are mimeographed texts of papers presented to a symposium on the Soviet "Take-Over Generation" in Munich, in September, 1965. Krylov cites some evidence from Soviet sources indicating that "nomenclature" workers are, in effect, above the law so long as they enjoy the favor of their superiors in the party apparatus. Although not fully convincing, his argument seems plausible. Lebed presents an interesting hierarchy of the various "nomenclatures," from the top down.

qualifications determine appointments to and tenure of executive posts. Not infrequently, failure of a factory or collective farm director leads not to demotion but merely to transfer to an equally good new job. Worst of all, party organizations often wink at or ignore malfeasance or even criminal practices of state officials. It is clear from press discussions of such matters that they occur because personal friendships and patron-client relationships are important in determining careers and life chances.

The supreme political leader — a Lenin or a Stalin, a Khrushchev or a Brezhnev — normally devotes more of his attention to shaping elite recruitment policy than to any other leadership role. Personal intervention from the top level has of course frequently brought about change in the highest Soviet decision-making bodies. The complexity of modern bureaucracy, however, forces even a Stalin to delegate some power in selecting key personnel and to develop routine procedures for appointing, assigning, promoting, or demoting the personnel on whose performance the political system's efficient functioning depends.

In the central committee there is usually a secretary who acts as the leader's deputy in organizational matters, including the selection of top-level personnel. Such a person — G. M. Malenkov, for example, in the last years of Stalin's lifetime, or A. I. Kirichenko and Frol R. Kozlov at different times under Khrushchev — is likely to be the second-ranking man in the entire political hierarchy, although no such post is explicitly identified. In addition, there is normally a specialist official like Khrushchev's personnel chief, the Ukrainian apparatchik V. N. Titov, who operates the administrative mechanism of upper-level leadership selection. One major subject of speculation about Soviet politics after Khrushchev's downfall and the downgrading of Titov which soon followed (although it was not made formal until the September, 1965 central committee plenum), was whether or not recruitment control had been sufficiently stabilized to permit the new leadership to hold a party congress. The failure to begin preparing for a congress in the summer of 1965 made it doubtful that N. V. Podgorny had been authorized to see to the selection of the delegates to a congress, an important task which normally has belonged to the top party leader's chief lieutenant, once his leadership has been firmly established. During the September, 1965 plenum, however, it was announced that the party's Twenty-third

Congress would be held in March, 1966, indicating that this problem probably had been resolved. The September 30 announcement that Titov had been assigned to Kazakhstan was accompanied by another, declaring F. D. Kulakov's "election" as a secretary of the central committee. It might therefore have been thought that Kulakov, a Great Russian, was brought in to take over Titov's job as chief personnel expert. But it soon became known that Kulakov, with his long background of party and government work in agriculture, had been made party central committee overseer, mainly in the RSFSR, invalidating such a hypothesis. After the December, 1965 plenum kicked Podgorny upstairs to the ceremonial position of titular chief of state, replacing Anastas Mikoyan, it seemed clearer than ever that Brezhnev was determined to control, as fully as his colleagues would permit, the new leadership that would be given formal authority by the forthcoming party congress. It then became known that another new secretariat member, I. V. Kapitonov, rather than Kulakov, had been picked by Brezhnev to handle top-level personnel details. As it was to be expected, Kapitonov delivered the report on the "mandate" of the delegates at the party's Twenty-third Congress.

Disregarding inconsistent details, which usually remain obscure to outsiders, we can clearly see that access to the command posts of Soviet society is controlled by executives of the major bureaucratic hierarchies. As a result, an official's tenure, especially in the middle and upper ranks of the party and state bureaucracies, depends upon such partly fortuitous factors as personal or organizational relationships with rising — or falling — stars in the political firmament. Political earthquakes in the highly integrated, but by no means completely homogeneous or harmonious leadership structure can have a shattering effect even on the peripheral officials.[4] A dictator's anger or fear, or even his whim, can cause heads to roll. An example was Stalin's 1936–1938 purges of his Trotskyite-Zinovevite-Bukharinite and other opponents, as well as the quieter but equally ruthless operations on a smaller scale connected with the "Leningrad Case" in the months following Andrei Zhdanov's death in 1948–1949. It must be remembered that data

---

[4] For a semifictional but highly plausible illustration, see the sketch entitled "The Party Secretary" in Raymond A. Bauer, *Nine Soviet Portraits* (New York, 1955), pp. 60–75.

essential for analyzing and understanding these events are still unavailable. Succession crises, lasting for years, during which a failing, floundering, or dying leader's lieutenants struggle for power, are another extreme and dramatic instability which in the past has wrought havoc with many careers.

The instability and caprice in Soviet politics sometimes, to be sure, have been greatly overemphasized. They are balanced by very important systematic, regular, and routine elite recruitment practices, to which we shall presently give our attention. To overlook the weak points, however, with the memory of Khrushchev's overthrow still fresh — seven years after he had consolidated the powers he had won in a complex succession struggle — would be to ignore a major source of possible future upheavals, which could even create fundamental change in Soviet society.

The Soviet elite's membership, selection, and fate are dominated by politics, but its functions are multiple, embracing as they do all kinds of social action. Among them the economic and productive function is perhaps second to the political one, and it is undoubtedly the most significant in the numbers of personnel that it involves. As Armstrong has put it, "Next to the maintenance of political control, the operation of the economy is the chief concern of the Soviet regime." And he correctly adds, "Indeed, the press and even party meetings devote more attention to economic matters than to the political and ideological questions." [5] The varied jobs, some requiring very special skills, in a highly integrated and centralized aggregation of bureaucracies, pose difficult elite recruitment problems. The party is aware of these problems, and is determined to cope with them, as we can see in such statements as that of Khrushchev at the Twenty-second Party Congress: "The promotion and training of cadres for various branches of party and state work and for economic and cultural construction is the most important obligation of the party organizations." [6]

The style and methods of selecting, assigning, and promoting leadership personnel decisively influence the elite's structure and capabilities. The party apparatus is responsible for this vital task and must judge the character and political outlook of potential

[5] Armstrong, *op. cit.*, p. 60.
[6] Quoted by P. F. Pigalev, *Mestnye partiinye organy — organy politicheskogo i organizatsionnogo rukovodstva* (Moscow, 1962), p. 35.

leaders, as well as their education, professional skills, and other characteristics, including age, experience, nationality, sex, etc. Whatever performance and qualification criteria are employed in recruiting the elite, their application requires that agencies for record-keeping and selection be set up and maintained. Since, like material resources, human resources are limited, the party leadership must decide how and where it can most advantageously deploy its cadres. Like Soviet policy in other areas, here it reflects at any particular time the party leadership's currently pressing preoccupations. Like Stalin, Khrushchev sought to contain within the party elite the emerging social formations created by rapid economic development. Probably because he relied less upon police terror as an instrument of rule than did Stalin and was thus partially deprived of a strong means of control, Khrushchev was less willing than Stalin to permit the semiautonomous state and managerial bureaucracies to develop; Stalin had controlled these by the elaborate, awe-inspiring mechanism of terror that will be forever associated with his name. As the Soviet economy became more complex, however, benefiting by the division of labor without creating unwanted ideological and political pluralism was more difficult for Khrushchev than it had been for Stalin. Khrushchev coped with the problem by such means as finding within the party apparatus appropriate and attractive opportunities for the growing army of Soviet "specialists." [7]

Although early in his administration Khrushchev curbed and disgraced the technocratically oriented hierarchs to whom Stalin had given vast power in administrating the Soviet economy, his recruitment policy for the all-important party apparatus and for the party as a whole permitted industrial managers and other skilled production specialists to gain unprecedented influence within the party. A significant editorial published in a central committee journal in 1964 expressed the view that the 1962 party reorganization "according to the production principle" had made it possible to promote more industrial and agricultural specialists to responsible positions in the party apparatus.[8] The article ex-

[7] "This is indicated by the editorial in *Partiinaya zhizn*, No. 10, May, 1964, entitled "The Apparatus of the Party Committee" which, while emphasizing the leadership over all branches of policy of the party apparatus, also pointed out that the party had "become specialized" to utilize production "specialists."

[8] Apparat partiinogo komiteta," *Partiinaya zhizn*, No. 10, May, 1964, pp. 3–6.

pressed regret that this trend had not developed as fully as would have been desirable. Now that the party apparatus' most important task was to increase production it was more than ever necessary that the apparatus include more persons trained as industrial specialists. The first of the three regular sections in each issue of the central committee organizational journal *Partiinaya zhizn* has long been headed "Leadership of the Economy," an arrangement, incidentally, which has survived Khrushchev's fall. The same journal stated that more than 70 per cent of the CPSU members were drawn from the "sphere of material production." [9]

Khrushchevian personnel policy reflected the increasing preoccupation with production which we perceived in political socialization and communication. It was also clear, however, that the party was determined to keep its control over social change and development. This aim was even reflected in university textbooks on constitutional and administrative law, into which were inserted sections concerned with the communist party's leading role.[10]

Before analyzing the practices and criteria which govern elite recruitment in the USSR it will be useful to describe in some detail the elite's major categories. Soviet secrecy makes it impossible to present a comprehensive profile, particularly of the middle and lower ranks of Soviet officialdom, whose obscurity contrasts sharply with the public attention enjoyed by their counterparts in nontotalitarian countries and also with the limelight in which the ruling few at the top of the Soviet pyramid bask. Even regarding upper-level leaders, though, most biographical information, especially the intimate facts which would be taken for granted in most countries, is not available.[11] Soviet sources divide organizations into two main types: "public" and "state." The first category includes the party, the trade unions, and also the hierarchy of Soviets which nominally governs the country; these are, at least formally, elective organizations. The "state" organizations are appointed and their employees, above certain legally defined levels,

9 *Ibid.*, No. 8, April, 1964, p. 9.
10 See Ya. N. Umanski, *Sovetskoe gosudarstvennoe pravo* (Moscow, 1960), pp. 115–18; G. A. Petrov, *Sovetskoe administrativnoe pravo* (Leningrad, 1960), pp. 18–24, 31–44.
11 Armstrong, *op. cit.*, pp. 3–6, 12–13. Because data on the elite of the Ukrainian Soviet Republic are more plentiful than those obtainable for the Soviet elite as a whole, Armstrong focused his study on the former.

are invested with legal authority. The public organizations and also the state organizations operate at these levels: (1) national, with headquarters in each of the fifteen constituent Soviet republics; (2) *oblast* or *krai,* usually translated as "province" and "territory," respectively, with headquarters in the several hundred oblasts and a few large krais (large, sparsely settled regions) of the USSR; (3) towns (the Russian word for town is *gorod*), often divided into a number of raions; and, (4) rural raions. Many rural raions were abolished in 1962, but they were re-established with somewhat altered boundaries and as a rule with larger areas after Khrushchev's fall. Below the raion level are local units of the party and other public organizations centered in factories and other industrial enterprises, collective farms and state farms, and also in governmental, cultural, and educational institutions. This lowest level of party organizations is known as the primary party organization, and may for convenience be abbreviated as "p.p.o."

The full membership of the party and other public organizations periodically elects delegates to representative congresses or meetings. The most important congresses of course are those of the All-Union Communist Party, which must be held once every four years, according to the statutes adopted in 1961. Primary party organizations hold annual "election and report" meetings. At each level, the congress or meeting elects a committee, presumably composed of the most meritorious and responsible members, which is vested with over-all policy-making and supervisory duties between meetings. These representative bodies, of which the most important is the Central Committee of the CPSU, in turn select smaller and more compact policy-making and executive committees to transact day-to-day business. The latter bodies, in their turn, select executives, of whom the vast army of party secretaries are the most numerous, and instructors as well as various other permanent, paid functionaries. At the p.p.o.'s level, most party secretaries are not paid functionaries but are dedicated, or at least zealous, party members, who in addition to their regular work perform their local party leadership jobs in their spare time. The full-time, paid party secretaries are known as "exempted" workers. It is probably at this level that the Soviet political elite begins, but it is really impossible to precisely draw the line between the elite's lower levels and the nonelite citizenry. Many exempted party secretaries are, or will become, members of the permanent party apparatus, and some rise to high posts.[12]

The Soviet authorities seek to confer appropriate prestige upon all who are elected to even the humblest office in the party, and in other organizations as well, and also upon all who participate actively, frequently, and effectively in party, trade union, or Young Communist League activities. Obviously close to Khrushchev's heart was reviving and expanding the voluntary, unpaid "activists" (collectively referred to in Russian as the *aktiv*).[13] A movement began in 1959 to introduce "public principles" on a large scale, with various objectives, among which was reducing the paid bureaucracy as much as feasible, in all kinds of organizations. It was certainly numerically impressive. By early 1962, according to Soviet reports, about 900,000 members of the party were working as unpaid "instructors" of party cabinets (the party cabinets assist propagandists by keeping records and preparing visual aids, charts, and other materials), and on various "commissions" of raion, city, and primary party organizations.

In addition, more than 2,000,000 party members held elective posts in party organs and also were reportedly carrying on "a great party work on the basis of voluntary principles." [14] Apparently this movement, meant to be symbolically effective and to mobilize manpower, is at least incidental in screening aspirants for political careers. The same editorial stated that it was becoming "a good school for preparation of cadres, and a means of establishing a reserve of experienced organizers and of party, Soviet and economic workers." These claims cannot be assessed without keeping in mind the criticism, which did not stop with Khrushchev's fall, alleging that party organizations failed to bring even the members of the aktiv, not to mention nonparty persons, "into participation in civic affairs."

Our evidence indicates that recruitment, as affected by the extension of "public principles," does not threaten the continued domination of the Soviet elite by the party apparatus but, in part, is intended to strengthen the apparatus by enlarging the pool of suitable applicants from which it can draw replacements. This

[12] Harcave, *op. cit.*, p. 9.

[13] The aktiv was defined in *Politicheski slovar* (Moscow, 1940), p. 18, as "the guiding cadres and the most active members of organizations."

[14] Pigalev, *op. cit.*, pp. 60–61; also *Pravda* editorial, Jan. 9, 1962.

will become clearer as we examine data on the relative weight of the party apparatus and other functional groups in the ruling political organs and the self-selective practices by which the apparatchiki thus far have succeeded in maintaining their preponderant influence. Re-emphasizing apparatchik prerogatives, in contrast to Khrushchev's populism, indeed seemed close to the Brezhnev-Kosygin team's heart.

The hierarchy of apparatchiki begins with the secretaries of large p.p.o.'s, which may have executive committees, several secretaries, instructors, and other functionaries on their staffs. It is probable that the first secretaries of large p.p.o.'s have gained in status in recent years as the many organizations which they head have grown. There were apparently 355,000 p.p.o.'s in the early 1950's, but as of the Twenty-second Congress in 1961 there were only about 300,000.[15] The growth in party membership during that interval makes it clear that many p.p.o.'s must have expanded substantially. The performance of p.p.o.'s and their secretaries is supervised by apparatus officials known as instructors, who report to the raion committees. Each instructor is responsible for and is expected to maintain liaison with a number of p.p.o.'s. In addition to raion committees (often abbreviated as *raikom,* and their secretaries as *raikomsec*), there are also instructors on the staffs of oblast committees (*obkom, obkomsec*) and central committees of party organizations of the republics, and some are also attached to the All-Union Party Central Committee. The higher-ranking instructors' work is analogous to, but more important than, that done by those at the raikom level.

According to an editorial, the instructors of the various party committees form the most numerous category in the party apparatus.[16] They must spend a large part of their time in the grass roots, doing organizational and political work. The editorial added that even more significant than the instructors' work was that of the "instructor-organizers" of the production collective farm-state farm administrations. (These were abolished after Khrushchev's fall.) Each of these officials, whose work was similar

---

15 Harcave, *op. cit.,* p. 20; *Materialy XXII sezda KPSS,* pp. 102, 288. The latter source also gives the following partial functional breakdown of p.p.o.'s: in industry, 31,830; in construction, 10,427; in transport, 15,938; in collective farms, 31,387; in state farms, 9,206. Kapitonov said at the Twenty-third Congress that there were 326,000 p.p.o.'s. This increase apparently was caused by the restoration of the rural raion organizations.

16 *Partiinaya zhizn,* No. 10, May, 1964.

to that of instructors, supervised a number of p.p.o.'s in collective farms and state farms. The instructor-organizers were expected to spend much time working "with people" on the farms and on the carrying out of party directives and instructions.

As is to be expected, at higher levels the party leadership and its inner core, the apparatus, are increasingly complex and their functions are more and more specialized. At each level and throughout the party structure generally, however, it is systematically attempted to closely coordinate and integrate "generalists" and "specialists," and "line" and "staff" functions. Thus at the raikom level there are departments for agitation-propaganda, personnel, organization-instruction, and other functions. These specialized departments are subordinate both to the territorial apparatus and to staff agencies, which are ultimately directed by central committee departments in Moscow.[17] In addition to apparatus officials, the bureaus, the executive bodies of raikoms and obkoms, and the central committees of both the constituent republics and the USSR as a whole, include officials of the state administrative and economic bureaucracies, high-ranking state security police officers, and in some cases important military commanders.

Police officials, military commanders, and officials in some other specialized fields, such as public health, education, and science, differ, in their relationship to the apparatchiki, from governmental and economic executives. Generally speaking, the party and state bureaucrats and most production chiefs make up what Rigby calls a "unified personnel pool." There is extensive interchangeability among these categories of officials. In contrast, the military in particular and also the officers of such different services as the security police and the diplomatic establishment belong to more or less sharply defined career services. Except for the armed forces, however, exceptions are easy to find, especially at the highest levels. Nikolai Ezhov was transferred in 1936 from his post in the central committee apparatus, where he headed the party control commission, to leadership of the political police. Also, two post-Stalin chiefs of the security services, Shelepin and Semichastny, had made their careers in Komsomol and party work before assuming leadership of the police. It should also

---

17 On this pattern, see Conquest, *Power and Policy, op. cit.,* pp. 37–53; Armstrong, *op. cit.,* Chs. VI and VII.

be kept in mind that the heads of such vital central committee agencies as those concerned with party organs and with "administrative organs" have much control over the police formations. Khrushchev assigned a number of party apparatus men to high positions in the Ministry of Foreign Affairs or to ambassadorial posts, perhaps because the apparatus was generally elevated over all chains of command upon Khrushchev's victory in the Stalinist succession crisis. This practice also enabled him to "kick upstairs" some high-ranking members of the apparatus toward whom the Khrushchev faction was not too favorably disposed.

Military officials and, still more, police officials differed from party apparatchiki, especially during the Stalin era. Perhaps the most significant difference was that the territorial chiefs of these services and also the territorial representatives of the procuracy (the closest United States equivalent to which is the office of the attorney general), were exempted from supervision and control by the local party organizations. In addition to these sensitive and potentially even dangerous bureaucracies, other special party and governmental agencies have been controlled directly from Moscow and, under Stalin, by the dictator himself. Those among the elite employed in what Stalin often referred to as the "punitive organs" diminished both in numbers and influence after his death, though the Soviet surveillance, inspection, detection, and detention apparatus is still very large. In its profusion of inspectoral agencies and functionaries, who help to prevent activities contrary to Moscow's interests at local levels or in specialized bureaucracies, the Soviet elite resembles that of the Russian Empire. Of course officials of even these agencies are subject to corruption, and even when incorruptible and efficient they often interfere intolerably with the work of those whom they are supposed to assist and supervise. Industrial executives' resentment of too many inspections may have been behind a bitingly sarcastic account of the arrival of commission after commission to investigate the same problem — that of assigning "young specialists" at a candy factory in the city of Kuibyshev on the Volga.[18] Such an item seemed to fit well into the post-Khrushchev regime's campaign to create conditions favorable to effective industrial management, although knowing the Russian and Soviet past we

18 *Pravda*, Jan. 23, 1965.

are bound to be skeptical about rapid progress in unshackling managers from bureaucratic controls.

Even under Stalin, the party apparatus was by far the largest element of the Soviet elite. But even its most prominent members lived in constant, numbing fear of Stalin and of the machinery of autocratic rule directed by his creatures, such as A. N. Poskreby-shev, head of his personal secretariat, and, until a year or two before his death, by Lavrenti Beria, whom Stalin had appointed head of the political police in 1938. Even these sinister figures, dreaded by so many, also lived in fear under Stalin's system of spying and intrigue, playing off his lieutenants against one another, in various combinations, depending on shifting circumstance and whim. Still, even during the Stalin years, eager and ambitious men strove mightily to rise in the party apparatus. The careful Harcave, who based his interpretation mainly on data from the Stalin era, was able to thus describe the prestige of even the relatively low-ranking first secretary of a raion: "It is generally recognized that he is not only the head of the party but also the head of society in the district." The party elite's predominant status was reflected in the lists of officials presented in the Soviet press. The names of party secretaries were given before those of chairmen of raion executive committees, the highest-ranking workers among the government officials. In every Soviet city, from Moscow and Leningrad to the small towns which are the nerve centers of agricultural districts, in the largest, finest, and best-located buildings, under Stalin and Khrushchev, and still today, were to be found the offices of the local party chiefs, or the highest party and governmental officials in the locality. Many buildings housing party officers and many "palaces" of the Young Pioneers are confiscated former residences of the tsar and the highest-ranking nobility.

Thus the new elite expropriated not only the property but much of the tradition and style of its predecessors. Certainly it is fond of physical symbols of authority and a heavy and solemn kind of pomp, as well as such obvious evidences of rank as the medal-covered chests of Soviet military greats. The elite of the toilers resembles the less vigorous, less efficient, but equally rank-conscious hierarchic order which it replaced.

The Soviet penchant for displaying the visible manifestations of political authority is most impressively exemplified in the military parades and political demonstrations held on the May Day and November 6 revolutionary holidays, not only in Moscow but in the public squares of Leningrad, Kiev, and other metropolises. The places of honor on these occasions are reserved for the party chiefs, flanked by their counterparts in the government, the police, and the armed forces.

Since Stalin's death the party apparatus' authority over both new elite elements and Soviet society as a whole is even greater than it was under Stalin. The party's direction and control have expanded greatly in agriculture, and party membership in the rural areas has grown by drawing especially on collective farm and state farm executive and professional personnel and also rank and file collective farmers. Whereas in 1939 only one collective farm in twelve had a p.p.o., and in 1956, 7,356 collective farms lacked them, by 1962 all collective farms had p.p.o.'s and many had more than one hundred members.[19]

We should keep our minds wide open to future developments in Soviet politics, including the possibility that Soviet "democratic centralism" may gradually become much less repressive than it now is. We should bear in mind, therefore, that the increase in the party's authority since Stalin's death has been accompanied by much improvement in the personal security enjoyed by the Soviet elite and indeed by the citizenry in general, and also by modestly increased freedom in discussing policy matters within the party, as well as by some increase in the responsibility, authority, and initiative of local party and government officials. Moscow at times allows lower party organization members to express some open opposition against the candidates picked, traditionally, by higher party bodies to lead the lower bodies. This happened on a noticeably large scale in 1957–1958, in preparation for the 1961 party congress, and also in the first months after Khrushchev's fall. Rigby has pointed out that although the "ephemeral shoots of responsible government" visible in 1957–1958 did not live long after the succession crisis was resolved, they might recur on a larger scale with the next succession struggle and might one day be consolidated. In any case, the party's increased authority has been accompanied by changes beneficial to the Soviet people, and, if more substantial positive political and social change occurs in the future, it probably will

19 Pethybridge, *op. cit.*, pp. 21–22; Pigalev, *op. cit.*, p. 69.

originate inside the party.[20] At least the style and tone of Soviet politics and administration have changed from the servile cringing before authority and the other abhorrent Stalinist features to the relatively businesslike spirit prevalent today in Soviet political and administrative life.

The trend toward a kind of gray flannel sobriety has indeed been more apparent since Khrushchev's removal. An irony of change in elite style was shown by Soviet criticism of Mao-Tse-Tung's "cult of personality," the Soviet portrayal of which resembled closely the formerly revered Stalinist rituals. Gone are the days when Stalin summoned the ambassadors of foreign powers to the Kremlin for conferences in the dead of night. Although the importance of such changes in atmosphere and appearance should not be exaggerated, they may be signs of a latent predisposition toward greater transformations.

The apparatchiki have always had a preponderance but never a monopoly of membership in the highest policy-making bodies of the party, such as the Politburo (which in 1952 became the presidium), the All-Union Central Committee, the central committees of the republic party organizations, and so on. In these bodies, in turn, memberships heavily overlap with those of the national and constituent republic councils of ministers, and with those of the executive bodies of the All-Union and Republic Supreme Soviets. Usually, however, the most important center of apparatus power has been the secretariat of the CPSU central committee. Each of its powerful secretaries supervises a major area of party and national policy and each is assisted by a large, expert staff.

The fusion of party and state bureaucracies and the formers' supremacy have been most strikingly manifested in the careers of men who rose to the Soviet power pyramid's apex. Thus Lenin was not just the master strategist of the revolution but also created the party organization of which Stalin fashioned his all-powerful party apparatus, and was the head of the Soviet government. As Lenin had, Stalin, Malenkov, and Khrushchev served both as party leaders (the latter three were supremely successful apparatus politicians) and also as heads of the Soviet government.

In Stalin's and in Malenkov's rise to power, exploiting the op-

[20] On this point see the interesting reflections by Rigby in his contribution to *Policy-Making in the U.S.S.R.*, *op. cit.*, pp. 18–20, 26.

portunities afforded by the party secretariat office was decisive;
it was of course not unimportant in the rise of Khrushchev. Malenkov, the least successful of the four, was also the only one who did
not enjoy a reasonably long tenure at the summit, simultaneously,
of both the party and the governmental machinery.[21] Both Stalin
and Khrushchev rose through the party apparatus and utilized
the secretariat as a springboard to power, but Stalin, especially
during and after World War II, elevated former party apparatus
men turned state bureaucrats, notably Molotov and Malenkov, to
the highest positions in the country. Khrushchev, who achieved
power in a struggle against men of such background, brought to
top positions mainly men whose careers had been built almost
entirely in the party rather than the governmental bureaucracies.
After Khrushchev became in 1958 head of the Soviet government,
its functions and prestige were expanded. Khrushchev developed
his version of a "brain trust," with nepotistic overtones. It was
manifested particularly in his son-in-law Aleksei Adzhubei's me-
teoric rise to a prominent policy-making post. Also, Khrushchev
sharply reversed his reliance upon the party central committee to
which he had turned for support in struggling against the anti-
party group. Indeed, during the last few years of his regime he
packed central committee meetings with crowds of chosen supporters and seemed to be seeking to turn that institution into a
mere sounding board for his policies. Often, he apparently ignored his presidium colleagues in making important foreign and
domestic policy decisions. Moreover, perhaps ominously, he began
to invoke Lenin's authority against "some comrades" who did not
share his policy preferences. In a word, as it became very clear
after his fall, Khrushchev had violated "collective leadership" and
other supposedly fundamental principles of party and state leadership and decision making. One crucial question for the Soviet
political future, however, is whether or not these principles can
be applied, and, if not, whether the instability which has characterized the political system in the past may not affect it in the
future so profoundly as to bring major changes or even evolution
toward another kind of system.

21 For a few days after Stalin's death, Malenkov was the highest-ranking
man in both the party and the government, but he apparently assumed that
the time had come when leadership of the state was more important than that
of the party. On this point see Pethybridge, *op. cit.*, who analyzes interestingly
the reasons for Malenkov's decision. See esp. pp. 35–36.

Although the peculiarly mixed fusion and differentiation in the Soviet elite has many disadvantages in the form of duplication, bureaucratic confusion, and waste, it does provide the nation with exceptionally rich leadership resources. Indeed, in a sense, it furnishes alternative governments, which fact perhaps explains how the system was able to survive Stalin's purges and the manpower losses of World War II as well as it did. More important, though, the Soviet combination of complementarity and rivalry among separate but interlocking bureaucracies has insured, and probably will continue to insure the top leadership in Moscow against possible undermining of the central power by other elite elements. Only those who hold the levers of central power have the panoply of instruments which penetrates and envelops all the other relatively specialized, isolated, and segmental hierarchies.

Although the fragmented elite and the correspondingly strong central party executive have the advantage of holding disintegrating forces in firm check (even now these forces are potentially powerful in the ethnically pluralistic USSR), there are equally great negative consequences. The system requires very powerful leadership at the center, to manipulate the power-strings and to keep hostile or dangerous coalitions and conspiracies from forming. In this ability, Stalin apparently was far better endowed than Khrushchev. A corollary result is unstable succession to top leadership. This instability can spread very far through the elite and can deeply affect the fate of all Soviet citizens and indeed that of all mankind.

In this uncertainty, whoever becomes head of the party machine is likely to aspire to become supreme national leader, partly out of ambition and partly for personal security. If he succeeds in making himself head not only of the party but also of the government and thus acquires additional formal and symbolic legitimacy, it will be difficult for him to prevent those around him from creating some sort of "personality cult," which in turn arouses envy and mistrust. This appears to have happened to Stalin and, in a very different way and degree, to Khrushchev. As of May, 1966 it was unclear whether Leonid Brezhnev would ever manage to be even another Khrushchev, but the revived title of general secretary conferred upon him stirred speculation.

Khrushchev's fall was engineered by, and also brought to power, a somewhat novel combination of leadership elements. In one sense the successor regime, characterized by dual executive power, reminded one of the Khrushchev-Malenkov relationship of 1953–1954. The holders of the two highest positions, party First Secretary Leonid Brezhnev, born in 1906, and Chairman of the USSR Council of Ministers, Aleksei Kosygin, born in 1904, differed more in their career backgrounds than had Khrushchev and Malenkov. Their relationship appeared to be more complementary and less competitive than that of Khrushchev and Malenkov. Although both Brezhnev and Kosygin had engineering training and managerial experience, their careers differed sharply. Brezhnev since 1937 had been a party apparatchik, with wide experience in political and military relations. Although preponderantly an apparatus man (his first period of service on the party secretariat began in 1956), Brezhnev also had high-level governmental experience, at home and abroad, as chairman of the USSR Supreme Soviet presidium in 1960–1963. During most of that time he was not in the secretariat and was politically eclipsed by the late Frol R. Kozlov. Brezhnev had joined the party presidium in 1957.

Kosygin never served on the secretariat, although his status in the CPSU was indicated by his election in 1939 to membership in the central committee and by his membership in 1948–1952 in Stalin's Politburo. Kosygin's career was impressive, however, because of his rich managerial, and governmental, administrative experience. He had served in a wide variety of posts before his jump in October, 1964 from first deputy chairman of the Council of Ministers (which he had held since May, 1960, when he also became a member of the party presidium), to chairman. He had been a factory director, a deputy head of the State Planning Committee (Gosplan), and had headed the ministries of textiles, light industry, consumer goods, and finance. His competence and involvement in increasing management efficiency in the national economy were indicated by his major speech at the All-Union Conference of Scientific Personnel reported in Soviet newspapers for June 15, 1961. Kosygin's career and his previously mentioned interests make it appear that he probably inspired the demands voiced after Khrushchev's fall for raising the quality of Soviet industrial output up to that of the best world models.

The Brezhnev-Kosygin team's accession to office posed many questions. An interesting one is whether or not it inaugurated a permanent or at least long-lasting arrangement in which the top party and government leadership would remain in the hands of separate executives, clearly subordinating government to party, but also with a better defined, semiautonomous sphere for government administration and personnel than had previously prevailed. This possibility at least for a time appeared to be heightened by the post-Khrushchev leadership's attempts to pull back from Khrushchev's practice of directly involving in the details of economic administration party executives at all levels. The new leaders appeared determined to more clearly divide party and state functions than did the fusion favored by Khrushchev.

No Soviet leader has shown any intent to do away with or fundamentally modify party apparatus control over the other elements of the Soviet elite. As long as the present system of surveillance and supervision exists, however, nonapparatus elements will be unable to realize even modest aspirations for functional and professional autonomy. Producing tensions and frustrations, party tutelage over managers and professionals will also continue to deprive Soviet society of the creativity and diversity which a genuine division of labor and a free market in goods and services, political programs and ideas would provide.

Painstaking recent studies of the Soviet elite enable us to perceive more clearly than we were able to not long ago its main features. Most available data cover participation by persons with such identifiable characteristics as membership in the party apparatus, the economic bureaucracy, the military officer corps, etc., in All-Union, republic and some lower-level party congresses and conferences. Analyzing representation in such bodies from the founding of the USSR until 1954, Rigby found that although the representation of persons working in the party apparatus had gradually diminished since the 1920's, it was still the largest category. The apparatchiki, he concluded, were "enormously overrepresented when compared with their rate in the mass membership." Rigby found that in 1927 party officials accounted for 67 per cent of the delegates to the congress held in that year, 60 per cent in 1930, 30 per cent in 1934, and 32 per cent in 1939. His analysis revealed that as of the early 1950's those whose careers had been spent primarily in the party apparatus made up more than 50 per cent of delegates to All-Union and republic congresses. The other two main categories, each constituting between 10 and 20 per cent of the congress delegates, were, respectively, industrial employees and officials of the armed forces and the police. Somewhat more than a quarter of the delegates to the Twenty-third Congress were apparatus functionaries.

Armstrong's analysis, covering both delegates to the Ukrainian party congresses and the membership of the central committee of the communist party of the Ukraine, from 1938 to 1956, yielded results similar to those mentioned above. By far the largest group — 39 central committee members in 1938 and 42 of those on whom data were available in 1956 — were party apparatus personnel. If we add to this group the closely connected category of state and trade union officials, their predominance is overwhelming. This study, like others of its kind, indicates that the relative importance of military and police officials in the Soviet elite diminished somewhat after World War II and particularly after the death of Stalin.[22]

For a time the prominence of Marshal G. K. Zhukov, as a political ally of Khrushchev and the first genuinely professional military man to achieve full membership in the party presidium, appeared to indicate increased political influence for the military. If there was such a trend, it was abruptly reversed with Zhukov's ejection from the presidium and from his official post as Minister of Defense in October, 1957. The military elite was subordinated anew to party control, both directly by the central committee through the political administration of the armed forces and less directly by the party organizations in the armed forces. A "populist" note was injected into statements on party-army relations, just as it had been applied to relations between the party leadership and other specialist bureaucracies. It was asserted that Zhukov was attempting to seal off the officer corps from Soviet society as a whole. Satisfaction was expressed that after his removal not only officers, as before, but also rank and file military personnel became increasingly active in the military party organizations.[23] With regard to the state bureaucracy as a whole and especially its economic segments, this trend became most conspicuous upon the establishment in November, 1962 of the party-state control commission, headed by party secretariat member and former police chief A. N. Shelepin. This new body, abolished in December, 1965, apparently was intended as both a centralized, bureaucratic

22 Armstrong, *op. cit.*, p. 15. See also Pethybridge, *op. cit.*, p. 31.
23 *XXII sezd KPSS i voprosy ideologicheskoi raboty, op. cit.*, pp. 265–67.

inspectorate and a "voluntary," public organization in a nation-wide struggle for efficiency and against corruption. It replaced and combined in one agency the old committees of party control and of state control. Such developments, when we consider the Khrushchevian demand that "Leninist norms" be restored and that the boundlessly proliferating activities be organized on "public principles," might be viewed as attempts by the leadership to strengthen its position with regard to the specialized bureaucracies by mobilizing the "masses" as auxiliary support for the party apparatus.

Analyzing the record of the All-Union Central Committee elected in 1961, we find the apparatus still supreme over other categories of members. To the members and alternate members elected in 1961 (about 70 per cent of the new central committee) we add party apparatchiki engaged in the increasingly complex supervision of agriculture and also those who had spent their careers partly in party and partly in state positions, finding once again that more than half the committee members were apparatchiki. As with all the central committees, the one elected in 1961 contained many economic officials, military and police leaders, and a handful of writers, scientists, and other groups, even including a few peasants. The central committee elected by the Twenty-third Congress is very similar in makeup.

It is clear that the apparatus continues to be dominated by those referred to by Armstrong as "generalists." These generalists do start their careers with increasingly good education, however, usually in engineering. Among the leaders whose rise was associated with the establishment of Khrushchev's regime and who are high in the post-Khrushchev councils one thinks of men like Leonid Brezhnev or Vitali Titov, both educated in engineering, or Nikolai V. Podgorny, also an engineer by training, with a background in leadership of Ukrainian industrial obkoms, or Petr Demichev, a chemical engineer. On the other hand, Alexander Shelepin majored in history and philosophy. Although the top party bodies are dominated by apparatchik-generalists like Brezhnev and Podgorny or by engineer-administrators like Kosygin, they also include many men who might be classified as theoreticians and communicators. Among such figures are: Mikhail Suslov, member of the secretariat since 1947 and in length of service by far its senior member; Leonid Ilichev, secretariat member since

October, 1961, and until the March, 1965 plenum, head of the Ideological Commission; and Boris Ponomarev, also a secretariat member since October, 1961 and head of the section which supervises relations between the CPSU and nonruling communist parties. Ponomarev, as an expert on party history, took a leading part in the December, 1962 conference which instructed Soviet historians on how best to contribute to communism's world victory.[24]

Party members generally, and apparatus men in particular, have shared in the rising educational qualifications which have affected the whole of Soviet society since World War II. As of 1956, more than two million party members, it was claimed, had secondary or higher education, and the rising educational level already was causing increased emphasis on "independent" methods in the adult political study program.[25]

According to first secretary V. P. Mzhavanadze of the Georgian party, 95 per cent of the secretaries of obkoms, gorkoms, raikoms, and other significant Georgian party levels had higher education.[26] With educational improvement many older party apparatus executives had been replaced by younger persons. Mzhavanadze reported that two-thirds of the secretaries of city and other senior party committees were under forty years of age.

More and more party apparatchiki have technical education. Many, especially the younger ones, are graduates of the Higher Party School, the curriculum of which has been revised to emphasize industrial administration and technology. According to Severyn Bialer, of twenty-four members — and alternates, in the presidium — of the top party executive bodies, nine had attended advanced party schools.[27] More and more party leaders have graduate degrees. Some, including Leonid Ilichev and Boris Ponomarev, even belong to the Academy of Sciences. Also, though men like Brezhnev and Podgorny probably could be best categorized as "line" officials, these two men and others like them are closer in background and probably in general outlook to industrial administrators than were either Stalin or Khrushchev. Although Armstrong presents evidence indicating that industrial managers

24 *Pravda,* Dec. 19, 1962, prominently reported Ponomarev's speech.
25 *Spravochnik partiinogo rabotnika, op. cit.,* p. 352.
26 *Partiinaya zhizn,* No. 23, Dec., 1964.
27 "Twenty-Four Men Who Rule Russia," *The New York Times Magazine,* Nov. 1, 1964.

in the Ukraine are excluded from making decisions "outside the sphere of enterprise management itself," and, in general, are distinctly subordinate to the apparatus hierarchy, the industrial administrators' point of view is at least indirectly represented at the highest party levels through such individuals as Brezhnev.[28]

RECRUITMENT PROCEDURES

Thus far we have been concerned primarily with the Soviet elite's structure and some of its characteristics and only secondarily with its recruitment. How do Soviet citizens get ahead in the world? In attempting to answer this question we shall examine formal and informal norms, regulations, and practices. We shall look into such criteria and attainments as education, social class, nationality, and others which have influenced or have the power to influence the likelihood that an individual will be admitted into the privileged strata of Soviet society. Party, state, and other executives may be either formally elected or appointed, but in practice the appropriate party authorities select both those who are elected and those who are appointed, or at the very least exercise veto power over all matters of assigning and promoting of cadres, even those of modest political significance.

The party has always had a network of cadres or personnel officials, supervised by sections of the secretariat, the titles of which have varied. Between 1939 and 1948 the personnel agency of the central committee was called the administration for cadres. In 1948 the functions of this agency were transferred to a newly created section for party, trade union, and Komsomol organizations, called in recent years the party organs section. This section, which in the 1930's had been titled the leading party organs section, has a division for the RSFSR and another for the non-Russian republics. It is by all indications the most powerful of the central committee staff agencies, as indicated by the relatively large number of heads of the republic party organs sections in the bureaus of republic party central committees. Its power is also reflected by the careers of such powerful Soviet leaders as Ezhov, Malenkov, Ignatev, and many others, who had previously worked in the cadres agency.[29]

Overt and specific reporting of the mechanics of cadre selection

[28] Armstrong, *op. cit.,* pp. 65–68, 50–51.
[29] Conquest, *op. cit.,* p. 40.

is relatively rare in the Soviet press. An interesting event occurred at the last session of the Supreme Soviet of the Russian republic in 1959. A. B. Aristov, then deputy to Khrushchev as head of the special RSFSR party bureau (headed since its establishment in 1956 by Khrushchev himself), made the following announcement:

> In connection with the great tasks which the supreme Soviet of the RSFSR is called upon to resolve, the central committee of our party has considered it necessary that the presidium of the Supreme Soviet of the Russian Federation be headed by a leading personality from the membership of the presidium of the central committee of the communist party of the Soviet Union. The central committee of the communist party of the Soviet Union recommends that Comrade Nikolai Grigorevich Ignatov be elected to the post of chairman of the presidium of the supreme Soviet of the RSFSR.[30]

Party committees at each hierarchic level maintain a "nomenclature" (*nomenklatura*) of key party, governmental, managerial, and professional posts for the filling of which they are responsible. The positions included in the nomenclatures of party committees, because of the functions performed by their incumbents, such as directors of scientific institutes and rectors of universities, cannot normally be filled by party apparatus members. In their personnel work, as in their other controls over socially significant groups, the party committees frequently are cautioned not to "duplicate" administrative agencies' work and not to interfere too openly in the selection of personnel for the latter. These warnings reflect the apparatus' tendency, inherent in its relationship with other elite formations, to go beyond its job of over-all coordination and get too deeply involved in specialized activities. They also mirror the friction, confusion, and sometimes the evasion and resistance that result when party authorities crudely or tactlessly perform their coordinating and inspirational mission.[31]

Leadership recruitment at lower levels can be drastically affected by changes in party and state supreme leadership. A persistent Soviet political behavior pattern that certainly is not compatible with orderly personnel selection is the ability of Beria, Malenkov, Kozlov, Khrushchev, Brezhnev, Titov, Shelepin, or other apparatus titans, to staff top posts with men whose principal qualifica-

30 *Pravda*, April 17, 1959.
31 Harcave, *op. cit.*, p. 26; Rigby, *Selection of Personnel, op. cit.*, pp. 145ff.; editorial in *Partiinaya zhizn*, No. 10, May, 1964.

tions are previous acquaintance and service with them.[32] On the other hand, it is important that we realize that the party, despite high turnover and frequent destruction of human material by personal and clique rivalry, has succeeded in training and developing cadres large enough and varied enough in skills to successfully direct an increasingly complex society and to cope reasonably well with the challenge of change in the international environment.

The methods used to match personnel to problems and circumstances have sometimes been costly and indeed brutal. Even the post-Stalin system has been characterized by very rapid turnover of elite personnel. Thus, Armstrong found that officials are generally replaced after less than three years of service in major posts in the Ukrainian apparatus.[33] The Khrushchev leadership strongly emphasized the need for systematic "renewal" of leaders and there is evidence that this policy was vigorously implemented. V. M. Churaev, Khrushchev's associate in the Ukrainian apparatus, who had been elevated to head the central committee department of party organs for the RSFSR, revealed in 1959 that the annual rate of replacement of p.p.o. secretaries was 30 to 40 per cent and that only about 45 per cent of raikom first secretaries had from one to three years of experience, whereas 19 per cent had occupied their posts for less than a year. A mere fraction of 1 per cent had worked on their jobs for more than ten years. Of the department heads in the obkoms, 46.8 per cent had from one to three years of experience, 9 per cent had held their positions for five to ten years, and none had done so for more than ten. In addition, Churaev pointed out that 35 per cent of the persons elected to the supreme party bodies at the Nineteenth Congress and 41 per cent elevated at the Twentieth Congress at the time of their election were newcomers to this exalted level of the hierarchy.

Churaev made a number of other significant points. Despite growth in the membership of the party as a whole, he noted, the party apparatus was being reduced, though its significance was increasing. Churaev cited Lenin's dictum that without an apparatus there would be no party. According to items which appeared in Soviet newspapers before Churaev's article was published, the personnel of central committees of republican parties in the ob-

[32] Armstrong, *op. cit.*, pp. 146–50.
[33] *Ibid.*, p. 143.

koms had been reduced by about 40 per cent. Only a little under 9 per cent of p.p.o.'s had full-time secretaries at that time — in the remainder the party secretaries were employed in regular production or office jobs, and performed their party duties in their off-the-job hours.

One of the most significant points made by Churaev was that the practice ("frequent in the past") of nominating candidates for party committees simply because they held managerial posts, was being abandoned. He presented particularly interesting data on the Chelyabinsk party organization. This organization, with 110,-000 members, had an obkom of 115 members, about 45 of whom were employed in industrial or agricultural jobs, as collective farm chairmen, turners and fitters, combine operators, miners, etc. The remainder were "secretaries of district committees and party organizations, economic executives, trade unionists, government workers and others." [34]

The portion of Churaev's article in which he criticized the more or less automatic awarding of high posts in the apparatus to successful industrial executives was doubly significant. It clearly reflected Khrushchev's determination to expand the party's managerial and entrepreneurial function. Conversely, it was antimanagerial, and, because of Khrushchev's subsequent fate, it takes on an interesting meaning, if only in the speculative haze of hindsight, which only a few commentators attached to it at the time. Khrushchev's effort to build what Sidney I. Ploss has named the "functional" party seems to have simultaneously antagonized both apparatchiki, forced to perform functions in which they felt uneasy, and industrial managers, deprived of a status they felt was their due.

It is difficult to see in detail how the frictions within the Soviet elite caused by Khrushchev's trying to infuse new entrepreneurial dynamism into the economy reflected apparatus and managerial tensions. Another way of looking at the matter is that frictions arose mainly from a painful retraining of administrators of all kinds, especially in the effort to rid them of the habit of administration by "command," in the semimilitary Stalin style. Under Khrushchev, and since his downfall too, difficulties in properly placing and developing "young specialists" have frequently been

[34] V. M. Churaev, "Development of Inner-Party Democracy in the Soviet Union," *World Marxist Review* (June, 1959).

mentioned, indicating that differences of outlook between the older generation of executives (and workers too, perhaps) and the better educated, probably more sophisticated younger cadres pouring from the institutions of higher education into the economy, may create adjustment problems in on-the-job relations.[35]

A comparison of recruiting policies in the Stalin and post-Stalin periods, despite resemblances such as continued rapid turnover, reveals significant, indeed striking, differences. Failures in performance or for incurring the supreme leadership's displeasure are penalized far less drastically than they were when arrest, imprisonment, exile, or even execution were common. Equally important, after Stalin's death the party strove systematically to promote functionaries with superior educational qualifications and performance records. It also conspicuously favored other desired attributes, such as "a feeling for the new" and such virtues as "tact" and "consideration." Apparently those dismissed were demoted because of reduction in staff in party and state or because they did not measure up to increasingly rigorous standards. It appears that many were given more training, and employment was found for them.[36] The CPSU leadership was transformed, at least slightly, from a semimilitary command structure to something resembling a political and economic civil service.

Perhaps the party's most impressive post-Stalin attempt to better the qualifications of leading personnel in all walks of life is the improving of the leaders' education. According to a major Soviet study,

In recent years the party has carried through a great work in the strengthening of party, Soviet and economic cadres. At the present time a majority of the party cadres possess the necessary knowledge and organizational experience. More than nine tenths of the secretaries of obkoms, kraikoms, central committees of communist parties of republics and almost three quarters of the secretaries of gorkoms and raikoms have a higher education. During the last five years the number of secretaries of raikoms and gorkoms with a higher education has increased more than threefold. With every year the number of engineers, economists, agronomists and other specialists among

[35] See Abramenkov and Tolstov, *op. cit.*, pp. 26–32, and the earlier cited article in *Pravda*, Jan. 23, 1965.

[36] See article by "Correspondent" in *Manchester Guardian Weekly*, Dec. 30, 1954.

the leading party workers increases. All this has produced positive results.[37]

The demand that both party and economic officials who lacked the desired efficiency and rectitude be weeded out was intensified after the party-state reorganization began in November, 1962. P. N. Demichev, then first secretary of the Moscow city party committee, since the November, 1964 party plenum has been an alternate member of the top party organization, specializing, despite his training as a chemical engineer, in high-level supervision of art and literature. He said, "We cannot close our eyes to the fact that many of our economic executives are products of the period of the cult of the individual, and that their early years too often left their imprints upon them." [38] Some directors, he complained, were still overfond to the point of rudeness of "bureaucratic" methods, and were afraid to exercise initiative. Sometimes they simply did not wish to try to explain the logic of their recommendations and instructions.

It was reported that in spite of current improvement in the educational qualifications of managers, only 45 per cent of the directors of major industrial enterprises had a higher education.[39] There were still directors, the article continued, who did not study, who "lagged behind life" and worked by crude methods, by giving orders and "shouting."

There is much evidence that Khrushchev was successful in maintaining the "Leninist" principle of party supremacy in the selection and the composition of the elite and yet at the same time in renewing, reshaping, and reforming it so that it could better serve his program of "transition to communism" at home and competitive co-existence abroad. It seems, though, to have aroused resentment among some elite elements. Apparently some industrial bureaucrats were dismayed and discouraged by Khrushchev's antiauthoritarian policies. Some party officials lacking in technical proficiency regarded the shift in their duties from exhortation to supervisory work in the economy as "depolitization of the party" — to borrow a phrase coined by Sidney I. Ploss.[40]

37 Pigalev, *op. cit.,* pp. 35–36.
38 *Pravda,* Nov. 21, 1962.
39 *Pravda,* Dec. 8, 1962.
40 Sidney I. Ploss, "Mao's Appeal to the Soviet 'Conservatives'," mimeographed study distributed by the Center of International Studies, Princeton University, March, 1963, pp. 2–3.

Also, the party's efforts to further rationalize and systematize recruitment procedures and to equalize opportunity to enter the upper echelons, still were hampered by other problems, not directly connected with the economy, but deeply rooted in the Soviet political culture and social structure.

Especially in the non-Russian republics, the party was forced to carry on a complex struggle against "family groupings," alliances for mutual protection or reinsurance, between party executives and other bureaucrats whom the party leaders were supposed to control. It is significant that one newspaper complained that "certain party committees in economic agencies sometimes violate the Leninist principle of selecting cadres according to their political and professional qualities." [41] Instead, the paper charged, some politically immature officials attempted to base the selection of cadres on birth or personal connections. Khrushchev himself, in his major address on "The Development of the USSR Economy and the Party Guidance of the National Economy," said that deficiencies in the economic planning agencies' work sometimes resulted from such factors as "friendship and nepotism." [42] The "mutual benefit associations," often formed by officials to protect themselves against pressures from above and to achieve at least the appearance of good performance, engage in such practices as falsifying output records. In a sense these are the lower-level counterparts of the patronage cliques brought to the top by successful leaders such as Khrushchev. Since survival, not to mention success, depends heavily on skill and luck in the choice — and sometimes the discarding — of friendships and political affiliations, and since all Soviet leaders in one way or another seem to be caught up in a tangled web of such relationships, it is difficult to see how the evils associated with them and often criticized by Khrushchev and other Soviet leaders can be eliminated.

Certain large social and occupational groups are still heavily discriminated against in their representation in the executive party bodies, especially at the top. For example, though 20 per cent of the party leadership are women, there are almost no women in the CPSU central committee and none in the presidium. Although Ukrainians are no longer as obviously discriminated against as they were under Stalin, proportionately their

41 *Kazakhstanskaya pravda*, Dec. 26, 1962.
42 *Pravda*, Nov. 20, 1962.

party membership is still below their percentage in the total population. Some other nationality groups, such as those of Central Asia and, in general, the Turkic nationality groups of Moslem background, are still seriously under-represented both in the party as a whole and in the apparatus. Despite constant efforts since the death of Stalin, and especially after the Twentieth congress, to bring more ordinary workers and collective farm peasants into the party, such elements are very poorly represented in the apparatus and in the party as a whole. Of the almost 3,000,000 members added to the party between the Twentieth and Twenty-second congresses, during which period membership rose from 7,215,505 to 9,716,005, 40.7 per cent were reportedly "workers," 23.7 per cent collective farmers, and the remaining 35.6 per cent "employees and students." About two-thirds of the employees were engineers, technicians, agronomists, and other specialists.[43]

In spite of such efforts, however, the party's composition remains unbalanced in its executive-managerial-professional elements; male-dominated, urban-dominated, Russian-dominated and, above all, dominated, penetrated, controlled by, and still primarily the instrument of its self-selected apparatus core — the elite within the elite of Soviet society. This composition did not change startlingly in the first two post-Khrushchev years. According to an important article, of the more than 300,000 members of raion and higher party committees, excluding the central committee, about 36 per cent were workers and peasants, a quarter were functionaries of "party and Soviet organs," and the rest were engineers, scientists, educators, factory directors, etc.[44] Kapitonov's report to the Twenty-third Congress indicated that the largest cohesive group among the delegates were the 1,024 "party workers." The party press expressed warnings about the tendency of party organizations to strive for representation of economic leaders and specialists to the detriment of their members' "political maturity." These warnings may have been a sign of worry that the professional party functionaries might be losing their preponderant influence.

43 N. Barsukov, *Borba Partii za moshchny podem narodnogo khozyaistva* (Moscow, 1963), p. 37.
44 *Kommunist*, No. 18, Dec., 1965, pp. 38–39.

CHAPTER VII

Policy Making: Leaders, Factions, and Issues

JOSEPH STALIN wielded enormous power and inspired almost unlimited awe. So great was his stature that it seemed to many that he had forever frozen Russia into a mold of despotism and put an end to normal political life. The memory of Stalin's awesome power so gripped the minds of even Western observers that until recently most found it difficult to fully understand that for years his despotism had concealed the infinitely complex intrigue and competition for political preferment and often simply for survival raging in the Kremlin. Moreover, Stalinism left an image of a political authority with absolute sway over its subjects, having spread the belief that despotic rule was permanent in Russia. After Stalin's death, however, new information and the obvious cut-and-thrust of the Russian political contest bared by the Stalin and the Khrushchev succession crises made it clear that, even when Stalin held his greatest influence, Soviet politics had been intensely competitive, that there were sharp differences over policy alternatives and the choosing of leadership personnel. To be sure, participation in Soviet political life, most of all under Stalin, was restricted to a group far more limited and more carefully screened than in almost any other system.[1] Since Stalin's

---

[1] Some analysts, notably Boris I. Nicolaevsky, for years had called attention to the peculiarities of Soviet high politics; but the work of men like Nicolaevsky, Franz Borkenau, and other pioneer "Kremlinologists" did not, until recently, receive the attention it deserved. Many of the informed speculations of

death, however, access to the Soviet decision-making process has become somewhat less restricted and more and more groups, with increasing openness and success, have been able to champion their special interests, sometimes publicly, and to a degree, professional and bureaucratic groups have successfully resisted Kremlin pressures for conformity to the leadership's demands. No longer is one man, or even, perhaps, one group, all-powerful.

Nevertheless, the formulation and execution of national policy in the USSR is still limited to upper-level party apparatus members. At times, a wider circle of persons approved by those who control the apparatus, serve by means of consultation or support. Despite its severe and obvious limitations, the Soviet political framework has room for a variety of political groupings and styles.

Post-Stalin Soviet politics has been primarily oligarchic. It is probably true that for a long time oligarchy prevailed even under Stalin, indeed, probably until the dictator's autocratic rule was consolidated in 1936–1938. From the great purge years until Stalin's death in March, 1953 the autocratic principle, always in conflict with the oligarchic or "collective" principle which, according to doctrine, is supposed to prevail, reached its maximum development. Because of his control over education and communication, Stalin was able to make his autocracy appear to be compatible with Marxist-Leninist ideology. Of course, it is possible to fit a wide range of structures and policies to that ideology, and also to the statutes of the CPSU and the constitution of the USSR. Both basic doctrinal texts and fundamental Soviet political documents are often and in many ways highly ambiguous, imprecise, and even irrelevant to the behavior which they are used to justify or explain.

Stalin and his official theorists, such as Andrei Vyshinski, construed the formulas of Soviet politics in the fashion best suited to justify an absolutist, autocratic style of leadership. Khrushchev, despite his political apprenticeship under Stalin, oscillated during his administration between a broad, "collective," and essentially

---

Nicolaevsky, in particular, have been confirmed by Soviet revelations, e.g., those in N. S. Khrushchev's "secret speech" and in Khrushchev's open address to the 1961 party congress. The publication in 1965 of a collection of Nicolaevsky's articles, previously available only in Russian, was a major contribution to our limited store of more or less solid knowledge of Soviet elite politics. See his book, *Power and the Soviet Elite* (New York, 1965), with a thoughtful introduction by George F. Kennan.

oligarchic style and a quasi-populist, but at the same time semi-dictatorial one. One of the numerous possible reasons for Khrushchev's fall was a growing fear among high-ranking party apparatchiki that his appetite for personal power was becoming so keen that it might endanger their personal interests and even their lives. It is still more likely that his Kremlin colleagues came to feel that his erratic, whimsical moods and methods threatened to disrupt the relationships without which apparatus rule over Russia cannot persist. In particular, "conservative" party leaders may have found that Khrushchev's experiments with various kinds of "popular" participation in public administration were both inefficient and subversive toward party and state authority in the eyes of the "masses." That this finding was accurate appears to be confirmed by the post-Khrushchev downgrading of the "state of all the people" idea.

The apparent failure of Khrushchev's neo-Leninist policies renders most Western students skeptical of the prospects for early, fundamental change in the Soviet system. Well into the second year after Khrushchev's fall the unstable, conspiratorial, but growing bureaucracy which prevails in the closed circles of Soviet elite politics seems likely to persist until a broader, deeper consensus can develop in Soviet society. Such a consensus, along with disclosure of how decisions binding on the community are made and with control of that process by law, still seems remote, but certainly it is less wildly improbable than it was fifteen or twenty years ago.[2] It may have been for this reason that Khrushchev's

[2] Robert C. Tucker, in his article "The Dictator and Totalitarianism," *World Politics,* XVII (July, 1965), pp. 555–84, argues that post-Stalin politics differs sufficiently from that of the Stalin era to be "pronounced, at least provisionally post-totalitarian." Whether or not one fully shares Tucker's emphasis upon Stalin's personality as shaping Soviet politics for many years, his formulation does characterize different stages in Soviet political development and suggests the possibility that if terror can be kept long enough from dominance in Soviet politics, there may be a further gradual unshackling of politics and of society, too. It is even possible that the gradually proliferating associational interest groups (pressure groups pursuing common goals) within the dominant Mexican ruling party, the PRI, may not be entirely irrelevant to speculation about future Soviet developments. Of course, a "Mexican" development for the Soviet polity would require that the Kremlin lose far more control over the various Soviet "interest groups" than it seems likely to do in the foreseeable future, and also an accelerated decay of the official ideology. Moreover, the Russian political tradition is more authoritarian than the Mexican. Still, one is tempted to speculate about possible emergence of Soviet pressure groups by such events as the Reuter's report, published in American newspapers Dec. 12, 1965, on a Moscow student demonstration demanding a public, legal trial for the arrested writers Sinyavski and Daniel.

successors held the Twenty-third CPSU Congress earlier than the most convenient time, considering the amount of unfinished business that confronted them. Perhaps a kind of "creeping constitutionalism" is at work.

In this chapter we shall examine power and policy conflicts among various cliques and factions in the Soviet political leadership, and such connections as we may perceive between social and economic trends and top-level political alliances and alignments. Students of Soviet politics have not as yet been notably successful in recognizing relationships between factional politics, on the one hand, and social trends on the other.

CLEAVAGES BETWEEN APPARATUS AND INTELLIGENTSIA

Throughout Soviet history relations between the two great sociopolitical formations in the system, the party apparatus and the intelligentsia, have been both cooperative and antagonistic. At all times the party apparatus has striven to spur and harness to its purposes the intelligentsia's creative potential. In a very real sense, the party has created the Soviet intelligentsia, and partly for this reason its leaders feel entitled to demand fealty from Soviet intellectuals. The intelligentsia's gradual growth, in numbers and in influence, has presented the apparatus with many difficulties. Soviet leaders who have advocated very strict and severe controls over the technical and creative intelligentsia may with some accuracy be categorized as "conservatives." Such leaders stress a relatively literal interpretation of official doctrines such as "partiinost" and socialist realism. On the other hand, some leaders have been predisposed by their functions, personal inclinations, or career associations to protect individual intellectuals or groups against the encroachment of party controls, or even to promote the interests of the intelligentsia as a whole against the party apparatus' normal tendency to contain and control it. They might fairly be described as "liberals" or "moderates" or "modernizers." Stalin, assisted by his political police organization and by such trustworthy aides as the sinister Alexander Poskrebyshev, who was for many years head of his personal secretariat, fought a by no means wholly successful battle to contain the increasing influence of the intelligentsia as a whole and of various groups within it. In many ways Khrushchev outwardly continued Stalin's anti-intelligentsia policies. He emphasized popular participation in administration, lacked sympathy with some Soviet lawyers who were trying to introduce in Russia a legal system of the Western type, and he tried, particularly in his educational reform of 1958–1959, to curb the growing privileges of the Soviet "new class." All of this leads us to think of him as a communist conservative or traditionalist — or perhaps it would be more correct to say that in his political outlook there was a strong streak of ideological revivalism.

Khrushchev pursued his objectives, however, apparently believing that they would ultimately lead to true Leninist goals, but the means he employed were very different from those used by Stalin. He had more confidence in the basic loyalty of all Soviet social elements to the Soviet system, including the intelligentsia, than his extraordinarily mistrustful and suspicious predecessor was capable of. Particularly after his victory over Malenkov, Molotov, and the rest of the "anti-party group," he sought active and willing support from the intelligentsia's progressive elements, apparently without great success. It was difficult for him to rally the intelligentsia behind him because of his crude personality and because some of his most fundamental policies threatened, or appeared to threaten, the interests of the privileged strata of Soviet society, to which, after all, the upper-income, highest-ranking intellectuals also belonged. Khrushchev also seems to have antagonized many party apparatus men because, despite his emphasis upon party supremacy over the other Soviet hierarchies, he tried to force the party to perform day-to-day administrative functions, lessening, it seemed to them, its ability to effectively exercise its traditional jobs, over-all control and indoctrination. In 1962, apparatus discontent became acute when he split the party into industrial and agricultural segments, causing great confusion and anxiety. He apparently lost whatever mass popularity he had enjoyed earlier in his leadership because in the early 1960's his at first rather successful agricultural experiments failed. Finally, his foreign policy frustrations, following initial successes, probably sapped his prestige in Soviet society, and were particularly irritating to the Soviet military establishment and their hard-line party allies. Failure is likely to be at least as costly to those upon whom the onus for it can be pinned in the Soviet system as in any other — unless its perpetrator is a dictator so powerful that even covert and muffled criticism carries a prohibitive price.

Access to participation in the political process is crucial to the Soviet system's future development and most important is the possibility of widening legitimate participation. Khrushchev failed to build a personal terror machine, and permitted and even encouraged broader participation in national policy making. To muster support for policies at which traditionalist party and state leaders looked askance, and to project his image as a leader concerned about public opinion, Khrushchev brought into top-level decision-making many more persons than had taken part in it under Stalin, drawing them from fairly diverse elite circles. It is almost certain that having eliminated terror as the basic instrument of social control, the top leaders in party and state, and perhaps also the top ruling bodies collectively, must widen the consensus upon which legitimate power must rest. Indeed, the reduced political use of terror has already brought about looser and weaker central controls over Soviet society.

We have now run into another fundamental problem: access and participation in Soviet politics are peculiar and limited, but in a sense politics of any kind is only partially legitimate, at least in theory, so long as Russia is ruled by men who subscribe to Marxism-Leninism. Soviet official doctrine offers no explicit theory to account for the Soviet version of what Western democratic theory regards as political man's normal proclivity to bargain, connive, and organize for group and individual advantage. This utopian myth does not and cannot prevent a strenuous and sometimes deadly political game from being played. It can partially conceal by euphemistic descriptions activities not compatible with ideological fictions. This stifling atmosphere inhibits scholarship in the social, legal, and political sciences. Thus Marxist-Leninist doctrine, by curbing critical analysis and free public discussion of politics, keeps alive political practices which would not be tolerated in a society which had no official political creed, and in which men had more nearly equal access to political influence and trusted one another more than Soviet citizens do.

It is vitally necessary that we recognize clearly and fully the differences between Soviet-style politics and the politics of the "open society," or the "civic culture." On the other hand, these differences should not be over-emphasized lest we forget that bargaining, the forming and dissolving of aggregations and coalitions, and the other universal political phenomena are ever present on the Soviet scene, even if barely visible. Even the highly defective Soviet source materials available to us, when closely studied, reveal that various leaders take broadly different approaches to fundamental domestic and foreign policy problems. Often these policies point to conflicting interests and preferences of rival cliques and factions ("factionalism" is so frequently criticized in Soviet sources that one suspects it is rife). As a rule, major policy disputes reflect conflicts of interest among combinations of powerful leaders drawn from a number of groups and chains of command. In other words, political alignments cut across formal patterns of organization. They do not often involve antagonism between the party apparatus and the majority of military leaders or well organized, cohesive groupings of rebellious writers, but rather involve tensions between, let us say, "modernizers" and "conservatives" or between "revisionists" and "dogmatists." They are also influenced, often, by the universal tendency of leaders and administrators to identify their own functional or administrative requirements with "higher" community and regime interests.

Personality clashes and power rivalries among leaders, the exigencies of adjustment involved in shifts of top leadership, such technological developments as atomic energy, automation, and computers, the shifting pressures of the international environment — these and many other factors affect the Soviet political system and alter the relationships among its actors, whose fortunes depend upon its workings. It is even possible that in time changing attitudes and relationships among the groups shaping the policy process could fundamentally alter the system. If such changes were to occur they eventually would be reflected in the structure and staffing of political institutions — for example, in the relations between party and state bureaucracies and the relative status of members of these two groups, as well as in the content and interpretation of doctrine. Although in political forecasting caution remains the better part of valor, particularly in Soviet affairs, the more accurately we can identify the players, rules, and strategies in the Soviet political game the more intelligently sensitive we may be to new and significant features.

Although there is still no fully developed theory of the Soviet or other political systems, our understanding is facilitated by a number of research accomplishments of recent years. We have made progress in identifying the major groups and persons in Soviet politics, the relative changes in power of the various groups, and the ways in which that power might change much more dramatically in the future.[3] Soviet studies have benefited not only by the application of group analysis but also by the perception — brilliantly exemplified in Barrington Moore's *Terror and Progress* — of underlying social trends, particularly in elite recruitment. Moore's three-part formula, identifying "power," "tradition," and "technical rationality," explains many policy and group relationships. Finally, Gabriel A. Almond's concept of "political capabilities," dealing with the relationship between political systems and their responses to internal and external environments, is most useful. We shall discuss its applicability to the forecasting of Soviet political behavior in our concluding chapter. Both Moore and Almond stress that policy modes are interdependent and how unlikely it is that all lines of policy will be developed simultaneously by any particular political leadership. Almond's broad categories, identifying the "regulatory," "distributive," and "responsive" capabilities of political systems seem particularly useful in sorting out the broad alternative policy "styles" in all political systems, including the Soviet one. Incidentally, the expression "style of work" recently has been used often by Soviet leaders, at the 1966 CPSU congress, especially.

Perhaps the most comprehensive categorization of "focuses of internal conflict within the Soviet system," and the groups engaged therein, is that of Rigby, who attempted in 1963 to refute

[3] Besides the studies by Robert Conquest and Roger Pethybridge, among the most valuable contributions to this literature are Thomas H. Rigby's article, "The Extent and Limits of Authority," *Problems of Communism*, XII, No. 5 (Sept.–Oct., 1963), pp. 36–41, and his article entitled "Crypto-Politics," in *Survey* (Jan., 1964), pp. 183–94; Myron Rush, "The Khrushchev Succession Crisis," *World Politics*, XV (Jan., 1962), pp. 259–82, and the series of "Occasional Papers on Soviet Politics" by Sidney I. Ploss. The papers distributed in mimeographed form by the Center of International Studies, Princeton University, will be referred to hereafter by number. Ploss has applied his "conflict" approach to the making of Soviet agricultural policy, particularly to "conservative" opposition to Khrushchev, in his *Conflict and Decision-Making in Soviet Russia* (Princeton, 1965). This study enlightens us on Khrushchevian pseudo-democratic, "utilitarian," and "empiricist" practices to which, several years before his fall, tradition-minded apparatus leaders had taken violent exception. Also pertinent is Marshall D. Shulman's *Stalin's Foreign Policy Reappraised* (Cambridge, Mass., 1963), which identifies relationships between Soviet foreign and domestic policy and the policy moves of Western nations, particularly the United States. See also Shulman's brief study, *Beyond the Cold War* (New Haven, 1966).

enthusiastic views projecting a relatively pluralistic image of Soviet politics. He listed twelve competitive or antagonistic relationships:

1. Between the principal leader (at present Khrushchev) and secondary leaders who have a common interest in setting limits to the former's power.

2. Between different individuals (and "groupings"?) within the secondary leadership, competing for influence over the principal leaders.

3. Between different aspirants for succession to the principal leader.

4. Between the inner leadership and the larger bodies from which its power formally derives: *e.g.,* Government Presidium *versus* Council of Ministers, and especially Party Presidium *versus* the Central Committee ("anti-party Group"), (1957).

5. Between subordinate officials and the occupants of superior echelons, whose posts they covet. This applies, for instance, to younger officials aspiring to positions like obkom secretaryships, which carry Central Committee status; to officials with Central Committee status aspiring to admission to the Presidium; to functionaries in the republics aiming at the republican leadership; to ministers and government committee chairmen coveting deputy premierships; and so on.

6. Between different sections of the bureaucracy, *i.e.,* between its major divisions [the party, the state administration, the army, and so on] or between particular units [*e.g.,* state production committees *versus* Gosplan departments *versus* sovnarkhozes; or raikoms *versus* Kolkhoz Production Directorates (1962); or the Party Presidium *versus* the secretariat (1957) or the Government Presidium (1953–1954?); or between different production branch units (*vedomstvennyi podkhod*)].

7. Between informal groupings of officials, usually based on past career associations and involving patron-client relationships, and either focussed on particular formal units or hierarchies or cutting across the formal structure.

8. Between the interests of one area and another, and between local and national interests (*mestnichestvo*).

9. Within groups entrusted with purveying different values (the arts, national culture, science, and even the official ideology), over the forms of orthodoxy; and between the purveyors of these values and the political leadership over the extent of the former's autonomy and influence over policy.

10. Between those cherishing such values and the official purveyors of them.

11. Between different occupational and skill groups over distribution of the national cake.

12. Between the "masses," valuing consumption, leisure, security and freedom, and the regime, valuing production, national power, development, and discipline.[4]

Of course we should not infer from this useful catalogue that disintegrative tendencies are likely to overbalance the powerful creativity, consensus, integration, and constraint contributing to the Soviet system's stability, persistence, and power. No responsible specialist would predict either civil war or a Soviet polity transformed into a constitutional democracy. It was pointed out long ago by Boris I. Nicolaevsky, and more recently by Robert Conquest, Roger Pethybridge, Carl Linden, Sidney Ploss, and Robert C. Tucker, among others, that in Soviet politics conflict over power and policy is "a fundamental, normal, and centrally important fact." [5]

It is also clear that in the Soviet world the ruling few and the elite as a whole still hold so much power over the "masses" that the supposed preferences of such large, unorganized social groups as workers, collective farmers, or the non-Russian nationalities probably have little effect on the political strategies of competing factions and bureaucratic cliques. Indeed, without political competition, relatively unrestricted social science research, and other channels for articulating and gauging public attitudes, it is probably difficult for the party leadership itself to adequately appraise Soviet "public opinion" at any given time. It does, though, constantly try to do so by using party, police, and other information-gathering channels, and increasingly by using various attitude surveys. In spite of continued party dictatorship, however, the still only partially articulated demands of the less privileged strata of Soviet society, especially for better goods and services, and the intelligentsia's desire that political and ideological controls be relaxed, have been better received by the post-Stalin regime, distinguishing it from Stalinist autocracy. Also, popular welfare has been involved in top-level power struggles. It is almost in-

---

[4] *Ibid.*, p. 36.
[5] The quotation is from Robert C. Tucker's "The 'Conflict Model'" in *Problems of Communism*, XII, No. 6 (Nov.–Dec., 1963), p. 59.

extricably associated with "peace" issues, such as the proper attitude toward a "detente" with the United States *versus* the Stalinist policy of achieving maximum state power by building the largest possible armaments and heavy industry. In his struggle with Malenkov, Khrushchev's position was closer to that of Stalin than was Malenkov's; and he successfully exploited the issue in wooing support among the Soviet military. But once he had thus consolidated his power, Khrushchev shifted to a policy whose rhetoric at least was more "revisionist" than that of Malenkov.[6]

SOVIET POWER STRUGGLE PARTICIPANTS

Among the many possible interactions between power struggles and policy formation in the Soviet Union the following are particularly significant: (1) the struggle among top-level politicians for dictatorial power, or for first place in a "collective" leadership, and the relationships between the dictator and potential heirs to his position; (2) the institutions of decision making and policy implementation within the dictatorship and the shifting balance of power and functions among them, as between the party presidium and the central committee, etc.; (3) difficulty in agreement and disagreement on major policy lines, for example between a stressing of heavy industry and a program directed more at consumers; (4) the part to be played in national politics by functional bureaucratic and other interest groups, such as the officer corps or the writers; (5) the interactions among regime policies; and (6) the attitudes and interests of the large, relatively unorganized social groups such as the "workers." Let us examine each major area in some detail, beginning with a very brief survey of Stalin's time.

All that is known about Stalin's dictatorship justifies the view that Stalin came about as close as is humanly possible to achieving absolute power, including the ability to commit a great state and an international ideological movement to life and death decisions. Stalin's power was vividly confirmed by the British political scientist John Erickson, reporting conversations in Mos-

[6] A good treatment of this and other issues in the Malenkov-Khrushchev struggle is contained in Pethybridge, *op. cit.;* see also Carl Linden, "Conflict and Authority: A Discussion," *Problems of Communism,* XII, No. 5 (Sept.–Oct., 1963), pp. 27–35, esp. pp. 29–30, and the contributions by Linden, Robert C. Tucker, and Wolfgang Leonhard to the continued discussion initiated by Linden's above article, in *Problems of Communism,* XII, No. 6 (Nov.–Dec., 1963). Myron Rush, in analyzing the succession problem cited above, also deals interestingly with political applications of policy differences regarding the allocation of resources.

cow with Soviet officials in 1963. The latter told Erickson that during the Soviet-German war Stalin directed combat operations by telephone calls to the fronts. During the final stages of the war, they added, "Stalin watched with unrelenting attention, imposing his decisions as he saw fit." [7]

It is often forgotten, though, that in its early stage Stalin's regime represented the triumph of one faction or a group of factions in the party apparatus over other factions, and that revulsion and resentment against his methods and policies, though suppressed and silenced, persisted throughout his reign. After Stalin's death Khrushchev (in his "secret" speech and in greater detail at the Twenty-second Party Congress) and other Soviet leaders, especially Anastas I. Mikoyan as well as journalists and scholars, publicly revealed political cleavages in elite circles. These had been suppressed by Stalin, though they were known to many inside Russia and were perceptively analyzed by knowledgeable outsiders such as Franz Borkenau and Boris Nicolaevsky. The following paragraph in the 1963 edition of the official party history is particularly significant:

> By the time of the Seventeenth Party Congress the cult of personality of Stalin had gradually taken shape. All of the successes achieved by the party and the people in the building of socialism had been associated with his name. Exceptionally fulsome praise of his services was manifested at the congress. Having become convinced of his infallibility, Stalin more and more departed from Leninist principles and norms of party life, violating the principle of collective leadership, withdrawing from the masses, and permitting his office to be abused. More and more forcefully were displayed the negative traits of his character: Rudeness, lack of loyalty toward leading party workers, intolerance of criticism, disregard for the collective opinion, the settling of problems by administrative methods. The abnormal situation which developed in the party in connection with the cult of personality gave rise to alarm among some communists, especially among the old Leninist cadres. Many delegates of the congress, particularly those who were acquainted with the testament of V. I. Lenin, considered that the time had come to remove Stalin from the post of General Secretary [of the party central committee] and transfer him to other work. [8]

[7] *Problems of Communism*, XII, No. 6 (Nov.–Dec., 1963), p. 53.
[8] *Istoriya kommunisticheskoi partii sovetskogo soyuza* (Moscow, 1963), p. 486. See also the article by L. Shaumyan on the twentieth anniversary of the seven-

That Khrushchev revealed that there was opposition within the party to Stalin and condemned its suppression had more than merely historical significance. It probably constituted acknowledgement (albeit retrospective) of clashing interests and opinions within the Khrushchev-led presidium and central committee. It also implicitly sanctioned the relationship between these bodies and the top party leader which was shortly to be turned against Khrushchev himself. As pointed out in Chapter I, the anonymous criticisms of the unnamed former leader after his fall in 1964 accused his predilection for a cult of personality, violation of the collective leadership principle, etc. An incidental irony of Khrushchev's critique of Stalinist political behavior was Khrushchev's attempt to retrospectively associate his name with the anti-Stalinist, "Leninist" members of the 1934 central committee — contradicting evidence in the stenographic report of the Seventeenth Congress that, more vociferously than most other delegates, Khrushchev extolled Stalin as a "leader of genius" and as the continuator of the work of Lenin.

One reason for Stalin's purges in 1936–1938 was his realization that respected party leaders such as Nikolai Bukharin, who opposed Stalin's terror and especially his brutal treatment of the peasantry, and also differed sharply from Stalin in interpreting fascism's international political significance, still enjoyed wide support in the CPSU. Perhaps Stalin feared that such leaders could interfere with the foreign policies on which he was preparing to embark, especially that in regard to Spain, and possibly even that they were a threat to his power.[9]

During and even after World War II, when victory over Nazi

teenth CPSU congress in *Pravda*, Feb. 7, 1964, which criticizes Stalin even more frankly than the above. Shaumyan accuses Stalin of eliminating the majority of the central committee elected by the 1934 party congress, and also of "destroying" more than a thousand delegates elected to that congress. He clearly identifies S. M. Kirov and his supporters as the true representatives of majority opinion in the party, and makes it clear that in his opinion Stalin led a minority faction opposed to truly "Leninist" policies. For a discussion of some doctrinal elements of Stalin's — and Lenin's — attitudes toward political opposition, see Frederick C. Barghoorn, "Soviet Political Doctrine and the Problem of Opposition," *Bucknell Review*, XII, No. 2 (May, 1964), pp. 1–29, esp. pp. 1–3, 11–16. It is significant that articles on Kirov, Vlas Chubar, and other victims of Stalin's "cult of personality," published shortly before the Twenty-third Congress, omitted indications that Stalin had done them in.

9 See the impressive analysis by Robert M. Slusser, "The Role of the Foreign Ministry," in Ivo J. Lederer, ed., *Russian Foreign Policy* (New Haven, Conn., 1962), pp. 218–27, and also George F. Kennan, *Russia and the West* (Boston, 1960), pp. 306–309.

Germany had won for Stalin unprecedented power and prestige, the dictator still considered it necessary to take prophylactic measures against potential challenges to his authority. Having hitherto held no governmental posts, except for the honorific one of Supreme Soviet deputy, Stalin decided six weeks before the USSR entered World War II to become chairman of the Council of People's Commissars, or chief of the Soviet government. During the war's first few weeks he also became chairman of the State Defense Committee and Commissar of Defense. In the autumn of 1941 he was named commander-in-chief of the Soviet armed forces, and finally, on June 26, 1945, he acquired the title of Generalissimo.[10] Thus Stalin moved to prevent the state and military bureaucracies from acquiring the administrative and political powers which their expanded functions and the national preoccupation with the war might have brought had he not taken these precautions. Even more striking were Stalin's moves following the end of the European war. These included his reminder to Soviet military commanders on the occasion of his famous toast to the Russian people, May 24, 1945, that a good foreign policy was as valuable as two or three army corps and his granting in July, 1945 of all rights and privileges of the Soviet army to political police personnel. Along with the latter act, Lavrenti Beria, then in charge of security matters, was elevated to Marshal of the Soviet Union. These and other related measures, including the removal of Marshal G. K. Zhukov from his post in Moscow to obscure provincial commands, reminded the Soviet army officer corps and other groups that severe repression would be visited upon those whom Stalin might suspect were disloyal or lacking in proper enthusiasm. At the same time, these actions indicated that Stalin was aware of the potentialities inherent in the social and occupational pluralism underlying Soviet political monolithism.

There is abundant evidence that Stalin's most ambitious and powerful lieutenants, while energetically serving him and outwardly professing unbounded loyalty to him, intrigued and maneuvered for his favor, for their own personal security, and also for backing for their preferred policies. Kremlin intrigue often sent repercussions throughout the Soviet land. From No-

10 John A. Armstrong, *The Politics of Totalitarianism* (New York, 1961), p. 148.

vember, 1951 to April, 1953 the upper levels of the communist apparatus in the Georgian Soviet Republic were rocked by purges and counterpurges reflecting Beria's vicissitudes in Moscow.[11]

The central thread of Soviet high politics between the Eighteenth Party Congress in March, 1939 and Stalin's death thirteen years later was Georgi Maksimilianovich Malenkov's struggle to get himself into a position which would assure his succession to Stalin. This story is obscure in many ways, as is always true in Soviet high politics, but its principal features are now visible. Malenkov, a well-educated man of culture, was above all a Kremlin "insider." In 1925 he began a career of uninterrupted service in the central committee apparatus. By 1939 he had achieved membership in the party secretariat. A specialist on personnel matters, he knew intimately the workings of the party and other bureaucracies, and was very close to security chief Beria. Malenkov also, so far as can be known, was inclined to value organizational efficiency and industrial productivity over ideological zeal.[12] It is true that Malenkov did not become a member of Stalin's politburo until 1946, and in seniority in that key body he was outranked by both Andrei A. Zhdanov and Nikita Khrushchev, both of whom became politburo members in 1939. He was probably the most influential leader after Stalin during almost the whole of the twelve years from the organization of the State Defense Committee on June 30, 1941, until Stalin's death, except for about a year in 1946–1947 during which he was deprived of his position as a member of the central committee secretariat.

Malenkov served on the State Defense Committee, which was headed by Stalin and which included such figures as V. M. Molotov, Anastas Mikoyan, Nikolai Bulganin, and other top leaders, and to which Khrushchev and Zhdanov never belonged. From Malenkov's return to the secretariat in 1948 he was the only leader besides Stalin with membership in the three main executive bodies of the Soviet political system — politburo, secretariat, and council of ministers. He delivered the major address at the Nineteenth Party Congress in October, 1952, indicating that he was still Stalin's heir presumptive. Besides Malenkov and general

[11] Conquest, *op. cit.*, Ch. VII, gives a masterful account of these events.
[12] See his biography in *Politicheski slovar* (Moscow, 1940), p. 326, and the sketches of him in Pethybridge, *op. cit.*, pp. 24, 26–28, and Conquest, *op. cit.*, pp. 79–109, 127, 185–86.

secretary Stalin, who saw to it that his own part in the proceedings far overshadowed those of all others (even though he did not deliver the main address for the first time since 1924), the other main speaker at the Nineteenth Party Congress was Khrushchev. By 1950, when Khrushchev was head of the party's Moscow obkom, he had apparently been selected by Stalin as a counterweight to Malenkov's power, or, as Myron Rush put it, as "counter-heir."

Until Andrei A. Zhdanov's death on August 31, 1948, however, not Khrushchev — who was serving as First Secretary of the Ukrainian Republic Party Organization — but Zhdanov was Malenkov's principal rival. A veteran apparatchik like Malenkov, Zhdanov since 1934 had headed the Leningrad obkom. For a time before the war and also during the few years which remained to him after World War II, Zhdanov headed the central committee department in charge of propaganda. It is evident that Zhdanov represented those in the party apparatus who gave highest priority among the tasks facing the party in the years immediately after the war to restoring strict ideological orthodoxy and conformity. In the international communist movement, he supported men like Marshal Tito of Yugoslavia, who at that time pressed for vigorous communist expansion, rather like Chinese communist policy after 1957.

It is not known whether Zhdanov should be credited with policy formation or should be seen merely as the exponent of policies which Stalin found it expedient to adopt for a time.[13] The so-called "Leningrad Case" is particularly significant because of what it reveals about Stalinist politics and because of its place in the post-Stalin succession struggle. In 1948–1949 a number of Zhdanov's close associates in the top party and state echelons were purged. Among the major victims were the politburo member, economist, and author, N. A. Voznesenski, central committee secretary A. A. Kuznetsov, the chairman of the Council of Ministers of the Russian Republic, N. I. Rodionov, and the secretary of the Leningrad obkom, P. S. Popkov. It was characteristic of this affair and of what it represents that V. M. Andrianov's role in it appears to have been important. The available evidence

[13] *Politicheski slovar, op. cit.,* p. 188; Armstrong, *Politics of Totalitarianism, op. cit.,* pp. 177–79, 193–201; Leonard Schapiro, *The Communist Party of the Soviet Union* (New York, 1959), pp. 507–10, 528–33.

links him to Malenkov, and he replaced Popkov as first secretary of the Leningrad obkom in February, 1949.

In September, 1953, Andrianov was removed from control of the Leningrad party organization, apparently because of the sharpening Malenkov-Khrushchev rivalry.[14] The obscure intrigues in which Andrianov figured illustrate the materials with which analysts of Soviet high policy (frequently referred to as "Kremlinologists") must work. In the kind of political analysis which Soviet source materials render inevitable, close attention must be given to: shifts in important party bodies, the amount and content of publicity given to this or that key figure, treatment in the press and in historical, political, and philosophical journals of institutions such as the State Defense Committee, or shifting formulas for ideological programs like the "Transition to Communism." Thus, Brezhnev's trip to the city of Gorki in September, 1965, to personally preside over the election of K. F. Katushev as head of the important Gorki oblast party organization, reflected the Moscow leader's increasing authority. Of course, Katushev's failure to win election to the steering committee of the Twenty-third Congress raised Kremlinologists' eyebrows.

The capricious execution of the Zhdanovites marked one stage in the covert struggle among Stalin's lieutenants. It was also one event among many in Stalin's last few years which led up to the ominous "doctors' plot" allegations.[15] The Tass announcement of this fabricated conspiracy stated that physicians who had treated some of the most eminent party, state, and military leaders had been arrested for criminal malpractice and for plotting, in collusion with Israel and the United States, to "wipe out the leading cadres of the USSR." It probably was intended to signal a new purge, perhaps as terrible as those of 1936–1938. Stalin's ability to plan such operations, together with his practice of dividing his politburo into various committees to deal with such matters as the dictator saw fit, never even inviting some politburo members to meetings (which Khrushchev denounced in his "secret speech" in 1956), indicate the kind of political regime inherited by his successors.

It is plausible to assume that the little band of at first badly frightened men who took power on March 6, 1953, were agreed

[14] Conquest, *Power and Policy, op. cit.,* pp. 95–96, 231–32.
[15] Reported in *Pravda,* Jan. 13, 1953.

that there must be an end to the reign of terror under which even the highest Soviet leaders had lived. On the other hand, it was inevitable that a political elite and a citizenry accustomed to the subservience which Stalin had so long exalted could, at best, move haltingly toward a less coercive and more responsive politics.

Before turning to post-Stalin Soviet politics, we shall indicate some connections between the events just summarized and the general analysis applied in this chapter. These events show that, even under Stalin, struggles for power simmered and sometimes boiled up. It is clear that under Stalin bureaucratic cliques conducted a struggle, mostly covert, for the dictator's favor. Their rivalries and intrigues became intertwined with policy disputes. Considering the importance Khrushchev gave to the Ukrainian and Leningrad party organizations, it is significant that the Leningrad organization was a major base of Zhdanov's power. If after Stalin's death one line of cleavage in apparatus politics appeared between Kiev and Leningrad, it appears that in the late Stalin years there was a similar cleavage between the Leningrad party organization and the Stalin-Beria party and police machine, staffed mostly by Georgians.[16]

Post-Stalin interest aggregation and articulation, and its effect on political structures and practices, may be most conveniently described in three phases. The first phase, from Stalin's death until Khrushchev's defeat of the "anti-party group" in June, 1957 has been characterized as an "interregnum," as a period of dual party-state power, or, more accurately, as the period of the Stalin succession crisis. During the second phase, from July, 1957 until some point difficult to determine with precision, Khrushchev ruled Russia. He may have done so as a dictator, but both personal inclinations and circumstances imposed limitations upon him which sharply differentiated his leadership from that of Stalin. A third phase clearly began with Khrushchev's fall. Since in comparison with the other two it is as yet brief, it would not be appropriate to discuss it in detail, although in this chapter and in the Postscript to Chapter X we have tried to characterize it. This third post-Khrushchev phase of Soviet politics has been marked thus far by the conspicuous absence of any leader whose stature or influence on his colleagues or country are comparable

---

[16] See the observations on this phenomenon in Armstrong, *Politics of Totalitarianism, op. cit.,* pp. 200–202.

to those of Lenin or Stalin, or perhaps even to that of Khrushchev. Pygmies appear to have succeeded to giants, although time will tell how this impression corresponds to reality and how much it masks our ignorance about the new leaders. Also, it is possible that, as suggested earlier, power slowly is beginning to diffuse, leading to what Barrington Moore once called the "bureaucratic state," which eventually will reach its full development.

Such a development might be characterized by a reaching for support by the top political leaders to lower party apparatus levels and also to the managerial, military, scientific, and other communities; by relative caution and pragmatic experiment in domestic and foreign policy; or by relative leniency on the part of victors in political struggles toward their competitors. It might also be marked by further reduction in the use of violence throughout society and by modest progress toward the "rule of law" in regulating relations among bureaucratic chains of command and between the state and the citizenry. Even these speculations presuppose other speculative assumptions, such as Soviet avoidance of large-scale international military operations.

Beria and Malenkov, Khrushchev's most powerful rivals in the struggle for Stalin's mantle, shared his general preference for looser, milder integration and control. All three differed notably in this respect from Lazar Kaganovich and Vyacheslav Molotov, and perhaps also from some important second-rank leaders like Mikhail Suslov and Frol Romanovich Kozlov. Some major differences between this pattern and that of the Stalin era can be sketched here.[17] Although centralized controls and coercive social mobilization were carried over from the Stalin era, the differences between that time and the post-Stalin period are sufficient to cause one to ask why Stalin's terroristic dictatorship survived as long as it did. Stalin's peculiar personality, in its mingled astuteness and ruthlessness, has seldom been equaled, and obviously is a possible answer. Also, Stalin had achieved supreme leadership at an early and vigorous age, and so had been able

[17] Conquest, *Power and Policy, op. cit.*, pp. 178–83, presents evidence indicating that Suslov, Kozlov, and other relatively junior leaders, including A. B. Aristov, had been selected by Stalin as key members of a new apparatus intended to replace that in which Malenkov, Beria, and Khrushchev were still dominant.

to devote many years to unrelentingly consolidating his power and fashioning an environment for its exercise.

The very success of Stalin's regime, in which complicity in actions which Khrushchev himself would later call crimes, and servile obeisance to the ruler, were required for survival, must have militated against any individual's developing the character and the personal authority necessary to replace Stalin. Myron Rush points out a broader consideration: Neither Lenin nor Stalin succeeded in selecting his successor, and it appears from the record that in the Soviet type of political system there is no clearly defined institutional pattern for either locating supreme authority or assuring an orderly succession. Whoever is to become the supreme leader must win his position by emerging victorious from a political struggle. In the Stalin succession crisis the victor was a leader high in the councils of the regime but, among the various contenders, he was least deeply implicated in the dictator's more sinister machinations. Perhaps the most important reason for the changed tone of Soviet political life after Stalin's death and one which shaped the post-Stalin period, was the increasing complexity and "modernization" of Soviet society, resulting from continuous and rapid economic and technological progress. As Wolfgang Leonhard has pointed out, the system established by Stalin and his followers in the late 1920's and early 1930's had become obsolete even before Stalin's death. Leonhard adds that "it was essential to free the party and state bureaucracy, the officer corps, the intelligentsia, as well as workers and kolkhoz farmers, from the fear that was crippling them, and give them at least some measure of personal security and a chance for personal initiative, if Soviet society was to progress." [18] To these underlying factors we should add the situation in the last years of Stalin's lifetime, as already described, and the probably increasing realization in the top levels of the Soviet elite that the USSR could not compete successfully with the Western "capitalist" powers without effecting important internal changes. Then it becomes easier to understand both the resolution of the Stalin succession crisis and the contrast between the Stalin and post-Stalin eras.

[18] Wolfgang Leonhard, "Internal Developments: A Balance Sheet," *Problems of Communism,* XII, No. 2 (March–April, 1963), p. 7. A similar thesis, but within a Marxist framework, was advanced by Isaac Deutscher in his provocative book, *Russia What Next?,* published about a month after Stalin's death.

Why did Khrushchev win the Stalin succession struggle and what were the main meanings of his victory? Broadly, Khrushchev won because his personality and skills, his career associations, and his political values enabled him to mobilize an effective majority of the upper-level party apparatus against the coalition of Malenkov, Molotov, Kaganovich, and other party presidium members who opposed him. This struggle is sufficiently well known to require only brief treatment. First of all, it is necessary to explain why Beria was so quickly eliminated from the ruling circle. Beria, together with Malenkov, and without consulting the other members of such top party and state bodies as the presidium or the council of ministers, had undertaken to allot the principal posts in the government which took office immediately after Stalin's death.[19] This action apparently aroused resentment and fear of Beria and also of Malenkov, particularly in Khrushchev's mind. The party leadership as a whole seemed united against Beria after the show of force by the police troops under his command around Moscow on the day of Stalin's funeral. Another reason was his attempt to gain support among the non-Russian nationalities by seeking to remove party leaders like L. G. Melnikov, head of the Ukrainian Republic party organization at the time of Stalin's death and for some time thereafter, on charges of "russification."[20] The specific pretext for Beria's destruction appears to have been the uprising in East Germany in June, 1953, which was blamed on him as the Soviet leader in over-all charge of security matters both in the Soviet Union and in Eastern Europe. The more fundamental causes were fears and vulnerabilities associated with his long career in the secret police. Beria's fall and the arrest and execution of many of his associates in 1953 and 1954 removed an important contender in the struggle for succession. They also signaled a drastic diminution in the autonomy and power of the political police in Soviet politics and in society generally. After Beria and his associate M. D. Bagirov were liquidated, the police were no longer represented in the party presidium, and in the central committee their representation was limited to I. A. Serov,

[19] Pethybridge, *op. cit.,* presents impressive evidence on this point. See esp. pp. 34–35 and 61.

[20] Armstrong, *Politics of Totalitarianism, op. cit.,* pp. 236–37, points out that although Melnikov's removal represented an attack on the Ukrainian party apparatus, it seems more likely that Melnikov himself was an adherent of Malenkov rather than Khrushchev.

who became head of the Committee of State Security, established in March, 1954. Serov was not re-elected to either full or alternate membership in the central committee elected in 1961. But his successor, A. N. Shelepin, who held the post of chairman of the KGB, the Soviet political police organization, from his replacement of Serov in 1958 until his promotion to the party secretariat in October, 1961, as well as Vladimir Semichastny, who replaced Shelepin as police head at that time, were elected, respectively, to full and candidate membership in the 1961 central committee. Shelepin and Semichastny are, however, party rather than professional police officials. The power of the police diminished in other ways, which will be discussed in Chapter VIII. In general, it ceased to be an instrument by which the dictator controlled the party and became only one of the instruments by which the party maintained its control over state and society.

The most important reason for Malenkov's defeat in the succession struggle, probably, was his close involvement, together with Beria and Stalin, in such episodes as the "Leningrad Case." Khrushchev, at first by innuendo and later openly, used that connection against him. Another factor that counted against Malenkov was his relative lack of political and administrative experience outside of Moscow. Unlike Khrushchev, he was unable to build up a large following among the territorial party secretaries. Conversely, Khrushchev's experience as a party officer in the field in the Ukrainian party organization probably gave him the advantage of wide acquaintance among territorial party leaders, especially in the Ukraine, and also a superior, highly useful understanding of the mentality of such people.

In the Khrushchev-Malenkov struggle a crucial factor was Malenkov's resignation from the secretariat of the CPSU on March 13, 1953. Malenkov as a result had to rely upon the state apparatus as his principal base of power, whereas Khrushchev was able to repeat Stalin's performance in utilizing the party secretariat as a springboard to supreme power. Why did Malenkov, voluntarily, it seems, surrender this advantage to his opponent? The answer apparently is that Malenkov considered the state machinery more advantageous for his purposes.[21] Malenkov may have counted upon gradually increasing the state bureaucracy's weight in Soviet affairs and, in particular, upon his

21 Pethybridge, *op. cit.*, pp. 27–28, 36–38.

excellent connections with Soviet industrial administrators. Khrushchev adopted some of Malenkov's most important policies, especially after 1958, which might tempt one to speculate that Malenkov's policies were in tune with the times, but that his record and personality did not fit him to effectively play the role which he selected for himself. The master of "government by card index" proved to be no match for the vital and magnetic politician Khrushchev, who, in turn, was to succumb to a coalition of his "gray flannel communist" colleagues. Formally elected First Secretary of the central committee in September, 1953, Khrushchev proceeded to enhance the secretariat's significance, to proclaim policies in agriculture and other fields which for a few years were attractive and deceptively successful, and then to strengthen the party central committee as a counterweight to the presidium and also to the council of ministers, in both of which bodies his opponents were firmly ensconced.

In his drive for power, he relied at first mainly upon support from his old associates in the Ukrainian party apparatus, upon the territorial apparatus generally, and also upon the armed forces. He apparently had excellent personal relations with Marshal Zhukov and other high-ranking army officers, who had scores to settle with the secret police and who resented their treatment at the hands of Stalin and his Kremlin entourage. Although his situation forced Khrushchev to pursue a political line which at first was far from "liberal," even from the beginning his political strategy had a "populist," antibureaucratic cast. In the eyes of the territorial party secretaries and the Soviet military leaders who in 1957 were to furnish him with the support necessary for his final victory over the "anti-party group," Khrushchev was the champion of a "new deal," which promised to overthrow an "establishment" which many Soviet citizens, at all levels of society, had good reason to hate.

"Conservatives" such as Molotov and Kaganovich, though they had sprung from the party apparatus, had settled during their many years of service under Stalin in the state bureaucracy into rigid, ossified habits of command. Against them, Khrushchev's advantages were particularly great. It was easy for him to mobilize support in the central committee against Molotov's stand-pat foreign policy line. Molotov's position clashed with Khrushchev's popular concept of "peaceful," but competitive, coexistence, which pointed a way out of the impasse in which, despite stirrings toward a more flexible policy during the last two or three years of Stalin's lifetime, Soviet diplomacy was still mired.

The whole "group," and "in particular, Comrade Molotov," were accused in the "resolution concerning the antiparty group of Malenkov, G. M., Kaganovich, L. M., Molotov, V. M.," of having displayed "sluggishness," and of having interfered with the carrying out of urgently needed measures "for the purpose of relaxing international tension." [22] More specifically, Molotov was accused of having opposed improving relations with Yugoslavia, concluding a state treaty with Austria, and "normalizing" relations with Japan, etc. Most important was the accusation that he had rejected Khrushchev's thesis that it was possible to prevent wars "under contemporary conditions." [23]

One thread running through the resolution's specific criticisms of the "group," in such fields as de-Stalinization, agriculture, industrial reorganization, and elevation of the Soviet standard of living, was that its members had clung to obsolete, bureaucratic methods of administration and that they had displayed a "contemptuous attitude toward the urgent interests of the broad popular masses." Probably an even more serious accusation, however, was the charge that the members of the group — "and Comrade Shepilov, who joined them" — had engaged in un-Leninist, conspiratorial methods of political struggle. Later, especially at the Twenty-first and Twenty-second CPSU congresses, those charges were spelled out in vivid detail. It was revealed that in June, 1957, "when the factionalists went over from open attack against the central committee," Bulganin (his was one of the names, together with those of Saburov, Pervukhin, and, finally, at the Twenty-second congress, Voroshilov) had placed his guard in the Kremlin in such a manner that without his permission nobody could attain access to "the government building, where the session of the presidium of the central committee of the CPSU was taking place." [24]

Before turning to the period of Khrushchev's predominance which followed the expulsion of the conspiratorial trio and

22 Quoted from p. 15 of text of the resolution in *Voprosy ideologicheskoi raboty, op. cit.*, pp. 13–18. The resolution was published in *Pravda*, July 4, 1957.

23 *Ibid.*, p. 16.

24 A. N. Shelepin's speech, *Pravda*, Oct. 27, 1961, p. 10.

Shepilov, their late-comer ally, from the central committee but not from the party, in June, 1957, a few observations are in order. First, Khrushchev's victory was not won without a hard struggle and for some six months, following the events in Poland and Hungary in the autumn of 1956, he was somewhat on the defensive. That was indicated by the zig-zag of policy in the vital industrial reorganization, which culminated, however, in his gaining his ends, since most of the industrial ministries were abolished in May, 1957. Second, neither in 1957 nor subsequently were the defeated subjected to court trial or the other penalties suffered by defeated Soviet politicians during Stalin's autocracy.

It is very interesting that the only party leader condemned in the 1957 resolution who was identified explicitly and in detail with a social group — namely, the "liberal" intelligentsia — was Dmitri Shepilov.[25] He was accused of making unsound public statements, especially at meetings of the Union of Soviet Writers. He was also accused of "flirting with demagogs," and seeking to develop a "platform" which was "broader" than that of the party. There is reason to believe that Shepilov and also Malenkov were better liked than Khrushchev in Moscow intellectual circles.[26] Khrushchev's "populist" inclinations have been linked to an anti-intellectual strain and also to close adherence in principle — though by no means always in practice — to the Lenin-Stalin-Zhdanov tradition of upholding the party's right to prescribe and control the content of the arts. Khrushchev was probably less orthodox in this field than Molotov, and apparently, both before and after 1957, he took a less doctrinaire attitude than such top-level ideology and communication specialists as M. A. Suslov or Leonid F. Ilichev.[27]

FACTIONAL POLITICS AFTER THE
ANTIPARTY GROUP'S DEFEAT

After Khrushchev's power had been consolidated in 1957, factional, bureaucratic, and policy struggles continued, but with greater restraint and less disturbing consequences than in the first

[25] See speech by N. M. Shvernik, *Pravda,* July 7, 1957 and editorial in *Kommunist,* No. 10, July, 1957 entitled "The Leninist Principle in Problems of Literature and the Arts," esp. pp. 16–21.
[26] Malenkov was also criticized in the above *Kommunist* editorial.
[27] For additional details on Shepilov as a link between Soviet intellectuals and ruling party circles, see Barghoorn, "Soviet Political Doctrine," *op. cit.,* pp. 7–8.

four post-Stalin years. Carl Linden, characterizing Khrushchev's political behavior, has written "Again and again one sees him returning to the same themes: Agriculture, consumer goods production, resource allocations, chemicals — the parts and pieces of his persistent and seemingly elusive quest for a more abundant Soviet society." [28] And Linden expresses the opinion that not only the difficult problems confronting Khrushchev but also "the lively opposition of political forces represented at the top levels of the Soviet regime" stood in the way of the smooth and successful fulfilment of Khrushchev's program.[29] Whether or not one accepts Linden's relatively heavy emphasis upon the resistance of "conservatives" such as Kozlov and Suslov to Khrushchev's policies, or the position of some other Sovietologists less inclined to stress the "welfare" side of Khrushchev's record, it is clear, from such indicators as top-level personnel shifts, and from significant contradictions and omissions in the Soviet media of communications that Soviet high politics continued to be characterized by contained pluralism, or, in other words, closed, oligarchic politics.

As in the Stalin era, at any given time, a very few party leaders most fully shared the chief executive's confidence, access to him, and some of his prerogatives of office. Although neither the selection nor the status of this inner circle was governed by legal or constitutional principles, a sharp struggle continued over the coveted objectives, the lieutenancies of supreme leadership. After Khrushchev, who retained, in addition to his other top executive posts, his vital position as party First Secretary, the position of senior member of the party secretariat still remained probably the second most important job in the country, and conferred upon its holder the possibility that on the death or disability of Khrushchev he might become his successor. Events were to prove the probability of any particular deputy leader's success rather low. From June, 1957 until January, 1960 A. I. Kirichenko was Khrushchev's first lieutenant in the party apparatus. Following Kirichenko's dismissal from the secretariat, Frol R. Kozlov became the ranking secretary. The secretariat at the June, 1963

28 In *Problems of Communism,* XII, No. 5 (Sept.–Oct., 1963), p. 27.

29 *Ibid.,* p. 28; see also the illuminating testimony of Robert C. Tucker and Vernon V. Aspaturian in Hearings before the Subcommittee on Europe of the Committee on Foreign Affairs, House of Representatives, Eighty-eighth Congress, 2nd Session, Part II (U.S. Government Printing Office, Washington, D.C., 1964), pp. 246–59.

party plenum was postponed for several weeks, causing speculation on policy disagreements in the Kremlin. L. I. Brezhnev returned to that key body after being absent almost three years. His
return and the concurrent appointment of N. V. Podgorny made
it appear that Kozlov's incumbency as second-in-command was
definitely and finally ended, although he was still listed as a member of the secretariat.[30] Kozlov had already run into rough political weather in 1962, and on May 4, 1963, *Pravda* reported that
because of illness he could not participate in the May Day celebration. Exactly a year before Kozlov experienced what most foreign specialists regarded as a genuine illness, he had suffered a
political defeat. Khrushchev personally presided over the Leningrad obkom meeting at which the main transaction was the
decision to transfer I. V. Spiridonov, a Kozlov ally, from the important position of first secretary of the Leningrad oblast party
organization, which he had held since 1957, to the ceremonial
post of chairman of the Soviet of the Union, one of the two houses
of the USSR Supreme Soviet.[31] Shortly thereafter, Spiridonov was
deprived of the membership on the central committee secretariat
which he had enjoyed since 1961. This transaction showed that
the power to personally nominate or — as in the Spiridonov case
— to participate in removing party executives at a lower level is
one prerogative of senior leaders. Press reports on the exercise of
this power sometimes give useful hints on elite politics.

Perhaps the most revealing episode in the Kozlov-Khrushchev
tug-of-war was the unprecedented alteration in the 1963 May Day
slogan regarding Yugoslavia. The slogan, one of thirteen characterizing the political physiognomy of the Communist-governed
countries of Eastern Europe and Asia, and also of Castro Cuba,
hailed all these countries, save Yugoslavia, for their part in the
"building of socialism." The description of Yugoslavia was similar
to those applied to such "bourgeois" countries as India, Laos,
Burma, Afghanistan.

The slogan appeared while Khrushchev was on vacation in
Georgia.[32] On April 11, the highly unusual step of "correcting" it
took the form of a *Pravda* note officially restoring Yugoslavia to

---

[30] *Ezhegodnik bolshoi sovetskoi entsiklopedii* (Moscow, 1960 ed.), p. 13;
(1962 ed.), p. 17; (1963 ed.), p. 19; Conquest, *op. cit.*, pp. 387–433.
[31] *Pravda*, May 4, 1962.
[32] *Pravda*, April 8, 1963.

the status of a "socialist" state. There is a striking coincidence between the slogan correction and other apparently related events, including the concurrent disappearance of Kozlov from public view, reports in Western newspapers that he had suffered a heart attack, and the rise in the political stock of Brezhnev and Podgorny. Also probably connected with this blow to Kremlin "conservatives" was the abated severity of attacks on literary nonconformists such as Evtushenko, which soon followed.

Following the June, 1963 appointment of Brezhnev and Podgorny to the secretariat, it appeared that there was an "heir" to Khrushchev (Brezhnev), as well as a "counter heir" (Podgorny). In July, 1964 Brezhnev resigned from his ceremonial position as chairman of the Presidium of the Supreme Soviet (equivalent to titular head of state) which he had held since July, 1960. This event gave rise at once to speculation as to whether or not his power would be increased as a result of his ability henceforth to concentrate more fully on his work in the secretariat. The spectacular events of October, 1964 were to indicate that such speculation had not been entirely idle.

These events, accompanied by other personnel shifts in the secretariat and other top-level bodies, were interpreted by some competent specialists as indicating tension between the relatively pragmatic, "reformist" party leadership elements headed by Khrushchev and the more "conservative" elements from whom, the evidence clearly indicates, Kozlov was for a time to receive his major support. In retrospect, these speculations take on an ironic cast because of Brezhnev's elevation to top party leadership, but they are not necessarily invalidated. Apparently almost the entire presidium "ganged up" against Khrushchev in the fall of 1964, and it is not impossible that Brezhnev was forced to betray his erstwhile patron and friend. All these speculations rested on data indicating that Kozlov's personal acquaintance, joint work experience, and patronage, had not linked him as closely with Khrushchev as were Kirichenko, Brezhnev, or Podgorny.[33] Also pointing in the same direction is the similarity between some features of Khrushchev's and Brezhnev's agricultural programs; both advocated establishing unions of collective farms.

[33] The evidence is examined by Conquest, *op. cit.*, pp. 179, 304, 347, 386–89; Carl Linden in his two articles in *Problems of Communism* already referred to; Ploss, Paper No. 1, p. 4; Paper No. 2, p. 2; Paper No. 3, p. 3; Ploss, *Conflict and Decision-Making*, *op. cit.*, pp. 471–72.

More fundamental than the fate of the individual participants in factional struggles were the issues regarding which policy disputes continued to rage throughout the Khrushchevian period. A number of salient issues were indicated by discussion at and decisions of party congresses and central committee plenary sessions, and by deliberations of numerous special meetings of party leaders with outstanding specialists representing the arts, the sciences, and other fields. Khrushchev apparently utilized these meetings both for consultation and for mobilizing elite opinion. Among these issues were:

1. Continuation of "de-Stalinization."
2. The problem of suppressing and removing from influential positions leaders regarded by Khrushchev as sympathetic to the "anti-party group."
3. The related question of the inner-party regime. Khrushchev favored an "anti-bureaucratic" line which, as pointed out in Chapter VI, apparently disturbed "traditionalist" elements still ensconced in the party, state, and economic bureaucracies.
4. Problems of the size, composition, and distribution of the national product. Khrushchev won only a partial victory for his relatively consumer-oriented program against the conservative "metal-eaters," who comprised a shifting coalition of party officials and industrial executives with a vested interest in heavy industry. Khrushchev favored stressing agricultural chemicals, plastics, etc.
5. Party apparatus-economic administration relations. Khrushchev, as indicated in Chapter VI, sought to subordinate the economic bureaucracy to the party but at the same time, in a sense, to "technocratize" the party by involving its cadres directly in economic production and equipping them with advanced engineering and business administration training.
6. Defense policy and party-military relations. Khrushchev pushed for weapons modernization and a considerable reduction in military manpower. Khrushchev's "more rubble for the ruble" weapons policy was opposed by conservatives in the armed forces, who apparently were also disturbed by his foreign policy.
7. Khrushchev's attempts to achieve a limited detente with the West. For some time he relied upon "competitive co-existence" for communism's ultimate victory, against the Chinese commu-

nists' bitter opposition. He met with varying opposition in the party and economic bureaucracy and in the officer corps of the armed services.

8. Cultural policy and the tightness of party control over writers and other creative intellectuals. Khrushchev seems to have favored leniency sufficient to arouse anxiety among "conservatives," which only partly satisfied the aspirations of the Evtushenkos and others among what one might call the intellectual "loyal opposition."

These are not all the major issues, but their political significance was and still is very great because they involve groups whose functions are exceptionally vital, and also because these problems cut across organizational boundaries, causing simultaneous challenges to several or many chains of command. For example, the allocation of resources impinges upon vested interests in many spheres of domestic and foreign policy. In addition to the very broad issues listed, there were others, more specialized, regarding which the leadership's actions affected with great immediacy the interests of particular groups. The educational reforms begun in 1958–1959 furnish a good example. Finally, we must give some attention to the relationships between major policy issues and the inarticulated interests of large social groups. There are two problems in the interlocking of policy making and policy disputes under Soviet conditions. First, the political significance of issues depends upon the power of the elite segments affected by alternative policies on these issues. Second, in a rough sense, power may be gauged by their representation in the party's central executive bodies, and to a lesser degree in those of the Soviet state.

The data presented in Chapter VI indicate that such groups as the party apparatus, the state bureaucracy, the economic bureaucracy, and military and police leaders are overwhelming compared with ordinary "workers" or "peasants." [34] If we add to this "representation" the relationship between group membership in the top-level decision-making bodies and the total size of the group involved, then such occupational groups as writers and scientists are surprisingly large.

[34] Sensitive to this "representation" issue, Soviet sources heavily stress the percentage of members of such bodies as the USSR Supreme Soviet who are directly engaged in "production." See *Deputati verkhovnogo Soveta SSSR, op. cit.,* p. 3.

In a sense, the importance of a political faction or an institutional or occupational group depends upon its access to the decision-making process. We should be careful, however, not to apply this principle too literally or mechanically. Conquest has perceptively noted, in discussing the political potential of the liberal Soviet intelligentsia and other forces pressing for change in Soviet society, "In every great established empire with an entrenched bureaucracy and police system, the opposition view, and that is to say the potential revolution, has been carried initially by intellectuals without access to the political machinery." [35]

In briefly examining major areas of policy making and policy dispute it is well to remind ourselves once again that the differences between Soviet "conservatives" and "reformers" are likely to be intra-apparatus differences in style, timing, and approach to common objectives. They may even be produced by personal idiosyncrasies, previous career associations, and other factors of little ideological significance. Leaders and officials such as Kozlov and Suslov, whose status had been well established before the rise of Khrushchev, might have been expected to feel jealous of Khrushchev's rapid rise. Consciousness of this kind of reaction may have impelled Khrushchev to issue his frequent injunctions that in selecting executives for the highest party and state posts the party should be guided by a proper balance between youthful vigor and expertise and mature experience and wisdom. It is safe to assume that not only the party apparatus but the upper strata of Soviet society generally continued their dedication to Leninist discipline, militancy, and the sacrifice of the present enjoyment of mass welfare to the future gains allegedly dependent upon the revolutionary transformation of society. From a more practical point of view there must be strong solidarity in the Soviet elite, above all in the party apparatus and the political police, because they realize their ideological objectives, their status, and perhaps their survival as functional social strata depend on preservation of the party's power and authority.

Khrushchev benefited by de-Stalinization and the demand that harmful remnants of the "cult of personality" be eliminated from Soviet politics, and from society generally. This slogan was ap-

[35] Robert Conquest, "After Khrushchev: A Conservative Restoration?" *Problems of Communism*, XII, No. 5 (Sept.–Oct., 1963), pp. 41–45. Quotation on p. 45.

plied to history and the social sciences as a demand for research and teaching combining the proper "party spirit" with intellectual independence — to enhance his personal authority, to discredit those obstructing his policies, and in general to facilitate "renovation" both in personnel and in administrative methods. On the crucial issue of the punishment to be meted out to his fallen opponents, Khrushchev was most enthusiastically supported by men like Alexander Shelepin who most obviously owed their rapid rise to association with or even selection by him. Khrushchev having fallen, we may speculate as to whether some of Khrushchev's proteges may not be more ideologically orthodox, ruthless, and anti-Western than he was. Some older party leaders, such as Mikoyan, Suslov, and Kosygin took a relatively moderate position and Kozlov, while paying lip service to Khrushchev's line (e.g., at the Twenty-second Party Congress) did not go along with the sharpest critics of the "group." [36] Also, he and Mikhail Suslov opposed Khrushchev's relatively consumer- and peasant-oriented policies on the allocation of resources.

One finds in "inner-party democracy" and other approaches of the Khrushchev leadership to internal party organization and functioning a pattern of paradox and contradiction similar to those just surveyed in the related area of de-Stalinization. Khrushchev's commitment to restoring "Leninist norms," particularly "democratic centralism," implied, at least in principle, respect for opposing views in the top party bodies incompatible with a purge of his opponents on the Stalin model. On the other hand, presumably it also involved commitment to an essentially elitist, antidemocratic political structure. Moreover, the requirements of administering the Soviet Union's domestic and foreign policies (in the absence of political democracy of the Western type, a market economy, etc.) required a leader with dictatorial or quasi-dictatorial powers. While restoring regular meetings of the CPSU central committee and other party bodies, and generally paying more attention to the rules and procedures laid down in party statutes,

---

[36] Wolfgang Leonhard, *The Kremlin Since Stalin* (New York, 1962), pp. 318–19 and *Problems of Communism*, XII, No. 6 (Nov.–Dec., 1963), pp. 62–63; Linden, in *Problems of Communism*, XII, No. 5 (Sept.–Oct., 1963), pp. 28–29, 31–32. Leonhard is less inclined than Linden to regard as the central thread of Soviet internal politics in 1960–1963 the struggle between pro- and anti-Khrushchev forces.

Khrushchev also manipulated the ambiguous doctrines of "collegiality" and "collectivity." [37]

In the hands of a strong leader controlling the central committee secretariat, these doctrines most often are used as weapons to enforce intermediate and lower party levels to comply with decisions made at the center. That this indeed was the use to which the doctrine of middle-level collective leadership was being put is shown by the emphasis given them after the November, 1962 bifurcation of the party committees into industrial and agricultural sections, together with a spate of articles in *Partiinaya zhizn* criticizing "some" party officials who had shown themselves unable to adopt "new" methods and especially those who opposed the promotion within the party apparatus of engineers and other technically trained persons. On the other hand, Khrushchev encouraged dissemination of the notion that he, like Lenin, was the kind of party leader willing to consider and to discuss points of view differing from his own.[38]

The problem of resource allocation, especially as it affects the balance between capital goods and consumer goods, is probably the most significant area of policy in its potential effect on the millions of ordinary people in the Soviet union who for years have been yearning for improvement in their relatively meager standard of living. In this area, Khrushchev borrowed the "consumerist" slogans to which Malenkov had laid claim during his brief period as head of the Soviet state. Just as Malenkov, in his speech to the Supreme Soviet on August 8, 1953, promised "abundance" to the Soviet people, so Khrushchev in 1957–1958, and for two or three years thereafter, was to talk of "overtaking and surpassing" the United States in per capita production of meat and dairy products.[39] Pledges of early achievement of abundant food-

[37] See editorial in *Partiinaya zhizn*, No. 22, Nov., 1963.

[38] Ploss, Paper No. 3, pp. 4–11, presents interesting evidence. See also statement in editorial, *Partiinaya zhizn*, No. 10, May, 1964, to the effect that one could argue any question at any time with Lenin. Ploss hinted that Khrushchev may have invoked some aspects of Leninism as a hedge against the possibility that he might be forced to appeal once again to the central committee, or even to a wider arena, to counter machinations of his "traditionalist" adversaries. See esp. pp. 35–36.

[39] Demands (which of course also implied promises) for agricultural production sufficient to catch up with the United States in meat, milk, and butter production first appeared in the 1957 resolution on the antiparty group; then in the May Day slogans in *Pravda*, April 13, 1958; and then, after being wat-

stuff production disappeared, following which, in June, 1962, there came bad news: prices for meat and butter increased by 30 per cent and 25 per cent respectively. By implication the decree announcing this unwelcome news blamed the increases on the necessity that the USSR hold its own in the arms race with the West.[40] It is impossible to appraise the effectiveness of such an attempt to blame the "imperialists" for failures that resulted, probably, from the Soviet economy's inability simultaneously to compete with the United States in the arms race and to rapidly raise the Soviet standard of living. In turn, this incapacity probably reflected basic characteristics of the excessively centralized Soviet economic system. It is clear that the Khrushchev regime was far more concerned about consumer needs and demands than was Stalin's. There is no doubt that Khrushchev's popular image was tarnished, and that consumer discontent increased in 1963, when poor harvests, resulting at least in part from bad weather, caused the Soviet government to purchase large quantities of grain from Canada, Australia, and the United States. Khrushchev's loss of popularity occurred although this action bespoke a solicitude for popular welfare which contrasted with Stalin's habitual ruthlessness.

Despite a mediocre record, at best, in improving the Soviet population's monotonous diet, the Khrushchev administration did succeed in significantly increasing the availability to the public of many consumer goods. In addition, the wages of the lowest-paid categories of workers and employees were raised, pensions were increased, and Khrushchev announced, in July, 1964, salary increases for Soviet physicians and school teachers (traditionally underpaid categories), and extension of the system of old-age pensions to collective farmers, thus bringing the pension system to a large and hitherto unprotected social group.[41] Despite its limita-

---

ered down to the demand only that the United States be surpassed in per capita production of "livestock products" in the Nov. 6 slogan published Oct. 13, 1960, disappeared.

[40] *Kommunist*, No. 8, May, 1962, pp. 3–9; see also comment on this action by Victor Zorza, *Manchester Guardian Weekly*, June 7, 1962.

[41] On the latter development, see comment by Zorza in *Manchester Guardian Weekly*, July 16, 1964; Frederick C. Barghoorn, *Soviet Foreign Propaganda* (Princeton, N.J., 1964), pp. 189–94, summarizes relevant developments during the years 1956–1963. See valuable material on Khrushchev's efforts to create a "communist welfare state" in articles by Alec Nove and others in *Problems of Communism* (Jan.–Feb., 1960), and by Alexander S. Balinky and others in the July–Aug., 1961 issue of the same magazine. For a good Soviet summary

tions, Khrushchevian progress in bringing the Soviet Union to at
least the earliest stages of the mass consumption economy, above
all in the hitherto abysmally neglected urban housing field, was
sufficient to raise difficulties in economic organization and economic policy with which more mature industrial societies have
long wrestled. There was the problem of permitting the use of
plant efficiency indices which might greatly increase productivity,
especially of consumer goods, but which would also require drastic
changes in Soviet economic planning.[42]

The November, 1962 party plenum's failure to institute the
kind of moves toward partially adopting a rational pricing and
planning system as advocated by some Soviet economists and managers may have been caused by the opposition to such policies of
"conservative" apparatchiki in the Kremlin. It now seems possible
that, because of the greater receptivity to the Liberman type of
policies displayed by Khrushchev's successors than by Khrushchev
himself, it may also have resulted from his reluctance to experiment with such "capitalist" methods. Khrushchev's reforms in
the economy (the most important being those of May, 1957 and
the party-state administrative restructuring of November, 1962)
were mostly confined to the administrative sphere. The Stalinist
system therefore was left almost untouched in other respects, but
this neglect may have reflected a consensus in the party apparatus.
From the party apparatus' point of view, definite moves toward
an economy based on the principles of price and profit, despite
possible advantages in spurring production of consumer goods
and services, could be disadvantageous in that they would give too
much freedom and potentially too much power to the economic
elite. Such a trend might have other disadvantages, too. Proposals
for greater flexibility of economic policy are likely to be associated with "consumerism," which whets appetites for the more
abundant life. An increased supply of consumer goods gives a certain freedom of choice to purchasers and makes it more difficult

---

of the Khrushchev record in this field, see the lead article in *Kommunist*,
No. 1, Jan., 1964, pp. 3–12.

[42] The article by Professor Evsei Liberman, in *Pravda*, Sept. 9, 1962 and the
lively debate which followed indicated how significant were the issues of
greater flexibility in planning and resultant increase in responsibility and
operational autonomy of managers of industrial enterprises, raised by Liberman. Besides Liberman's article, and the important article by Nemchinov,
Pravda, Sept. 21, see also *Pravda*, Sept. 13 and Sept. 16; *Pravda*, Oct. 12. See
also Harry Schwartz, *The New York Times*, Nov. 25, 1962.

for the party to rule by coercion. For the idea — to which Khrushchev gave some encouragement — develops that superior effort should be rewarded materially, whereas under Stalin punishment for failure was emphasized more than reward for success. Then too, increasing the supplies of consumer goods creates marketing difficulties, and puts an increasing premium upon managerial and administrative skills. It reinforces tendencies toward elevating the economic administrators' functional autonomy. Such potentially unsettling developments are not unrecognized, as we may see in the slowness to adopt proposals of Liberman and others, despite their popularity among the Soviet technical and professional elite. Other indications appear in policy statements, heavily stressing communal or collective, rather than individual use of major appliances, and also in the continued strain of austerity in official statements describing the communist future.

Perhaps the most crucial problems confronting the Soviet leadership in the allocation of resources — which includes, but is bigger than, the question of how far to move toward a consumer-oriented economy — revolve around the ideological and sociopolitical consequences of alternative policies toward the military establishment. Rapid progress toward a consumer-oriented economy would require that emphasis be shifted from production for national power to production, and distribution, for popular welfare. That might undermine ideological militancy and arouse dangerous resentment among military professionals and others committed to a "conservative" policy line. A full-scale Soviet "new deal," never really attempted by Khrushchev, despite his "populist" political style, would unite against its proponents all the conservative and orthodox elements among the elite, divided though they are on various issues. Party apparatchiki, police cadres and military officers, and probably also most industrial executives share a vested interest in social discipline and in keeping alive popular hostility toward the "imperialists." These groups also benefit from a hierarchic organization of society and the legitimizing of their status and power derived from a semimilitarized economy.

The foregoing interpretations are and must remain, speculative since Soviet sources inform us so poorly of Soviet military leaders' reactions, and those of military professionals generally, toward arms reduction and its logical ultimate result, disarmament. Some military leaders were disturbed by, and covertly opposed, the reductions in the Soviet armed forces which occurred in 1955–1959. Western analysts detected similar responses to Khrushchev's 1960 plan for a large additional demobilization, which, mainly because of international political tensions, was only partially implemented. It was also apparent after the limited nuclear test ban agreement was signed in July, 1963 that Soviet military leaders were afraid that the agreement would create illusions regarding the extent of the "detente" which, according to much comment in the Western press, it signaled or initiated.[43]

Apart from the threat to the officer corps' vested interest posed by reductions in force and related measures — which Soviet propaganda argues, not very convincingly, is not an issue in a "socialist" society — many other issues of civil-military relations are involved in the problem of allocating resources. These include questions about the military budget, such as the size of the armed forces and other technical and economically important questions, the proper relationship between the military leadership and the party in formulating defense policy, and such intangibles as the way in which journalists, and poets and novelists too, should present to the public the armed forces' "image." The firmly established Soviet tradition of political supremacy in military affairs and political control over the armed forces is generally accepted. But one leading American specialist has expressed the view that renewed emphasis on these doctrines in recent years, especially after the Cuban crisis of October, 1962 showed increased tension between the military and political leadership.[44]

An interesting aspect of the Soviet military as an interest group is the military leaders' effort to see to it that men of words render proper appreciation of their contribution, both past and present, to national greatness. From time to time Soviet sources report sharp discontent over the image of the military, partly but by no means exclusively related to its supposed influence on the incoming stream of recruits for compulsory service.[45]

[43] The fullest and most expert discussion of the above and related matters is in Thomas W. Wolfe, *Soviet Strategy at the Crossroads* (Cambridge, Mass., 1964). On military reaction to the demobilizations, and especially to disarmament, see esp. pp. 30–37, 46, 238–42. See also the above-mentioned articles by Carl Linden, and Ploss, Papers Four and Five, and Tucker, testimony before House Committee on Foreign Affairs, *op. cit.*, pp. 250–61.

[44] Wolfe, in Ch. VIII, discusses this question thoroughly and judiciously.

[45] See the speech by M. Kh. Kalashnik, deputy chief of the Main Political

Khrushchev's purge of Marshal Georgi K. Zhukov and some of his close associates in October, 1957 was impressive evidence of the strength of Khrushchev and of the party machine generally over the military as an interest group. But it also required replacing some of the Soviet military leaders most closely associated with Khrushchev by new men, and may have helped, indirectly, to pave the way for Khrushchev's downfall. This too is speculation, but it is clear that, although the Soviet military had no open or major part in Khrushchev's fall, seven years after that of Zhukov, they also did nothing to prevent it. Zhukov's limited and little-publicized rehabilitation after Khrushchev's fall is difficult to appraise. Such events as including his name among signers of an obituary published in the main Soviet military newspaper in February, 1965 probably were indirect reproaches to Khrushchev and also gestures of appeasement to the officer corps generally — or perhaps mainly to elements associated at various times with Zhukov. Incidentally, but perhaps not insignificantly, Zhukov's partial rehabilitation was a mark of the relative leniency and "normalcy" of post-Stalin Soviet politics.

Some features of Khrushchev's foreign policy undoubtedly irritated and even dismayed many Soviet military leaders and their "conservative" supporters in other segments of the party-state machine. One thinks of the U-2 episode in 1960, the Cuban missile crisis of 1962, and also the possible broad effects on military and civilian leadership circles of Khrushchev's inept handling of relations with the Chinese communists. Militant and mistrustful elements in the party and other bureaucracies were undoubtedly disturbed when Khrushchev and President John F. Kennedy, in 1963, negotiated a partial detente in the United States-Soviet relations. They were constrained, however, by the wide popularity of the detente and were forced to oppose its implementation covertly and cautiously.

Obviously, a large increase in the influence of militant "conservatives" in either country could destroy the tender shoots of limited collaboration nurtured by Kennedy and Khrushchev. So

---

Administration of the Soviet Army and Navy, in *XX sezd KPSS i voprosy ideologicheskoi raboty, op. cit.,* pp. 263–71, and the discussion in Wolfe on a speech in which Marshal Malinovski in 1964 criticized an allegedly "pacifist" approach by Soviet writers to World War II.

too could other factors, such as Soviet yielding to Chinese communist pressures. Whether or not and how much Khrushchev's successors were predisposed to such a "conservative" direction was one of the liveliest subjects of political speculation after his removal. Despite a tendency, perhaps temporary, to revert to such pre-Khrushchev principles as withdrawing the party apparatus from the close involvement in economic administration advocated by Khrushchev, but denounced by his successors as conducive to confusion, Khrushchev's heirs, at least in 1964 and 1965, did not jettison his economic and social policies. They did undo all his major administrative reorganizations.

Less impressive, perhaps more reluctant, more cautious, and probably more efficient than Khrushchev, the Brezhnev-Kosygin-Podgorny-Shelepin-Suslov oligarchy remained committed to priority for Soviet national interests and welfare over any substantial sharing either of wealth or risks with the Chinese-led elements of international communism. So long as this orientation persisted, one could not attribute to the post-Khrushchev leadership a reversion to militant communist "conservatism."

In the complex, delicate, and often imponderable field of international relations that is sometimes described as "cultural relations," judging by evidence supplied by well-informed American scientists, educators, and others, the Khrushchev administration and its successors have experienced divided counsels. Despite his pioneering initiative in widening Soviet contacts with the "bourgeois" world, Khrushchev also made it clear that he did not intend to permit their influence to become so pervasive or intimate that they could reinforce "cosmopolitan" and "alien" attitudes, especially in literary, artistic, scientific, and student circles. There was an obvious fear that if this happened on a large scale Soviet internal propaganda would be seriously weakened.

When Western governments pressed for more, longer, and less restricted exchanges of graduate students and scholars in such "sensitive" fields as the social sciences and philosophy, they found that "conservative" party, police, and state officials were uneasy about any proposals which would fundamentally alter the "closed" Soviet communication system. Soviet skittishness about widening and deepening intercultural channels of communication was of course heightened by Moscow's desire not to add verisimilitude to

Chinese charges that Russia and America were working hand in glove against the "people's revolution" in Southeast Asia and other underdeveloped areas.

In comparison with the party apparatchiki, ensconced in the presidium, the secretariat, and other controlling agencies of the party machine, or with high state, economic, or military leaders, even the most influential members of the "creative" (*tvorcheskaya*) and "technical" (*tekhnicheskaya*) intelligentsia seem to have little access to and participation in shaping national policy. Moreover, most members of most of the "free" professions, such as writers, composers, artists, or actors (journalists are a conspicuous exception) do not aspire to political authority or influence. As shown by the increasingly voluminous Western scholarly literature on the politics of the arts and sciences in Soviet Russia, however, Soviet professionals demand favorable conditions for the exercise of their skills, adequate logistic support in the form of equipment, material incentives, health and recreational facilities, and educational and training procedures for young members of their professions. They also speak out more negative desires such as keeping interference by party, state, and police control agencies from crippling their creativity and hobbling the exercise of their skills.[46] Successful members of the most prestigious professions, especially natural scientists and writers, with lawyers and physicians well toward the bottom of the order, are probably the best off of any group in Soviet society, except perhaps the most successful party apparatus men. They enjoy a disproportionate share of all except narrowly political rewards. The word "success" must

[46] In addition to the above-cited works of Barrington Moore and Harold Swayze, see Nicholas DeWitt's article "Politics of Soviet Science," *The American Behavioral Scientist*, VI, No. 4 (Dec., 1962), pp. 7–11; Mark G. Field, "Soviet Science and Some Implications for American Science and Society," *Journal of International Affairs*, XIII, No. 1 (1959), pp. 19–33; Caryl T. Haskins, *The Scientific Revolution and World Politics* (New York, 1964); also useful were the articles by R. F. Marshak and Eugene Rabinowitch in the *Bulletin of the Atomic Scientists*, Jan. and March–April, respectively, 1958. On recent developments in Soviet social science, with some attention to their political significance, see George Fischer, *Science and Politics* (Center for International Studies, Cornell University, 1964) and Ralph K. White, "Social Science Research in the Soviet Bloc," *Public Opinion Quarterly*, XXVIII, No. 1, pp. 20–26. In addition to Swayze's exceptionally important systematic work, the book and periodical *Output on Soviet Literature* is too voluminous to list. The books and articles of George Gibian, Victor Erlich, Patricia Blake, Max Hayward, Robert Conquest, and many others, and numerous translations from Russian into English which have appeared in recent years make it easier for a non-Soviet scholar to acquaint himself with Soviet literary politics than with almost any other current Soviet topic.

of course be used with due appreciation of its ambiguity. Far more nonconformity was tolerated after Stalin's death than before, and up to a point it was even encouraged. But the vilification of Pasternak and the exile of his friend Olga Ivinskaya on apparently trumped-up charges, or other cases such as the conviction of the young poet Josif Brodski for "parasitism" indicated that those who, unlike Evtushenko, were nonconformists in the practice of their profession as well as in their attitude toward the official ideology and party-approved norms of everyday life, were in danger not merely of official ostracism but also of police action.[47] It was noteworthy and characteristic of the post-Stalin practice, though, that many of Russia's most distinguished intellectuals pleaded Brodski's cause both with the court which sentenced him and with the CPSU central committee.

The situation of successful Soviet intellectuals and professionals improved greatly after Stalin's death. Khrushchev offered them a kind of junior partnership in his attempt to revitalize Soviet society. Although even the most favored Soviet scientists were far from being as free as their Western European and American colleagues, they were gratified by many post-Stalin policies, especially by much easier access to foreign publications and to their foreign colleagues. Although the establishment on April 12, 1961, of the State Committee on Coordination of Research and Development appeared to diminish the autonomy of the highest-ranking organization of Soviet scientists and scholars, the Academy of Sciences of the USSR, knowledgeable American scientists and diplomats queried by the writer believed that by 1963–1964, and especially after Khrushchev's fall, the Soviet scientific community's leadership had succeeded in recovering at least some part of the professional autonomy threatened by this supercoordinating body. In 1954, Barrington Moore said that about the best that scientists and other intellectuals could expect was to achieve "some minimal degree of autonomy within the system." This statement still seemed valid, but, especially for such favored categories as physicists, conditions had perhaps improved more rapidly than Moore had foreseen.[48]

After Stalin's death, even social scientists were partially freed from the restraints formerly applied to them. One of the by-

---

[47] See Patricia Blake in *The New York Times Book Review*, June 21, 1964.
[48] Moore, *Terror and Progress, op. cit.*, p. 153.

products of the vogue for "cybernetics" was heavily utilitarian but nevertheless impressive revival of research, and especially of applied research, in sociology, social psychology, labor psychology, and other social science fields. Perhaps the most vital center of such activity is the "Public Institute for Social Research" in Leningrad, in which members of the Academy of Sciences, the faculty of Leningrad State University, and also party and administrative leaders cooperate in studying such eminently practical problems as the economic and psychological causes of labor turnover. Scholars associated with this Leningrad center are also seeking to apply advanced data processing methods to legal scholarship. The latter endeavor, led by Professor Kerimov of the Leningrad University law faculty, was begun under the general direction of the distinguished electronic engineer, academician A. I. Berg.[49] The party's trend toward using social science for practical purposes was reflected significantly in N. G. Egorychev's address to the Twenty-third Congress. He urged that an institute for the study of propaganda be established.

The case of Shepilov appears to be the only one in which, even indirectly, the attitudes and interests of Soviet intellectuals had substantial influence at the highest levels of the political struggle. Nonetheless, Soviet intellectuals, working together with allies and sympathizers in the party apparatus, were able to exercise a kind of veto power over the adoption or implementation of policies which appeared to threaten their interests. In some ways and on some issues Khrushchev himself fell into this category. In literature, a good example was the partial blunting of the cultural crackdown which began in the fall of 1962 and culminated in the "ideological" CPSU plenum in June, 1963. Soviet scientists and their allies in the educational bureaucracy succeeded in reducing some deleterious effects of the 1958–1959 educational reform upon the teaching of mathematics and the natural sciences in Soviet primary and secondary schools.[50] (V. P. Elyutin, minister of higher education since 1955, is also a member of the party central committee and a chemist by professional training.) The debate on the educational reform afforded an opportunity for advocates of a

[49] Some of the work of this institute is described in D. Rozhin's article, *Izvestiya*, Oct. 25, 1963.

[50] DeWitt, *Education and Professional Employment in the USSR*, esp. pp. 5–21.

relatively "humanistic" approach to education, such as Ilya Ehrenburg, to express their views publicly.

There was no corresponding improvement in the opportunities of the large groups such as industrial workers, the Soviet peasantry, or the mass of people of the non-Russian nationalities, all poorly represented in the higher councils of the regime and having little access to channels of communication. These groups all benefited, of course, from the reduced use of terror and from Khrushchev's partial shift of Soviet economic policy toward "consumerism." The role of Soviet trade unions, however, did not substantially increase.

As Albert Boiter and Jay D. Sorenson have made clear in carefully documented studies, Soviet workers, following Stalin's death, were frustrated by the growing gulf between their rapidly building aspirations (stimulated by Khrushchev's de-Stalinization policies), and the very modest satisfaction which the regime was able — and willing — to give them.[51]

Industrial workers benefited greatly from the 1956 repeal of the oppressive 1940 legislation forbidding unauthorized quitting of jobs and imposing severe penalties for lateness to or absence from work. Also, the rights of trade unions, especially on paper, were increased by resolutions adopted at the March, 1959 and October, 1963 congresses of the All-Union Central Council of Trade Unions. According to Sorenson, because the trade unions were represented on the bureau of the Council of National Economy, and as a result of other post-Stalin changes, "The balance struck between management and labor under Stalin has been altered." Moreover, Sorenson pointed out, varied proponents of labor reform, including those dominant among trade union leaders, some anti-managerial party apparatchiki, "modernizer-economists of the 'Liberman' stripe," and apparently N. S. Khrushchev, favored measures to further increase trade union prerogatives and to improve labor's standard of living and comfort — all were opposed by party "conservatives" and by most factory managers.

On the other hand, the rise in the Soviet standard of living, or in the power of unions or of workers in any capacity to bargain collectively, was not sufficient to keep labor unrest from growing.

[51] Jay D. Sorenson, "Soviet Workers: The Current Scene," *Problems of Communism,* XIII, No. 1 (Jan.–Feb., 1964), pp. 25–32; Albert Boiter, "When the Kettle Boils Over . . .," *ibid.,* pp. 33–43; see also Anthony Sylvester's contribution to the same issue, esp. pp. 47–48.

The workers' principal negative response was large-scale quitting of jobs, leading to an expensive increase in labor turnover. In addition, serious strikes (in effect illegal, since strikes "have no status in Soviet law") occurred in 1959 at Temir Tau, Kazakhstan, and in 1962–1963 on a larger scale, especially at the South Russian city of Novocherkassk in June, 1962, apparently in protest against a factory production speed-up occurring at the same time as increases in food prices.[52] It is possible that Soviet purchase of foreign grain in 1963–1964 was partially motivated by a desire to palliate labor discontent, which may have been fanned to the hottest ever by the poor food situation, beginning in the autumn of 1963.[53]

How much more active and significant future worker grievances may become in Soviet politics than they are at present is unpredictable. Thus far the gestures and minor concessions resorted to by Stalin's successors, combined with the use of armed force when it proved necessary, have kept the situation under fully effective control, without a return to the brutal controls imposed by Stalin.

One reason for the relative effectiveness of these measures is the Soviet doctrine that active, open class struggle is legitimate only in a "capitalist" society. This theory probably is still generally accepted, with great intensity by the managerial and party elite, but also, on the whole, by workers. Apparently, many city workers and peasants regard themselves as "simpler" than and morally superior to their more privileged fellow-citizens of intelligentsia status. The regime's policy of periodically staging public criticism of privileged "bureaucrats" and intellectuals seems to divert to these targets of mass envy some of the hostility which the less privileged might otherwise feel for the party.[54] To supplement the traditional labor controls of force and propaganda the Soviet authorities now seem increasingly committed to the use of systematic attitude surveys and other applied social science techniques.

The largest segment of the population, the farmers, has the least representation in the party and government and the fewest channels by which to bring its grievances and aspirations to the

---

[52] The statement regarding strikes is quoted from Harold J. Berman, *Justice in the U.S.S.R.*, rev. ed. (New York, 1963), p. 358; Boiter, pp. 35–38.

[53] Boiter, *ibid.*, p. 43.

[54] See Inkeles and Bauer, *The Soviet Citizen, op. cit.*, pp. 314, 319.

party leaders' attention. Collective farmers do not belong to unions, and of course have no organization equivalent to those through which farmers in the United States can bring pressure to bear upon legislators. There is little doubt, though, that the moods of the collective farmers are closely observed by the rural party organizations, the Ministry of agriculture, and the secret police network of informers. In spite of the poverty of its organizational resources, exceptional even by Soviet standards, the collective farm peasantry has proven to be one of the most difficult social forces for the party to control.

Post-Stalin policy toward the peasantry, and the response thereto, was basically similar to relations between the party and industrial workers. Diminished use of coercion was accompanied by partial economic reforms, especially by an attempt to increase the individual's material stake in the system. Propaganda activity was intensified and party penetration of these groups was increased by recruiting a bigger percentage of new communists from among them. This effort may have somewhat reduced "social distance" between the regime and the worker and peasant "masses," which certainly does seem to have been one of Khrushchev's objectives.

With regard to the non-Russian nationalities, especially the Ukrainians, Khrushchev instituted symbolic concessions and administrative and political reforms, widened access to party membership, and increased participation in party, state, and also military policy-making activity.[55]

Especially after 1956, however, nationality policy, in the main, has been a milder, more tactful continuation of Stalinist policy. Still, the current version of "Leninist nationality policy," has permitted influential members of non-Russian national groups to resist, for a time, and perhaps to blunt the particular Moscow-originated measures which threatened to further erode local cultural patterns. An example was discussed in the section of Chapter II dealing with nationality patterns.

---

[55] Armstrong, *Politics of Totalitarianism, op. cit.,* pp. 342–44, offers useful data and interpretations regarding this matter.

CHAPTER VIII

Implementing Public Policy

THUS FAR we have dealt with the goals and perspectives of the groups and agencies that make national policy. Top party leaders, executives of party and government agencies, and cliques and factions representing combined elite interests and perspectives are the principal political authorities who convert what they regard as community needs into decisions which must be obeyed by the citizenry. The aspirations and needs of larger, less well organized occupational and social groups, as we have pointed out, also are taken into account in making public policy.

In the USSR the political "inputs," or demands for official, legally binding decisions, are fed into the political machinery in a fashion different from that of more "open" societies where it is relatively easy to form organizations and to agitate and lobby for the most varied group goals. In the Soviet system, in contrast, access both to the political arena and to the channels and operations by which policy is translated into plans, rules, regulations, and routines is far less free than in more pluralistic, less centralized regimes. Administrators who are not subjected to or supported by pressure groups, lobbies, opposition parties, or criticism by a powerful, independent press, are much more dependent upon and subordinated to political leaders than those in parliamentary democracies. Civil servants work under the surveillance of party organizations, which are supposed to "verify," or check up on their performance. The civil servant in the Soviet Union is the party's agent, rather than the public's servant, as he is, in theory at least, in Britain or the United States.

258

If we did not emphasize that the party's top command and its professional cadres are prone to intrude into spheres which administrators claim as their own, we would be blinded to an essential feature of the Soviet system. To overlook the vital contribution to the regime's maintenance, indeed, its survival, by bureaucrats and bureaucratically supervised functionaries, employees, clerks, and specialists, is to exaggerate the differences between the Soviet polity and others. The party itself is, after all, a bureaucracy. Its operations require nonpolitical as well as political skills, habits, and routines. Still more indispensable are housekeeping, record keeping, and a myriad of specialized techniques, some requiring unusual talent and long training, in order to provide essential services such as public health, utilities, police protection, education, and the like. The rapidly growing, state-directed economy urgently needs highly qualified managers, economists, accountants, and engineers. That education and scientific research need dedicated professionals, including many kinds of administrators, is obvious.

To be sure, party leaders and functionaries are expected to spur, inspire, and coordinate the multimillion-person army of Soviet civil servants. The latter, many of them party members and graduates of educational institutions which teach the doctrine of party supremacy, are as predisposed as the Kremlin can make them to playing second fiddle to their party bosses. Moreover, though party executives are increasingly equipped with education appropriate to their supervisory jobs, it must seem to many administrators and specialists, especially to the most highly trained and creative, that the apparatchiki are superficial generalists. Mutual irritation and even contempt can result, especially if normal differences of perspective are compounded by personality clashes or other troubles. Thus the all-powerful political leader cracking the whip over the pliant bureaucrat, or galvanizing him to voluntarily perform herculean feats by the contagion of example, no longer exists. Still, in the Soviet politician-civil servant relationship the former still retains great predominance, but his position is not completely unchallenged and indeed seems to be slowly diminishing. It should not be supposed that the relationship between the party hierarchy and other functional groupings is full of sharp and constant antagonism. Latent, usually suppressed, and intermittent, antagonism is contained and overshadowed by a division of labor which is apparently tolerably satisfactory to all.

The Soviet civil servant's worst days of subjugation to political authority (to the dictator himself, in effect) fell during the late Stalin era, from about 1934 on. The governmental economic bureaucracy and others were Stalin's cowed, submissive, often inefficient, and sometimes corrupt or even obstructive servants. Stalin's power and aura of authority gone, the USSR was left without an effective legitimating and mobilizing agency. This lack was made more serious by the challenging, delicate leadership and coordination difficulties facing the more and more complex economy and society. It may have seemed to Khrushchev that if the party did not take the initiative in tackling the issues confronting the country, other forces might. Certainly as a committed Marxist-Leninist he could not contemplate with equanimity the dangers of either stagnation or challenge to party hegemony by state and economic bureaucrats. Khrushchev's solution to these problems was to transform the party from a primarily mobilizing and indoctrinational organ into what Sidney I. Ploss has called the "functional," utilitarian party. In a sense, Khrushchev tried to replace Stalin's autocracy, which had ruthlessly but effectively supplied the innovative, entrepreneurial energies needed for economic growth, with a rejuvenated CPSU, capable, he may have hoped, of doing the job done in the United States by the combined efforts of private enterprise and big government.

Cliques of bureaucrats, allied with conservative party leaders, prevented Khrushchev from converting the party apparatus into a "functional," utilitarian production agency. There is reason to believe that similar forces succeeded in limiting the post-Khrushchev liberalization of Soviet economic administration to the cautious (in the long run probably unworkable) compromise between bureaucratic centralism and managerial autonomy decreed by the September, 1965 CPSU plenum. Generally, central government officials, especially those in the Council of Ministers, and economic planners and industrial executives gained more authority after Khrushchev's ouster. Traditionally the administrative bureaucracy has been able to obstruct party policies which it found impracticable or inimical to its interests and also has ignored or frustrated the ordinary Soviet citizen's yearning for efficient, courteous public services. This negative behavior, in a way, is the bureaucracy's revenge for its widely despised role in the community. Fundamental, constructive change in relations between politician and administrator will only be possible when Soviet economic and governmental executives have been freed from the controls which still prevent them from exercising their creative initiative for innovation.

Soviet political doctrine, state administrative law, and administrative practice have always distinguished between the separate spheres of competence of the CPSU and the state and government organs, but the line of demarcation between them has been fluid and shifting.[1]

The party's direct involvement in administration, and even in routine governmental operations, has varied. During the Khrushchev period it became more and more involved. According to Barrington Moore's division of Soviet social direction controls into positive political controls, negative political controls, and technical controls, Khrushchev's emphasis on increased party involvement was logical.[2] As terror came to be used less and less for social control following Stalin's death, and as the national economy's more complex facets continued to grow (especially the scientific research establishment), it was felt that the party's creative, entrepreneurial, and inspirational work should be enhanced. The drive to improve the party's innovating and creative performance also spread to the civil service. Many statements and measures reflected the Kremlin's acute need to replace obsolete routines and stodgy bureaucrats by modern methods and educated, imaginative, and efficient personnel. Responding to a shortage of trained manpower caused by war losses and industrial expansion, the party leadership campaigned vigorously in both party and government bureaucracies to increase individual and organizational efficiency and to reduce swollen administrative and clerical staffs. In part, the Khrushchev and post-Khrushchev emphasis on the "public" organizations and nonprofessional community service in the "all-people's state" was a response to the

[1] See I. I. Evtikhiev and V. A. Vlasov, *Administrativnoe pravo SSSR* (Moscow, 1946), Ch. I, esp. p. 6; G. I. Petrov, *Sovetskoe administrativnoe pravo* (Leningrad, 1960), Chs. I. and II, esp. pp. 41–45; Yu. Kozlov, *Sovetskoe administrativnoe pravo* (Moscow, 1964); Ya. N. Umanski, *Sovetskoe gosudarstvennoe pravo* (Moscow, 1960), p. 22; *Ezhegodnik bolshoi sovetskoi entsiklopedii, 1963* (Moscow, 1963), pp. 11–24; V. M. Marchuk, *Organy gosudarstvennogo upravleniya USSR* (Kiev, 1964).

[2] *Terror and Progress* (Cambridge, Mass., 1954), Ch. 1.

manpower shortage. Also, "voluntary" service to society increasingly replaced police and terror as instruments of social control.

The traditional and still dominant doctrine on party-government relationships is that although the party exercises leadership (*rukovodstvo*), government agencies are responsible for administration (*upravlenie*). That is to say, decisions are the party's prerogative, but implementing policy is the task of government. High-level party and government agencies, usually centered in Moscow, share in seeing to it that government administrators and experts, if need be on pain of severe sanctions, do in fact execute Kremlin policies. Some of Khrushchev's administrative experiments challenged this principle, but toward the end of his tenure he was forced to revert toward it, and major pronouncements by his successors reaffirmed its indispensability to the Soviet system's proper functioning.[3]

In a sense, Soviet experience in administrative rule making and rule adjudication has revolved around uncertainly defined relations and spheres of "leadership" and "administration." When the Moscow leadership wants to push forward a drastic new social and political program, as in Stalin's collectivization campaign in 1929–1931, or when it feels that stagnating national efforts must be revitalized, as in Khrushchev's agricultural reorganizations from 1953–1958, it calls for increased party apparatus involvement in day-to-day administrative and control functions, sometimes including petty housekeeping details. The party pulls back its cadres from excessive involvement when it seems that party-led campaigns are arousing resentment among the "masses" and that resentment is being directed against the party, rather than toward government officials. It does so also when the party cadres are needed elsewhere, or become so involved in administration that the Kremlin fears they may lose perspective, hurting party discipline.

To regard the party and governmental organs as perfectly synchronized parts of a single smoothly working mechanism, or as twin horses docilely obeying a driver in the Kremlin, is to suc-

[3] The distinction between "leadership" and "administration" in Soviet usage is excellently discussed by Leopold Haimson in Margaret Mead's, *Soviet Attitudes Toward Authority* (New York, 1951). The editorial in *Partiinaya zhizn*, No. 23, Dec., 1964, was one sharp, important criticism of Khrushchev's conception of party-government administrative cooperation, especially of his Nov., 1962 reorganization, blaming him for "pushing the party committees into replacing the economic-administrative organs."

cumb to fallacious reasoning. But it is still more incorrect to assume that party and government are enemy camps, vying for power, with the government civil servants on the side of order and legality and the party apparatus championing permanent and total revolution. There is no such dichotomy because, first, there are numerous clique and functional differences within the party and the governmental bureaucracies (aggregations of bureaucracies, to be exact). These often cause power rivalries or policy disputes, involving several party and state agencies. Another of the numerous variables that this simplified view of Soviet bureaucratic politics ignores is the overriding common elite interests and political styles which most Soviet bureaucrats and probably most of the elite share as compared with that of the vast masses of clerical, industrial, and agricultural workers over whom they exercise control, guidance, supervision, and influence.

Foreigners who have intimately experienced Soviet life, such as Western participants in student exchange programs, often comment on the relative passivity that Soviet citizens display toward the political authorities and the widespread indifference toward the political system's upper levels. Perhaps more striking and convincing is the apparently complete passivity with which most of the Soviet population accepted Khrushchev's removal. Soviet publications contain a wealth of guarded but interesting and significant indications of widespread political apathy, even among members of raion party committees. Typical was a long "party life" article sharply criticizing an apparently widespread practice of the apparatchiki who head party organizations.[4] They do not even bother to give assignments for party work to enthusiastic members of party bureaus and, when they do, simply ignore the efforts of nonapparatus activists to do their bit for the cause.

That the post-Khrushchev leadership was troubled by political apathy, especially among the vital Komsomol members and also among youths generally, was shown in an article by Komsomol first secretary Sergei Pavlov.[5] He noted that youths were growing up in conditions that rendered their political training difficult. Among these he included youths' increasing remoteness from the heroics of revolution and war and the effect of problems in the international communist movement. He had numerous prescrip-

[4] *Pravda*, Dec. 8, 1964.
[5] *Partiinaya zhizn*, No. 5, March, 1965.

tions for creating identification with the polity and active political participation. Most of them revolved around the view that such positive attitudes could develop only if party and government leaders offered youths meaningful and responsible opportunities in solving the great practical economic problems facing the country. This, and not mere indoctrination, asserted Pavlov, would teach youths to think broadly and in a statesmanlike fashion.

Regardless of the sincerity or the feasibility of Pavlov's prescriptions, there is little doubt that the ills he sought to cure were real and serious. His diagnosis, like much other evidence, tells us something about the relatively poor support which the Soviet citizenry offers to the political system. Evidence of the kind offered here is of course fragmentary and unsatisfactory, but no other kind can be assembled. In turn, however, this evidence reinforces the indirect and partial evidence of defective citizen involvement with government symbols and practices, which even top-level Soviet officials feel must be publicly deplored.

Apathy, inadequate emotional support for the polity, and related states of mind, sometimes involving escapist, destructive impulses such as alcoholism, hooliganism, and even crime, are factors in the environment in which Soviet public administration functions. Their continued presence reflects unfavorably on the performance of the Soviet civil service. A government which, despite Khrushchev's years of trying to popularize and "democratize" it, remains massively unresponsive and incapable of eliciting either active, spontaneous demands or lively, enthusiastic support from the citizenry is suffering from grave defects and handicaps, even from the carefully censored, official Soviet point of view.

As with other areas of performance officially admitted to be less than satisfactory, the rather cool relationship between citizen and government is held to be a temporary survival of the "old world" of capitalism. Hope is expressed that if all good communists will unite to do away with apathy and irresponsibility, the Soviet people will come to identify their personal interests with those of society. One may venture to guess that this kind of support for party and state will develop only when the administrative apparatus puts an end to surly service in shops and service agencies, to the poorest quality and most limited assortment of goods and services now available in any major industrial country, and to such frustrations as the five-year average wait to obtain contact lenses, described by an ailing laboratory scientist in a letter to the editor.[6] It is only fair to note that *Izvestiya*'s reply to this letter sharply criticized the Ministry of Health for its attitude toward "a problem, which, as we see, worries millions of people."

The administration would have to be much more responsive to the population's obvious, though only partially articulated desire for more and better goods and services, and also for livelier newspapers, more courteous public servants, greater opportunity to travel to other countries, and many other "cultural" benefits which the party has taught the citizenry to desire. Just how much more it would have to give the people before it could dispense with the enormous machine for coercion and suppression upon which it leans so heavily, we can only speculate. Khrushchev apparently hoped that exhortations, combined with loosened administrative bonds, and enhanced opportunities for the populace to participate in peripheral and ceremonial administrative acts would induce the people to give lively support to the party's policies by "voluntarily" backstopping the party-state machines. Beginning in 1960, this hope was frustrated and the growing governmental responsiveness to public demands was arrested, though it may have been revived by Khrushchev's successors in the summer of 1965. That revival increased efficiency in satisfying specific wants for goods and services but could not compare with Khrushchev's attempt to rekindle emotional identification with the regime among the masses.

Obviously, the Soviet formula for public administration emphasizes the party's "leadership," grounded as it is in party control of political indoctrination, and also the selecting of government personnel. After the Party-State Control Committee was established in 1962, primary party organizations normally had an officer — usually one of the deputies to the secretary of the organization — who supervised party-state control activity in the enterprise or other "collective" over which his party organization exercised leadership. Though party directives activate the administrative machine, it is not usually required that Soviet citizens conform on penalty of fines, deprivation of liberty, or other sanctions, until the directives have been translated into laws, decrees, or administrative regulations by legally constituted government institutions.

[6] *Izvestiya*, April 7, 1965.

To be sure, these agencies, units, and groups are guided from within by groups of party members, the leaders of which transmit to their colleagues and subordinates the operational and propaganda directives of party organizations to which theirs are subordinate.

National economic plans are formulated by the highest party leadership but acquire the force of law only after complicated administrative bargaining and consultation and legislative enactment. One reason why there is in the Soviet Union a formal government with authority to employ force if necessary to secure obedience to its commands, is that the communists early found that neither ideological conviction nor sheer force would alone enable them to do the positive and negative work of governing a complex, rapidly modernizing society. It was found almost from the first days that a legitimate authority was also necessary, namely, the "state," endowed with the symbolic majesty of a duly constituted and publicly acknowledged agency for social control.

Another major reason for the development of a vast and complex formal machinery of government was referred to by Moore. He pointed out the need for a trained, disciplined, organized, and suitably specialized and differentiated body of officials capable of complex rational calculation, social control, and other functions. It is difficult to believe that the Soviet communists will achieve much more than token (or fictional) success in their professed objective of eventually replacing the present machinery of state, law, and bureaucracy by voluntary, public organizations. If the party, together with its affiliated and subordinate mass organizations, is ever fully to replace the present system of governmental organizations then it will itself be transformed into a state. Such a transformation would be highly undesirable from the point of view of present Soviet political doctrine, since it would deprive the party of its uniqueness as an ideological, inspirational organization. It would also gravely affect administration. The more the party becomes involved in planning and executing policies other than those crucial for maintaining or strengthening the Soviet system at home or abroad, not to mention routine administrative and supervisory matters, the less effective its long-range policy planning will be. It will also be more vulnerable to the negative impressions upon the public of the myriad everyday mistakes of rank and file functionaries, and to the loss of respect and confidence engendered by many of its representatives' actions.

Barring the replacement of party dictatorship by a system more responsive to the Soviet public's demands, a highly duplicative and wasteful Soviet administration consisting of parallel party and state bureaucracies probably will persist. There is some danger that Britons or Americans, observing the Soviet administration from the perspective of their systems, in which "political" and "governmental" are much more sharply differentiated, may exaggerate the Soviet model's inefficiencies. The interconnection of party and state and party domination of the state confer upon Soviet public administration exceptional unity of control and uniformity of ideological perspective. Great inefficiency may result at lower levels, because of difficulty in communication between the center and the periphery; post-Stalin reforms have been aimed at ameliorating such difficulties. But the Soviet administrative system has the advantage of concentrating effort upon objectives that have highest priority in the calculations of the party leadership, though factional strife at the highest levels, as well as bureaucratic sloth at lower levels, often limit this advantage. Also, the advantages in mobilization of such a system depend greatly upon the party leadership's skill, judgment, and energy. A highly centralized and tightly coordinated system such as the Soviet bureaucracy can get maximum utility out of some policies, but it can also destroy the usefulness of others.[7] The spasmodic production of "dysfunctional outputs" seems to have been increasingly characteristic of the system in the last two or three years of Khrushchev's leadership. In a different way, the system was also increasingly ineffective in the late Stalin era, although then its malady was not Khrushchevian "organizational itch," but incipient paralysis, as Stalin's creative energies waned, but his awestruck lieutenants dared not put forward needed new programs. The rather colorless proceedings of the Twenty-third CPSU Congress and the post-Khrushchev failure to vigorously reform the economy, despite wide discussion of reform proposals in the press, made some analysts of Soviet

[7] On some of the pitfalls in attempting to appraise by "Weberian" and other Western criteria the character and effectiveness of the Soviet bureaucracy, see the contributions of Merle Fainsod and Carl Beck to Joseph La-Palombara, ed., *Bureaucracy and Political Development* (Princeton, N.J., 1963), and also the remarks in the first paragraphs of T. H. Rigby's article, "Crypto-Politics," in *Survey* (Jan., 1964).

affairs suspect that again the system may be faced with the danger of succumbing to immobilism.

In addition to its peculiar relationship with the ruling political party, other characteristics distinguish the Soviet government from its counterparts in more pluralistic systems. An obvious but only too easily forgotten characteristic of Soviet public administration is the practice, not yet dead, of investing even seemingly minor government acts with ideological sacredness. Both oral and written Soviet official communications regarding the processes of government explicitly relate them to Marxist-Leninist doctrine. It is constantly proclaimed that social, and particularly political institutions, such as the army, the Soviets, or the courts, are "schools of communism." Administrative reorganizations, such as that which led to the bifurcation of the party apparatus after the November, 1962 party plenum, are likely to be hailed for their "contribution to the theory of Marxism-Leninism." [8] Such statements can take on an ironic tinge, as in November, 1964 at this particularly significant manifestation of Khrushchev's mania for reorganization, when the example extolled becomes the example deplored. The most significant difference between public administration in the USSR and its American or West European counterparts is the sheer massiveness of Soviet government and its effect upon the citizen's life. The extensiveness of governmental functions is suggested by official statements. A major text on administrative law proclaims that "On the basis of and in the execution of laws, Soviet state organs organize the defense of the USSR, strengthen its power and independence, exercise leadership over the building of the armed forces, conduct, on the basis of a state monopoly, foreign trade, protect state security, assure public order, strengthen and develop socialist property, protect the life, health, the rights and lawful interests of citizens, organize the satisfaction of their social and cultural needs, and take measures looking toward the constant elevation of the material prosperity of the Soviet people." [9]

---

[8] Marchuk, *op. cit.,* p. 5.

[9] V. A. Vlasov and S. S. Studenikin, *Sovetskoe administrativnoe pravo* (Moscow, 1959), p. 9. A similar catalog of governmental activities, with more emphasis upon welfare functions and upon Soviet "democracy," is contained in Part Two, Section III, of the 1961 Party Program. For valuable comment on the party's conception of contemporary and future Soviet governmental and administrative functions, see Herbert Ritvo, *The New Soviet Society* (New York, 1962), pp. 165–88. In post-Stalin, as compared to Stalin-era Soviet writ-

To further remind ourselves of the mass and reach of the Russian government we should recognize that it is far more deeply involved in the economy and in cultural policy than are most other governments. But the party adds to these burdens difficult responsibilities flowing from its self-imposed revolutionary mission of ideological indoctrination and social transformation. It also has the arduous task of trying to raise an economy which is still backward, particularly in the amenities and comforts, to a level not merely equal to, but superior to that of the most advanced industrial economies of the West. A governmental apparatus which performs as many significant functions as that of the Soviet Union, and which generates such relentless demands upon its citizens, requires a ponderous array of administrative and watchdog agencies.

Another distinctive feature of Soviet public administration is the administrative representation of ethnic and cultural factors in the society. The cultural self-consciousness and the habits of communication of the non-Russian ethnic subcultures are accommodated by federalist elements in the state structure and by the use of local languages in educational, law enforcement, judicial, and commercial establishments and other institutions, which work better for that reason. Moscow regards concessions to the non-Russian peoples' national sentiments as transient expedients, the need for which will diminish, accompanying the hoped-for erosion of the attitudes and traditions that still make them necessary.[10] There are formidable administrative safeguards against the potentially dangerous political demands that the aspirations of the non-Russian nationalities may engender. The theory and practice of the party as a single, unified organization is essential to contain these centrifugal urges, but contrasts with and substantially modifies the formal federalism of the constitutional structure. Countervailing centralism, especially in such non-Russian

---

ing on state, government, and law, the positive and "creative" functions of government have increasingly been emphasized, and the regulatory and coercive functions of government have been played down.

[10] Professor A. I. Lepeshkin, of the Institute of Law, Soviet Academy of Sciences, gave an authoritative expression of the Soviet theory on federalism, reflecting with a certain candor its instrumental, temporary place in long-range Leninist perspectives. The paper, entitled "Problems of Development of Soviet Socialist Federation," was presented to the Oxford Round Table Meeting of the International Political Science Association in Sept., 1963. Professor Lepeshkin kindly supplied the writer with a copy of this enlightening paper.

political units as the Turkic-populated Central Asian republics, where cultural distance is greatest between the indigenous population on the one hand and Russians and other Slavs on the other, is accomplished by assigning Russians or other non-natives to sensitive, though usually disguised, posts in the party apparatus, the security police, and any other positions that will help maintain Moscow's influence. The Soviet system of stationing military units far from their native communities serves as another check.[11]

Despite obvious limitations, ethnic federalism in Soviet public law and administration should not be dismissed as insignificant. A relaxing of central administrative controls, particularly in the important Ukrainian Soviet Republic, in 1956 and 1957, was prominent among Khrushchev's policies. The propaganda and psychological significance of this theme is made evident by a long series of measures and statements.[12] Westerners who, like this writer, have taken part in official cultural exchanges involving Soviet officials and intellectuals of non-Russian republics have been able to observe that the latter have strong ethnic pride, which may take the form of touchiness in the presence of Soviet citizens from other republics. On an exchange visit to Kiev University in 1961, we were impressed by the earnestness with which our hosts sought to persuade the Yale University group not to proceed on a tour of the Caucasus and the Russian Federation after leaving Kiev, but to spend the entire available time in the Ukraine. Georgian officials in Tbilisi also displayed coolness toward the Ukrainian professor who accompanied our party as a guide and who had to obtain from the Tbilisi authorities hotel accommodations, etc., for himself and for us.

Although the problem of adapting administrative forms to national structure is separate from that of centralization *versus* decentralization, the two are closely related. The administrative functions of the constituent Soviet republics and even more so those of the local government units within each republic, were

11 The application of this control system to Central Asia is described in detail in Michael Rywkin, *Russia in Central Asia* (New York, 1963), esp. Chs. VII, VIII, and IX. See also William H. Riker, *Federalism* (Boston, 1964), pp. 38–41, for a highly original interpretation.

12 See Part Two, Section IV of the 1961 party program and the statistical and other material on the participation of numerous representatives of non-Russian nationalities in the Soviet of Nationalities, the lower house of the Supreme Soviet, *Ezhegodnik bolshoi sovetskoi entsiklopedii* (Moscow, 1963), pp. 11–13.

enhanced by Khrushchev's decentralizing policies in 1956–1959, though these measures remained within the framework of centralism in policy planning and formulation and local responsibility for policy execution as established by Lenin and Stalin. However, even the modestly increased authority of the republic party and governmental apparatus during Khrushchev's earlier leadership was partially curtailed, consequently playing down nationality as a political and administrative factor by means of the recentralization measures of 1961–1963. Among these the establishment of unified economic administrations for Central Asia and the Caucasus and of special party units for these areas were most important. The Central Asian Economic Administration, however, was abolished after Khrushchev's fall. Post-Khrushchev administrative centralization probably further diminished the republics' political weight compared with that of Moscow, especially in economic administration. The post-Stalin leadership frequently proclaimed that it was bringing about both the "flourishing" and the "rapprochement" of the nations of the USSR. In practice, this formula seems to reflect a desire to elicit the non-Russian nationalities' enthusiastic support for a unified national policy of economic and cultural development. On the positive side, post-Stalin nationality policy featured such psychological boons to non-Russians as the turning over of the Crimea by the Russian to the Ukrainian republic in 1954. However, efforts to administer with tact and with consideration for the sensibilities of the local populations the political units inhabited mostly by non-Russians ran counter to other major trends. As under Stalin, authoritative comment on nationality questions continued to emphasize, though in less menacing language, that although national and cultural factors would be taken carefully into account, they would not be permitted to interfere with the further "rapprochement" of Soviet nationalities or with the development of the unified economy of the country, "organized and developing in accordance with a single state plan." [13] Pavlov referred approvingly to industrial and construction projects involving the movement of many people from various Soviet republics to others. He particularly referred to Central Asia, and quoted a statement by Khrushchev at the November, 1962 party plenum predicting that

[13] E. Pavlov, "Rastsvet i sblizhenie sotzialisticheskikh natsii," *Kommunist*, No. 18, Sept., 1962, pp. 40–50. Quotation on p. 47.

the "exchange of qualified cadres among the nations" would increase in the future. His article, like many others of recent years, hinted at tensions and irritations among non-Russian peoples resulting from increasingly close contacts among Russians and non-Russians, brought about by population movements incidental to the continuing economic integration of the country. As remedies for problems arising in relations among and within national political units, the author prescribed faithfulness to the centralist, "internationalist" principles of the CPSU and a personnel policy eschewing "national isolation," in favor of proper "business-like and political attributes." Behind such cryptic advice lay the realities of continued "Europeanization" of Transcaucasia, Central Asia, and Kazakhstan, and particularly the latter, where the influx of outside settlers has been heavily stimulated since 1954 by the settlement of the Virgin Lands in the northern part of this huge, semidesert area. In October, 1963 the writer noticed that most factory workers whose names and photographs were displayed in a square in Alma-Ata, Kazakhstan, in honor of their good work performance appeared to be Slavs, though most herders and collective farmers similarly honored had Asiatic names and features. The exceptionally high priority given by Stalin's successors to economic productivity and efficiency may have further exacerbated traditionally difficult relations between the central Soviet administration and the non-Russian chiefs of local administrative units. Tension already caused by problems connected with new construction, and tendencies toward heightened economic integration, above all in projects involving more than one republic, may have been increased by clashes between administrators sent into Kazakhstan from Russia and the Ukraine with non-Slavic party and government officials linked both by mutual bureaucratic self-interest and by ethnic and kinship bonds. Such speculation is supported by very heavy turnover among party and government officials in Kazakhstan, Central Asia, and Transcaucasia since the death of Stalin and also by criticism of party and state organizations in these areas for allowing their personnel policy to be influenced by kinship, regional preference, and personal loyalty.[14]

The CPSU leadership has a formidable arsenal of instruments

[14] See *Central Asian Review*, VII, No. 4 (Dec., 1959), Pavlov, *op. cit.*, and *Pravda*, March 25, 1963.

for formulating and executing policy. These controls may conveniently be divided into the following categories: (1) organizational controls, involving the deployment of executives and specialists as considered most appropriate by the leadership for fulfilling current policy goals; (2) personnel controls, including the training and assignment of officials; (3) control by incentives: the planned employment of rewards and deprivations, both ideological and material, commensurate with efficiency and loyalty; and (4) control over the bureaucracy through public organizations. The latter category has been more heavily emphasized in the post-Stalin era than ever before, although it has always been important to Soviet communism. There are also negative controls, exercised mainly by police organs, which will be discussed in Chapter IX.

ADMINISTRATIVE AGENCIES

Since a mere list of party and government administrative agencies would require many pages and would soon be made obsolete by the Soviet system's propensity for organizational reshuffling and relabeling, it seems sensible to limit discussion of structural patterns to broad problems and tendencies.[15]

Let us recall here that the party rules partly directly and partly indirectly, and that the state structure through which policy is administered is itself divided into two pyramidal hierarchies, one headed by the USSR Council of Ministers and the other by the Presidium of the Supreme Soviet of the USSR. (See the charts following Chapter X.) According to the constitution, the Council of Ministers is "responsible" to and "accountable" to the Supreme Soviet. With its associated committees, commissions, and other agencies (collectively designated by the Soviet constitution as the

[15] Historical background and details are available in the excellent studies of Fainsod, Hazard, etc., and in the extremely valuable study by Louis Nemzer, "The Kremlin's Professional Staff: The 'Apparatus' of the Central Committee, Communist Party of the Soviet Union," *American Political Science Review*, XLIV, No. 1 (March, 1950), pp. 64–85, and also in two studies issued, respectively, by the Subcommittee on National Policy Machinery, U.S. Senate, and the Subcommittee on National Security Staffing and Operations. The first of these studies is entitled *National Policy Machinery in the Soviet Union* (Washington, D.C., U.S. Government Printing Office, 1960); the second, *Staffing Procedures and Problems in the Soviet Union* (Washington, D.C., U.S. Government Printing Office, 1963). Up-to-date organizational and personnel studies and charts are made available to the public from time to time both by U.S. government agencies and by such private organizations as the Institute for the Study of the USSR, in Munich.

"government"), it overshadows by its endowment of operational powers the body which stands at the apex of the nationwide system of "legislative" organs to which the Soviet form of government owes its name — the Supreme Soviet of the USSR. The governmental and administrative functions of the Council of Ministers and its subordinate organs are indeed vast.[16]

There is clear evidence that the "rule-applying" agencies have much more weight than the formal "rule-making" agencies (more realistically, "rule-enunciating" agencies). The ministers, whether those of the central government in Moscow or those of the counterpart councils of ministers of the fifteen constituent republics, are extremely busy, full-time officials, whereas deputies to both the USSR Supreme Soviet and the supreme Soviets of the constituent republics work at full-time jobs in industry, agriculture, the professions, etc., and probably devote only a few weeks of each year, at most, to their parliamentary functions. On the other hand, it would be a mistake to regard as politically and psychologically insignificant the Supreme Soviet's symbolism, its continuity with the revolutionary past, or its impressive constitutional prerogatives, including the exclusive right to issue national legislation in order to generate an aura of legitimacy. Also significant are its powers to appoint such powerful officials as the USSR procurator, roughly comparable to the Attorney General of the United States, but with far greater authority, and to elect the members of the USSR Supreme Court and other important officials. To many Soviet citizens — including some members of the intelligentsia, so far as this writer could determine by conversing with professors of Kiev University in March, 1963 — the Supreme Soviet's "sovereignty," despite what we know about party control over it, seems very real and important. It is in the bicameral structure of the Supreme Soviet that the "Leninist nationality policy"

16 This is indicated by the charts and lists in Yu. Kozlov, *Sovetskoe administrativnoe pravo, op. cit.* As of 1964, the Supreme Council of the National Economy (established in March, 1963), directed, under Gosplan (State Planning Committee), fifteen state committees for four industrial fields and, under the Gosstroi (State Construction Administration), thirteen state committees. Through its subordinate Council of the National Economy, it supervised the network of local councils of national economy (*sovnarkhozy*) and other important bodies. In addition, through state committees for procurement, irrigation, etc., and the Ministry of Agriculture, the Union Committee for Agriculture, and other organizations, the Supreme Council, headed by D. F. Ustinov, a First Deputy Minister of the Council of Ministers, directed another vast network of agencies.

receives its most impressive symbolic and ceremonial manifestation.[17] Both the ministerial and the Soviet pyramids extend down from Moscow to the republics, autonomous republics, and lower. At the oblast, city, and still lower levels, the executive committees of the Soviets are the backbone of local government. There are three main groups of ministries: (1) all-union ministries, the heads of which, in Moscow, directly exercise control throughout the entire USSR; (2) union-republic ministries, coordinated from Moscow but administered in each republic by counterpart ministries in the republic capitals; and (3) republican ministries subordinated to the councils of ministers of the fifteen republics. From Stalin's death until Khrushchev's fall, many all-union ministries were converted into union-republic ministries. Together with the many industrial ministries abolished in 1957 and the turning over of numerous administrative functions to oblast and city Soviets, this conversion brought about extensive decentralization of operations.

Khrushchev's administrative decentralization, even at its height, was never as important as it was sometimes held to be in the West — or as Khrushchev claimed it was. In the first place, there were countertrends, such as the establishment in 1954 of the All-Union Ministry of Higher and Specialized Secondary Education, which greatly increased Moscow's control over Soviet higher education. Second, most union-republic and even republic ministries have always been coordinated by bodies and agencies located in Moscow. Although there is no all-union administrative agency for primary and secondary education, educational policy and education throughout the country is supervised by the Academy of Pedagogical Sciences of the RSFSR, in the national capital. Many national administrative agencies have local offices attached to oblast, city, and even lower-ranking Soviets. By the administrative principle known in the Soviet Union as "dual subordination," these local field offices are responsible both to the Soviets to which

17 Deputies to the "upper" house of the Supreme Soviet, the Soviet of the Union, are elected on the basis of one deputy for every 300,000 citizens. Deputies to the Soviet of Nationalities are elected on the following basis: 25 from each union republic, 11 from each autonomous republic, 5 from each autonomous region, and one from each of the very thinly populated but territorially enormous national areas. Elections to the Supreme Soviet are held every four years. The election scheduled for 1944 was not held, but was postponed until Jan., 1946. A Supreme Soviet election took place in March, 1962, and another should have in March, 1966, but was postponed until June.

they are attached, and to the next higher echelon of their own ministerial or committee chain of command. This important feature sharply distinguishes local government in the USSR from those of England or the United States. It is true, as the Soviet press frequently asserts (particularly at election time), that millions of people participate in various ways in Soviet local government. Also, local government units are the lowest levels of a chain of command extending ultimately to Moscow, and the acts of these units and agencies are subject to review by upper echelons. Like the actions of all government agencies in the USSR, they are also subject to controls exercised both by the appropriate levels of the party organization and by a number of agencies of the national government. The party-organized, one-candidate elections of Supreme Soviet and lower soviet deputies, as well as the elections of judges of the people's courts, the lowest level in the judicial system, facilitate rather than obstruct unified administration. The elections do serve important propaganda and even recreational purposes.

Within the broad framework of government operations, party-directed but duplicative and indeed at times quadruplicative and even quintuplicative, which has existed almost from the first days of Soviet power, there have been wide variations in organization. One of the impressive strengths of the Soviet administrative system has been its ability to adapt to changing circumstances. At the same time, the vice of the system is its tendency to respond exaggeratedly, even frantically, in unison with prescriptions and pressures emanating from Moscow. Khrushchev's "corn-hog" agricultural program was applied to soil and climate areas for which it was not suited, and probably in a way not desired by Khrushchev, partly because of the "bandwagon" tendency seemingly built into the highly conformist responses of Soviet middle- and lower-level bureaucrats once a "campaign" is launched from on high. Today, denunciations of Khrushchevian "subjectivism" assail the ear in chorus, but one suspects that the ailment and its concomitants have not yet been cured.

Among the major organizational challenges affecting both party and state administrations the following are highly significant: (1) how extensively the party apparatus, especially the central committee apparatus, should organize special departments to supervise industrial and agricultural production, and whether such "production-branch" units should be responsible for assigning the personnel necessary to carry on their activities or whether personnel controls, information, propaganda, and other activities should be conducted by special central committee "functional" units; (2) how much responsibility for control of various nationwide activities should be centered in Moscow or delegated to republic and lower territorial organizations, both party and state; (3) how directly the party should be involved, if not in operating, at least in supervising and applying ceaseless pressure upon state organizations, especially in the field of production; (4) how far agencies responsible for the performance of functions should be trusted to fulfill their responsibilities without the surveillance of watchdog agencies of the inspectorate type, often operating directly out of Moscow, in the persons of officials not responsible to the appropriate territorial state, or even party, units. The economic police functions of the security agencies under Stalin were a prime example of the latter task. In addition, the Soviet leadership has had to prevent dangerously expensive expansion of staffs, within both party and state bureaucracies, and the related problem of assuring the best possible performance among the numerous and varied apparatuses under its control.

The first of these problems has been referred to in Soviet sources as a choice between "functional" and "production-branch" forms of organization. In fact, it appears that the problem has been one of choosing between maximum effectiveness of political "input" activities and those giving maximum production "output." A "functional" plan was enforced between 1930 and 1934, but there was a turn toward the alternative "production-branch" set-up between 1934 and 1939. It was followed, however, by another switch to "functionalism" at the Eighteenth Party Congress and then again a return to the "production-branch" model after Andrei Zhdanov's death in 1948.

These switches of emphasis apparently reflected the different outlooks of intensely "ideological" leaders such as Zhdanov and more production-conscious party leaders like Malenkov. It also seems that the alternation between these two emphases reflected a sense of urgency regarding political loyalty and ideology during the crucial early years of industrialization in 1930–1934 and the even more critical years when World War II loomed. During the other periods mentioned, apparently it was believed that the type of party administrative organization necessary was that which would best facilitate rapid economic development.[18] Basically, the "production-branch" model re-established in 1948 has persisted.

Regardless of varying emphasis upon central party control of, and involvement in, governmental functions, the party has always had central committee sections or subsections for allocating resources and determining their use and distribution. These have dealt with such fields important to the Kremlin as applying party organizational and ideological policy to the armed forces (through a special political administration), supervising party organizations within the armed forces, as well as mass direction and coordination of the media of mass communication, educational institutions, the scientific research establishment, and one other vital and sensitive sector, the police, prosecution, and judiciary agencies. The latter control is exercised by the powerful and relatively little-publicized section for administrative organs. Next to the section for party organs, and that for supervising propaganda and agitation, the section for administrative organs is probably the most important central committee administrative agency. Finally, there are special central committee sections for dealing with foreign communist parties. Their scope and the publicity given them increased after Stalin died. This trend may have reflected the Kremlin's determination to exploit worldwide social ferment to further expand communism's influence wherever possible. Probably more important, though, was the increased pressure of administrative work and negotiations required by Moscow's effort to cope with increasingly complex relations with foreign communist parties as a result of Sino-Soviet rivalry in the communist movement throughout the world.

The central committee apparatus keeps both the party as a whole and the various government bureaucracies under constant scrutiny. In the pages of *Pravda* and other newspapers, and most of all in the central committee magazine *Party Life* (*Partiinaya zhizn*), the central committee conducts a continuous, systematic public review of party operations. In addition to its editorial section, which, from the summer of 1963 until Khrushchev's removal, directed its fire mainly against the Chinese communists,

18 This interpretation is based partly upon data in Nemzer, *op. cit.*, esp. pp. 80–82.

Party Life contains sections which deal with the following topics: "leadership of the economy," "party-organizational work," and "ideological work." Other sections specialize in such topics as internal party matters and international communism.[19] Thus the party press, in conjunction with other forms of organized pressure, backstops and assists the party and also the state administrative agencies, though its relationship to the latter is likely to be more one of pressure than of assistance.[20] Also used for organized pressure are the "discussions" which follow announcement by the party leadership that it regards certain policies as desirable and which, through "mass campaigns," lead up to the enactment of legislation by the Supreme Soviet.

At all times the central committee apparatus — and of course the supreme party leader, whenever he feels in a strong enough position — reserve the right to intervene directly in administrative matters, often, in fact, in the minutiae of administrative operations. They do so particularly in mass communication, where, as pointed out in Chapter V, the party is of great administrative importance.[21]

The weight in Soviet public administration of various kinds of "inspectorates" is rooted in Russia's centuries of experience with the ways of centralized bureaucracy. It undoubtedly reflects also the requirements of a political authority which has made exceptionally rigorous demands upon its citizens and the natural tendency, in response, toward evasion whenever enforcement of controls has not been effective. The need for such controls, particularly over officials whose jobs make it possible for them

[19] No. 15, Aug., 1964 contained editorials on the importance of improving the services available to Soviet citizens. Incidentally, they severely criticized numerous local government agencies, attacked the Chinese communist leadership, and covered other fields. In the economic section was a discussion of personnel problems in industry, a laudatory article on a former army officer who had voluntarily taken a job in a Siberian city as a factory worker, a discussion by the editor E. I. Bugaev on a "seminar" of secretaries of party committees of production collective farm-state farm administrations in Latvia (entitled "Style and Methods of Work of the Party Committee"). In the party-organizational section and in the ideological section were items on overcoming "survivals of the past" among Soviet people, another on "historical-revolutionary films," etc.

[20] Wolfgang Leonhard, in *The Kremlin Since Stalin* (New York, 1962), esp. pp. 21–24, discusses such "campaigns" as instruments by which the party mobilizes both the administration and the public.

[21] Numerous illustrations of this point are contained in *O partiinoi i sovetskoi pechati* (Moscow, 1954), and in *Voprosy ideologicheskoi raboty* (Moscow, 1961).

to turn a dishonest ruble, is heightened by scarcities and by the absence of a free market which would make black marketing and graft less lucrative than they have been traditionally — and still are. Both the party and the state bureaucracy were extensively fragmented under Stalin, who made the political police his main agency of government. But, mistrustful even of his police chiefs, he set up such special watchdogs over the police as the agency headed at the time of the dictator's death by the dread, shadowy figure, A. N. Poskrebyshev. These, of course, were traits that had been developed by both pre-Soviet and Soviet experience. They were also, above all, a product of the dictator's own extraordinarily suspicious personality. Fortunately, that baneful influence has vanished from the Soviet scene.

The party and police inspection services kept the administration, during the Stalin era, so awe-struck by the authority in Moscow that, although fraud and corruption were never eliminated, the possibility of subversion and open political opposition were reduced almost to nothingness. The terrifying official image of the relationship between inspection organization personnel on the one hand, and even the most highly honored citizens serving in posts of responsibility on the other shows in an account in the military newspaper *Red Star*.[22] It tells how a Red Army colonel, holder of many decorations, reacted with abject fear to an investigator's unfavorable analysis of his work and finally burst into tears.

The atmosphere in which such an episode could be favorably reported (perhaps fabricated by the press) has not existed for a number of years. Criticism within the Soviet press of excessive reliance upon "command" methods of leadership and administration has been profuse. Nevertheless, there seems to be a very strong tendency to evade and violate official controls, especially on the part of officials in a position to benefit by fraud. The party leadership attempts to eradicate or at least to check such damaging activities by maintaining special central control agencies, from time to time establishing new ones. This situation encourages the "snooper" type of citizen, who fairly often takes it upon himself to play the part of an unofficial detective or policeman. He some-

---

22 "The Party Investigator," Sept. 25, 1946. A. E. Lunev, *Obespechenie zakonnosti v sovetskom gosudarstvennom upravlenii* (Moscow, 1963), pp. 117–128 provides much detail on the structure and work of inspection services.

times does so in a fashion which elicits official press rebukes, such as one pillorying a factory official who arbitrarily arrested four of his female employees for alleged theft.[23]

Some of the fundamental agencies of the national government, particularly in the economic field, are mostly "watchdog" agencies, which check on the behavior of government personnel. They include the economic planning agencies, the Ministry of Finance, and other government departments. The name, of course, much more accurately describes such an agency as the Party-State Control Committee, which existed from November, 1962 until December, 1965. It was replaced by a new "mass" agency, named "Organs of People's Control," the latest in a long line of economic and administrative surveillance agencies, the earliest of which was the Commissariat of Workers and Peasants Inspection. By a decision of the Twelfth Party Congress in 1923 this agency was merged with the corresponding party organization, the Central Control Commission. In 1934 the two agencies were again divided into a governmental organization, the Commissariat of Soviet Control, later renamed the Commissariat of State Control, and a party agency, which was renamed the Party Control Commission.[24]

At the Twentieth Party Congress in 1956, Khrushchev complained that the state control organ, which by that time had become a ministry, was functioning poorly.[25] In November, 1956 V. M. Molotov was appointed head of this ministry, but in August, 1957, after Molotov's removal from all positions of major responsibility, G. V. Enyutin replaced him as its head, and its name was changed to Commission of Soviet Control. Enyutin, a veteran party apparatchik with long experience both as a territorial secretary in the Ukraine and as an inspector-overseer working out of the Moscow central committee, served until some time in 1962. He then became head of the RSFSR section of the Party-State Control Committee, under A. N. Shelepin. Apparently the 1957 reorganization of the state control agency, and particularly the change in its name, was meant to create the impression, cherished by Khrushchev, that in controlling the bureaucracy public organizations were to be relied upon increasingly, with staffs recruited

---

[23] *Komsomolskaya Pravda,* April 16, 1965.
[24] *Istoriya kommunisticheskoi partii sovetskogo soyuza* (Moscow, 1963), pp. 374, 485.
[25] *Pravda,* Feb. 15, 1956.

mainly from nonprofessional, unpaid helpers. An expanding system of volunteer "controllers" was organized in Soviet factories, and as early as 1959 it was claimed that in the Russian republic alone there were 37,000 of these "controllers."

By a Supreme Soviet resolution in July, 1961, the organization was renamed the Commission of State Control. Thus it was altered by more openly identifying it as a state disciplinary and economic police agency. Also in 1961, the agency, previously empowered only to impose fines, was given the right to impose penalties for violating the regulations which it enforced of up to three years' deprivation of liberty. These changes coincided with Kremlin agitation over discoveries of major frauds and widespread falsification of reports by industrial and agricultural officials. Also at that time Soviet authorities began to impose the death penalty more frequently for so-called economic crimes. The replacement of the State Control Commission by the still more powerful Party-State Control Committee, headed by powerful party secretariat member Shelepin in November, 1962, was followed by a massive, continuous publicity campaign against violators of state economic discipline. This campaign took such forms as full-page articles and periodic publication of a Party-State Control "list" in *Izvestiya*. These measures were designed to fit such activities into Khrushchev's dogged effort to impart to public administration an aura of popular participation and support. At the same time, they were in effect an admission that there had been disappointingly little progress in suppressing violations of economic discipline, and revealed that Moscow-centered machinery was being strengthened to assure that government directives and regulations were fulfilled, particularly in the economic sphere. That they were needed indicates that the post-Stalin attempt to revitalize primary party organization control over the managing of factories and trade and construction enterprises, the subject of an important central committee resolution of June 26, 1959, had not yet achieved satisfactory results.

Changes in the mechanism for controlling the fulfilment of state administrative regulations did not involve abolishing the central committee agency for making sure that party members and party organizations observed the program, statutes, and directives of the party. The name of this agency was changed, at the Twenty-second Party Congress, from Committee of Party Control to Party Commission. Immediately after the Twenty-third Congress, Arvid Pelshe replaced N. M. Shvernik as head of this agency.

The party plenum held on December 6, 1965, abolished the powerful Party-State Control Committee, and instituted the above-mentioned, apparently less powerful "Organs of People's Control." The resolution establishing the new "people's control" organs said nothing of the new bodies having jurisdiction over party activity, indicating that they were meant to give the party leadership control over the state machine rather than both the party and the state bureaucracies. Thus the last of Khrushchev's major organizational innovations was reversed. This change represented another of the post-Khrushchev steps toward restoring the late Stalin demarcation of functions among party, state, and "public" agencies. It seemed to indicate that the leadership was determined to permit neither state nor public organizations to interfere in the administration of the party machine. The Party-State Control Committee's abolition was important because of the presumably negative effect it had, at least temporarily, on the power position of the man who had headed it, Alexander Shelepin. The man chosen to head the new agency, Pavel Kovanov, was relatively junior in party status, at the time of his appointment being only a candidate for membership in the Central Committee.

The leaders who followed Stalin apparently felt that one way to facilitate the CPSU's control over a more complex society was to greatly expand its membership. Between the Nineteenth Congress in October, 1952 and the plenum of November, 1962, party membership grew by 50 per cent, an extraordinary rate of growth, resulting in a membership of almost 11,000,000 by the latter date.[26] As previously noted, membership increased to 11,500,000, by late 1964, and reached more than 12,000,000 by 1966. However, expansion in party membership was accompanied by a rigorous and evidently successful attempt to reduce both the number of party members employed as apparatus functionaries, and also the size of the apparatus. An important step in the pruning campaign was a central committee resolution of May 21, 1957, prescribing that in primary party organizations with less than one hundred members, party work should be conducted by secretaries not ex-

[26] Herbert Ritvo, "Party Controls Reorganized," *Survey* (Oct., 1963), p. 88.

empted from their regular jobs. Noting that the number of paid workers of primary party organizations, compared with 1940, had increased by almost five times, the resolution stated that this growth was incompatible with the party's effort to increase communists' initiative and to cut the cost of the paid apparatus.[27] The thinning out of the party apparatus was part of a larger operation designed to reduce both the economic and the psychological costs of the top-heavy bureaucracy through which Stalin had ruled Russia. Administrators and office workers in all fields were transferred by the thousands to factory and farm work. The Soviet armed forces also were affected by this effort to increase the proportion of the working population directly engaged in material production. Marshal F. I. Golikov, at the time chief of the armed forces political administration, reported to the Twenty-second Party Congress that more than 200,000 of the Soviet servicemen who had been "put on the reserve" had gone to work on "construction projects of communism" and that thousands of officers had started working, after demobilization, "in the sphere of material production." [28]

If Stalin regarded the Soviet Union as a gigantic barracks, Khrushchev seems to have thought of it as one big factory. The indications are that his successors are even more inclined in this direction. By May, 1962 Frol R. Kozlov was able to report that, in comparison with January 1, 1956, when for each 1,000 communists working in industry, construction, and transport, 130 were employed in the administrative apparatus, by January 1, 1961, the number so employed had been reduced to 46. The remainder were engaged directly in production.[29] By 1963, there were only a third as many full-time apparatchiki per 1,000 party members as in 1940.[30]

The campaign to pluck party, government, and economic administrators out of their chairs and put them to work at the factory bench was accompanied by what appears to have been a vigorous effort to compel the Soviet labor force as a whole, its administrative officers most of all, to increase their efficiency.

27 *Spravochnik partiinogo rabotnika* (Moscow, 1957), pp. 440–41.
28 *Soviet News,* London, Nov. 1, 1961, p. 122; *Manchester Guardian Weekly,* Dec. 30, 1954; item in *Pravda,* June 10, 1955, entitled "Concerning Swollen Staffs and Kibitzers," examining the situation which necessitated drastic cuts in "non-productive" office staffs.
29 *Kommunist,* No. 8, April, 1962, p. 12.
30 Ritvo, *op. cit.,* p. 89; Pigalev, *op. cit.,* p. 60.

Khrushchev and his successors have done everything possible to spread abroad the idea that leaders and specialists in all fields could win promotions, or even hold their jobs, only by "getting results." A prime example of the result was the leapfrog of leaders in the Ministry of Agriculture from 1954 on. The struggle to replace "old" methods and men by those with a feeling for the "new" brought on nationwide campaigns popularizing modern methods of administration and production and a struggle, to use the language of a headline, "To Achieve the Greatest Results with the Least Costs." [31] Bureaucratic "comebacks" can occur in the Soviet Union, however, as proven by the return to that post in February, 1965 of V. V. Matskevich, fired by Khrushchev as Minister of Agriculture in early 1961. A related event was the rise to full central committee membership in November, 1964 of P. M. Masherov, long an associate of the anti-Khrushchev, pro-Matskevich leader, K. T. Mazurov, who in March, 1965 achieved full presidium status.

If the Soviet leadership actually succeeded in effecting the impressive manpower savings and increased administrative efficiency indicated by the Soviet press, this result may have been achieved partly because of Khrushchev's streamlining of the party, state, and economic bureaucracy. It may have owed much also to the rapid promotion of younger and better educated executives in the party and other apparatuses. The Khrushchev "renewal" of cadres was carried out on the whole in a businesslike manner, and was not accompanied by wholesale imprisonment or disgracing of displaced individuals as in Stalin's time. On the contrary, it appears that there was a systematic effort to retrain displaced officials for new jobs and to assist them in making difficult adjustments. [32]

[31] *Pravda,* May 22, 1964. This lengthy article reported an all-Russian conference on problems in the industry and construction economy, in which such party luminaries as A. P. Kirilenko, N. V. Podgorny, V. N. Titov, and A. N. Shelepin participated.

[32] This impression is given in the above-mentioned report in the *Manchester Guardian Weekly,* as well as in an article by Paul Wohl in *The New Leader,* April 17, 1961, and also by Khrushchev's statement that there was a place in Soviet executive ranks "for vigorous young men and for experienced older men." The Party's effort to suggest that solicitude was being shown for worthy party members who had to be transferred from one kind of work to another was exemplified in the article in *Partiinaya zhizn,* No. 15, Aug., 1964, entitled "Vsegda na perednem krae," describing the model behavior of a demobilized army captain who sought factory employment in far-off Omsk, and was rewarded by the appropriate party organization. That there may have been anxiety and resentment among senior party and government executives be-

According to Soviet sources, a vast program "drawing communists to the carrying out of party work in the capacity of non-professionals, in the form of public activity" accompanied the drive to effect administrative economy in the party and other echelons of society.[33]

Early in 1962, after the above trends were given fresh impetus by the Twenty-second Party Congress, it was asserted that more than 50,000 party members were working as nonprofessional instructors of party committees, 105,000 as nonprofessional lecturers, and more than 80,000 on permanent commissions of raion party committees. In all, it was claimed that almost a million party members were engaged in activities of this kind — in addition to more than two million communists who, as members of elected party organs, were doing party work.[34]

Party members thus engaged in furnishing unpaid assistance to the professional party apparatus did all sorts of work, as propagandists and lecturers, assisting the "ideological commissions" set up in local party organizations, serving on commissions to assist the professional apparatus in recruitment into the party, and assisting the apparatus in controlling industrial organizations. Such activities were further expanded after the Party-State Control Committee was established, when its "groups of assistance" were formed. It was stated that their tasks were "to actively influence the perfection of the apparatus of ministries and departments, to help the party organizations train civil servants in the spirit of high responsibility for the matters entrusted to them, and instill a solicitous attitude toward the requests and letters of the working people," etc.[35] These groups of public "controllers" brought the party into public administration in a fashion which

---

cause of pressure to replace them by younger men was indicated by a number of post-Khrushchev press statements signed by such senior party leaders as V. P. Mzhavanadze, head of the Georgian party organization, G. Popov, first secretary of the Leningrad city party committee, and others, which criticized the excessively rapid replacement of veterans by youngsters. See *Pravda,* May 25 and May 30, 1965, the latter containing an article on this subject by the head of the Lipetsk city committee. These statements of course may have had political rather than administrative motivations, but in the Soviet context they obviously had important implications for administration.

33 Pigalev, *op. cit.,* p. 60.

34 *Ibid.,* pp. 60–63.

35 N. Sidorov, "Kontrolery v sovetskikh uchrezhdeniyakh," *Partiinaya zhizn,* No. 8, April, 1964, p. 34.

seemed to violate the still honored principle of separating party and state administrations.[36]

It appears that the attitudes of some members of the growing nonprofessional party apparatus which began to take shape after 1959 aroused anxiety in the professional party apparatus. In 1964 some unpaid secretaries of primary party organizations in industrial enterprises were said to believe that their superiors on production jobs did not have the right to punish them for violations of work discipline but must report such matters to the appropriate party authorities. The central committee's main organizational journal sternly reminded such party activists that the Ninth Party Congress had laid down the principle that communists working in industrial enterprises enjoyed no special privileges, but, on the contrary, bore special responsibilities. This organ stressed that although some economic officials attempted to "get even" with subordinates who outranked them in party status, the party organizations in these rare cases had "sufficient rights to correct the economic leader in good time." [37] An editorial even went so far as to declare that party organizations should not hesitate to eliminate the nonprofessional apparatus where it was superfluous.[38]

These and other items in the Soviet press indicated that the hopes entertained during the first flush of enthusiasm following the Twenty-second Party Congress that party functions would more and more be transformed from professional to "public" activities might not soon be realized. Several problems were apparently posed by expanding the nonprofessional party apparatus at the expense of the paid apparatus. It appeared that there was a tendency to transfer the burden of paying for the work of the party apparatus from the budget of the party central committee to the budgets of state and economic institutions. Perhaps more important, excessive self-confidence and authority given to the nonprofessional activists might challenge the authority of the party apparatus itself. Finally, there was a danger that nonprofessional party workers' officiousness might aggravate relations between the party apparatus and the managerial bureaucracy.

[36] Ritvo, *op. cit.*, pp. 87–88, has some pertinent observations on how the establishment of the Party-State Control Committee affected the principle of separation of party and state administration.
[37] *Partiinaya zhizn*, No. 8, April, 1964, pp. 47–48.
[38] *Partiinaya zhizn*, No. 10, May, 1964.

The episodes mentioned touch, albeit tangentially, on matters of basic significance for the Soviet system. However visionary it may appear even to its own leaders, the party is doctrinally committed to ultimately eliminating government as a bureaucratic, coercive part of society. On the other hand, for the foreseeable future it requires an efficient apparatus, both within the party organization itself and in the government bureaucracy, to survive and flourish. The party leadership also apparently feels it necessary to impose upon all Soviet citizens, including party members, strict and indeed severe state discipline. It is significant that the rules adopted by the Twenty-second Party Congress included the provision, carried over from earlier versions only slightly amended, that if a party member commits an indictable offense he must be expelled from the party and prosecuted in conformity with the law.[39]

In spite of the Soviet system's revolutionary origins and pretensions, it has gradually built up stable, graded civil service agencies whose personnel display many similarities of function, organization, and outlook to their counterparts in non-Soviet polities.[40]

Khrushchev's neo-Leninism aroused irritation and anxiety in some administrative services, particularly among industrial administrators and some party apparatchiki, and also among judges, lawyers, and law enforcement officials perturbed by the party's limited but potentially threatening ventures in popularizing law enforcement. It did not undermine the bureaucracy and probably was not intended to do so, but rather was designed to check or reverse "conservative" tendencies. In particular, Khrushchev apparently disliked and feared tendencies among officials to develop styles of life and behavior different both from those of the territorial party apparatchiki from which he had emerged and from those of the working "masses." Accordingly, he sought to reduce the advantages enjoyed by children of highly placed officials and

---

[39] See Section I, Article 12, of the 1961 party rules adopted at the Twenty-second Party Congress.

[40] No fully satisfactory book-length treatment of the Soviet governmental bureaucracy as a whole is available. However, valuable material is contained in *Staffing Procedures and Problems, op. cit.*, and in Alf Edeen, "The Civil Service: Its Composition and Status," in Cyril E. Black, *The Transformation of Russian Society* (Cambridge, Mass., 1960), pp. 274–92. See also the articles in Parts Two and Three of Black, Ch. XII of Fainsod, *How Russia Is Ruled*, and pertinent material in Moore, *Terror and Progress*, and Armstrong, *The Soviet Bureaucratic Elite*. Soviet texts on administrative law also contain much useful, if not very detailed, material.

professionals in obtaining the educational qualifications which so generally determine access to Soviet society's upper echelons. To be sure, in Khrushchev's own family, his son-in-law, Aleksei Adzhubei, was editor-in-chief of *Izvestiya* and similarly, the sons of top-ranking government officials such as Andrei Gromyko or Mikhail Menshikov served, at early ages, in important posts in the Soviet foreign affairs bureaucracy, indicating that a rigorous and consistent campaign was not being conducted against the privileges of the "new class." Adzhubei's status, of course, but not that of the nepotistic "new class" generally, fell, together with that of his father-in-law, in October, 1964.

The seriousness of the problem of stratifying status and rank in an economy expanding as rapidly as that of the USSR, with its high social mobility, should not be exaggerated. However, Khrushchev's concern about such matters points to social tensions which must be taken into account if we are to understand the Soviet government bureaucracy's characteristics and social position.

The Soviet communists built a state and military bureaucracy because they needed such formations in order to govern, defend, and consolidate their revolutionary new order. They entered upon this task intensely suspicious and hostile toward those members of the old tsarist bureaucracy whom they were forced to employ as civil service bureaucrats and experts, especially during the first ten or fifteen years of the Soviet regime, when there was still a desperate shortage of trained manpower of all kinds. In 1957 it was pointed out in an authoritative Soviet publication that for nearly two decades the dominant element in the Soviet civil service had been "persons who originated in the petty-bourgeois group, formerly the exploiting classes." [41]

To deal with this situation, the regime practiced self-protective discrimination and vigilant surveillance toward administrative functionaries and their children. At the same time it made it easier for able, ambitious children of industrial workers and peasants to be recruited into and rapidly advanced within the administrative ranks, particularly in such sensitive branches as the military officer corps and the political police. However, the vastly expanded civil service resulting from industrialization in the 1930's and the development of an administration much of

[41] *Partiinaya zhizn*, No. 20, Oct., 1957, p. 58, quoted by Edeen, p. 284.

which was drawn from worker and peasant backgrounds, led to the dropping of discriminatory practices such as the preference for admission into the party formerly given to children of workers and peasants. Still, as late as 1941, Georgi M. Malenkov considered it necessary to denounce the choosing of functionaries for party and administrative organs according to the person's "family tree" and proletarian origins rather than his practical and political qualifications.[42]

As Edeen notes, "During the 1930s many rules and stipulations were once again introduced for the purpose of gaining control over and at the same time granting authority to the powerfully expanding and differentiated administrative apparatus." [43] Along with party apparatchiki, military officers, and successful scientists and artists, the civil servants now became members of a privileged elite. Some members of the industrial working class and party officials of working class origin still hold a certain contempt for "bureaucrats," and even for creative intellectuals and other persons who do not earn their living either by political work or with their hands. It appears, though, that the pervasive party controls and the persisting proletarian ideal, together with Russian nationalism, limit the divisive effects of bureaucratic rank consciousness.[44]

We must mention again the extensive interlocking and overlapping of the party and other bureaucracies at the upper levels. At the very highest levels the various hierarchies are just about fused. As one study notes, the top 15 to 20 per cent of government positions, including all key "national security" positions, are controlled by the party, the secretariat of which is directly involved in selecting a number of the most important officials. According to the same study, however, assignments to the remaining 80 to 85 per cent of government posts "are completely within the purview of the employing agency, subject to compliance with existing classification schedules, tables of organization and service regulations." [45] A number of agencies, in addition to the party secretariat, have a hand in staffing the governmental bureaucracy. The

[42] *Ibid.*, pp. 284–86.
[43] *Ibid.*, p. 286.
[44] Pertinent comment on these problems is contained in the contributions of Robert A. Feldmesser and George Fischer to Black, *Transformation of Russian Society, op. cit.*
[45] *Staffing Procedures, op. cit.*, p. 17.

Ministry of Finance determines the wage fund of ministries, state committees, and enterprises. The State Staffing Commission (*Gosudarstvennaya shtabnaya komissiya*), established in 1941, establishes tables of organization and salary schedules for government agencies, as well as standard job descriptions, fixing ceilings on the staff size, etc.[46] The State Committee on Labor and Wages works out uniform salary scales and prepares drafts for legislation on salaries and wages.

The Central Statistical Administration gathers, collects, and disseminates manpower statistics and maintains a central personnel file. The Party-State Control Committee also shared control of the civil service through its responsibility for detecting violations of laws, government regulations, and party directives. In the Ministry of Higher and Specialized Secondary Education is a department that plans the training and placement of graduates, collecting requests from government agencies for graduates of the institutions of higher education under its jurisdiction, matching these requests with the expected output of each educational institution, and allocating the graduates according to priority among various educational institutions.[47]

The Soviet educational system has a major though indirect part in recruiting government servants and increasingly in recruiting people for every type of career. Partly for this reason, Soviet young people compete intensely for acceptance by the leading universities and institutes. Various bureaucracies have their own service schools, including the party apparatus, the military services, the KGB, the Ministry of Foreign Affairs (Higher Diplomatic School), the Ministry of Foreign Trade (Institute of Foreign Trade), and others.[48] Of course, they also draw on the stream of graduates of regular institutions of higher education. A directive issued in June, 1960 required that these institutions, before the end of the school year, set up placement commissions with ultimate responsibility for placing graduates. These commissions include school and local government officials, trade union and party representatives, and often representatives of agencies seeking to recruit personnel for sensitive fields, such as the diplomatic service, the

[46] Fainsod, *op. cit.*, pp. 415, 519, gives a good description of this agency, the title of which he translates as Central Establishments Administration; see also *Staffing Procedures, op. cit.*, p. 18.

[47] *Staffing Procedures*, pp. 18–19.

[48] *Ibid.*, p. 32.

KGB, and the military establishment. There are special procedures for earmarking the promising aspirant, who may be sent to the school operated by the agency that chooses him.[49] Once the aspiring young official has cleared the first hurdles by obtaining the necessary education and being accepted into a branch of government service, his or her advancement depends upon seniority, staying out of trouble, and quality of performance on the job. There is a much higher proportion of women in the civil service, as in the labor force generally, than is found in other countries, although its highest rungs are still overwhelmingly dominated by men. Positive incentives for superior performance, besides salary increases and other material incentives contingent on promotion, include numerous rewards designed to confer personal satisfaction and public recognition.[50] There is a corresponding array of fines, reprimands, and more severe penalties for negligent, faulty, or, worse yet, criminal conduct in public office.[51]

Since the death of Stalin the Soviet leadership apparently has sought to increase organized social pressure upon officials to assure exemplary performance of their duties. Centrally administered rewards, especially material ones, and prestige rewards, such as Lenin prizes, orders, medals, personal ranks and titles, etc., as well as deprivations in the form of prison, exile, and even execution, are still much used in controlling Soviet public administration. Some cruder forms of both rewards and penalties are less used. By a Supreme Soviet decree of July 12, 1954, personal ranks were abolished for most civilian positions. They are retained, however, in the military services and also in the diplomatic service and for prosecutors and criminal investigators.[52] And, as Edeen suggests, the contrast between Stalin and post-Stalin treatment of demoted or retired executives, many of whom now live comfortably on pensions, involves "a return to methods which correspond somewhat to the prerevolutionary order." [53] If this proves to be a stable trend, it may turn out that the "Leninist" Khrushchev may actually have promoted, in public administration and in society generally, trends far more "conservative" than those favored by

49 *Ibid.,* pp. 32–33, 57–62.
50 See Petrov, *op. cit.,* pp. 211–13, 272–87.
51 *Ibid.,* pp. 213–26, 261–67.
52 Petrov, *op. cit.,* p. 213.
53 Edeen, *op. cit.,* p. 290.

Stalin, who is often credited with having introduced a measure of stability in the society and in the polity.

We have had to ignore many legal and organizational aspects of Soviet public administration, but one deserves brief mention: ministries and other administrative agencies normally attempt to combine the advantages of "one man rule" (*edinonachalie*) and "collegialness" (*kollegialnost*). Most Soviet administrative agencies are headed by a chief, who may have the title of minister, chairman, chief, etc., with full personal and, under certain conditions, criminal responsibility for his agency and his staff. "One man rule" is balanced, however, by providing the chiefs of administrative agencies with "colleges" of advisers, usually consisting of deputy ministers and a handful of other high-ranking officials, to clarify responsibility by the widest possible range of expert opinion.[54] The alternation of these two organizational styles in the state bureaucracy finds a certain parallel in the ebb and flow of popularity in the party organization of "collective leadership." It appears that in handling this and other broad administrative problems the Soviet system has been moderately successful. It continues to suffer, in the opinion of many, from overcentralization, poor coordination, and other inadequacies probably inherent in the continued effort of an elitist, centralized, and bureaucratic political party, however large, and however much its leaders may seek to keep it open to those of talent, to operate an increasingly complex, maturing industrial society.

Let us now examine Soviet industrial and agricultural administration. Even more fully than it was under Stalin, the Soviet leadership is committed to the view that the future of Soviet Russia and of mankind in general will be determined by the Soviet economy's productivity and efficiency. This emphasis upon the production battle is perhaps most strikingly indicated by the concentration of more than 70 per cent of the party's membership in "the sphere of material production."[55] It would be inappropriate to analyze here in detail the principles and techniques upon which the operation of the Soviet economy is based. But to understand Soviet economic organization requires some knowledge of two fundamental characteristics of the economy. In spite of the

[54] For a discussion of these points see Petrov, *op. cit.*, pp. 158–62.
[55] *Partiinaya zhizn*, No. 8, April, 1964, p. 9.

many important changes since Stalin's death, essentially the Soviet economy still runs by the allocating of resources by administrative decision rather than by a market mechanism. Its operations are still governed by a priority system that gives preference to capital goods and military and scientific development over consumer goods. Because of the way in which these principles are applied, consumer sovereignty, in which condition the producing of goods is determined by the combined prices made in the marketplace by millions of consumers, cannot develop in the Soviet Union.[56] Since Stalin's time, the leadership obviously has been keenly aware of shortcomings in the economy, particularly in agriculture, and of general dissatisfaction caused by shortages and low-quality consumer goods and, to judge by frequent complaints in the press, extremely bad performance of laundry, dry cleaning, and other service industries.[57] The party has been attempting to improve this very bad situation, but one gets the impression that much of its effort is devoted to organizational and hortatory activity, and not to fundamental changes in the balance between consumer goods and services and other economic outputs or the kind of structural reform which might bring radical improvement.[58] For some years now there has been a debate that may be of great future significance but is at present difficult to evaluate. The subject is the crucial economic problem of the method by which and the agencies by which economic plans are drafted. However, even the most far-reaching proposals thus far discussed in the Soviet

[56] A valuable analysis of post-Stalin developments in the operating principles of the Soviet economy is Harry G. Shaffer, "What Price Economic Reforms?" in *Problems of Communism*, XII, No. 3 (May–June, 1963), pp. 18–26; see also Rush V. Greenslade, "Khrushchev and the Economists," in *ibid.*, pp. 27–32; Abraham S. Becker's extremely careful study "Soviet Military Outlays Since 1955" (RAND Memorandum RN–3886–PR, Santa Monica, July, 1964) indicates that as of 1962, Soviet military expenditures were considerably higher than in 1955. This trend has interesting implications regarding Soviet economic policy generally and in particular, of course, for the Soviet standard of living.

[57] See the lead editorial in *Kommunist*, No. 1, Jan., 1964, which noted on p. 11 that the Soviet Union's population was forced to devote to self-service activities the "astronomical" total of one hundred billion man-hours a year, and also pointed out that of 127 hours a week of "non-working time" only 20 hours, or approximately three hours a day were devoted to leisure, while 31 hours a week were devoted to domestic work and self-service and 14 hours a week to getting to and from work, etc. See also the startling figures on the lack of leisure time of Soviet workers in S. G. Strumilin, *Problemy sotsializma i kommunizma v SSSR* (Moscow, 1961), pp. 374ff.

[58] See the second lead editorial in *Partiinaya zhizn*, No. 17, Sept., 1964, devoted to the work of party organizations of Moscow service industries.

press, including the well-known schemes of Evsei Lieberman, now partially adopted, do not go very far toward suggesting that a "socialist market economy" be established, such as has existed in Yugoslavia for a number of years.

Experiments with market economy techniques took on added impetus after the downfall of Khrushchev. It is true that Khrushchev had encouraged discussion of proposals that managers be given an incentive to concern themselves about quality, as well as quantity of output. Traditionally, industrial establishment managers had been interested mainly in achieving global plan targets and were thus tempted to concentrate on the items easiest to produce, and also to understate their plants' capacities in order to make the best possible showing by overfulfilling a plan drafted in Moscow. His successors, going further in their economic thinking, and tinkering, appeared to be committed to policies which would give plant managers, at least in some industries producing consumer goods, incentives to produce goods tailored to consumer tastes. Even if there were much progress in this direction it would still leave investment and other crucial levers of economic control completely in party hands.

Certainly much strenuous effort was devoted to the structural reorganization in the direction of Soviet industry, construction, and agriculture after Stalin's death, particularly in the years 1957–1964. Until 1958, the trend was toward reducing the work of Moscow-centered agencies in administering agriculture, and toward increased reliance both on local party officials of the units and on farms themselves. In agricultural administration the Ministry of Agriculture's influence began to be reduced in the autumn of 1953 and that of the rural party apparatus was increased. In 1955, the agricultural planning system was modified so as to better take into account local conditions and to facilitate more active participation in planning by the collective farms. The first phase of reorganization in agricultural administration ended in 1958 with the Machine Tractor Stations (MTS) abolished; a few years earlier special party units had been established to control them more effectively.[59] This step and the 1955 planning reform

[59] Howard R. Swearer, "Changing Roles of the CPSU under First Secretary Khrushchev," *World Politics*, XV, No. 1 (Oct., 1962), pp. 20–43, 26–27. Also very useful in the preparation of the section of this chapter was Dr. Swearer's unpublished paper, "Agricultural Administration under Khrushchev," prepared for the Kansas University Conference on Agricultural and Peasant

survived all subsequent reversals, and together these measures gave to agricultural administration a great deal of new flexibility. Apparently the 1958 reforms of agricultural organization were motivated mostly by the realization that excessive party involvement in agricultural management had begun to produce harmful effects, including a loss of "that detached critical attitude toward management demanded by partiinost, or party spirit." [60] In 1957, abolition of the agricultural and other specialized departments of the raion party organization was begun. In March, 1962, finally, the raions were abolished as administrative units in the countryside and amalgamated into large districts, within which agriculture was henceforth to be administered by so-called territorial production collective farm-state farm administrations.[61] After Khrushchev's fall, however, along with the undoing of other Khrushchev organizational measures, the raions were restored, although not exactly in their earlier form. Generally, the new raions corresponded in size to the territorial collective farm-state farm production administrations. Beginning in November, 1962 the party organizations below the republic level were divided into agricultural and industrial networks and the Soviets, or local government agencies were similarly divided. Judging by post-Khrushchev press comment this change created much administrative confusion and anguish. It may also have had the advantage, which Khrushchev claimed for it at the November, 1962 party plenum, of facilitating assignment of party secretaries to the type of work for which their experience and talents best fitted them. It was thus a step toward increasing the party apparatus' administrative efficiency. One obvious disadvantage of this change is that it greatly increased the number of party organizations within the country and thereby made supervision, paper work, and control much more difficult. It also tended to distract the apparatus from its traditional work, mobilizing and coordinating other bureaucracies and the general public.

Studies done by Sidney Ploss and Howard Swearer indicate that during the confused years 1958–1962 a power struggle took place

Affairs, Sept., 1963, a copy of which he furnished to the writer. See also, especially on top-level political reverberations of shifting agricultural policies, Sidney I. Ploss, *Conflict and Decision-Making in Soviet Russia* (Princeton, N.J., 1965), Chs. V, VI.

[60] Swearer, *ibid.*, p. 27.
[61] *Ibid.*, p. 30; Fainsod, *op. cit.*, p. 401.

between the Khrushchev faction in the party apparatus and a coalition of anti-Khrushchev leaders, allied with the Ministry of Agriculture. The Ministry obviously was the loser in this struggle, for in 1961 it was stripped of most of the powers it had retained after earlier reforms. It was reduced to an educational and scientific organ, and, as previously noted, V. V. Matskevich was dismissed as minister. However, the ministry was avenged after Khrushchev's fall. In line with the recentralizing trend beginning in 1960 and 1961, a unified State Committee for Agricultural Procurement was formed to contract for purchases from the collective farms and care was devoted to isolating its inspectors from local pressures.[62] Other centralized agencies, including a new Agricultural Equipment Association, were entrusted with controlling and supervising national agricultural policy. To assure central party guidance, an organizer from the oblast party committee was placed in each territorial production collective farm-state farm administration, and was charged with assisting primary party organizations of collective farms and state farms in "organizational and mass-political work." [63] By 1962 a new unified bureaucracy had been created to administer agriculture, but differences of opinion persisted about how to coordinate the work of party and state agencies in the agricultural field. These were indicated by such signs as postponement of a central committee plenum from mid-December, 1960 to mid-January, 1961, and published articles expressing views at variance with those of Khrushchev. In the meantime, in the party, especially in the party organization leadership in Kazakhstan and Central Asia, turnover of high-level cadres became very heavy and there also occurred the veritable leapfrog of Ministry of Agriculture leadership. Above all, agricultural output lagged until finally the disastrous harvest of 1963 forced Khrushchev into the politically disadvantageous step of buying Western wheat — a step to which his successors, albeit on a smaller scale, also resorted in 1965.

Western experts agree that close to half the Soviet population still makes its living in agriculture. The Soviet collective or state farmer remains under very tight organizational and political control. Workers on state farms, unlike their countrymen in the collective farms, draw salaries or wages like factory or office workers,

[62] Swearer, *op. cit.,* p. 30.
[63] *Ibid.,* p. 31.

depending on whether they belong to management or to labor. The Twenty-third Congress recommended, however, that collective farmers in the future also be paid a wage. Many rural residents are, by occupation, workers, and like industrial workers, they belong to trade unions.

The economic well being of Soviet collective farmers, compared to that of industrial workers, has somewhat improved since Stalin's day. This relative improvement is not necessarily an absolute rise in living standards (some experts think they have actually declined since about 1960); it resulted from the higher prices paid to farmers for their produce and from other measures. Social security benefits, formerly reserved for city dwellers, were extended to the collective farmers in 1964. Khrushchev spent a great deal of time traveling about the Soviet countryside assuring the peasants of his interest in their welfare. On the other hand, he was more loath than his successors appear to be to permit collective farmers to devote much time and energy to cultivating the limited "private" plots upon the productivity of which much of the Soviet food supply still depends. Post-Khrushchev farm policy was more "liberal" than that of Khrushchev in some respects although it remains to be seen if the new leadership will develop a long-range program for fundamentally improving agricultural performance and the farmers' welfare compared with that of the urban population. Toward that end, Khrushchev was at least groping, and some powerful members of the post-Khrushchev leadership, including Mikhail Suslov and K. T. Mazurov, seem to have been opposed to it. It was also significant that F. D. Kulakov, the party secretariat member charged with supervising agriculture by the September, 1965 central committee plenum had earlier opposed Khrushchev's policies, and been downgraded by him.

In industry, Khrushchev's overriding objective apparently was to strengthen pary control and simultaneously to increase productivity.[64] The decentralization measures of 1957, establishing about one hundred councils of national economy to replace the economic ministries that formerly directed most industrial, construction, and related functions, seemed very successful for a time, but had the disadvantage of encouraging "localism," or the hoarding by factory directors and other economic officials of resources

---

[64] Swearer, *op. cit.*, pp. 32–34; Jeremy R. Azrael, "Politics and Management," *Survey*, No. 49, Oct., 1963, pp. 90–101; Barsukov, *op. cit., passim.*

in their regions. Also, the boundaries of the councils of national economy generally coincided with those of the oblasts, encouraging collusion between the heads of the councils and the obkom party leadership. Two early measures were designed to curb activities deemed objectionable by the party leadership and at the same time to replace "administrative" methods of economic leadership by the ideological inspiration which Khrushchev saw in the influence of the party, the trade unions, and the Komsomol.[65] These were the decree of April 24, 1958, providing penalties for "localist" offenses, and the establishing in 1959 of commissions in primary party organizations of production and commercial enterprises to assist the party organizations in exercising their "right of control" over the economic administrations.

Even more important was the consolidating and great reduction of the councils of national economy following the November, 1962 plenum. The jurisdictions of obkom secretaries and heads of councils, which formerly coincided, were separated. Perhaps the most fundamental of Khrushchev's initiatives in industrial management was his attempt to enhance the party's entrepreneurial role by bringing into the lower ranks of the party apparatus many successful industrial managers and practicing engineers, as distinguished from party officials with engineering education but with little or no experience in their profession.[66] This "specialization" of the party apparatus promised to energize the economy by replacing executives cowed by years of Stalinist terror with fresh, highly trained, businesslike production leaders. There were significant risks, however. It was possible that the party apparatus would become so production-oriented that it could not properly perform its other functions and that an influx of relatively non-ideological specialists, as Leonid F. Ilichev apparently feared, might sap the ideological dynamism of the apparatus as a whole.[67] Such fears were among the factors responsible for the restoring of a more traditional party organization, presumably conducive

---

[65] *Vedomosti verkhovnogo soveta,* May 28, 1958, p. 499; *Zapisnaya knizhka partiinogo aktivista* (Moscow, 1960), pp. 149–65; Barsukov, *op. cit.,* pp. 36–37.

[66] Azrael, *op. cit.,* pp. 94–96; useful insights on the party apparatus as an industrial coordinating body are also contained in Jerry F. Hough, *The Role of the Local Party Organs in Soviet Industrial Decision Making,* unpublished Ph.D. dissertation submitted to the Faculty of Arts and Sciences of Harvard University (Cambridge, Mass., 1961).

[67] Azrael, *op. cit.,* pp. 97–101.

to tighter control over the managerial elite, by the post-Khrushchev regime.

Although the Soviet industrial administration changes so frequently as to soon render obsolete any particular set of titles and names, we shall briefly describe the structure established in March, 1963. That set-up was still in effect two years later, but it was altered by the September, 1965 party plenum. Until September, 1965 the operational command of the Soviet economy was headed by the Supreme National Economic Council. Its chairman, from its establishment until March 26, 1965, was the engineer and veteran military production executive, D. F. Ustinov, who rose to candidate membership in the presidium and entered the party secretariat at the March, 1965 plenum. He was replaced in his Supreme National Economic Council chairmanship by V. N. Novikov, also a military engineer, and, judging by available biographic data, long an associate of Ustinov. Novikov, just before his promotion, was chairman of the Supreme Soviet Presidium's Commission for Economic Problems, and prior to that was head of the State Planning Committee. He became a member of the party central committee in 1961. The Supreme National Economic Council, abolished in September, 1965, was subordinate to the USSR Council of Ministers, which, besides its first deputy chairmen and deputy chairmen, has scores of ordinary ministers, as well as heads of various state committees and commissions; most of these officials are concerned with economic matters. Ustinov served as Commissar of Armaments during World War II, and Novikov as a deputy commissar in that industry. In 1952 Ustinov became a member of the CPSU Central Committee, and in 1957 a deputy chairman of the Council of Ministers. When Ustinov became Chairman of the Supreme National Economic Council in March, 1963, he was also made one of the three first deputy chairmen of the Council of Ministers, serving together with Anastas I. Mikoyan and A. N. Kosygin, both veteran party leaders with vast experience in industry and trade, but he was not made a member or an alternate member of the party presidium. Western experts speculated as to whether or not Khrushchev, though he had promoted an official with military background to the highest economic coordination job in the USSR, considered it necessary to refrain from permitting a man who might be regarded as representing the military point of view in Soviet politics to achieve presidium status. Ustinov was elevated at the March, 1965 plenum, and K. T. Mazurov, veteran Belorussian party leader and opponent of Khrushchev's agricultural policy, was promoted from candidate membership in the presidium to full membership, as well as to the post of First Deputy Chairman of the Council of Ministers of the USSR. These seemed to foretell partial restoration of the Stalin administrative scheme, in which the dominant party apparatus chiefs ruled more by virtue of their authoritative posts in the state than, as Khrushchev desired, by direct involvement as party leaders in economic and administrative functions. Another striking symptom of this "conservative," bureaucratic revival was a decree of February 24, 1965, returning V. V. Matskevich to the post of Minister of Agriculture, from which he had been removed early in 1961. He, like Mazurov, favored tight, centralized control over the economy.

Until the Supreme National Economic Council was abolished following the September, 1965 plenum, it coordinated the work of a number of state committees, including the very important State Committee for Coordination of Scientific Research. The latter was established by decree in 1961 [68] and was headed from June of that year until October, 1965 by central committee member K. N. Rudnev, an electrical engineer with many years of experience in defense industry; he was replaced in October, 1965 by the thermophysicist V. A. Kirillin. There are also committees for defense technology, electronic technology, inventions and discoveries, standards, measures, and measuring instruments, atomic energy, medium machine building (generally assumed to have charge of Soviet military atomic energy development), and many others. Even more important than these committees, however, is the State Planning Committee (Gosplan), which is responsible for long-range economic planning. Like other major economic and administrative agencies, Gosplan was subordinated to the Supreme National Economic Council from early 1963 until late 1965. The Party-State Control Committee, whose head, Shelepin, was also appointed deputy chairman of the Council of Ministers in November, 1962, is another important agency of economic direction. The control machinery described above was augmented by the recentralizing of the bureaucracy begun in 1960–1961. That involved numerous other measures, the most important of

[68] *Pravda,* April 12, 1961.

which took effect after Khrushchev's downfall. By a series of Supreme Soviet decrees, among which the most significant were those published in the official gazette of the Supreme Soviet, a number of state committees of military significance (aviation technology, electronics, etc.) were elevated to centralized, all-union ministries.[69] Prior to this the important Civil Air Fleet, also a partly military agency, had become a ministry. And in February and March, 1965, new ministries, such as the all-union Ministry of General Machine building, were established by decree.

The most important "re-centralization" measure was the post-Khrushchev undoing of Khrushchev's division of the party, the Komsomol, the trade unions, the Soviets, and other structures into industrial and agricultural networks. Reuniting these and other hierarchies into single chains restored the pre-1957 structure of Soviet public administration.

It seemed clear that one objective of the March reorganization, which removed the key military production agencies from their previous links with the regional economic councils and re-created a separate, streamlined defense industry, was to put the Soviet defense industries in a better position to obtain scarce resources and to ready itself to meet the exigencies of possible international crises. It may be that the military and industrial reorganization, together with other recentralization measures, reflected the influence of men like Kosygin and Ustinov, with their background in centralized industrial planning and production under Stalin. Perhaps it was also a response to pressures emanating from high military circles.

Thus the March, 1965 plenum added powerful impetus to economic and administrative recentralization. The September plenum and the October, 1965 Supreme Soviet session carried the job much further.[70] The Gosplan was strengthened organizationally and many industrial ministries, both of the centralized all-union and slightly more centralized union-republic variety, operating in all major parts of the national economy, replaced Khrushchev's councils of national economy and his two upper-level bodies, the Supreme National Economic Council and the National Economic Council. Fashioned after the three-tiered Stalin

69 *Vedomosti,* March 10, 11, 1965.

70 For a discussion of the compromise between centralism and autonomy arrived at in the Sept., 1965 reforms, see Michael Tatu, "Soviet Economic Reforms," *Problems of Communism,* XV (Jan.–Feb., 1966), pp. 28–34.

era models, the ministries were intended to serve as the principal links between the Council of Ministers and the primary economic enterprises throughout the country. Kosygin's and Brezhnev's speeches at the plenum highly praised the "branch" system of economic organization and quoted Lenin on the socialist economy's need for centralized direction, lest anarchy develop.

The tightening of Moscow's formal administrative control was somewhat balanced by the September–October reorganization, which called for increased use of material incentives, profits most of all, in stimulating the work of both management and labor. It was stressed more than ever that production quality would be improved by better incentives. Perhaps the reform's most important feature was that it freed plant managers from some detailed controls that Gosplan formerly exercised over them. Doubtless these measures promised to reward excellence. At the same time, cost accounting techniques were stressed and Kosygin's address introduced the principle that state capital investments in enterprises should be regarded as "loans" rather than grants. These seemed to foreshadow stern fiscal controls that would ferret out and discourage the incompetent. As Tatu points out, the reforms went about as far toward "liberalizing" the Soviet economy as could be hoped for under the existing political circumstances of continued party dominance over the managerial elite.

The September–October decisions were connected with but not necessarily limited to the Brezhnev-Kosygin team's attempt to increase the national wealth. The number of changes in top party leadership was surprisingly small, but that was not true of the state administration. Thus, Nikolai Baibakov, an oil industry expert, at one time was head of Gosplan but for years had been relatively obscure. He returned to lead that powerful agency, from which P. F. Lomako was transferred. Of the twelve members of the Presidium of the Council of Ministers, which includes the chairman, first deputy chairmen, and chairmen of the Soviet "cabinet," eight were either promoted, transferred, or demoted. The major promotion was that of the relatively young and personable D. S. Polyanski to the small circle of first deputy chairmen. Perhaps inspired mainly by administrative considerations, this reshuffle appeared also to be partly motivated by the Brezhnev-Kosygin predilection for anti-Khrushchev, moderately "conservative" personnel appointments.

The tightening of Moscow's control over the vast territorial administrative machine late in Khrushchev's time and after his fall did not necessarily imply early restoration of controls of a fully Stalinist temper. For one thing, a year and a half after Khrushchev's demise, there had been no sign of a return to active, large-scale terror as a major administrative technique. Perhaps a better sign of possible long-term evolution, the leadership was attempting to supplement hierarchic command methods of control, especially in economic administration, using the profit motive more and more. The impetus of profit was applied to many economic enterprises, which, in a number of consumer goods industries, were encouraged to seek profits by producing not what state planners ordered them to manufacture, but what consumers wanted. And executives were told more candidly than ever that income and advancement depended on efficient and high-quality performance.

In addition to its cautious experiments with various economic incentive schemes, the new leadership was also encouraging limited rational and empirical approaches in economics, psychology, law, and other social-science disciplines, the findings and techniques of which could contribute to effective public administration. That these developments, lumped by Soviet political leaders, economic administrators, and researchers under the general title "cybernetics," were important was indicated by the increasing amount of their precious space that the major party periodicals gave to them.

In the spring of 1966 the post-Khrushchev regime, still outwardly "collective" and smoothly consensual, was displaying a combination of administrative ingenuity and cautious deliberativeness which set its behavior apart from that of either the Stalin or the Khrushchev styles.

ADMINISTERING SCIENCE AND CULTURE

The complexities of Soviet scientific, educational, and cultural administration are such that we must confine our study of them to a few major post-Stalin developments. And we must bear in mind that these took place within an environment displaying close continuity with the Stalinist past. The party, though it exercises supervision through the central committee as well as through territorial and other party organizations, has recognized that it must grant some professional autonomy to scientists, artists, and educators (at least to those employed in the leading institutions of higher education). Paradoxically, the autonomy of natural scientists may have been reduced by Khrushchev, who was deeply interested in having scientific research make the greatest possible contribution to national defense and to economic productivity. Scientists and professionals, nonetheless, generally enjoyed better treatment in the post-Stalin era because capricious, unpredictable intervention into scientific and cultural matters, often bringing the direst consequences to its victims, had been abandoned. Khrushchev and his successors, in frequent consultation with leading representatives of the various professions, have sought to elicit cooperation among party, government, and professional elites.

One such practice is shown by the prominent coverage given a speech on agricultural problems by the senior party literary spokesman and highly respected writer, Mikhail Sholokhov.[71] The establishment in 1961 of the State Committee for the Coordination of Scientific Research and other administrative measures showed the pragmatic bent of Soviet scientific administration and also a belated effort to sharply focus the national scientific effort and achieve maximum coordination. For the first time, a powerful agency was established to achieve cooperation between such bodies as the Academy of Sciences of the USSR, the Ministry of Higher and Specialized Secondary Education, the State Committee on Automation and Machine Building, and other important organs. Shortly after this powerful committee was established, mathematical physicist Mstislav V. Keldysh, who had made outstanding contributions to Soviet aviation and space efforts as president of the Academy of Sciences, was brought into the committee, undoubtedly strengthening the coordination of the national scientific effort. Because of the military research backgrounds of both Keldysh and Rudnev, head of the Coordination Committee, its outlook became more distinctively military.[72]

During the post-Stalin period, the party offered a kind of limited partnership to creative intellectuals in literature as in science,

71 *Pravda,* April 15, 1965.

72 Expert comment on these developments will be found in Caryl T. Haskins, *The Scientific Revolution and World Politics* (New York, 1964), pp. 81–91, and in *Staffing Procedures and Problems,* pp. 36–46. See also Nicholas DeWitt, "Politics of Soviet Science," *The American Behavioral Scientist,* VI, No. 4 (Dec., 1962), pp. 7–11.

in the process of "building communism." But at the same time it sought to strengthen the machinery by which it guided their activities. That this combination of policies was slightly contradictory was proven by the establishment in 1958 of the Writers Union of the RSFSR. The purpose, apparently, was to weaken the traditional influence of the Moscow organization of the USSR Writers Union by creating a new control body.[73] As we suggested previously, both Khrushchev and his successors were willing to grant writers and artists much greater professional autonomy and to continue providing them with satisfactory material compensation for their work (in line with the generally low standard of living of the whole country, of course). In return, they expected creative people to respond with enthusiastic support for official policy. In particular, they wanted help in reviving ideological enthusiasm among youths. The post-Khrushchev leadership frequently criticized the former leader's "subjective," changeable cultural policies. Their hope, evidently, was to replace Khrushchev's sometimes lenient, sometimes harsh, often spasmodic interventions in artistic and literary matters by carefully considered committee decisions. They also wanted to prevent publication of ideologically subversive books, such as Solzhenitsyn's *One Day in the Life of Ivan Denisovich* (permission to publish it had been granted by Khrushchev).

We might apply a similar generalization to the Soviet regime's current policies in the social sciences, although here the problem is not coping with the rebellious moods of a courageous minority but overcoming the sterility, dullness, abstractness, and, above all, the ignorance on the part of Soviet social scientists, of modern concepts and methods resulting from the atmosphere created by Stalin's "cult of personality." [74] The Khrushchev, and especially the post-Khrushchev leaderships showed determination to apply, in economic administration and control over the labor force, empirical social science techniques. How much they can benefit by

[73] Harold Swayze, *Political Control of Literature in the USSR* (Cambridge, Mass., 1962), pp. 199–223.
[74] On the post-Stalin organization and developing social sciences in the USSR, see George Fischer, *The New Soviet Sociology, op. cit.;* Ralph K. White's "Social Science Research in the Soviet Bloc," *Public Opinion Quarterly,* XXVIII, No. 1 (Spring, 1964), pp. 20–26, and George L. Kline, "Philosophy, Ideology, and Policy in the Soviet Union," *The Review of Politics,* 26, No. 2 (April, 1964), pp. 174–90. Kline deals mostly with philosophy, but has some perceptive comments also on social science.

this limited use of applied social science, without freedom to criticize the basic assumptions of society, polity, or economy, remains to be discovered.

Like the internal administrative arrangements we have examined, the Soviet conduct of external affairs is uniquely formed by the political culture and system it is designed to protect and expand. Soviet foreign policy shares much with the policies of other states, since all the world's more than one hundred sovereign nations must operate in an international arena which even the most powerful cannot fully control. However, both the organization and the ideology of the Soviet system require a special kind of foreign policy behavior. The enormous concentration of political functions at the party summit produces an exceptional capacity to mobilize national resources in pursuit of foreign policy objectives.

Concentration has the corresponding effect, however, of severely limiting the responsiveness and accommodativeness of Soviet diplomacy, in dealing with adversaries as well as with allies. Personnel charged with the conduct of foreign relations are required to entertain expectations regarding the "capitalist" world which must imbue them with anxiety and mistrust, as well as with contempt, moral indignation, and condescension, tinged perhaps with envy. Their attitude might be described as both antagonistic and manipulative with respect to an environment which probably inspires in their minds both envy and fear. They are taught that they represent a social system destined to become universal, and also that it is their duty to facilitate the Marxist-Leninist mission by all means compatible with the survival and preservation of the Soviet base of the world revolution. Those who administer political, economic, cultural, and other transactions between the Soviet Union and societies in which the desired transfer of power to communists has not yet occurred are trained to operate within, and also against, those societies, but to maintain toward the servants of the "imperialist" elites (as they look upon established, noncommunist officialdom) a correct but wary and coolly detached posture.[75]

[75] On various aspects of the problem sketched here see Alexander Dallin, ed., *Soviet Conduct in World Affairs* (New York, 1960); Marshall D. Shulman, *Stalin's Foreign Policy Reappraised* (Cambridge, Mass., 1963); J. M. MacIntosh, *Strategy and Tactics of Soviet Foreign Policy* (New York, 1962); and relevant portions of Fred C. Ikle, *How Nations Negotiate* (New York, 1964); Frederick

A corollary problem is the Soviet leadership's strong sensitiveness about sharply defining and strictly maintaining ideological boundaries between the Soviet citizenry and foreigners, whether at home or abroad. This attitude applies especially but by no means exclusively to foreigners known to be or suspected of being opposed to whatever policy objectives the CPSU is pursuing at a particular moment. This guardianship over Soviet citizens' attitudes and sentiments, required for maintaining that boundary, is reflected in formidable administrative controls over international and internal communication. One is the distinction in Soviet administrative law between "sanitary" and "legal" controls at frontiers, and a law punishing unauthorized crossing of the Soviet border by deprivation of liberty for one to three years. The political attitudes of Soviet personnel employed abroad by sensitive agencies dealing with foreign affairs, such as the Committee of State Security, the Ministry of Foreign Affairs, or the Ministry of Foreign Trade, are of great interest to the government. Within the secretariat of the CPSU Central Committee is a special Department for Travel Abroad by which "every individual of whatever rank who is proposed for an overseas assignment must be cleared." [76] According to our most recent information, this agency was headed by Alexander Panyushkin, who had served both in the police apparatus and, throughout most of his career, in the Ministry of Foreign Affairs. He had been Ambassador to China and to the United States and his educational qualifications included graduation in 1938 from one of the highest Soviet military academies.[77]

C. Barghoorn, *Soviet Foreign Propaganda* (Princeton, N.J., 1964); and, for a Soviet official view, F. G. Zuev, *et al., Mezhdunarodnye otnosheniya i vneshnyaya politika SSSR* (Moscow, 1961). The book by Colonel A. I. Seleznev, *Voins i ideologicheskaya borba* (Moscow, 1964), is interesting for its relative frankness in describing the Soviet approach to "psychological warfare" and the latter's relationship to military policy.

[76] On Soviet attitudes toward international communication, see Frederick C. Barghoorn, *Soviet Cultural Offensive* (Princeton, N.J., 1960), pp. 99–124, and also Barghoorn, *Soviet Foreign Propaganda, op. cit.,* pp. 220–25; and see Seleznev, p. 17, on the alleged exploitation by "imperialist" governments of any and all acts of communication between their citizens and Soviet citizens. See also the criticisms of the "imperialists," for allegedly seeking to build "bridges" to the "world of socialism," the better to undermine it, in *Kommunist,* No. 3, Feb., 1965, p. 7.

[77] *Staffing Procedures and Problems, op. cit.,* Chart 3; *Who's Who in the USSR* (New York, 1962), p. 576. See also report of Panyushkin's taking part in an official party which greeted A. N. Shelepin on his return from a trip to Korea, *Izvestiya,* Aug. 22, 1965.

A number of other party and government agencies perform important functions in Soviet external relations. These include (1) communication agencies, such as the official telegraphic agency TASS and the Novosti Press Agency, both of which are important in Soviet foreign propaganda work, (2) economic organizations such as the State Committee for Foreign Economic Relations, and (3) organizations supervising exchanges of artists, scholars, and other "cultural" personnel and materials with foreign countries. Among the latter are the powerful governmental organ, the State Committee for Cultural Relations with Foreign Countries, and the "public" organization, the Union of Soviet Societies for Friendship and Cultural Relations with Foreign Countries, and many others.[78] It is explicit in communist doctrine and Soviet legal principles that all such organizations promote the party's aims and policies. A number of training and research institutions, which help to prepare Soviet citizens for careers connected with international relations and also facilitate the gathering of intelligence, the planning of foreign policy, and international propaganda activities, are growing in importance.

An Institute of International Relations, nominally under the Ministry of Foreign Affairs but apparently operated by the Ministry of Higher Education, trains Soviet citizens for work in the Ministry of Foreign Affairs, various research organizations, Intourist (the official tourist agency), etc. It also trains students from "friendly" countries, the majority presumably from the "socialist" countries of Eastern Europe. It has its own publishing house, and among its publications is an English-language pamphlet, "On Diplomatic Practice," obtained by the writer in Moscow in 1963, designed to familiarize future Soviet foreign service personnel with English diplomatic language.[79] The ideological tone of this pamphlet shows in a section by John Gollan, General Secretary of the British Communist Party, which describes the "class setup" of the British Foreign Office in the language one would expect from its author. Another institution about which foreigners have been able to acquire only scraps of information is the Diplomatic School, operated by the Ministry of Foreign Affairs for its own personnel. Other important training programs are provided by

---

[78] For further details on these and other organizations, see Barghoorn, *Soviet Foreign Propaganda, op. cit.,* Ch. VIII.

[79] International Relations Institute Publishing House (Moscow, 1963).

the Foreign Trade School, operated by the Ministry of Foreign Trade, and the Military Institute of Foreign Languages, under the Ministry of Defense, and by various language and area programs. Among these, the Oriental Faculty of Leningrad State University and the Institute of Oriental Languages of Moscow State University rank high. Apparently special party recommendations are required for entrance into these elite language programs.

One of the most important research organizations in the foreign relations field is the Institute of World Economics and International Relations of the Academy of Sciences of the USSR. Its director (as of September, 1964) was Anushavan Agafonovich Arzumanyan, a leading Soviet economist. One of its officers was a son of Anastas Mikoyan, the affable Sergo Mikoyan, who traveled in the United States shortly after Khrushchev's fall, visiting university centers of economic and international relations studies. This institute, which has hundreds of researchers on its staff, publishes the important journal *World Economics and International Relations* and many books as well. Very important also are the area study institutes of the Academy of Science, including the Institute of Orientalogy, the Institute of the Peoples of Africa, and the Institute of the Peoples of Hispanic America. Apparently the work of these institutes is coordinated with that of the Institute of World Economics and International Relations. There is evidence that these agencies frequently perform research assignments for the CPSU Central Committee.

CHAPTER IX

Soviet Justice

As FAR AS history can inform us, no society can keep its stability and function effectively without a definite system of enforceable rules prescribing its members' conduct toward one another and toward their fellow members who are authorized to act in the name and the interest of the community. Adherents of anarchism, or at least some who so designate their political beliefs, seem to think that the antisocial behavior which law and its enforcement are designed to prevent is produced by the very regulations and restraints upon which most men believe that society must rely to preserve public order. Some socialist doctrines, including Leninism, share the anarchist vision of a law-free, coercionless society, but hold that this state can come to be only after the present "capitalist" society has been replaced by a "communist" one. As outlined in Lenin's major work, *State and Revolution,* and in subsequent Soviet doctrine, the new society will have new norms, appropriate to an order freed of exploitation of the propertyless by those who own the means of production which, according to Marx and Lenin, was the source of coercion. Until now, however, socialist governments have not proven that a state-directed economic system will pave the way to a society that needs no laws, courts, or law enforcement agencies. Soviet experience has, if anything, proven the opposite.

Those who regard constitutionalism and the civic political culture's other benefits as more humane and, eventually, more effective than any dictatorship or oligarchy are likely to feel that the Leninist attitude toward legitimate coercion is fallacious.

First, its utopian appeal distracts attention from serious political problems. Second, its "class struggle" morality justifies, even encourages, extremes of coercion, as we have seen in the lawless behavior of Stalin, or even Lenin.

Thus, those who believe in responsible and responsive representative government are not likely to be satisfied with Soviet interpreting and enforcement of legal rules. And they probably will not agree that it can be significantly improved without fundamentally reforming the system in which it is enmeshed.

Americans, especially, often feel that attributing to Soviet political behavior any characteristics of "law" or "justice" is an absurd misconception or even deliberate deception. Certainly this attitude is not entirely unjustifiable. The "rule of law," in the American sense, cannot be said to work in a political system in which, as dramatically demonstrated once again by the sudden and mysterious fall of Khrushchev in October, 1964, there are still no enforceable legal or constitutional rules for selecting even the top political leaders. And in this system these leaders, while in power, can make, interpret, or even break laws, regulations, and other rules, including some previously proclaimed by themselves.

For weighty reasons Americans tend to be mystified and disturbed by the Soviet version of the judicial process. Soviet behavior in international relations has imprinted upon the American mind an image of lawlessness, which can easily be extended to areas where it may not be relevant. For cultural and historical reasons, Americans and most other English-speaking peoples find it more difficult than continental Europeans to understand Soviet legal behavior, which has been heavily influenced by continental doctrines and practices. One significant feature shared by Soviet and continental legal systems is the prolonged, searching pretrial investigation of suspects in criminal cases by trained investigators, during which the accused is normally not represented by legal counsel, and in which both accused and counsel lack many opportunities and prerogatives that should be available to them according to the "Anglo-Saxon" tradition. Such features of English and American law as trial by jury, presumption of innocence, habeas corpus, etc., are also wholly or partly lacking both in continental European and Soviet law, though Soviet jurists claim that in their system the accused is provided with equivalent or better protection of his rights and interests.

Americans are repelled by the practices and techniques of Soviet prosecutors. Basic to their revulsion, however, is their over-all judgment that the Soviet political system is dictatorial and that therefore there can be little justice in Russia. Where laws are made by and interpreted in the interests of rulers unchecked by popular custom or representative institutions, how can legal adjudication in the courts be consistent and fair? So goes the argument which to most Americans, including this writer, seems difficult to refute.

Some leading Western specialists on Soviet law and some general theorists on jurisprudence, however, warn that we should not allow ourselves to be blinded by our justifiable aversion to basic features of Soviet judicial behavior. Legal rules and regular, careful procedures for applying and interpreting them, at least in matters that are not politically sensitive, have long been important in the Soviet governmental process, and their significance has much increased since the death of Stalin. These scholars say that from our point of view Soviet law may be bad law, but it is law nonetheless.[1] Soviet legal rules and the procedures for adjudication differ significantly from those of noncommunist systems. Moreover, as an instrument of social control, law is less important in that system than in those of Britain, the United States, and other countries in which the "civic culture" prevails. Berman suggested this in his distinction between the respective spheres of "law" and of "terror" in the Soviet Union. He wrote that law "was for those areas of Soviet life where the political factor was stabilized. Terror, whether naked or (as in the purge trials of the late 1930s) in the guise of law, was applied when the regime felt itself threatened."[2] Berman and other scholars have described how after Stalin's death a partial curb was applied to the power of the political police to arrest, detain, interrogate, exile, or execute suspects, often without trial or any form of due process of law and all too often using fabricated evidence and confessions exacted by threats, deception, or force. It would be hazardous to predict whether Soviet legal behavior will further evolve toward

[1] See pertinent sections of Herbert Hart, *The Concept of Law* (Oxford, England, 1961) and, among leading specialists on Soviet law, the writings of Harold J. Berman, esp. his major study, *Justice in the U.S.S.R.* (New York, 1963), and his introduction to Berman and Spindler, *Soviet Criminal Law and Procedure* (Cambridge, Mass., 1966).

[2] Berman, *Justice in the U.S.S.R.*, *op. cit.*, p. 66.

impartiality, consistency, and stability, or will be arrested or accelerated by Khrushchev's absence. He did much to bring about such reforms as were effected in this area, especially from 1956 to 1960, when reform was most evident. More than any other he revealed, in his "secret" speech of February, 1956 the truth regarding the police terror under which most Soviet citizens had lived for so many years. The post-Khrushchev regime's first year and a half provided a modicum of encouragement that there would not be a relapse into Stalinist lawlessness.

However, the sentencing in February, 1966 of Soviet writers Andrei Sinyavski and Yuli Daniel to confinement in corrective labor camps for allegedly slandering Soviet society in their writings reinforced Western doubts — including those of prominent European communist intellectuals — about the quality of Soviet justice. To be sure, these men were treated far more humanely than they would have been by Stalin. They were tried in a court, defended by counsel, and allowed to plead not guilty. On the other hand, they were sentenced not for actions but for merely expressing opinions. Moreover, many features of their case, including long secret interrogation and pretrial vilification in the party-controlled press, represented, by Western standards, the unscrupulous application of defective laws. From the scanty information that has reached the West, we find that those detained in jails and labor camps have been treated much better than they would have been in the heyday of Stalinist caprice and brutality. But this improvement was modest, and its shaky ideological and institutional foundations inspired anxious speculation as to its durability. The codes of conduct binding upon Soviet citizens and the consistency, predictability, and equality with which they are interpreted and enforced still depend on the good will, determination, and skill brought by the CPSU leadership to their self-imposed task of selecting, training, organizing, and supervising personnel in these varied but related jobs.[3] To be sure, the strengthening

---

[3] A valuable discussion of party control of law enforcement agencies by the late N. R. Mironov appeared in *XX sezd KPSS i voprosy ideologicheskoi raboty* (Moscow, 1962), pp. 229–37. Mironov in August, 1959 was appointed chief of the Section for Administrative Organs of the CPSU Central Committee, which supervises the procuracy, courts, police, and state security agencies. He was killed, together with the Chief of Staff of the Soviet Army, Biryuzov, and other Soviet officials in an airplane crash in Yugoslavia a few days after Khrushchev's downfall. As of early 1966, no successor to Mironov had been identified in the Soviet sources available to this writer.

since Stalin's time of the party's and the procuracy's control have extended due process of law or at least have restricted capricious police action.[4] The use of terror was much diminished and limited concessions were accorded "liberal" Soviet jurists who had demanded improved procedural regularity, although these were partially offset by establishing "non-courts and impolice." These were agencies of "public" participation in police and judicial activities whose operations were fraught with danger in the opinion of those who sought to institute a style of legality less "revolutionary" than that which had flourished under Lenin and Stalin.[5]

One problem was not attacked in any fundamental sense, however, by post-Stalin reforms of rule making, rule application, and rule adjudication. That was the basic conflict between dictatorship and a genuine rule of law. Soviet legal reforms have, to a distressing degree, represented a dictatorial system's borrowing for its own special purposes some of the symbols, concepts, and techniques developed by political systems in which law is felt to be not an instrument of the ruling political party but a body of legal norms, serving the citizenry's interests and binding upon all citizens, including the political elite. In the legal systems of pluralistic, citizen-controlled polities, citizens, either as individuals or as members of legitimate interest groups, can question and on occasion contest in the courts the actions of their duly constituted government officials — as well as those of private citizens. Such a conception of legal rules and procedures remains remote from the still dominant Soviet concept of party-created, party-enforced, "socialist legality."

Some needs of the Soviet system are filled by selective borrowing of "bourgeois" legal ideas and a few practices, but such borrowings displease some elements in Soviet society. The ideas and prac-

[4] On the Soviet procuracy see the important study by Glenn G. Morgan, *Soviet Administrative Legality* (Stanford, Cal., 1962).

[5] The expression "non-courts and impolice" was coined by Professor Leon S. Lipson of the Yale University Law School for a paper delivered at the 1963 annual meeting of the American Political Science Association. For informed comment on the background and content of post-Stalin legal reforms, see Lipson's articles, "The New Face of 'Socialist Legality,'" in *Problems of Communism*, VII, No. 4 (July–Aug., 1958), pp. 22–30, and "Socialist Legality: The Mountain Has Labored," in *ibid.*, VIII, No. 2 (March–April, 1959), pp. 15–19. See also Darrell T. Hammer, "Law Enforcement, Social Control and the Withering of the State: Recent Soviet Experience," in *Soviet Studies*, XIV, No. 4 (April, 1963), pp. 380–97; Jeremy Azrael in "An End to Coercion?" *Problems of Communism*, XI, No. 6 (Nov.–Dec., 1962), pp. 9–11, presents valuable material on the coercion exercised by the police and other agencies.

tices borrowed may seem overly sophisticated to a citizenry most of whom are still relatively unversed in legal subtleties. In 1956–1957, there were attempts to bring Soviet "legality" closer to Western standards, undoubtedly pleasing many legal scholars and lawyers. They may have seemed threatening, though, to police cadres accustomed to great freedom in their work, safeguarding the "conquests of the revolution," and also to many "hard liners" not only throughout the system of legal administration, but also in the party apparatus. Men of such kidney were bound to be disturbed by the possible undermining of ideological conformity and social discipline if the party's right and capacity to employ even the instrument of terror, should "historical necessity" require it, were to be given up. The zig-zag course of post-Stalin legal reform, and the complex backing and filling in the amorphous area of social controls, coercion generally, and culture especially, revealed pressures for the loosening up of Soviet society. But these pressures were countered by vested interests, entrenched habits, ideological convictions, and vigilant determination to resist innovations in organization and doctrine. Change was accepted only if there were convincing evidence that it would not weaken Soviet party and state apparatus control of the internal socioeconomic environment and their ability to cope with the external environment, abroad. Harold J. Berman wrote:

> But the long-range problem of government in the Soviet Union is whether Soviet leaders are willing and able to establish not merely a season, or a climate, or a policy, of freedom and initiative, but also a legal and institutional foundation which will make freedom and initiative secure from their own intervention.[6]

The Soviet leadership was reluctant, perhaps unable, to rapidly and decisively solve this "long-range problem." After Stalin's death the special board (*osoboe soveshchanie*), a police body empowered since 1934 to impose punishments without court proceedings, was "abolished" in a peculiar manner. This dreaded agency, which had condemned thousands to death or forced labor camps without legal proceedings, was referred to as abolished in Soviet sources in 1956 and again in 1957.[7] But the 1934 laws empow-

---

[6] Harold J. Berman, "The Dilemma of Soviet Law Reform," *Harvard Law Review*, 76, No. 5 (March, 1963), p. 950.

[7] On this point see esp. Vladimir Gsovski and Kazimierz Grzybowski, *Government Law and Courts in the Soviet Union and Eastern Europe*, Vol. I (Lon-

ering police agencies to punish out of court apparently were not overtly and finally repealed.[8] It appears that the political police ceased to practice punishment without court proceedings, or practiced it on a very limited scale, after the death of Stalin; it seems also that the leadership did not wish to deprive the police and itself of the right to revert to this practice if it were deemed necessary.

Another extralegal practice of the Soviet political police was the use of deception and fabrication in alleged political crime cases. It had been denounced at great length by Khrushchev in his secret speech. But that it has survived was proven by this writer's arrest on what can only be described as trumped-up charges of espionage, after he was forcibly seized on the street in front of the Metropole Hotel in Moscow, about 7:30 in the evening of October 31, 1963. The belief that fabrication of reality is a legitimate weapon in the "class struggle" did not die with Stalin.[9]

Let us now examine in some detail how Soviet law and its interpretation and enforcement by police, prosecution, courts, and bar distinguish Soviet political behavior from that of other types of political system, since the party leadership obviously feels that this behavior is essential for the maintenance and further development of the system.

A difficult ideological problem is posed by crime and other violations of the norms of community living prescribed by the party leadership and enacted into laws. Because Marxism-Leninism associates these evils with capitalism, there is no place for them in a socialist society. Since the Twenty-first Party Congress in 1959, it is officially proclaimed, society has been engaged in the "full-scale" construction (*razvernutoe stroitelstvo*) of communism. But the

---

don, 1959), pp. 577–79; see also Ritvo, *The New Soviet Society* (New York, 1962), p. 176, quoting a Soviet radio broadcast referring to thousands of arrests, many of them followed by torture and shooting, sanctioned by a special board of the NKVD in the Dagestan area of the Caucasus during the last four months of 1937 alone.

8 Other peculiarities are connected with this matter. Professor Berman and other foreign visitors were told that the board had been abolished, several years before any such action was mentioned in the Soviet press, but they were also told that the law abolishing it was "secret." See Berman, "Soviet Law Reform — Dateline Moscow 1957," LXVI, *Yale Law Journal*, pp. 1191, 1192; and Berman, *Justice in the U.S.S.R.*, pp. 396–97, note 5.

9 A perceptive discussion of the "social prophylaxis" practiced by Soviet police, especially during Stalin's purges, appears in F. Beck and W. Godin, *Russian Purge and the Extraction of Confession* (New York, 1951), pp. 231–37.

optimism about rapid social progress implied by such language waned, apparently, in 1965 and 1966. At the Twenty-third Party Congress, references to the 1959 congress, at which the "transition" figured prominently, were conspicuously absent. Crime and the agencies and instruments for its prevention, detection, and punishment remind the party leaders of the less than complete success of their attempts at socialization. Press articles on the crime problem often include demands that party, trade union, and other organizations, as well as the "collectives" of factories, improve their crime prevention educational programs and supervisory activities. Between the improvement in human behavior promised by official doctrine as a fruit of the beneficent "socialist" environment and the reality of widespread crime and corruption, the contrast is embarrassing. It makes the Soviet authorities secretive about crime statistics, although figures on alleged increases or decreases in crime are released fairly often. More fundamentally, the utopian outlook of Marxism-Leninism inhibits the objective study of crime.

There are signs that some Soviet legal scholars and administrators are beginning to realize how valuable systematic and accurate recording and scientific analysis of crime statistics can be, at least for use within the bureaucracy. An article by Yu. Kasatkin, head of the court statistics division of the USSR Supreme Court, deplored the neglect (attributed by implication to Stalin) of proper "Leninist" gathering and analysis of crime statistics and urged that it be remedied, and also that "violations of moral norms" be studied, as well as crimes, and that their causes and the conditions which contribute to them be analyzed.[10]

It would probably be unrealistic to attribute to the contrast between ideals and achievements in the Soviet struggle against crime a significant weakening of Soviet ideological conviction. After all, such basic sources of doctrine as Lenin's *State and Revo-*

10 *Izvestiya*, Nov. 12, 1964. M. Vilenski, a Soviet lawyer (*advokat*), discussed the related subject of defects in reporting court cases by court secretaries, who, he pointed out, are neither jurists nor stenographers (*Izvestiya*, Nov. 18, 1964). It appears that one significant negative consequence of the doctrinal presumption that "socialism" somehow prevents or inhibits crime is a tendency of law enforcement officers to fail to make arrests, lest the statistical record of their jurisdictional area appear less favorable than others. Z. Kruglova, a secretary of the Leningrad party committee, sharply criticized this and other practices (*Izvestiya*, Aug. 22, 1965). The legal scholar V. Kudryavtsev (*Izvestiya*, Nov. 24, 1965) demanded that the study of — and policy toward — crime be based solely on "scientific," statistical evidence.

lution offer grounds for the view that the struggle to transform human behavior may require a very long time. It can always be asserted that in the past insufficient effort has been devoted to this struggle and that the work must be redoubled in the future. Recent Western analysis of Soviet justice in action, especially the brilliant reporting of George Feifer, indicates that after Stalin's death the faith that "communism" can conquer crime was revived.[11] Paradoxically, this renewed faith, after the optimistic period of reform from 1956 through 1959, was accompanied by renewed severity of punishment, including extension of the death penalty to crimes, especially "economic crimes," previously not so punished.

Though it seems logically contradictory to increase the severity of and expand repressive measures when society is allegedly progressing toward communism, the contradiction may make psychological sense. Several writers have commented on the "sense of exasperation" felt by the Soviet leaders because the relative leniency of the early post-Stalin years actually led to an increase in crime. With the movement toward communism the continued blemish on the body politic of large-scale crime becomes increasingly repulsive, and there must be a temptation, regardless of logic, to fall back on draconian measures to eliminate it — or to abandon exaggerated claims of rapid progress and realistically admit that a certain amount of antisocial behavior is inseparable from civilization, a position very hard for Leninists to accept.

As we have said, there is a fundamental ideological problem in the very existence of law, and of law enforcement agencies which apply coercion and, if necessary, violence. The struggle against crime requires that there be "law" and a "state," and yet the state as a coercive agency, according to Marxism-Leninism, is destined to "wither away" once full communism is achieved. The 1961 CPSU program introduced an additional complexity by proclaiming that the dictatorship of the proletariat in the Soviet Union had been replaced by the All-People's State.[12] Perhaps it can be said of these dilemmas that, though they may be troublesome even to Soviet communists, and though they furnish polemical ammu-

[11] George Feifer, *Justice in Moscow* (New York, 1964), *passim*, and esp. Ch. XVI.

[12] For a perceptive and lucid discussion of the main ideological problems in Soviet doctrine regarding law and the state, see Ivo Lapenna, *State and Law: Soviet and Yugoslav Theory* (New Haven, 1964).

nition for anti-Soviet propaganda, they probably will not undermine the morale of Soviet law enforcement officials or impair
their self-righteousness. This author was able to observe the latter
at first hand during more than two weeks of KGB hospitality in
1963 — it seems still to flourish.

When one asks a Soviet lawyer or legal scholar if he believes
that when the state finally disappears, lawyers will no longer be
needed, he is likely to smile and reply that all that is very far in
the future or that lawyers will "always" be needed. Such an attitude may not necessarily be incompatible with Marxism-Leninism.
It can be argued that the state as a system of organized coercion
will indeed some day be relegated to a museum of antiquities, but
that law as a system of social norms, and lawyers and other trained
personnel skilled in interpreting these laws, may be needed indefinitely. This is not the place to discuss further such intricacies
of theory, though some acquanitance with them makes it easier
to understand many Soviet legal doctrines and practices.

The ideological challenge posed by crime probably worries
Soviet leaders less than its potential threat to public order, which
could undermine the social and political system. The increasingly
severe laws and punishment of recent years prove the strong effect
of crime upon economic productivity and efficiency. Because the
Soviet economy is administered by governmental agencies, economic behavior has political and legal connotations which are
absent in other systems. It has often seemed very difficult to distinguish between the inefficiency or poor performance of an
ordinary collective farmer, a factory worker, or a high-ranking
executive, and crime.[13]

In Stalin's time, at any rate, it was almost impossible for a
Soviet industrial executive to do work required of him by the

---

[13] Berman, *Justice in the U.S.S.R., op. cit.*, pp. 144–51; Feifer, *op. cit.*, pp.
306–22; A. V. Benediktov, *Grazhdansko-pravovaya okhrana sotsialisticheskoi
sobstvennosti v SSSR* (Moscow, 1945), p. 264, lists in its index thirteen categories of "criminal responsibility" for economic activity, beginning with "output of poor quality production." It was also interesting that a decree of April
26, 1958 imposed "criminal responsibility," in some cases, for the failure of
some enterprises to fulfill their responsibility of supplying other enterprises,
in other economic regions, with various materials, products, etc. The criminal
law aspects of the establishment in Nov., 1962 of the Party-State Control Committee, headed by Shelepin, who had previously served as chairman of the
KGB, were equally intriguing. On these, see A. E. Lunev, *Obespechenie
zakonnosti v sovetskon gosudarstvennom upravlenii* (Moscow, 1963), esp. pp.
89–95, and George L. Kline, "Economic Crime and Punishment," *Survey*, No.
57 (Oct., 1965), pp. 67–72.

government without violating the law in various ways and at various times, and it seems reasonable to assume that conditions remain similar, especially if we recall post-Stalin prosecution of many managers of industrial and trading establishments for "economic crimes." [14] Thus the range of possible criminal activity in the Soviet Union is enormous. It includes acts such as theft or murder, which are considered to be crimes in all civilized countries, and others which, under the Soviet economic system, are regarded as economic crimes against the state and are usually punished more severely than are "private" crimes.[15] Some "economic crimes," such as the case tried publicly in March–July, 1962 in Frunze, capital of the Kirghiz Soviet Socialist Republic, have involved relatively high government officials, factory directors, and other members of the Soviet elite.[16]

The modal characteristics of the Soviet criminal appear to be as follows. He is a young collective farmer or factory worker who disturbs public order or commits a theft (usually under the influence of alcohol), is tried in a People's Court (the lowest of the four levels of ordinary Soviet courts), and receives a relatively stiff sentence (by American standards), of confinement for one or more years in a labor colony (until about 1956 known as a "corrective labor camp").[17] The four levels of Soviet courts are: the People's Courts, which try almost all cases, both criminal and civil; the city or oblast courts; the supreme courts of each of the fifteen Soviet republics; and the Supreme Court of the USSR. Some cases, such as murder with aggravating circumstances, counterfeiting, and desertion, are tried in the first instance in oblast or, as in Moscow, in city courts. The decisions of People's Courts can be appealed, both by the defendant and by the agencies of prosecution, to higher courts. In minor cases no representative of the procurator's

[14] See Joseph S. Berliner, *Factory and Manager in the USSR* (Cambridge, Mass., 1957), Chs. X, XI, XII.

[15] Feifer, *op. cit.,* pp. 306–308 has an interesting discussion of this point.

[16] See the discussion of this case in *Jews in Eastern Europe,* II, No. 1 (Dec., 1962), pp. 16–19 (published by European Jewish Publications, Ltd.). See also Lunev, *op. cit.,* p. 90.

[17] Mironov, *op. cit.,* p. 230; Feifer, Chs. I and II and esp. p. 32; Kruglova, *loc. cit.,* stressed alcohol as a factor in leading young Leningrad factory workers into crime. See also examples of antisocial, potentially criminal behavior described by Professor K. S. Yudelson in his *Sud tovarishchei* (Moscow, 1965). Soviet literature gives so much attention to crime as related to alcohol, one wonders why the authorities make it so freely available. Of course, it is an important source of profit to the state, and perhaps it is felt that restrictions would only spur bootlegging.

office is present, and the defendant is often unrepresented by counsel. The role of the presiding judge thus is most important in the ordinary Soviet court trial. This description, by and large, applies to all judicial levels.

Between the People's Courts and the higher courts there are some important differences. Judges of the People's Courts are elected; higher court judges are appointed. In the People's Courts there is also organized "public participation," which is absent from the higher courts. The judge in a People's Court trial is assisted by two "lay assessors," chosen by election from factories, places of residence, etc. As far as we know, the judges, more and more of whom have legal training, dominate the proceedings. In occasional, exceptional cases, one or both of the assessors succeed in influencing the judge's verdict. Regular courts above the People's Courts level have three judges. Important political cases such as the trial of U-2 pilot Francis Gary Powers in August, 1960 or that of Oleg V. Penkovski in May, 1963 are tried by the military collegium of the USSR Supreme Court. Also, even since Stalin's death, there have been special and rather irregular proceedings and tribunals in very important political cases, as in the trials of Lavrenti Beria and Mir Dzhafar Bagirov in 1953 and 1956, respectively.[18]

It is probably true, as Berman, Feifer, and others maintain, that in most nonpolitical cases Soviet courts — mainly the People's Courts — are tolerably fair and consistent, despite excessive informality, by Western standards, and a lack of procedural methods for safeguarding the rights of defendants. It is difficult to quarrel with or, unfortunately, to verify Feifer's opinion that most Soviet citizens feel that justice is done in the courts, although they often feel that sentences are excessively harsh or, sometimes, too light. Without attempting a detailed comparative appraisal of Soviet and "Western" standards of justice, we shall indicate some strengths and weaknesses of the Soviet court system.

Before a case reaches a Soviet court its decision has already been pretty much determined by the preliminary investigation, conducted partly by the police and partly by investigators of the procuracy. In political cases, and also in cases involving accusations of major so-called economic crimes, the preliminary investi-

18 Gsovski and Grzybowski, *op. cit.,* Vol. I, pp. 579–85, give a detailed analysis of these cases.

gation has been conducted by KGB investigators since May, 1961.[19] When the preliminary investigation in a Soviet criminal case is conducted by the fearsome KGB, there is little doubt that the results of the investigation have determined the verdict and punishment to be meted out to the criminal, though the KGB, as an agency of the USSR Council of Ministers, in its turn is subject to the highest party and state authorities. Presently, we shall discuss Soviet pretrial investigation. Even in ordinary cases, where there is no question of treason, espionage, or other "state" crime, that system exerts enormous influence on legal decisions. But first, we must say something about the "educational" and other functions of Soviet court trials.

The activities of Soviet courts most fully reported to the public (in a highly laudatory tone) reinforce the propaganda and adult political socialization work of the family, the schools, the mass media, the trade unions, and other institutions, including the "comrades' courts." To be sure, police and courts provide socialization with legal teeth, the lessons of which may be underscored by detention and exile. The Soviet court, it appears, does double duty as a propaganda agency. It seeks, as the trial proceeds, to teach the transgressor the error of his ways and to point out to him the path he must follow if, after completing his sentence, he is to be an "honest," public-spirited Soviet citizen. With its authority to impose sanctions for violating community behavior, it is exceptionally well placed to disseminate to the general public party doctrines and current positions on law as an instrument of social control.[20] The educational work of Soviet courts is exercised within the framework of party policy, regarding not merely law enforcement but policy generally. Like other responsible citizens,

[19] *Vedomosti verkhovnogo soveta* (Moscow, 1961), No. 260, Item 270, discussed in "Economic Crimes in the Soviet Union," Staff Study, International Commission of Jurists (Geneva, 1964), pp. 12–13, 21. This report takes the position that the 1961–1962 developments in criminal law, of which the economic activity of the KGB was one feature, really "undid" the 1956–1959 reforms.

[20] *Justice in the U.S.S.R.*, *op. cit.*, pp. 299–308. Feifer's *Justice in Moscow* provides a wealth of illustrations of the educational, or as Berman puts it, the "parental," role of the Soviet court. It is not without interest that in the last few years Soviet criminologists have increasingly emphasized the priority of the home and family in giving children a moral training which will safeguard them against the possibility of their becoming criminals. See "The Youth's Fate" (*Sudba podrostka*), in *Izvestiya*, Aug. 19, 1965, by G. Minkovski and V. Pronina. The authors are identified as members of the staff of the All-Union Institute for the Study of the Causes and Prevention of Crime of the Procuracy of the USSR.

Soviet judges, most of them party members, are expected to keep themselves informed on matters political by reading the general press and also by following such special legal publications as *Sovetskoe gosudarstvo i pravo* (*Soviet State and Law*).

Through the press, both legal and general, and also through party organizations and the local government agencies of the communities in which they work, judges are informed of the severity with which at any given time the central party authorities consider that particular transgressions should be punished. Published guidance for judges, police officers, and others engaged in legal activities appears in a great many forms. N. R. Mironov, chief of the Division of Administrative Organs of the Party Central Committee, warned against what he regarded as harmful tendencies toward excessively lenient treatment of dangerous criminals, connected with the turning over of some forms of law enforcement to nongovernmental agencies.[21] Interestingly enough, he said that one reason for the May, 1961 legislation instituting the death penalty for serious economic crimes was that Soviet authorities felt this step would counteract growing tendencies toward excessively lenient enforcement.[22] While the party struggled to orient law enforcement officials and to mobilize them as educators of the citizenry, Mironov revealed bribe-taking and other offenses committed by prosecutors, judges, and attorneys, even in Moscow. To prevent such lapses, the party's watchdog over the law enforcement agencies prescribed the traditional Stalinist remedy, "political and ideological hardening," to overcome a "narrowly professional" point of view which still put a barrier, according to Mironov, between many public officials and the country's general political life.[23]

Such propagandistic exhortations by party leaders, as well as by high judicial and police officials, are very numerous.[24] Lengthy

21 In his address to the Dec., 1961 All-Union Conference on Problems of Ideological Work.

22 See also Mironov's article on strengthening "socialist legality" in *Partiinaya zhizn*, No. 5, March, 1962. The same point was made very forcefully by Kruglova in her article in *Izvestiya*, Aug. 22, 1965.

23 Mironov, *op. cit.*, pp. 231, 235.

24 See the article by A. Sokolov, head of the Leningrad Administration for the Protection of Public Order (*Ministerstvo okhrany obshchestvennogo poryadka*, often referred to as MOOP): "Humanism Is Not All-Forgiveness," *Izvestiya*, Sept. 2, 1964. See also "Juridical Science on the Level of New Tasks," *Pravda*, Aug. 4, 1964, commenting on a central committee resolution demanding improved juridical scholarship and education.

columns are frequently devoted by the main Soviet newspapers, especially *Izvestiya*, to resolutions and decisions of the Supreme Court of the USSR and the procuracy, the two main agencies which guide and supervise the court system.[25] Then too, judges, prosecution officials, police officials, lawyers, and legal scholars are expected to contribute to the "law-consciousness" of the Soviet public by writing articles, delivering public lectures, taking part in the "political enlightenment" program, etc.

All this legal education activity inside and outside the courts is certainly important. But to the Western European or American observer interested in the politics of Soviet justice and how it affects the citizen's legal and civil rights in relation to the political authorities, the propagandizing of judges or other judicial officials is not the legal system's most striking feature. More impressive is the gathering and appraising of intelligence by the pretrial investigation. The latter influences the materials used by judges in court trials so strongly that "To an observer it seems that the trial is a reconstruction not so much of the crime as of an earlier reconstruction of it, that it has all been said before." [26] Apparently this unbalance is caused by the control granted to police investigators, who are in charge of a suspect for up to twenty-four hours after his arrest, to the procuracy's investigators, or, in "political" and in some serious "general" crimes, to the KGB, who may then carry on the investigation for several months. This writer was told by the KGB investigator assigned to his case, while he was held incommunicado in the KGB Inner Prison (Lubyanka), that according to law the pretrial investigation might last for nine months. These officials have so much control over the detainee and limit access to him and to witnesses so tightly that the investigation constitutes judgment on the case. It is difficult to know whether the police still have as free a hand in investigating criminal cases as they did before the new Fundamentals of Criminal Law, Criminal Procedure and Law on the Judiciary were adopted in 1958.[27] The 1958 Fundamentals provided for continuing in

[25] See *Pravda's* report of Oct. 21, 1964 on a USSR Supreme Court plenum, in which R. A. Rudenko, general procurator of the USSR, took part, or the extremely interesting item on the same subject in *Izvestiya*, April 15, 1965, which dealt with instructions on how guidance of Comrades' Courts by People's Courts should be exercised.

[26] Feifer, *op. cit.*, p. 86.

[27] Gsovski and Grzybowski, *op. cit.*, Vol. I, p. 859, cites an article in *Izvestiya*, July 2, 1957, complaining about the apparently widespread but

many crimes the old dual system, under which the police made one inquiry and investigators supervised by the procuracy made another. As far as we know, neither regular police or procuracy investigators, nor those of the KGB, have made use since Stalin's death of physical violence, torture, and other methods vividly described by Khrushchev in his secret speech. These agencies still have at their disposal, however, an array of pressures that can shape the suspect's testimony in a desired direction. One highly significant legal formality lacking in Soviet criminal procedure is the right of counsel for a suspected or accused person until the preliminary investigation is completed.

The 1958 Basic Principles of Criminal Procedure of the USSR and the Union Republics, as well as the 1962 statute on the Advokatura (legal counsel) of the RSFSR, regulate the accused person's right of defense and the rights and duties of advocates at the preliminary investigation.[28] Pre-1958 Soviet rules on criminal procedure did not mention the lawyer's duties at the preliminary investigation. That defense counsel is provided at all at this crucial stage of the judicial process represents progress in safeguarding the rights of the accused, by Western standards, but this progress, judging by the language in the relevant legislation, is limited. Section 22 of the Basic Principles of Criminal Procedure states that

> Counsel for the defense may participate in a case from the moment the accused has been given notice of the closing of the preliminary investigation, and the accused is given access to [the records] of the proceedings [which have taken place].

In criminal cases of minors, as well as of persons who, on account

---

illegal practice of police agencies taking over the whole of the preliminary investigation in "almost all criminal cases." An article in *Izvestiya*, April 17, 1965, devoted mainly to examples of humane and "cultured" performance of their duties by Leningrad police officers, cited one case in which a police investigator, by interceding on behalf of a young man convicted for the second time of theft, whose case he had investigated, prevailed upon the judge to impose a minimum sentence. This episode underscores the continued centrality of the investigatory function of the police — in this instance, so far as we can know, to the benefit of an "honest," but "confused" wrongdoer.

[28] For articles on this subject, see Z. Szirmai, ed., *Law in Eastern Europe*, No. 3 (Leyden, 1959), containing, on pp. 118–19 and 124–25, the relevant articles of criminal procedure, and Lawrence M. Friedman and Zigurds L. Zile, "Soviet Legal Profession: Recent Developments in Law and Practice," *Wisconsin Law Review*, No. 1 (1964), pp. 32–77, which on pp. 39–41 and 61, presents, in English translation, the pertinent articles from the statute on the Advokatura relating to participation of defense counsel in the preliminary investigation of criminal cases.

of a physical or mental deficiency, cannot themselves safeguard their right to be defended, a counsel for the defense will be called into the case from the moment the accused has been informed of the charge brought against him.[29]

This section is a welcome addition, along with others governing defense counsel's activities and stressing the advocate's duty, defending "the laws and legal interests of citizens, enterprises," etc. (such provisions were absent from the 1939 statute which the 1962 legislation replaced). As during Stalin's time, though, Soviet law does not require that officers charged with preliminary, pretrial investigation contend with defense counsel until their job is done and they have decided whether or not the accused shall be bound over to a court for trial, except in special cases as indicated in the language quoted above.[30]

Provisions for right to counsel found in Soviet legal codes and referred to in law textbooks are vague, and set no limit to prolonged interrogation prior to counsel's taking up the accused's defense.[31] According to the 1958 Basic Principles, Section 13, the accused has "a right of defense" and the investigator, the procurator, and the court must safeguard his right of defense "from the moment he has been informed of the charge brought against him, and safeguard the protection of his personal and property rights." [32]

So far as it has been determined, defense counsel begins to take part in a Soviet criminal case only at the trial or very shortly before the trial opens. It is safe to assume, for that reason, that the defense attorney's work, especially if a case is "political," begins so late as to be of limited value to the client.

During investigation, and before the suspect has been formally accused, he is so completely subject to investigating authorities that, particularly if they abuse their powers, he may be pressured

29 Szirmai, *op. cit.*, p. 125. The Russian text of this article is given on p. 124. The above quotation reproduces Szirmai's translation of the first two paragraphs of Section 22, referring to a brief explanatory statement on p. 155.

30 Section 13 of the Basic Principles of Criminal Procedure, stipulating that investigators, procurators, and courts must safeguard the accused's rights of defense, in the manner and by the means established by the law, appears to be less significant than section 22, although it is not unimportant.

31 Ya. N. Umanski, *Sovetskoe gosudarstvennoe pravo* (Moscow, 1960), p. 342, refers to "the most democratic" principle, guaranteeing an accused the right to defend himself and "to have a defender." The right to defense is guaranteed by the constitution but the constitution does not spell out in detail how the accused may exercise this right.

32 Szirmai, *op. cit.*, pp. 118–19.

or cajoled into statements, or even a confession, which will set the tone of his subsequent trial. The average prisoner's isolation, his sense of helplessness, and his inability to cope, in legal knowledge and probably in general intellectual capacities, with his interrogators, put him at a disadvantage intolerable to anyone acquainted with Western legal systems when they are functioning properly. In appraising Soviet legal practices we must of course keep in mind the all too frequent breaches of legality in the United States in such areas as civil rights. Such failures of "bourgeois" justice are treated to countless commentaries in the Soviet press. Fortunately, they also interest, in the United States, many organs of the press, interested groups of citizens, lawyers and legal scholars, and in general so many independent forces of citizenship that there is no genuine counterpart in a political and legal system of the Soviet type. There is no doubt that Stalin's death was followed by a massive effort to eliminate abuses in police and judicial investigation. The instruments of correction were wielded, however, by a ruling party which, while Stalin was in power, had been unable or unwilling to prevent flagrant violations of legality. No fully independent countervailing forces guaranteed that police and prosecutors would not slip back into a state of mind in which even the procurators who, according to the law, were supposed to control the police and security agencies, "themselves feared those organs, over which they exercised supervision." [33]

From May through December, 1964, the Soviet press carried discussions of proper relationships between the judicial role of prosecutors and of judges. Even in cases that did not involve crimes against the state, some prosecutors felt that arrest and investigation raised a presumption of guilt and that the courts' job was merely to determine the degree of the accused's guilt and to sentence accordingly. Worse yet, according to distinguished jurists and officials, some judges accepted this narrow conception of their duties.[34]

[33] Mironov, *op. cit.*, p. 233.

[34] Important contributions to this discussion are those of Professor M. S. Strogovich, *Literaturnaya gazeta*, May 23, 1964, G. Filimonov, *ibid.*, Aug. 18, 1964, O. Chaikovskaya, *Izvestiya*, Sept. 10, 1964, and A. Gorkin, *ibid.*, Dec. 2, 1964. Filimonov, an assistant procurator who was sharply criticized by Chaikovskaya, unsuccessfully sued her. The tone and proportions of the contributions indicated that the party was on the side of those seeking to prevent abuses of authority by prosecutors.

A. Gorkin, chairman of the USSR Supreme Court, pointed out in his three-column contribution to this significant discussion that an "accusatory inclination" could lead to abuses of both investigation and sentencing, and might even cause the innocent to suffer, while the guilty remained unpunished. From the point of view of proponents of "legal rationality," the tone of this published exchange was encouraging, on the whole, including Gorkin's statement that "there could be no return" to the day when, in accusations of "state crimes," the accused's guilt was essentially decided by the investigatory organs. Publication of Gorkin's article after Khrushchev's fall was an encouraging sign that the impetus toward continuing or at least maintaining the reforms achieved earlier had not ended with Khrushchev. Also heartening was an article by the liberal scholar R. D. Rakhunov, published in the September 22, 1965 issue of *Pravda,* demanding a number of fundamental reforms in legal procedure.

Many questions remained, however. Would Khrushchev's successors desire and be able to maintain the scrupulous respect for the law, as set forth in principles and codes, preached by Gorkin? How effective could such exhortations be when, it is generally agreed, the procuracy gets the best legal talent, leaving the rest to the courts and the bar? How could even capable judges, day in and day out, cope with even a few procurators who have ideas such as those criticized by men like M. S. Strogovich and Gorkin?

Certainly the outside observer can find no easy answer to such questions. We feel justified in keeping a qualifiedly positive perspective. It appears that Stalin's successors realized increasingly that judicial abuses, like other defects of the political system, were dysfunctional, because they were bad for morale and they undermined faith in legitimate authority. Also, an increasingly educated and no longer terror-numbed legal intelligentsia might gradually become a powerful force for legal rationality and consistency, especially if its members could press the appropriate party and state authorities to work for improvement in judicial practices and in the professional training of prosecutors, judges, and lawyers. The drive for improved training has become stronger in recent years, bringing stricter educational requirements, vigorously reviving all branches of legal scholarship, and applying to that field of advanced Western social science theories and techniques. The penetration of Western scientific thinking in

Soviet legal scholarship remains a minor but hopeful aspect of the scene, exemplified in the writings of such scholars as M. S. Strogovich and R. D. Rakhunov.

If Soviet criminal law procedure, especially in pretrial investigations, has aroused misgivings in the West, it is partly because the Soviet authorities have not seen fit to disclose adequate data on these areas, or to permit even one qualified foreigner to observe them.[35] For that reason we shall refer briefly to the writer's interrogation by KGB investigators (*sledovateli*) from the evening of October 31 through 2:00 P.M., November 16, 1963, in the Lubyanka Prison in Moscow. It must be borne in mind that this account is based on memory, since the accused was not permitted to make any notes. And, since this was a KGB investigation of alleged espionage, it may not necessarily represent the type of investigation that would be conducted by procuracy or ordinary police investigators in nonpolitical cases.

In the Soviet Union there are two kinds of "police." The ordinary police are known as the militia (*militsiya*) and, since 1962, have been controlled by the Ministries for the Protection of Public Order in each republic and autonomous republic of the USSR. Like the KGB, the procuracy, and the courts, these agencies are under the Department of Administrative Organs and are also, it is believed by some specialists on Soviet affairs, under the Party Organs Department of the Central Committee which, beginning in 1962, was associated with or supervised by the Central Committee Commission on Organizational and Party Questions.

This writer's encounter with Soviet justice began with abduction by plain-clothes men and forcible removal to a militia station. After sitting for five or six hours in the militia station, in very tightly fitting handcuffs, he was taken in an automobile to the Lubyanka, where for the next sixteen and a half days he was held in absolute isolation from the outside world, and was only released after President John F. Kennedy personally intervened. Except for the period of handcuffing, there was no roughness or brutality. On the other hand, frequent requests for permission to communicate with the United States Embassy and occasional references to right of counsel were met only with what appeared to be amused explanations that such requests were contrary to

35 Feifer, *op. cit.*, p. 90, notes that as far as pretrial investigation was concerned, "direct knowledge was denied me."

Soviet law. The writer distinctly recalls that he was informed that failure to reply to the questions put by his interrogators would be punished by six months' imprisonment and that false testimony would be punished by imprisonment of two years.[36] The accused was given to understand that he would make it easier for himself at his forthcoming trial (every effort was made to convince him that indeed he would be tried) if he would make a full confession of his "guilt." The experience was made terrifying by the fantastic isolation in which the accused was held — he never saw another prisoner and knew nothing about the reaction of his own government or the American public to his detention until he was able to talk to fellow passengers on a British European Airways plane flying from Moscow to London — and by a variety of psychological pressures employed by the interrogators, but it is only fair to state that in many ways it was also interesting.

The episode can be called interesting partly because the chief interrogator was a man of wit and humor. After formal interrogation he would often engage in long, speculative conversations with the accused. During these conversations, the chief interrogator, and at times his assistant and the interpreter who was present throughout the proceedings, conducted for the most part in Russian, set forth the official Soviet point of view on all questions discussed, though they sometimes did this in a more informal, relaxed, and less rigid fashion than might have been expected. The "whole man" and "educational" aims of Soviet justice, of which much is made by some American scholars of Soviet law, were evident in the proceedings. Despite such annoyances as twenty-four hour illumination of the cell and inspection through a peephole every few minutes, also throughout day and night, as well as the threat implicit in the entire situation, all of which made the experience trying in the extreme, the administrative regulations posted in great detail on the inside of the cell door were carefully observed, for the most part.[37] On the other hand, every element

[36] According to Feifer, *op. cit.*, p. 88, an accused person is not criminally responsible, either during his investigation or at the trial, for refusing to talk or for giving "wrong testimony."

[37] This author noted a general similarity of the tenor of his treatment with that accorded to Francis Gary Powers in reading, subsequent to his release, the account of the U-2 affair given in the book by Thomas B. Ross and David Wise. A link with the Russian past was one of the prohibitions posted on the door of the writer's cell prohibiting tapping to communicate with other prisoners — a favorite practice of Russian revolutionaries during the tsarist era.

in this "case" seemed to rest upon illegality. Although the writer
knew nothing of military affairs, he was accused of having had in
his possession military intelligence data, in the form of photographs, which actually had been thrust upon him by a total
stranger just prior to his abduction. He was never confronted
with his alleged accomplice. The other three charges against him
had to do with his service in 1943–1947 in the American Embassy,
as a diplomat, his service as a State Department officer interview-
ing Soviet refugees in West Germany in 1949–1951, and his alleged activity, as a tourist, in gathering intelligence data for the
United States Government. All represented what appeared to the
accused to be completely unwarranted inferences from data which
had obviously been carefully and patiently gathered for many
years and incorporated in a dossier which was drawn upon, obviously, to provide background for the interrogation.

This writer does not profess to be able to identify the motives
for this action, though it seems most plausible that he was to
be used as a hostage, in retaliation for the arrest of a Soviet citizen
in the United States. Its legality, by Western standards, was
dubious in the extreme. This episode, like other apparently arbitrary actions of the Soviet security authorities against American,
British, and West German citizens, some with diplomatic status,
indicates that when the authorities suspect even the slightest
threat to the political regime's security (as perhaps this writer's
excessively active sociological curiosity was construed), expediency can take precedence over legality far more easily than it can
in the American system.

Thus far we have said little about Soviet attorneys and how
they defend the rights of accused persons. From our account of
the Soviet judicial process it appears that, though he dominates
the proceedings once the case comes to court, the judge is overshadowed by the investigator, whose skills and efforts have so distinctly shaped the judgment before the matters are entrusted to
the public arena of a court. What room and weight are left in this
scheme of things for counsel for the defense?

It can be asserted without fear of expert contradiction that
there are no Soviet equivalents either to celebrated American trial
lawyers such as Clarence Darrow, Samuel Liebowitz, or Edward
Bennet Williams, or to the wealthy Wall Street corporation attorney. But before we look at the Soviet equivalent to the Amer-

ican lawyer in "private" practice, we must mention the categories to which, broadly, the title "lawyer" applies in Soviet usage. Of the 78,700 persons classified in Soviet official sources as of 1959 as "juridical personnel," 23,000 were listed as judges and procurators. There were also thousands of "jurisconsults," roughly equivalent to "house counsel" in the United States, who are on the payrolls of Soviet industrial and other state enterprises. Apparently no global figures are available on the number of "advocates" (*advokati*), but this writer was told by the chairman of the Leningrad College of Advocates during an interview in March, 1963 that there were 14,000 members of his professional group in the Soviet Union at that time.[38] The consensus among American specialists on Soviet law is that the ablest graduates of the Soviet university law faculties are recruited for the procuracy, or go on to graduate training and become teachers, or even, if they are extremely successful, are taken into the Institute of Law of the Academy of Sciences. There is no doubt that the training and education of all Soviet jurists has improved greatly since World War II ended. To be sure, following the postwar spurt in training legal personnel, filling gaps caused by severe war losses, fewer such personnel were turned out. Today the number of advocates and other legal workers probably is about the same as it was just before World War II. That the Soviet legal profession, in its size and growth, is so modest compared with the engineering field crudely but not insignificantly indicates the relatively low status of lawyers in the Soviet social and political system. Still, persons with legal training may achieve high rank in such relatively powerful organs of the bureaucracy as the procuracy and the KGB, whose cadres are one of the most important "career" services of the Soviet civil service.

With improved education and the post-Stalin emphasis on

[38] Most of the figures above are from Friedman and Zile, *op. cit.*, pp. 47–48, 69. Figures on enrollment in law faculties of Soviet institutions of higher education are contained in Seymour M. Rosen, ed., *Higher Education in the U.S.S.R.* (U.S. Dept. of Health, Education and Welfare, Washington, D.C., U.S. Government Printing Office, 1963), p. 101. Incidentally, Rosen's data indicate a significant decrease in enrollment, if 1961–1962 figures are compared to those for 1950–1951, or 1955–1956. The total number of "lawyers" in the Soviet Union, with a population some thirty or forty million greater than that of the United States, seems small when compared to the 286,000 members of this profession in America. For figures on the size of the profession in the United States, see Martindale-Hubbell, *Law Directory*, 1961 edition, and *Statistical Abstract of the United States*, 85th ed. (Washington, D.C., U.S. Government Printing Office, 1964).

"socialist legality," Soviet lawyers gained professional conscious-ness. Berman was very strongly impressed by the "cohesion" of all kinds of Soviet jurists, which was based, he reported, on pro-fessional ties, a variety of common activities, and "their common vested interest in the preservation of legality." [39] Soviet lawyers and legal scholars were unable, however, to prevent such negative developments as the extension of the death penalty, which re-sulted in the execution of more than 250 Soviet citizens from May, 1961 to May, 1962, and perhaps a greater number from June to December, 1962. A particularly backward step, according to the Western conception of the "rule of law," was retroactive applica-tion, in some cases, of the death penalty. When asked to explain the July, 1961 decision instituting this practice, one leading Soviet jurist reportedly replied, "We lawyers didn't like it!" [40]

In fact, the lawyers' aspirations met numerous frustrations, one of which is particularly interesting. Toward the end of 1958 four jurists proposed in the main Soviet legal journal that an All-Union Association of Lawyers be established. It would include those employed in the procuracy, jurisconsults, advocates, and also teachers and researchers. Despite enthusiastic support in let-ters to the editor of *Sovetskoe gosudarstvo i pravo,* this proposal was not adopted.[41] The 1962 RSFSR statute governing the organ-ization, rights and duties, compensation, and supervision of advo-cates appeared to accord them increased autonomy, exercised through the "colleges of advocates." Actual legal practice was or-ganized in "consultation offices," through which the profession deals with such matters as recruiting advocates, disciplining erring members of the profession, etc. But the statute supplied no functional parallel to American-style bar associations in cover-age of the profession. And, more significant, it left to government authorities control both over enforcing professional standards and over "the schedule of fees to be charged for legal services and the conditions under which gratuitous legal services are ren-dered." [42]

---

39 Berman, "Dilemma of Soviet Law Reform," *op. cit.,* pp. 944–45.

40 *Ibid.,* p. 949.

41 Friedman and Zile, *op. cit.,* pp. 37–38.

42 For the latter provision, see Friedman and Zile, *op. cit.,* p. 45. For other important provisions of the Statute on the Advokatura referred to above, see pp. 50, 52, 57, 63, and esp. pp. 66–67. The latter pages contain a translation of Article 42 of the Statute and the authors' comment that "The present article goes a long way toward prescribing regular disciplinary proceedings; it at-

As Feifer describes them, on the basis of his extensive first-hand observation, the status and image of Soviet courtroom defense attorneys probably would seem dismal to most of their colleagues in noncommunist countries. Successful lawyers, and even lawyers in general, certainly are better off financially than are judges or prosecutors. The head of the Leningrad College of Advocates told this writer in March, 1963 that it was possible for an outstanding lawyer to earn 450 rubles a month, four or five times as much as a skilled Soviet factory worker earns. Also, more than half the lawyers in the RSFSR are members of the party; presumably their discontents are partially mitigated by a sense of identity with the ruling elite and by the party's efforts to relate day-to-day legal activity to long-range ideological goals.[43] On the other hand, advocates live well, by Soviet standards, and, by various means, they usually succeed in receiving for their services sums greater than specified by the official schedule of fees. This practice, if it is not carried too far, seems not to lead to reprisals by the government, but it casts a "bourgeois" shadow upon their public image. Although elderly judges or procurators sometimes become advocates for financial reasons, there apparently is very little movement in the other direction.

Like judges and procurators, Soviet advocates are subjected to periodic social pressure "campaigns" such as the one begun in 1961–1962 for more severe punishment for criminals. Subjected to this frequent, direct political intervention in law enforcement, lawyers, as Feifer puts it, play "second fiddle in the courtroom." Apparently, they often feel hampered in trying to marshal, for the defense of their clients, the resources afforded by Soviet law and procedure. Affecting not only the lawyer's work but the situation of the accused in a Soviet court, "A Soviet trial is so conducted that the lawyer's concluding statement is more often a collection of mitigating circumstances than a denial of guilt or a

tempts to set out some sort of 'due process' for advocates accused of violations." Ultimate control over advocates in the Russian Republic, prior to 1963, was vested in the RSFSR Ministry of Justice, as well as in the Council of Ministers — the latter with respect to some important matters. In 1963, the Ministry of Justice of the RSFSR and of other republics was abolished, but this agency was replaced by a juridical commission of the Russian Republic. Presumably, the same change occurred in the other republics of the USSR. On this point, with regard to the RSFSR, see *ibid.*, pp. 44–45, 47, 50, 56, 66.

[43] Friedman and Zile, *op. cit.*, give some figures on party membership, based on Soviet sources.

presentation of purely legal arguments." [44] The defense which the lawyer can give his client is therefore limited, and part of the Soviet lawyer's art must be "sensing the limits." [45]

An outside observer, studying Soviet judicial decisions, gets an almost overpowering feeling of systematic pressure by concentrated political authority upon the criminal and upon those who investigate, defend, and judge him. This feeling is still further reinforced when one takes into account certain features of the system discussed further on in this chapter, particularly the procuracy's functions. The courts, advocates, and procurators can lodge various kinds of protests regarding the legality of sentences and the procedures leading up to them through the administrative mechanism which links the entire court network into a system, at the apex of which is the Supreme Court of the USSR.

Of these three main agencies of Soviet justice, the procurators are by far the most highly trained, centrally organized, and powerful. In the whole area of applying and interpreting legal norms, the procurators seem to be second in real power only to the KGB. According to legal formalities, even the KGB is not permitted to make an arrest or begin an investigation without the written permission of an appropriate procuracy officer. Presumably, the procuracy has a special agency for liaison with the KGB. The procuracy, originally established by Peter the Great, was abolished in 1864 as incompatible with the liberal forms of legal reforms then instituted, but was restored by the Soviet government in 1922. The legislation under which it presently operates was adopted in 1955.[46]

The procuracy is a hydra-headed, bureaucratic, legal creature. Procuracy officers conduct pretrial investigations in criminal cases, leaving "political" investigations to the KGB, and act as government prosecutors in court. It also has departments charged with exercising "general supervision" over the legality of all governmental operations, including courts, local soviets, councils of national economy, and other economic, administrative agencies, etc.

---

44 Feifer, *op. cit.*, p. 239.
45 *Ibid.*, p. 252.
46 On the procuracy's powers and structure see V. S. Karev, *et al.*, *Organizatsiya suda i prokuratury v SSSR* (Moscow, 1961), Chs. IX, X; a detailed history and analysis of procuracy operations, devoted mainly to its "general supervision" over administrative legality, is contained in Morgan, *Soviet Administrative Legality, op. ct.*; see also Berman, *Justice in the U.S.S.R.*, pp. 238–47; and Feifer, *Justice in Moscow*, Ch. V.

But it does not supervise enactments and practices of the USSR Supreme Soviet, the Council of Ministers of the USSR, or the policies and practices of the CPSU. Essentially, the procuracy assures that high-level party and state policy is carried out and prevents middle and lower ranking officialdom from arbitrarily exercising its power. Perhaps its most important administrative function, as distinct from its legal operations, is combating graft and corruption in the Soviet economy.

To assure the procuracy's authority and to keep it independent of local party and government ties which might entangle it in local collusive combinations, the procuracy is tied closely to the top party and government command. The General Procurator of the USSR, in accordance with Article 114 of the USSR Constitution, is appointed by the Supreme Soviet of the USSR for seven years. The General Procurator, in turn, appoints procurators of union republics for five years. The latter appoint procurators of the administrative regions within their republics, except for deputy procurators of union and autonomous republics and some other high-ranking procuratorial officials, who are appointed by the General Procurator. In late 1965, the General Procurator of the USSR was Roman Andreevich Rudenko, who, according to official Soviet sources, had worked in the procuracy since 1929, after a few years of labor in a sugar mill and serving in Komsomol and government administrative duties. In 1944 Rudenko became procurator of the Ukrainian Republic. In 1953 he rose to General Procurator of the USSR. In 1961 he became a member of the CPSU central committee. The photograph of Rudenko in the 1962 Official Directory of Supreme Soviet Deputies showed him in his uniform, presumably that appropriate to his rank as Actual State Counsellor of Justice. His education was listed as "incomplete higher," but included an honorary Doctor of Juridical Sciences degree from Humboldt University in East Berlin.

Except for his relative lack of formal education, Rudenko's characteristics and career seem rather typical of the procuratorial service's upper ranks. The procuracy provides its officials with the professional training necessary to inculcate in them zeal in defense of party and governmental values and with status and authority sufficient to inspire awe among potential and actual lawbreakers. Soviet procurators undoubtedly often defend the accused in court cases and sometimes defend ordinary citizens whose rights have been violated by public officials, but their principal work is defending the party's interests, both directly as criminal investigators and prosecutors and indirectly as watchdogs over judges, lawyers, and administrators. The Soviet procurator is formidable, particularly in fostering "law-consciousness" and also in providing something of a substitute for the functions performed in the American system by judicial review.

On the other hand, the procuracy was unable to prevent the truly fantastic orgy of illegality which flourished under Stalin. Despite its objectionable features from the British or American point of view, its strengthening since Stalin's death may be viewed as one constructive step toward more consistent and predictable judicial behavior. Still, even the post-Stalin procuracy suffers from many deeply rooted defects, including some secrecy in making and disseminating administrative and other rules and relatively poor, though improving, legal training of its cadres.[47]

In exercising its "general supervision," the procuracy has always found it difficult to deal with industrial enterprises. Procurators usually lack the economic and accounting skills needed to cope with the refined techniques by which Soviet industrial administrators often evade bureaucratic regulations which keep them from fulfilling government planning directives or frustrate their desire for personal enrichment, or both. In seeing that the activities of industrial and other economic administrators are legal, the procuracy overlaps the work of such agencies as the Ministry of State Control and the Ministry of Finance. It cannot, however, encroach upon the work of agencies that check on the economic activities of enterprises, institutions, and organizations.[48] It seems very difficult to distinguish between defective economic performance and legal violations for which the procuracy, when it discovers them, is obliged to institute criminal proceedings. In fact, neither the economic control agencies nor the procuracy, even in the post-Stalin period, have prevented economic illegality to the satisfaction of the party. Signs of that disapproval were the estab-

[47] Morgan, *op. cit.*, Ch. 9, esp. pp. 188–89, cites USSR General Procurator Rudenko, in 1956, as saying that "A major bar to public knowledge of Soviet laws is the lack of well-codified laws that are known to the public and convenient for use." Morgan notes that citizens can hardly be expected to obey laws unknown to them and that the procuracy "can hardly exercise effective supervision over the observance of the laws when procurators know nothing of the laws because they cannot obtain them."

[48] Karev, *op. cit.*, p. 202.

lishment in 1962 of the Party-State Control Committee and the turning over of detection and preliminary investigation in major cases involving "economic crimes" to the KGB in recent years.

There are two major organizational challenges to the consolidating and further improvement of Soviet rule application and rule adjudication, of which we have described some features. The lesser of these, albeit interesting, significant, and disturbing, is the movement for "popular participation" in law enforcement represented by the *druzhina* (variously translated into English as "people's guard," "people's police," etc.), the comrades' court (*tovarishcheski sud*), and the antiparasite assembly. The greatest threat to the development in the Soviet Union of a judicial process of the "Western" type, however, is still probably the powerful agencies of intelligence, surveillance, detection, detention, and investigation, of which the KGB forms the inner core. This machinery, in turn, reflects fundamental features of the Leninist political culture, such as the belief that the bitter struggle between "socialism" and "imperialism" will continue for a long time and that the "socialist" states, as long as this struggle continues, must defend themselves against foreign espionage and subversion by vigilantly guarding frontiers, safeguarding state secrets, and ferreting out foreign agents and their supposed accomplices.

These grim tenets of Leninism, then, seem to be associated in the party leaders' minds with maintaining a powerful political police mechanism. The more optimistic of Marxist-Leninists, though, envisage, along with progress toward communism, that administrative and coercive governmental agencies will gradually be replaced by the more "democratic" machinery of the developing "all-people's state." That will lead logically to a limited transfer of law enforcement from regular police, court, and prosecution agencies to the "public." "Scientific" jurisprudence, as interpreted by Western or, from many indications, Soviet jurists, looks upon both KGB practices and "popular" justice as negative phenomena, though party discipline inhibits Soviet legal scholars and practitioners from expressing their doubts. A tear in the web of concepts and behaviors symbolized by the phrases "equal justice," "rule of law," and "due process" must make uneasy those who desire a legal order in which no violation of law will go unpunished and no punishment will be meted out to one who cannot be proved to have violated a clearly defined rule. Some of the ideas professed by Soviet jurists in recent years are threatened by (1) the vigilantism of nonprofessional police and courts and (2) the potential abuse inherent in judicial investigation secretly conducted by police agents who exercise physical control over those whose actions they are charged with investigating.

Presumably, if Khrushchev's successors do not repudiate the policies inaugurated under his leadership, the regular judicial practices described in this chapter will continue to be applied in most criminal and civil cases. The dread hand of the KGB will fall upon those who, whether Soviet citizens or foreigners, are suspected of being dangerous to the military, economic, or political security of the state. Logically, if political and social stability at home and "peaceful co-existence" between the Soviet Union and states with "different" social systems abroad flourish (the ambiguity and difficulties of measurement involved in these concepts are obvious), then the power of the political police may be expected to gradually diminish. Finally, satisfactory progress toward "communism," increasing economic abundance, and voluntary and joyous acceptance by the citizenry of the "rules of socialist communal living" will gradually expand noncoercive citizen activity in interpreting and applying norms of behavior at the expense of both the regular judicial system and the political police organization. These are some speculations inspired by contemplating post-Stalin trends in Soviet justice. Of course, the difficulty of even the most modest contingent forecasting should not be underestimated. The outside observer (and perhaps the Soviet observer) has only limited, inadequate, and carefully processed information, particularly on the most sensitive political police and "popular" law enforcement practices.

Perhaps the best clue to the party's hopes for nonprofessional law enforcement was contained in Khrushchev's report to the Twenty-first Party Congress in 1959. Khrushchev declared that the withering of the state, if understood "dialectically," was "the problem of the development of socialist statehood into communist public self-government." [49] Here also Khrushchev suggested that the means that "social organizations" had for coping with "violators of socialist legal order" were not inferior to those possessed by the militia, courts, and procuracy. He expressed hope that the assuring of public order and security might be fulfilled "along parallel lines" by state institutions such as the militia and the courts, and by "social organizations." He went on to say that such a process was already occurring, adding that "the apparatus of the militia has been sharply cut and the apparatus of the organs of state security has been especially sharply curtailed." [50]

Khrushchev mentioned the "people's militia" and the "comrades' courts," and also referred to "organs similar to them." He thus identified some existing "social" or "civic" forms of public participation in applying and adjudicating rules of social behavior. He did not specifically mention what one might call nonlegal law, which probably posed the most serious threat to due process in Soviet society's treatment of violators of public order. These were the laws which some Soviet republics had already passed in 1957 and 1958 to deal with "parasites." In 1961 revised antiparasite laws were enacted in all fifteen republics.[51] The practice of "parasitism" was defined loosely in the various enactments prescribing penalties to deal with it, and persons committing a wide variety of offenses were punished as "parasites." Broadly, persons so punished were individuals who evaded or refused to perform work regarded by the authorities as socially useful. The quasi-public organizations praised by Khrushchev apparently flourished in the next few years.

It was said that by the spring of 1963 there were 130,000 units of the druzhina, or people's guard, with a membership of 5,500,000 — well over 2 per cent of the Soviet population.[52] In the same year, more than 197,000 comrades' courts were reported.[53] Reviving and expanding such non-professional agencies was but one

[50] *Ibid.*, p. 104.

[51] On the antiparasite laws, see the astute comment by Leon Lipson, "The Future Belongs to . . . Parasites?" *Problems of Communism*, XII, No. 3 (May–June, 1963), pp. 1–6.

[52] Dennis M. O'Connor, "Soviet People's Guards: An Experiment with Civic Police," *New York University Law Review*, 39, No. 4 (June, 1963), p. 580. As O'Connor explains in detail, the people's guard is not to be confused with the traditional auxiliary militia, one form of which Khrushchev apparently had in mind in his above-quoted reference. Various nonprofessional, citizen units for assisting the police, especially in rural areas, have existed since 1924. On the history of these units, see *ibid.*, pp. 580–87.

[53] Harold J. Berman and James W. Spindler, "Soviet Comrades' Courts," *Washington Law Review*, 38, No. 4 (Winter, 1963), p. 895, referring to *Pravda*, Nov. 13, 1963. This valuable article includes a translation of the 1961 RSFSR Statute on comrades' courts.

method of increasingly involving the Soviet public in widely varied activities for backstopping party and government operations, some of which were referred to in earlier chapters. In the legal field alone, these developments also included "the expansion of the auxiliary use of lay accusers and defenders, representing civic organizations, in criminal trials; the scheduling of more and more regular court sessions in places of public assemblage like union halls or clubs; and the placing of certain defendants under the tutelage of civic organizations vouching for their correction and for their proper re-education." [54] This vast endeavor, particularly in law enforcement, has achieved only modest success compared with the avowed party objective of transferring old functions to new structures and transforming the functions themselves. It appears that thus far there has been less a replacement of the police, courts, and procuracy by "social organizations" than a division of labor, in which relatively unimportant matters are handled by the auxiliary organizations while professionals continue to deal with important matters. Also, the regular police and courts have come to exercise more guidance over public organizations than originally planned.[55] Although these nonprofessional bodies and units are not direct arms of the party, it has been clear from the beginning that they were to be the party's instruments for facilitating the "transition to communism." We must keep this perhaps obvious point in mind, lest "social," "public," and "civic," constantly repeated, create the false impression that replacing some coercion by "persuasion" necessarily, under Soviet conditions, will bring relaxed supervision of the individual's life by organized social agencies.

New, "voluntary" agencies of social control may well have brought more rather than less surveillance and interference by worker over fellow worker, colleague over colleague, and neighbor over neighbor. On the other hand, Soviet sources have frequently reported that surveillance and deterrence by the people's guards and the social pressure exerted by the comrades' courts, such as public criticisms of an individual's conduct by "tens or hundreds

54 Lipson, "Parasites," *op. cit.*, p. 4.
55 Thus, it is reported that "As a result of experience the guards have come under increased police management while performing police functions." O'Connor, *op. cit.*, p. 594.

of one's fellow-workers or neighbors," have reduced crime substantially.[56]

AUXILIARY JUDICIAL AGENCIES

A brief description of the people's guard, the comrades' court, and the machinery for dealing with "parasites" will make it easier to appraise their place in Soviet justice. People's guard units are established on the initiative of the party, Komsomol, or trade union organizations. Volunteers for membership must be at least eighteen years of age. Apparently the units have far more Komsomol or party members than the community average.[57] Groups of guards' units are supervised by a staff selected by the local party committee. There are units in places of work and residence and also in universities and other educational institutions, and special units in frontier areas.[58]

Guards perform their unpaid labors during off-duty hours. Persons admitted to the guards receive an identification card, lapel pin, and handbook.[59] Each guard's unit is subordinated to a "commander" (*komandir*), and under each komandir a number of patrols serve. Members of the patrols wear red armbands. Patrols do such work as assisting the police in directing traffic, deterring public disorder in restaurants, clubs, etc., conducting "raids" to detect shortchanging of customers in stores, and many other activities. They have authority to demand identifying documents and even to detain or arrest citizens. Apparently guards have often had to decide whether to take action equivalent to police action or to report infractions of public order to the regular police. There have been conflicts of jurisdiction between guards and the regular police. Since the guards normally have little knowledge of law, relatively limited police skills, and are unarmed, they sometimes find it difficult to describe their functions and some guards have been murdered. In 1962, penalties provided by Soviet law

---

56 Berman and Spindler, *op. cit.*, pp. 895–96; O'Connor, pp. 605–607.

57 Hammer, *op. cit.*, p. 384; O'Connor, *op. cit.*, p. 590.

58 O'Connor, *op. cit.*, pp. 590–91. On special Guards' units in restricted frontier areas, "representatives of the local organs of the KGB and also of the frontier troops" participate and, one would suppose, supervise. See A. G. Khazikov, *Sbornik normativnykh aktov po sovetskomu administrativnomu pravu* (Moscow, 1964), pp. 498–99. O'Connor cites on p. 591 two Soviet references regarding Guards' cooperation with security personnel.

59 O'Connor, *op. cit.*, p. 590.

for resisting regular police personnel were extended to include guards.[60] It appears that from 1959 to 1964 the guards were successful in deterring or punishing "obvious or minor infractions," especially when such people as retired policemen or chauffeurs turned to directing traffic or other work for which their previous professional experience had fitted them. Soviet society may have gained something "from the experiment in redistributing police functions," i.e., the guards, but the most obvious conclusion is that the experiment proved that professional skills and standards are necessary to those who exercise police functions.[61]

COMRADES' COURTS

According to Soviet legislation, "comrades' courts are elected social agencies charged with actively contributing to the education of citizens in the spirit of a communist attitude toward labor and socialist property and the observance of the rules of socialist community life, and with developing among Soviet people a sense of collectivism and comradely mutual assistance and of respect for the dignity and honor of citizens." [62] As Berman and Spindler note, they are called "social" rather than "state" agencies "because they are not staffed by civic servants but by volunteers and because they are conceived to perform a persuasive rather than a coercive function." [63] Although comrades' courts may impose small fines and even recommend eviction from an apartment or other rather serious measures, the language used in legislation governing them and in reporting their activities avoids conventional legal terminology. Thus, a person charged with an offense is described not as an "accused" but as a "person brought before the comrades' court." Hearings of comrades' courts are informal, and are usually held in the "social room" of a factory, apartment house, neighborhood, or collective farm. Lawyers do not usually participate in the argument and the judges are not civil servants but "neighbors or fellow-workers, who, however, may be given

60 O'Connor, *ibid.*, pp. 593–610.
61 O'Connor, *ibid.*, pp. 613–14, in by far the most comprehensive study available, reached the above conclusions.
62 Berman and Spindler, *op. cit.*, pp. 587–88, translating the first sentence of Article I of the 1961 RSFSR Statute on comrades' courts. Berman and Spindler translate the Russian name for this institution as "comrades' court"; others as "comradely court."
63 *Ibid.*, p. 842.

some elementary training in law." [64] The members of comrades' courts are elected "by open ballot" at meetings "called by factory, plant or local trade-union committees, the boards of collective farms or the executive committees of local soviets." [65] They consider a variety of cases, including violations of labor discipline, unwarranted personal use of state or collective farm property, "petty hooliganism, petty speculation, petty theft of state or social property, if committed for the first time," etc., drunkenness in public places or at work, and many other infractions or offenses against public order.[66] A 1963 amendment included "petty hooliganism," etc., bringing certain minor crimes under the jurisdiction of these institutions for the first time.[67] Broadening the auxiliary courts' jurisdiction apparently created some discrepancy between the RSFSR statute regarding them and the Criminal Code. More disturbing from the point of view of legal precision was Paragraph 9 of the statute, which provided for "other anti-social acts not entailing criminal liability." [68]

Cases may be brought before comrades' courts upon recommendation by people's guard units, trade union committees, executive committees of local soviets, or by state agencies, including courts or the procuracy — and also "upon the initiative of the comrades' court itself." [69] If they are "convinced of the necessity of holding the offender criminally or administratively responsible," comrades' courts may turn a case over to the appropriate state agencies. The statute governing comrades' courts also provides that a judge of the people's court may review certain of their decisions, including those involving fines. It appears that "judicial and procuracy workers and lawyers" are sharing increasingly the work of councils of chairmen of comrades' courts, which facilitates the "exchange of experience" among comrades' courts.[70] Presumably, the mechanism for supervising the comrades' courts prevents their usurping the regular courts' functions. According to one expert's opinion, if a case which came before a

[64] *Ibid.*, p. 843.
[65] *Ibid.*, referring to Article III of the Statute.
[66] *Ibid.*, pp. 863–65.
[67] *Ibid.*, pp. 867–68.
[68] *Ibid.*, p. 872. Berman and Spindler, however, appear to feel that Paragraph 9 does not imply, at least intentionally or technically, a return to the doctrine of "analogy" eliminated from Soviet criminal law in 1958.
[69] *Ibid.*, p. 875.
[70] *Ibid.*, pp. 889, 892, 893–94, 898.

comradely court were not "trivial" it would be in the regular courts or in the antiparasite tribunals.[71]

In their comprehensive study, Berman and Spindler saw these dangers in the comradely courts' work: (1) abuse of their functions by party organizations; (2) degradation of law, resulting from possible encroachment by nonprofessional judicial agencies; (3) dulling the sense of legality, which might result from "a strong likelihood that the persons participating in comrades' courts proceedings, whether as members of the tribunal, persons charged with offenses, complainants or spectators, will think of the proceedings as embodying correct legal methods for reaching just decisions" (which they consider most significant); and (4) "the most serious danger" inherent in "the possibility that they will pry into the personal affairs of Soviet citizens and will be an instrument for imposing conformity of thought and behavior in all spheres of life." [72]

Other competent scholars take a dimmer view of the comrades' courts, seeing them as one instrument used by the Soviet regime to find a substitute for political police capabilities reduced after Stalin's death.[73] Our incomplete data suggest that the anxiety expressed when the people's guard and the comrades' courts began their expanded activity around 1959 was only partially justified. It also seems that these social agencies have created a great deal of confusion and have brought about many abuses. Paradoxically, they have failed to justify the worst fears as to the damage they could inflict on Soviet judicial behavior, mostly because certain standards of legal procedure and some supervision by duly constituted official agencies have been successfully imposed on them.

THE ANTIPARASITE ASSEMBLY

The antiparasite edicts undoubtedly represented the most dangerous threat to the post-Stalin reforming of law and legal pro-

[71] *Ibid.*, p. 900.

[72] *Ibid.*, pp. 898–910, and esp. pp. 902, 905. Berman and Spindler's weighing of the pros and cons identifies many relevant problems.

[73] See the articles by Lipson and Azrael previously cited in this chapter. These are also commented upon by Berman and Spindler, *op. cit.*, pp. 844–45, 901.

cedure.[74] Fortunately, their effectiveness was reduced greatly by an amendment dated September 20, 1965, which is discussed later in this chapter. The edicts strongly mixed "popular" and conventional justice, with overtones of traditional Stalinist arbitrariness. They provided for issuing a warning to a "parasite" (a person who leads "an anti-social, parasitic way of life," whether employed, for appearance's sake, in a regular job, or living on the proceeds of such activities as "the exploitation of land plots, automobiles or housing," etc.) by "a social organization or state agency." If this warning is ignored, it must be followed by either a "social sentence" handed down by a "collective" of workers or employees, or, for persons without employment, by a people's court order for "resettlement in specially designated localities." The basic sanction was exile for not less than two or more than five years, with compulsory labor at the place of exile.[75]

The antiparasite legislation did not provide for right to counsel or other normal rights and procedural guarantees, and the offenses with which it dealt were not officially categorized as "crimes." In addition to dramatizing the "He who does not work, neither shall he eat" theme, the antiparasite laws may have had more specific objectives, such as combating the tendencies of some privileged members of the younger generation to seek to live an easy life, perhaps at the expense of affluent parents.[76] Whatever its motives, the antiparasite legislation lacked important provisions for protecting the rights of the accused: the right to counsel, the right of appeal, and even the right to appear and defend himself. To Soviet legal scholars and others who championed "strict legality," it must have seemed a partial defeat. On the other hand, it may have been welcomed by diverse elements in Soviet society, ranging from poor and honest workers through members of the older generation of party members (probably including Khrushchev himself) uneasy about how susceptible

[74] An English translation of the RSFSR edict is contained in Berman, *Justice in the U.S.S.R.*, pp. 291–94.

[75] Lipson, "Parasites," *op. cit.*, points out that, strictly speaking, the punishment is not "exile," but eviction, or "ex-settlement." The amendment referred to above abolished the provision for exile, except for the city of Leningrad and the oblast and city of Moscow.

[76] This is one of the hypotheses advanced in Lipson's discussion of Soviet "parasites."

many young Soviet citizens are to "bourgeois" values, to hard-nosed policemen impatient with legal niceties.

POLICE FORMATIONS

This chapter would be incomplete if we did not examine the ordinary police, or militia, and the KGB. These police agencies are semimilitary in their training, organization, and the terminology they use to designate rank. Their methods of surveillance, detection, arrest, detention, investigation, and their other work significantly influences the tone and character of rule application and rule adjudication in the USSR. The KGB is particularly important, for its personnel, as already noted, still handle the vital preliminary investigation of persons suspected of particularly serious crimes. Also, despite more effective party supervision applied to its establishment, which was drastically curtailed following Stalin's death, the KGB is heir to a tradition of police power and practice the memory of which probably still evokes awe among the citizenry, particularly those old enough to vividly recall the purges of the late 1930's.

Since the militia, as well as the KGB, the procuracy, and the courts, apparently was supervised, on the administrative level at least, by the same party official, the late Nikolai Romanovich Mironov, we begin our survey of the police agencies with a brief biographical sketch. According to the official directory of Supreme Soviet deputies, Mironov was born in 1913, a Russian by nationality. He became a party member in 1940, and was graduated from the Dnepropetrovsk State University. In 1945, after military service in World War II, he began a career in "leading party work." From 1951 through 1959 he worked in the organs of the MGB [77] and the KGB, assuming a post as "chief of a section of the CPSU Central Committee" in that year. *Pravda* for August 8, 1959, identified Mironov as a Major General.

Placing Mironov, a veteran party and police apparatchik, in the party's operational control post over the entire Soviet judicial, police, and legal apparatus reflected party control over these highly coordinated agencies as well as the continued prestige and influence in the post-Stalin period of men who were, one might guess, not unsympathetic toward Soviet career police officials' political point of view. As we have seen, almost a year after

[77] Ministry of State Security (Ministerstvo Gosudarstvennoi Bezopastnosti).

Mironov's death no successor had been announced. For a time, apparently, A. N. Shelepin performed Mironov's work along with his many other political and investigatory and control tasks. It was reported that "a conference of the chiefs of the sections of administrative organs of the communist parties and the Ministers for the Protection of Public Order of the union republics" was attended by very high officials, including Chief Procurator R. A. Rudenko, five of the ministers concerned, and by Shelepin, who reportedly delivered an address, the content and even the title of which were not reported.[78]

The Soviet press often publishes brief items containing bits of evidence on organizational and personnel links between the party leadership and the police agencies. One of these reported a conference devoted to "important problems of the further improvement of the activity of the capital's militia." [79] Among the participants listed were V. E. Semichastny, chairman of the KGB, V. S. Tikunov, Minister of Protection of Public Order of the RSFSR, Rudenko, N. G. Egorychev, First Secretary of the Moscow City Committee of the CPSU, and other high government and party officials.[80]

The Soviet militia, highly centralized in party control and ideological direction, is formally decentralized in operation. Each constituent republic and autonomous republic of the USSR has its Ministry for the Protection of Public Order, to which the militia units are subordinate. At the oblast and city level, these units are subordinate to the executive committees of the soviets.

In many ways the Soviet militia resembles police forces in noncommunist states. Its work includes traffic direction, maintaining normal public order, apprehending criminals, etc. Both its func-

---

[78] *Pravda*, April 10, 1965.

[79] *Pravda*, Aug. 2, 1964. As mentioned previously, *Izvestiya*, Aug. 22, 1965, reported on the party that greeted A. N. Shelepin on his return from North Korea. Among those listed were: V. E. Semichastny, KGB head; A. S. Panyushkin, head of the committee screening Soviet citizens for travel abroad, and P. V. Kovanov, then deputy chairman of the Party-State Control Committee and (after that agency was abolished) head of the "Organs of People's Control." There seems to be a kind of "police community" in the USSR, to which such persons belong, or with which they have close ties.

[80] On the basis of news items in *Izvestiya*, Oct. 27, 1959, and *Sovetskaya Estoniya*, Oct. 10, 1958, Tikunov can be identified as a former Komsomol leader who, like Nikolai Shelepin and Vladimir Semichastny, moved up from youth leadership to police work. According to *Kommunist tadzhikistana*, May 23, 1959, Tikunov at that time was a deputy chief of the Central Committee Department of Administrative Organs.

tions and its organization, however, have some interesting peculiarities. The militia administers such crucial instruments of social control as the Soviet internal passport system. Established in 1932, it closely resembles (like so much in Soviet administrative and police practice) features of the prerevolutionary order once fiercely denounced by the bolsheviks. All citizens who have reached the age of sixteen and who reside in specified categories of urban community must have an internal passport and must present the passport, upon demand, to the militia or other appropriate authorities. Standard Soviet legal textbooks describe the passport system as important for preserving public order and state security.[81] Persons proceeding from their place of residence to other parts of the Soviet Union must, within a period specified by law, register their passports with the appropriate personnel of hotels, apartment houses, etc. In addition to the strict and complicated passport system, the militia administers many other controls. These include procedures for obtaining permission to have and use printing, mimeographing, typewriting, and other reproduction and communication equipment, as well as photographic equipment and also guns, explosives, etc.[82] Such police controls over communication reinforce the controls over the press and literature described in Chapter V. They help to explain the difficulties and dangers experienced by some Soviet citizens, including young writers, who in the post-Stalin era provided foreigners with copies of literary manuscripts unpublishable in the USSR because they did not conform to the party line on literature.

To all the controls administered directly by the police agencies must be added other practices which, though administered by cadres departments of factories, mines, retail establishments, etc., must make the Soviet citizen aware of the government's power to exercise surveillance and control over him. We cannot know whether or not these practices arouse resentment, especially among the majority who know little about systems in which they do not exist.

[81] See V. A. Vlasov and S. S. Studenikin, *Sovetskoe administrativnoe pravo* (Moscow, 1959), pp. 272–75.

[82] *Ibid.*, p. 276. A more recent, but very brief treatment of these functions is contained in Yuri Kozlov, *Sovetskoe administrativnoe pravo* (Moscow, 1964), p. 264. One reason for the increasingly rare descriptions of police functions in Soviet legal literature may be the criticism leveled by reviewers against earlier textbooks on state and administrative law for allegedly presenting the Soviet administrative system at if it were the system of a "police state."

Perhaps the most important of these other controls is the labor book (*trudovaya knizhka*) which all workers must present to the cadres departments of their places of employment when they are employed. These are a source of information to employers (and, one may assume, in certain cases, to the legal authorities) on the individual's work record. During the last year of Khrushchev's leadership there was talk of replacing the labor book by a "labor passport" system, which would be administered not only by the factory authorities but also by designated workers of each factory or plant. Like so many of Khrushchev's proposals, the "labor passport" plan had pseudodemocratic aspects, but these might have been offset by the increased group surveillance over the individual which it implied. In any case, the plan seems to have been dropped.[83]

The activities of the Party-State Control Committee and those of its less powerful but still massive successor agency, the "Organs of People's Control," to which the press devotes a vast amount of space, could hardly fail to make the ordinary citizen — and particularly the managerial elite — feel the daily confrontation by a ubiquitous network of controllers and informers. To be sure, this committee's staff are mostly "volunteers." They serve in the "groups" and "posts" of the committee, in industrial enterprises, and also in institutions of higher education, and in cultural, medical, social welfare and, apparently, in agencies of all kinds. As of September, 1964 there were 260,000 "groups" and 500,000 "posts," and in these networks more than 4,000,000 "representatives of the toilers," including even housewives, students, and persons on pension, were doing their bit as "people's controllers." [84]

This popular participation in preventing illegality is supervised with the greatest care. In economic enterprises it is one of the organization's main functions — in primary party organizations a deputy secretary devotes most of his time to heading the "group of assistance to the organs of party-state control." [85]

Small wonder that, heartily encouraging what it holds to be socially useful snooping, the party sometimes feels that it must warn the citizenry against "improper" tale-bearing, anonymous letters, and "playing at detective"!

[83] For a typical discussion, see *Izvestiya* editorial, March 5, 1964.
[84] *Kommunist*, No. 13, Sept. 1964, p. 123.
[85] *Partiinaya zhizn*, No. 4, Feb., 1965, pp. 30–31, describing the structure of party organizations in institutions of higher education.

The militia is assisted in its exceptionally comprehensive, penetrating, and varied surveillance and detection work by "a vast army of insignificant people on whose activities the whole organization is not infrequently dependent."[86] These informers, most of them unpaid, include janitors, building superintendents, and members of voluntary associations for assisting the militia, mostly Komsomol and young party members. In some of its politically sensitive functions, especially those involving foreigners, appropriate militia personnel collaborate closely with and occasionally are supervised by KGB officers.[87]

In the first three or four years after Stalin's death, the militia, like the KGB, was severely criticized in the Soviet press for abuses committed in performing its functions. In recent years, however, it has been much praised, especially in articles by police officials, for improving its training and the style of its work. Typical of such favorable publicity was a long article by I. Golovchenko, Minister for the Protection of Public Order of the Ukrainian republic, on "Soviet Militia Day," a new Soviet national holiday established by a Supreme Soviet decree of September 26, 1962, and since celebrated annually.[88] He noted with satisfaction that "the main mass" of new militia personnel had higher or specialized secondary education. Presumably, some were graduates of MOOP educational institutions, for Golovchenko noted that the Ministry had at its disposal educational establishments. He paid tribute to the "personal" interest taken by Khrushchev in the militia's work, one result of which was that "the ranks of the militia are being replenished by the best representatives of the party and the Komsomol, specialists with higher juridical education." In 1963, he wrote about 2,500 members of the Komsomol and party had been assigned to work in the militia.[89]

A year after Golovchenko's article was published, A. Aksenov, who had held since 1960 the same post in the Belorussian republic, reported that during the preceding year more than 2,500

86 A. Lunin, "The Lower Echelons of the Soviet Militia," *Bulletin*, Institute for the Study of the USSR, II, No. 11 (Nov., 1955), pp. 3–7. Quotation on p. 3.

87 Lunin, p. 6, presents some details on militia-KGB collaboration.

88 *Pravda*, Nov. 10, 1963.

89 It is interesting that the issue of *Pravda* which published Golovchenko's article also included, on p. 4, the photograph of a militia officer with two members of the people's guard, simultaneously celebrating the worthiness both of state and "public" law enforcement efforts, and underscoring their close relationship.

officials of the Belorussian MOOP had studied such subjects as criminology and the "economy of various branches of production" in secondary and higher educational institutions. He also stated that in Minsk and other large Belorussian cities part-time legal and political "universities" had been set up for Ministry workers. Like many of his executive colleagues in both police agencies (the KGB and the MOOP), Aksenov rose to police eminence from a leading Komsomol position.[90]

After Khrushchev's fall, the Soviet leadership augmented the militia and undertook to enhance its prestige. V. Tikunov (Minister for the Preservation of Public Order of the RSFSR), in an authoritative article in the central committee's organizational journal, asserted that the former "underestimation" of the militia had been corrected and that many new recruits, including members of the Young Communist League and former military service personnel, were being brought into the militia.[91] Larger police forces were necessary because, he explained, since the end of World War II many new towns and settlements had been established, and the population had grown. But many statements, including Tikunov's, indicated that the real reason was the Soviet Union's acute crime problem. That conclusion seems safe, since Tikunov said that the police forces had been underestimated because of failure to realize what state the maintenance of public order was in. He also referred to numerous criminal actions, and his language was pessimistic and harsh, suggesting that party and police leaders were indeed worried about controlling the more unruly elements.

A significant disclosure in this article was that in militia units with more than fifty staff members, deputy commanders for political education work had been appointed. Although Tikunov stressed cooperation between professional law enforcement person-

---

90 Above article in *Izvestiya*, Nov. 12, 1964.
91 V. Tikunov, *Na strazhe obshchestvennogo poryadka, Partiinaya zhizn*, No. 20, Oct., 1965, pp. 15–21. Tikunov's article shows a frankness unusual in Soviet discussions of police matters. At the beginning of his discussion, he notes that "earlier," the NKVD and later the MVD, as administrator of "internal affairs," dealt not merely with preserving public order in the narrow sense but also with such matters as organizing municipal services and amenities, resettling people, verifying the carrying out of the orders and resolutions of the central and local organs of authority, etc. It is not entirely clear whether such a reminder of the enormous powers of the dreaded Stalinist police agencies was intended as an indication of post-Stalin improvement or, perhaps, as a slightly veiled threat.

nel organizations and the public generally, the establishment of a special political control agency, together with other hints in the article, seemed to reflect the Kremlin's intention to strengthen Moscow's control over the entire national police system.

Far more formidable than MOOP, the regular police force, is the KGB, or Committee for State Security, current designation for the powerful Soviet national political police agency attached to the Council of Ministers, USSR (Komitet Gosudarstvennoi Bezopasnosti pri Sovete Ministrov, SSSR). In its present form, this agency dates from a decree of March 13, 1954.[92] The KGB is the successor to the MGB, the NKGB, and the other Soviet state security agencies, extending back to the Cheka, which was established in December, 1917 to perform intelligence and counter-intelligence functions and administer summary justice to "enemies of the people." [93]

The security agencies were of great importance in consolidating the communist regime.[94] In spite of its sinister heritage, and the potential danger that it might revert to earlier practices, the KGB's position in the polity differs significantly from those of its predecessors. Foreign diplomatic missions were able to assemble information on numerous major developments that confirmed Soviet official statements on post-Stalin changes and improvements in security police methods and operations. The special boards were abolished; forced labor as a major instrument of national economic policy was abandoned; hundreds of thousands of both "ordinary" and "political" exiles were returned from camps; Beria and many of his henchmen were executed; and party control, as well as partial procuracy control, was re-established over arrest, investigation, etc.

92 Text in *Trud*, April 28, 1954, p. 2. Also available in other Soviet publications.

93 Gsovski and Grzybowski, Vol. I, p. 565. From the early days of the Soviet regime there has been a special agency of the KGB type, functioning within the complex of law enforcement and political police agencies. During the last years of Stalin's rule there was the MGB and the larger, but less specialized, and presumably less powerful MVD — Ministry of Internal Affairs. Since 1954 the corresponding pair of agencies has been the network of ministries for Protection of Public Order, and the KGB. For historical background, see Gsovski and Grzybowski, Vol. I, pp. 564–84, Fainsod, *How Russia Is Ruled*, (Cambridge, Mass., 1963), Ch. XIII, and Simon Wolin & Robert M. Stusser, *The Soviet Secret Police* (New York, 1957).

94 An illuminating account of their part in the Soviet political system's development is in *Entsiklopediya gosudarstva i prava*, Vol. III (Moscow, 1927), pp. 1174–78.

The KGB is still a terrifying and terrible instrument of political control but, unlike Stalin's and Beria's police, it is not used only capriciously and often senselessly to instill terror. Stalin had operated a police system and a political hostage system — he forced his colleagues to live under his watchful eye in the Kremlin. Neither his fellow members of the politburo or the secretariat, nor, for that matter, the top leaders of the police, could be confident from one day to the next of avoiding sudden imprisonment, torture, or death. After his passing, even Soviet citizens of the highest rank could enjoy personal security.

The political and quasi-judicial powers of the KGB remained formidable, probably far more so than many Soviet jurists wished. In 1957 and 1958 jurists suggested that all pretrial investigatory functions be turned over to the procuracy; they were not heeded. The KGB was assigned "preliminary investigation in cases concerning state crimes, assigned by the law to its jurisdiction and in some cases [the conduct of] inquiry." [95] As noted earlier, the KGB often assumes leadership in detecting and investigating persons suspected of currency speculation, large-scale embezzlement of state property, smuggling, etc.[96] Semichastny, chairman of the KGB, in a long article dedicated to the 45th anniversary of the "organs of state security of the Soviet Union," stated that his men were "helping" in the struggle with "bribe-takers and embezzlers of socialist property." [97] The KGB's prominence in the struggle against "economic crime" may be categorized as one retrogressive tendency discernible in some sectors of Soviet law enforcement after 1961. It does not seem arbitrary to regard any substantial expansion in Soviet political police activity as threatening further development of the law enforcement style which seemed to be emerging in the early post-Stalin years. Another negative indication was that the security police sought to utilize the "public meeting" provision of the antiparasite laws to intimidate persons holding or perhaps even those suspected of holding unorthodox political, ideological, or aes-

[95] Karev, *op. cit.*, pp. 224–28, with organizational chart on p. 225.
[96] The Soviet Weekly *Nedelya* in its Aug. 26–Sept. 1, 1962 issue, reported an interview with a group of KGB investigators, in which the agency's activity in such cases was referred to. An English translation of that article was published in the *Current Digest of the Soviet Press*, XIV, No. 25 (Sept. 26, 1962), pp. 12–14.
[97] *Pravda,* Dec. 20, 1962.

thetic views.[98] Even when political loyalty or ideological perspective were not involved, legality seemed to be endangered by the security authorities, which might use the opportunities offered by the antiparasite laws to bypass formal legal proceedings. Such dangers receded somewhat in the year after Khrushchev's dismissal. Soviet jurists apparently were more and more successful in restricting the antiparasite laws to the rules and principles of normal legal procedure. They gained a substantial victory in September, 1965, when the Supreme Soviet of the Russian republic drastically amended the RSFSR antiparasite laws of May 4, 1961, sharply limiting and defining far more clearly, the behavior to which it applied. Except in the city and oblast of Moscow and the city of Leningrad, it legally abolished the banishing of convicted "parasites" to "specially designated places," mainly in the far North and Siberia. In an equally positive step toward the rule of law, the amendment provided that only administrative agencies of government or regular courts could punish persons who wilfully refused to perform "socially useful labor." Thus, apparently, Khrushchev's vision of summary justice administered by assemblages of outraged workmates or neighbors ingloriously died.

Those who hope to see the day when Russians will enjoy the legal security possessed by citizens of other civilized countries can derive comfort from the foregoing developments, but these improvements must be balanced against other factors, such as the post-Khrushchev increase in the regular police forces, continued demands for harsh measures against all "anti-social elements," and continued glorification of the KGB.[99]

98 Azrael, "Is Coercion Withering Away?" *op. cit.*, p. 13.
99 The text of the amendment to the RSFSR antiparasite law is in *Vedomosti verkhovnogo soveta RSFSR*, No. 38, 1965, Item 932. I am indebted to Mr. Albert Boiter for interpretation of this amendment furnished in private conversation and in an unpublished memorandum. See also Mr. Boiter's article, "Comradely Justice: How Durable Is It," *Problems of Communism*, No. 2 (March–April, 1965), esp. pp. 83 and 91–92. The post-Khrushchev trend toward eliminating the extralegal potential of the antiparasite legislation contrasts with evidence that, under Khrushchev, state security officials sought to increase the powers and the severity of punishments imposed by antiparasite assemblies, on which Theodore Shabad reported in *The New York Times*, Sept. 11, 1963. One is tempted to believe that it was amended because of unfavorable publicity abroad about such notorious applications of the antiparasite law as occurred in the case of Joseph Brodski. Frequent press criticism of alleged coddling of parasites in exile indicates, however, that this form of unconventional justice was ineffective and perhaps even politically inconvenient, since it may have facilitated the dissemination of antiparty attitudes. Such speculation is suggested by articles like the one in *Komsomolskaya*

By the publicity given the KGB in the post-Stalin era, including Khrushchev's statements, we can see that the party leadership desired to keep its prestige and authority high. In his report to the Twentieth Party Congress he first suggested that the Soviet "public" should have an important part in enforcing correct behavior (his statement on this subject to the Twenty-first Congress was much more detailed). He also had some highly laudatory things to say about the security police. He noted that because, following the exposure of the "Beria gang," a number of other cases were re-examined, "some comrades began to show a certain distrust of workers of the state security agencies. This, of course, is incorrect and very harmful. We know that the overwhelming majority of our Chekists consists of honest officials, devoted to our common cause, and we trust them." [100]

It is significant that Khrushchev chose to refer to the political police as "Chekists," [101] a word with terrifying connotations, implying that the leadership, and he also, were determined to continue wielding the "proletarian sword" against both internal and external enemies. Tributes to the state security agencies for continuing the "glorious traditions of the Cheka" also stressed party control of these agencies, as contrasted to Stalin's "personal control," and for their alleged devotion to "the strictest observance of socialist legality." [102]

Those who believe that effective and consistent justice, personal security, and civil liberties can flourish only where political authorities willingly submit to legal limits, cannot fail to be disturbed by the beneficent image of the KGB projected by the CPSU leadership. One scholar with much experience in the Soviet Union has pointed out that "Now, as under Stalin, every sizeable

---

Pravda, Nov. 16, 1965, entitled "Litso tuneyadtsa v profil i anfas" (The Ne'er-do-well, Profile and Full Face).

[100] *XX sezd Kommunisticheskoi partii* (Moscow, 1956), Vol. I, p. 95.

[101] There is an extensive tradition surrounding this word. To it are linked such names as those of Feliks Dzerzhinski, Genrikh Yagoda, and N. I. Ezhov. For years Beria was honored as the leader of the Soviet Chekists. In 1946, this writer purchased in a bookstore on Gorki Street, in Moscow, the scores of two songs entitled, "Song of the Chekists" and "Song about Marshal Beria." The Beria song included the suggestive phrase, "warmed by Stalin's friendship." The writer was told by a member of the Moscow press corps that the censors had killed a story which he had attempted to send regarding these songs.

[102] See Semichastny's article in *Pravda,* Dec. 20, 1962, and the greetings extended by the Central Committee and the Council of Ministers published on the following day.

plant, farm, military unit, office and higher school has its own *spetsotdel* (special department)." [103] There is no reason to doubt that this statement is correct. It points to an enduring, all-penetrating complex of secret police informers, whose operations must intimidate all but the boldest or, perhaps, the most foolhardy Soviet citizens. But Soviet citizens, especially young people of intelligentsia background in cities such as Moscow and Leningrad, feel free to express unorthodox opinions. That they do so in conversing with foreign tourists makes one think the police agencies and their party supervisors are unwilling, or perhaps even unable to impose the unrelenting coercion which prevailed under Stalin. Intellectuals who openly reject the Soviet system are still subject to police action, as we can see in what can only be called the persecution of such people as Joseph Brodski, Boris Pasternak's friend Olga Ivinskaya, Andrei Sinyavski, and Yuli Daniel, or others who could be cited. Indeed, coercion in the broad sense remains massive, though it has assumed new forms, such as semivoluntary participation in settling the Virgin Lands of northern Kazakhstan and Siberia, or in vast construction projects.[104]

Personal and political rights and freedoms as they are understood in constitutional democracies are not likely to develop under the shadow of a police agency such as the KGB. Not only does it have the legal right to arrest, detain, and interrogate, but a great many armed, highly trained men are at its disposal, some in uniform, some not. In recent years the KGB apparently has controlled the highly trained and honored frontier forces (*pogranichniki*). The overlapping functions of the two formations require close collaboration.[105] The KGB is responsible, subject

[103] Azrael, "Coercion," *op. cit.,* p. 9.

[104] Azrael, pp. 13–17, discusses nonpolitical coercion.

[105] On this point, and on the KGB's post-Stalin role, see the illuminating article by S. Volin, "Cheka posle Stalina," in *Sotsialisticheski vestnik,* May, 1958, pp. 95–101, esp. p. 96. Fainsod, *How Russia Is Ruled,* p. 93, states that "The security police, border guards, and internal-security troops are subject to the control of the KGB." Fainsod's view is confirmed by A. E. Lunev, *op. cit.,* p. 116. However, according to S. Wolin and R. Slusser, *The Soviet Secret Police* (New York, 1957), p. 384, the "border and internal troops" were controlled by the Ministry of Defense for a time after Stalin's death. For two examples of the favorable publicity given to the frontier troops, see items in *Pravda,* Feb. 15, 1957, on the celebration of the thirtieth anniversary of this formation (this item linked the pogranichniki with the history of the Cheka and with the name of Dzerzhinski); and *Pravda,* May 28, 1964, with lengthy stories and several photographs, under the title "Today is the Day of the

to the procuracy's approval, for bringing suspects "to criminal responsibility." The laws governing the violations committed by these suspects seem to have been drafted with excessive looseness, though they are more precise than those of the Stalin era which they replaced. Article 65 of the Criminal Code of the RSFSR defines espionage as

> The transmission, and also the theft or collection with the intention of transmitting to a foreign state, foreign organization or their agents of information constituting a state or military secret, as well as the transmitting or gathering on the instruction of a foreign intelligence agency of other information to be used to the detriment of the interests of the USSR.

The penalty for this crime, if the espionage is committed by a foreigner or by a stateless person, is deprivation of liberty for from seven to fifteen years, with confiscation of property, or by death and confiscation of property.[106] This broad definition of espionage, together with other criminal laws, such as the one directed against "anti-Soviet agitation and propaganda," enable the KGB to take action (either directly or indirectly, perhaps working through the antiparasite laws) against persons not directly involved in what might be considered antistate activity in most countries.

To its weighty domestic job as an arm of the party leadership, and also as a semiautonomous political interest group, the KGB adds important foreign policy functions. In the fall of 1964, dramatic but hitherto obscure episodes in the history of the KGB's predecessor organization were brought to the world's attention by the glorification of the Soviet spy Richard Sorge for his services as a Soviet secret agent in Japan from 1933 to 1941. The KGB is the main counterintelligence and foreign espionage agency of the Soviet state, although other agencies, such as the

---

Frontier Guard." The border guards' duty, safeguarding Soviet military (and political) security, is mentioned in legal textbooks. The severity with which the USSR punishes illegal border crossing is shown by the fate of the American Newcomb Mott, who in 1966 received an eighteen-month sentence for that offense. His death in transit to exile (whether by suicide, accident, or murder is unclear) prevented him from serving that sentence.

[106] Text of Article 65 translated from *Ugolovny kodeks RSFSR, Kommentarii* (Leningrad, 1962), p. 146. Pp. 144–87 are devoted to "commentaries" on offenses against the Soviet state.

military intelligence units of the Ministry of Defense, also gather and interpret foreign intelligence. It is at least possible that at times the KGB's semi-autonomous activities significantly influence Soviet foreign policy. By arresting or detaining foreign citizens, even persons with diplomatic passports, as it did a number of times in 1963 and 1964, and accusing them of espionage, the KGB, perhaps in collusion with one or another faction of the party leadership, may be able to heighten tension between the Soviet Union and "imperialist" states. KGB leaders and "conservative" Soviet ideologists frequently warn that foreign tourists, scholars, or diplomats might be spies in disguise, suggesting joint action by interested groups to prevent what they may feel to be dangerously relaxed restrictions on communication between Soviet citizens and "bourgeois" foreigners. There is a faint possibility that differences between Khrushchev and the KGB and its supporters in the party presidium and secretariat on the handling of "cultural relations" and other issues may have contributed to his downfall. As bureaucratic interest group, as ally in top-level factional strife, or as loyal and faithful executor of the policies of whoever happens to be the supreme leader of the party and the state, the KGB is associated, internationally as well as domestically, with deprivation, tension, and conflict.

Soviet citizens undoubtedly fear the KGB, but to the extent that they have accustomed themselves to the dominant political culture they must accept it as a necessary evil in a world divided by ideological and class struggle. They must entertain varied and contradictory attitudes toward the KGB and the other ways of enforcing acceptable behavior. Unfortunately, the very practices dramatically symbolized by the KGB's techniques make it impossible for us to systematically and empirically investigate these practices or citizens' attitudes toward them. We know enough, however, about "socialist legality" to enable us to draw some modest conclusions to this necessarily brief discussion of rule adjudication in Soviet society. After Stalin's death there were impulses toward a "scientific," consistent, and humane justice. These impulses were supported, up to a point, by the party leadership, headed by Khrushchev. Progress toward the "rule of law" was checked and balanced by the curbed, curtailed, and supervised, but still very powerful political police machinery. It was also impeded and frustrated by the movement for popular participation in social control, just how much, it is difficult for the outsider to judge. Finally, though the citizen could breathe much more freely than he could under Stalin, he was likely to be haunted by terrifying memories of the past and perhaps troubled by forebodings about the future.

CHAPTER X

Prospects for Soviet
Political Development

MEN FIND it overwhelmingly difficult to understand the past. They quail before the task of forecasting the future. Forecasting, by and large, is a projecting of trends which the forecaster perceives to have been active in the past. To be sure, the political or social forecaster may postulate, with varying comprehensiveness and precision, the necessary and sufficient conditions which will permit the structures and processes which he has studied to persist into the future.[1] Perhaps it is enough to say here that some encouraging progress has been made in developing theories about forecasting and some impressive results have been achieved, especially by economists, but most of the work of constructing a theory that will enable us to precisely and accurately forecast the political, social, or even the economic and technological future, remains to be done.

Nevertheless, we are prone to speculate. The future, after all, is the only part of life that is left for us to live. Decisions, whether those of individuals solving intimate personal problems or those of statesmen committing their nations to fateful choices among alternative courses of action, involve speculation about the future. So long as the theoretical speculations of scholars on Soviet society's future are clearly labeled as the mixture of con-

---

[1] An excellent inventory of social prediction methods is the article by Daniel Bell, "Twelve Modes of Prediction — A Preliminary Sorting of Approaches in the Social Sciences," in *Daedalus* (Summer, 1964), pp. 845–80.

jecture, subjective preference, and something approaching scientific method that they are at best, they can be useful. One may hope that careful and systematic thinking about the future implications of past and present realities may contribute to rational and wise public policy. Such thinking must be contingent and conditional. It must be understood that new trends may nullify present assumptions and require new and fresh revisions — and revisions of revisions.

If we wish to better understand the present and increase our sensitivity to the potentials of the future we must search for the best analytical tools, and we must first of all be aware of our biases to avoid distorting our perceptions and analyses. Until recently, one variety of biased prediction of which Americans seemed particularly fond was that the Soviet regime might collapse because of widespread popular discontent. This tendency was related to a widespread assumption that American political institutions are norms toward which all peoples, including those of the Soviet Union, aspire. Similarly, journalists, statesmen, and scholars from time to time foresaw the Soviet system's failure, or even its collapse, because it lacked the market economy or religious freedom of America or Western Europe. World War II diminished, but did not completely destroy, receptivity to such theories. They were succeeded by hopeful predictions that the Soviet Union would "evolve" toward attitudes, behavior patterns, and even institutions congenial to conservative, or liberal Western preferences. Some were Marxist or pseudo-Marxist, such as those of Isaac Deutscher, who optimistically saw early democratization of Soviet internal political life resulting from what he mistakenly assumed to be a rapid rise in the Soviet standard of living. Predictions about the USSR's political future that are based on an assumed "affluence" raised doubts, because of Soviet agriculture's poor performance in recent years, reflected in anxious Soviet commentaries. However, we cannot assume that the Soviet agricultural problem is insoluble. Khrushchev's successors seem to have tackled it with determination and skill. Certainly a substantial increase in agricultural productivity would help mightily in solving a host of problems and in raising the level of general welfare in Russia. Non-Marxist predictions of Soviet evolution stress the Soviet population's improved education, the presumably increased influence of natural scientists and other highly trained professionals on policy formation, etc. This kind of analysis, based on the belief that there are certain secular, long-term trends, often associated with the view that all industrial societies have much in common, is useful. Like any single-factor analysis it is of limited value in prediction, and if combined, as it often seems to be, with a tendency to overlook the hostility and aggressiveness of Soviet political culture toward the "bourgeois" West, it may encourage dangerous complacency. Harold D. Lasswell has applied his pessimistic but useful "Garrison State" version of trend analysis to Soviet-Western relations. This approach, stressing the violence inherent in the arms race, is a good antidote to the complacency engendered by simple technological determinism.

Perhaps the best known and most comprehensive interpretive scheme was set forth by Crane Brinton.[2] He compared major revolutions since the seventeenth century, including the bolshevik revolution, with social illnesses that, though traumatic, are also regenerative. Another approach to Soviet society that is helpful in prediction is to regard revolution as a powerful disturber of a society's equilibrium, from which the society may recover, but by which it is permanently affected. George F. Kennan, in his famous "X" article of 1947, and Nicholas Timasheff, in _The Great Retreat,_ similarly concluded that revolutionary extremism in Russia was impermanent and that prerevolutionary attitudes and behavior would be returned to, at least in part.

Although many interpretations of the Soviet system implicitly or explicitly predicted change, many others assumed that Soviet politics would remain essentially unchanged. A notable example is an article by Bertram D. Wolfe, who provided for significant, but not fundamental, change by distinguishing between "change in the system" and more "superficial," or "within system" change.[3] Wolfe's powerful article should warn all among us who are prone to "too ready self-deception" in interpreting Soviet political episodes which arouse hope but actually represent no diminution in the Soviet party apparatus's power monopoly. Without rejecting Wolfe's salutary realism, however, we may take within-system changes as preconditions for eventual and more fundamental change.

[2] _The Anatomy of Revolution_ (New York, 1938).
[3] "The Durability of Soviet Despotism," _Commentary_ (Aug., 1957).

Though all the interpretive schemes and hypotheses referred to have contributed to an understanding of Soviet politics, none was as successful in accounting for and tentatively predicting the continuity and change in Soviet political behavior since the death of Stalin as the method applied by Barrington Moore.[4] Moore forecasted that the CPSU's dictatorship over Soviet society would continue, but that if the political system were to cope with the economic and other tasks confronting it, it would have to be guided in recruiting the elite less than in the past by crude indicators of loyalty to the leadership and more by such criteria as technical rationality and professional skill.

Recently, Gabriel A. Almond has incorporated in an interpretive scheme Moore's "principle of limited possibilities," designing comprehensive categories to account for both the persistence and stability of political systems and political adaptability and change.[5] For anyone who seeks indicators of possible changes in the political system's performance, Almond's key concept is political "capabilities." These are the patterns of a political system's performance, encompassing both its "internal" social environment and the "external" environment, which is more or less the international political system or the "foreign" world. These are shaped by the "input" of demands and supports fed into the polity and by the latter's corresponding "output" of policy. Both the inputs and outputs, in turn, are influenced by the way in which the junctions of elite recruitment and political socialization are performed. These patterns can be changed by changes in technology, science, economic conditions, international pressures, etc. The effect of changes in the internal or external environment depends upon, among other things, the leadership's reaction or adaptation

[4] *Terror and Progress.*

[5] Bell applies the phrase "principle of limited possibilities," borrowed from anthropologist Alexander Goldenweiser, to Moore's method. The most comprehensive version of Almond's approach to political development is in his article in *World Politics* (Jan., 1965), entitled "A Developmental Approach to Political Systems." A partial version of some of the ideas in that article appeared in *The American Behavioral Scientist* (June, 1963). Another leading exponent of the "systems" approach to political analysis, David Easton, argues in *A Systems Analysis of Political Life* (New York, 1965) that all political systems must be able to adapt and change if they are to survive. A major analytic and research effort would be required to test the applicability of Almond's and Easton's theorizing to prediction of Soviet development in a truly systematic fashion. However, even without such an effort, one's thinking about the prospects for polities which used to be conceived of in the crude and rigid categories of "totalitarianism" — categories which, unless applied with many qualifications, inhibit analysis — can be greatly stimulated.

to them. Partly for this reason, the king's or dictator's personality may have a good deal to do with political stability or instability.

Almond suggests five categories of political capability: the extractive, regulative, and distributive capabilities, which are the political system's outputs into the internal and external environments; the responsive capability, a relationship between inputs coming from these environments and outputs; and the support capability, which includes the relationship between material support, loyalty, etc., of a society to its ruling political system and the demands which the system makes upon the society. It seems to be assumed in this analytic framework that, since the political system has limited resources of capital, skills, and the like at any given time, priority of effort in developing or exercizing one or more political capabilities will require that others be minimized. Moreover, this approach also implies that the capabilities must be developed in a definite order. Thus, there can be no regulative system without an extractive or revenue-raising system and no distributive or allocative system without a regulative capability. The more elaborately each required system is developed, the more fully the more complex, dependent capabilities can be developed. Political capabilities of a system depend on one another and on the internal and international environments.

Almond points out that this approach, of which the main elements have been very briefly summarized above, will have to be further elaborated and extensively tested on historical and contemporary data before it can be developed into a comprehensive theory. Even at the present stage of our knowledge, however, the "systems" approach has the merit of sensitizing our thinking to change. Changes in the Soviet polity have occurred in startling profusion and promise to occur with increasing rapidity, more and more deeply influencing what seemed a few years ago a rigid system, easy to describe and unlikely to develop, except by warlike foreign expansion, internal collapse, or a combination thereof.

In October, 1964 the Soviet Union entered its second post-Stalin succession crisis, through the first year and a half of which it passed much more smoothly than it did through the corresponding phase of the Stalin succession crisis. Robert V. Daniels noted that this may have been the first time in Russia's history that the established ruler was voted out of office.[6] There were no visible signs of significant unrest or disorder in the Soviet population during the first half year after Khrushchev's removal. The new leadership in Moscow was carefully controlling responsiveness to elite demands at home and carefully modulating pressure on both its Chinese Communist rivals and its Western adversaries. It appeared that, like Khrushchev, the new leaders were committed to maintaining a powerful but not grotesquely overdeveloped capacity for regulation and coercion. At the same time, they sought to make the system more responsive to growing popular demand for consumer goods and services, and for more and better recreational and cultural facilities — with the Kremlin still firmly controlling their allocation and "mix," and the means of providing them. But Khrushchev was being condemned (though not by name) for "improvisation," for "hare-brained schemes," and for "subjectivism," and, in general, for attempting to go too far too fast, suggesting a sober, conservative aversion to excessively fast innovation.

The relative caution of the new administration in Moscow seemed to be produced, in part, by its oligarchic, "collective" nature. It was apparent that a systematic effort was afoot to maintain a smooth consensus in the party presidium and in the other top echelons of the political system. How long the collective leadership, under the dual command of Leonid I. Brezhnev heading the party chain of command and Aleksei Kosygin heading the government, could be maintained was anybody's guess. Observers could only speculate as to whether Brezhnev, Nikolai Podgorny, Kirill Mazurov, Dmitri Polyanski, Alexander Shelepin, or perhaps some other presidium member as yet relatively unknown in the West might win unchallenged sway over the Soviet polity's destiny. One young man on the make in 1965–1966 was Moscow party secretary N. G. Egorychev.

Throughout 1965, Brezhnev appeared to be gradually consolidating his position, although even after his election as general secretary in April, 1966, just after the Twenty-third Party Congress, he probably had far less authority than Khrushchev once held, let alone the naked power of the mightiest revolutionary despot, Joseph Stalin. The December 6, 1965 central committee

[6] Preface to *Russia* (Englewood Cliffs, N.J., 1964).

plenum abolished the Party-State Control Committee, headed by Shelepin, and also deprived Shelepin of his government position as Deputy Chairman of the Council of Ministers. Nikolai Podgorny was made chairman of the Presidium of the Supreme Soviet, replacing the ailing Anastas Mikoyan, who failed to gain re-election to the newly re-established Politburo. Also, the old and feeble N. M. Shvernik was replaced in the new Politburo and in the post of chairman of the Party Control Committee by the Russianized Latvian A. Ya. Pelshe, a former secret police officer. The plenum seemed to be taking some power from two of Brezhnev's competitors. Presumably, the ceremonial functions of the Soviet "presidency" would keep from Podgorny the kind of party power which had caused some Western analysts to regard him as a potential threat to Brezhnev. Nevertheless, subsequent to this change in Podgorny's status, he continued to enjoy a very favorable press in the USSR. As for Shelepin, he lost control of an agency which had enabled him to ferret into both party and government affairs throughout the nation.

It is possible, as some Western analysts suggested, that Shelepin was shorn of some power because his extensive experience in police and other administrative and control activity had stirred fear as to what he might some day do to the fortunes and lives of his colleagues. Rumors emanating from Soviet sources in September, 1965 had indicated that there was talk in top Soviet circles of his replacing Brezhnev as head of the party apparatus. Some thought that such rumors were set in motion by the rather liberal-minded Anastas Mikoyan. The likelihood that a person with Shelepin's background might become head of the party could well have aroused fear of a return to something approaching Stalinist practices. Whether or not such fears were widespread and regardless of Alexander Shelepin's destiny, the December plenum reminded students of Soviet politics once again of a fundamental Soviet dilemma. Like all political systems, that of the Soviet Union requires strong and effective leadership. On the other hand, there is an exceptionally great danger that, under Soviet conditions, a ruthless leader, taking in hand all the engines of control, may become a menace to his peers and a scourge to the country. Although Stalin's great abuse of power need not mean that the same would happen if the delicate equilibrium of post-Khrushchev collective leadership were to collapse, in mid-1966 that possibility continued to haunt the memories of the citizens of the Soviet Union and indeed of all thoughtful men.

V. V. Shcherbitski, apparently a Brezhnev protégé, like Brezhnev had served in the Dnepropetrovsk oblast committees of the Ukraine. That he was named as a candidate for membership in the party presidium indicated that the Brezhnev influence and that of the "Ukrainian" group of party leaders was still strong or getting stronger. Another important result of the December, 1965 plenum was the appointment of Ivan V. Kapitonov as a secretary of the central committee. Information released during the December plenum regarding Kapitonov, as well as his previous career, indicated that he was to serve as Brezhnev's cadres officer in the preparations for the forthcoming party congress to be held in March, 1966.

Shcherbitski, a candidate member of the presidium in 1961–1963, and Kapitonov, who for a time in the 1950's headed first the Moscow city and then the Moscow oblast party organizations, both recovered lost ground with their new appointments. These comebacks are difficult to evaluate, as are those of such men as P. M. Masherov and Vladimir Matskevich, and also Nikolai Mikhailov. The latter, after several years of obscurity, in the fall of 1965 was named head of the State Press Committee. It may be that they benefited by a trend toward compensating persons who had fallen afoul of Khrushchev. The reversing of these careers that had seemed to falter may show that post-Stalin personnel selection is still evolving toward relative stability, so that a fall from Kremlin favor and ensuing demotions need not signify disgrace and ruin. But the obscurity surrounding such important personnel changes once again reminded outside observers that Soviet politics lives in an abnormally secretive and conspiratorial atmosphere.

The December plenum's doings seemed to show that power rivalries were becoming more apparent, but that in the top party spheres there was a relatively solid consensus and "collective leadership" still prevailed. This estimate was confirmed by the Twenty-third Congress. Soviet political history indicated, however, that sooner or later both party and government machines would have a single leader. If this were to happen, perhaps when the presidium members came to face a difficult decision and had to commit themselves to policy and factional choices, the exceptional calm prevalent in Moscow in early 1966 could easily be disturbed. Without visibly perturbing the leadership, Moscow had taken a harsh verbal stand against United States policy on a number of especially complex and acute issues, i.e., the Congo, Santo Domingo, and Vietnam, while maintaining its traditional wariness toward United States proposals regarding the chronic and crucial German and disarmament problems. Major surveys of the world scene, such as the editorial in the first issue of *Kommunist* for 1965, during the early months of the year continued to reiterate the Khrushchev line that "peaceful coexistence" was the basis of Soviet foreign policy. But as tensions mounted over Vietnam, Soviet statements pointed with increasing frequency to the dangers of a larger war, and the December, 1965 Supreme Soviet session voted a modest increase in the military budget. Attacks on the United States were balanced by intermittent friendly gestures, such as the relatively generous recognition accorded American astronauts Cooper and Conrad in August, 1965.

When the Soviet leadership faces difficult policy choices, the likelihood increases that a leader endowed with dictatorial ambitions will come to power. On that probably sound though somber assumption, we can see that the conditions confronting the USSR in 1965 and early 1966 in both domestic and foreign affairs may well have spurred some leaders to demand dynamic and militant leadership. Some ambitious and concerned politicians experiencing such feelings might have found the comparatively cautious and colorless Brezhnev-Kosygin leadership wanting in boldness and flair. Collective leadership and caution in both domestic and foreign policy remain the order of the day, however. Trying to balance between militant communist China and "imperialist" United States, Moscow was still committed to difficult, devious competition with China in revolutionary and subversive activities, and opposition to United States policy in Vietnam. Using mostly diplomacy and propaganda, it was still keeping risks as low as possible and, despite Chinese charges of United States-Soviet "collusion," trying to avoid slamming the door on possible later revival of the Kennedy-Khrushchev "detente." Probably the most reassuring aspect of the Soviet-United States relationship in 1965–1966 was the effort made on both sides to maintain not merely formal diplomatic relations but also a variety of scientific, educational, cultural and other contacts. Despite Vietnam, these mutually beneficial links remained unbroken. Their continuation and further development was supported with varying degrees of enthusiasm by different groups in both countries. Perhaps their most ardent champions on both sides were to be found among natural scientists and also among scholars in the social sciences and the humanities.

Polities which enjoy or aspire to the Anglo-American "civic culture" are vitally interested in any change of Russia's political style from coercion to a more "responsive" pattern, both internally and externally. The more responsive a political authority is to the pressures and demands of individuals and groups at home, the more likely it is to be accommodative in its external relations. We would be mistaken if we assumed that similar internal regimes assure international harmony (the pre-World War I rivalry between Germany and England suggests the contrary), but we are justified in feeling that in the nuclear age government responsiveness to popular domestic demands for peace and material prosperity lead to domestic and international stability. The peoples of Western Europe and the United States, then, have still another reason for hoping that the Soviet leaders' traditional domination over the citizenry will gradually be reduced. Such a transformation would obviously be to the advantage of countries that enjoy a civic political culture. International tensions would be greatly reduced and worldwide welfare would rise much more rapidly if the governments of both highly developed and less well off nations were freed from the pressure of internal warfare, latent or actual, and from the threatening nuclear holocaust. A transformation in Russian attitudes and behavior might work miracles with these problems and the political, administrative, and psychological stresses that they cause. What, then, are the prospects that the Soviet political system might be transformed, becoming more responsive to the noncommunist world's aspirations?

When one speculates about Soviet political trends, one becomes involved not only in complex political systems theory but also in perceiving the contours of the huge and mostly uncharted international political system. If a genuine world community is ever to replace the present shifting, precarious balance among cooperation, antagonism, and anarchy, all political systems, not just that of Russia, will have to learn to respond to one another. That this change is necessary is still little recognized by noncommunist societies, and in the closed Soviet polity is recognized almost not at all — at least it is not objectively analyzed and explicitly discussed. Soviet political doctrine still is preoccupied with the demand that the noncommunist societies transform themselves according to the Soviet model. We can tell from experience that the resources invested and the risks undertaken will be limited, however, as long as the noncommunist societies, and above all the strongest of them, the United States, keep furnishing evidence that further communist expansion will be prohibitively expensive.

It seems, then, that Soviet demands upon the external political environment can be restrained most effectively, and perhaps can be transformed, by stability in the noncommunist world. Lasting stability in the external political environment might alter or perhaps atrophy the Soviet ideological propensity to seek international conflict and expansion, thus profoundly affecting Soviet political culture. Joined to other, internal influences, it might bring about a shift from power, coercion, and discipline toward material and other pleasures, and perhaps even from Marxist asceticism toward increased freedom of groups and individuals to express their demands.

How responsive outside influences can make the Soviets depends on (1) demonstrating that coercive outward pressures are futile; (2) persuasion and cooperation in mutually beneficial works, substituting for the outward pressures nondestructive or less destructive forms of competition; (3) skilfully confronting Soviet fears of foreign hostility with realistic, constructive, mutually beneficial programs. Expanded Soviet-non-Soviet communication at all levels, using all media, will help to disarm suspicion, if it is conducted in good faith on both sides and if it is associated with constructive policies. Communication may be particularly effective if it strengthens the influence of those within the Soviet elite who are most favorably disposed toward cooperative relationships with noncommunist societies. It must avoid ideological polemics and seek to intimately, informally exchange professional experience.

It may be that Soviet political relations with communist China and with communist parties generally, both ruling and nonruling, affect Soviet external politics more strongly than Soviet relations with the noncommunist governments. Empirical modes of thought in time may encroach upon Soviet dogma, weakening the belief that the Soviet formula for revolutionary social change must be universally adopted. Tendencies toward ideological and political fragmentation in the international communist movement encourage this viewpoint. For some time, though, Sino-Soviet rivalry may force Moscow to manifest an ideologically respectable, orthodox Marxist-Leninist point of view. Polycentrism and other pluralistic forces are bound to sap Russian faith in Marxist-Leninist "science" and its power of prediction. If these forces persist long enough they will favor empirical rather than dogmatic and "prophetic" thinking in Russia and other communist-ruled countries. Of course, none of the influences yet mentioned can be expected to bring rapid change in Soviet political culture or behavior. From Russia's bitter and tragic past come many memories of foreign hostility and cunning, which are reflected in party dogmas. For a long time to come, Soviet communists and most Soviet citizens, especially those of Great Russian ancestry, probably will feel that political centralism, stern social discipline, and an authoritarian, conspiratorial political style are essential to national welfare and national survival. The political system described here is anything but open to the kind of communication that might dispose Soviet society to free dissemination of "bourgeois" ideas. Khrushchev and his successors were, in fact, much disturbed by the negative byproducts of Soviet-Western cultural exchanges and were determined to counteract them. Two significant articles [7] called upon writers and artists to reject any "group" attitudes which might distract them from their obligations toward the party, and another demanded that writers produce science fiction that would inspire efforts to "bring nearer the communist future." [8] Later statements, perhaps designed to reassure the "creative intelligentsia," emphasized that party guidance must be exercised with tact and perspective and specifically repudiated both Stalinist and Khrushchevian "subjectivism." The gist of the post-Khrushchev regime's rather vague pronouncements on literature and the arts was a plea for "rational" political controls, probably representing a careful compromise. On the whole, the same appraisal seemed to fit the pronouncements of the Twenty-

[7] *Pravda,* Nov. 22 and 27, 1964. See also Alexander Chakovski's blast against ten years of Khrushchevian "subjectivism," in *Kommunist,* No. 4, March 1, 1966.

[8] *Izvestiya,* Nov. 24, 1964.

third Congress, but by then the balance had swung somewhat more to the conservative side than it had in late 1964.

It will be interesting to observe the congruence or contradiction that may arise because of the party communication cadres's commitment to maintain ideological orthodoxy and the growing party leadership program to apply selected, empirical, social science practices to education, industrial management, law enforcement, and other areas of public policy. It seems prudent to assume that most Soviet citizens will continue to protect their peace of mind by rejecting information that sharply differs from the picture of reality that the party's socialization and communication programs press upon them.

It seems, however, that those dominant within the party leadership have decided to emphasize Marxism-Leninism's empirical and analytical side instead of its dogmatism and ritualism, and have done so increasingly since Khrushchev's fall. This interpretation alone would account for the many articles on social science that the most authoritative newspapers and magazines published in the first few months of 1965, and also the increasing sophistication with which "socialist realism" is being applied to cultural controls.[9]

Social scientists and other intellectuals still must defend their borrowings of Western techniques by referring to them as service to the party's objectives, but within that framework they can strike blows against dogmas of yesterday and those who allegedly defend them today.[10] Perhaps all we can expect from such efforts for the present is further development of guided empiricism and controlled spontaneity. Such partial freedoms might turn out to have been among the preconditions for the fuller freedoms of an as yet obscure future.

Recent Soviet advocacy of empirical and utilitarian approaches to scholarship and culture are especially significant because they help to consolidate the gains made during de-Stalinization.

Because of the empiricist revival, Soviet thought appears to be facing up to social realities which for generations could not be investigated or publicly discussed. Belatedly, and timidly by Western standards and even by those of communist Yugoslavia, it is

[9] See A. Rumyantsev's important article, "The Party and the Intelligentsia," *Pravda,* Feb. 21, 1965.

[10] See the remarkably bold (by previous Soviet standards) article on applied social research by V. Shubkin, *Kommunist,* No. 3, Feb., 1965.

being recognized that social groups are differentiated not just by economic factors, but by cultural and historical influences as well. Most important, if the party is to effectively guide Soviet society, it must inform itself fully and accurately about the needs and aspirations of workers, young job applicants, consumers, etc., whose attitudes and problems Soviet social researchers are now studying and whose energies the authorities wish to most effectively mobilize. It is possible that in posing significant questions about group attitudes and other social problems, and assembling the data needed to answer them, social scientists may help to unshackle Soviet thought and culture from the thralldom still hanging heavy over it.

The demands and aspirations of the Soviet citizen can influence the political system only if they can be brought to bear upon the making of policy. They must be expressed and communicated, and if they are to influence and ultimately to transform the political system they must formulate programs and exert pressure on behalf of the demands of interest groups that have direct or indirect access to the national bodies that make decisions. To make these statements is to suggest how far the Soviet system is at present from the perspectives and practices of the civic political culture. And yet, it has come surprisingly far, in the few years since Stalin's death, from the glacially constricting, terroristic despotism. The changes which have already occurred nourish the hope that there may be others, much greater and more positive, over the next few generations. It may be objected that such speculation is dangerous, since it may dull our vigilance against present dangers. There may be such a tendency, but it will not be troublesome if we ferret out and critically examine the evidence upon which either Soviet or non-Soviet statements regarding Soviet political evolution are based.

It seems unlikely that in the near future the party apparatus will be forced to surrender its overwhelming preponderance of power. This is indicated by many pieces of evidence and perhaps most strikingly by the absence from the post-Khrushchev presidium of any representatives of the Soviet armed forces. To be sure, D. F. Ustinov, an experienced military production executive, was elevated to membership in the party secretariat at the March, 1965 plenum, possibly strengthening military influence in top-level policy making. But more likely, it reflects the new leadership's intention to achieve greater sophistication and balance (e.g., between nuclear weapons and other arms) in over-all military policy. The party cadres will continue to rule Russia, but they are inevitably influenced by changes in society, if only because the party includes most of the ablest, most energetic, and ambitious members of Soviet society. It is apparent that both Khrushchev and his successors were concerned about maintaining unimpaired party control over society while spurring its productive efforts, above all in the economic sphere. After Khrushchev's fall it became more apparent than ever that his colleagues in the leadership were deeply dissatisfied with his policy of directly involving the party apparatus in economic administration. Apparently it was feared that the party apparatus might lose some of its ideological zeal as a result of such involvement.[11] At the November, 1964 central committee plenum the post-Khrushchev leadership moved to return to a more traditional relationship between the party apparatus and the economic administration. At this plenum and that of March, 1965, leadership promotions and demotions replaced a number of "Khrushchev men" with individuals identifiable as opponents (or victims) of Khrushchevian policy moves, and demonstrated a related advancing of "conservative" apparatchiki. Particularly significant was the elevation at the March plenum of the veteran Belorussian leader, Kirill T. Mazurov, from alternate to full membership of the party presidium. Mazurov also became, at this plenum, a First Deputy Chairman of the USSR Council of Ministers.

Mazurov's Belorussian apparatus colleague, P. M. Masherov, was one of eight alternate members of the central committee who achieved full membership at the November, 1964 plenum. Four of the eight, including army political overseer A. A. Epishev and political police boss Semichastny, were veterans of the Ukrainian party organization. They partially balanced the continued disproportionate top-level representation of the "Ukrainians," not all of whom were ethnically Ukrainians, but whose large share in the top party posts may cause resentment among ambitious aspirants for power brought up in the Moscow, Leningrad, and other major party organizations.

11 The dissatisfactions and doubts regarding Khrushchev's Nov., 1962 party reorganization are discussed in the editorial in *Partiinaya zhizn*, No. 23, Dec., 1964.

The March plenum removed Leonid Ilichev as head of the Ideological Commission of the central committee, which was soon replaced by an ideological section. Judging from reports published on Soviet Press Day, which is celebrated every year on May 5, Petr Demichev, educated as a chemical engineer, seemed to have replaced Ilichev as top propaganda officer of the regime, with Mikhail Suslov still the senior authority on the official Marxist-Leninist creed. These assignments appeared still to be in force in the weeks following the March–April, 1966 party congress.

By early April, with the downgrading of Vitali S. Titov, once Khrushchev's formidable cadres specialist, the new leadership apparently had settled most of its personal scores with Khrushchev's inner circle — and with others against whom the new "ins" may have had grudges. A new phase of the post-Khrushchev era seemed to be starting. It was marked by the faint beginnings of Brezhnev's pre-eminence, although his lack of flair seemed to cast doubt on his ability ever to act the part of a Stalin or even a Khrushchev. Brezhnev did clearly dominate the March plenum, however, and during the celebrations in May of the twentieth anniversary of the defeat of Nazi Germany, he further overshadowed his presidium colleagues. Kosygin went to Berlin to preside over the East German part of this vast Soviet-bloc political commemoration, while Podgorny represented the Soviet Union in Prague, and other leaders did similar jobs elsewhere in the area. This division of labor left Brezhnev at the center of the Moscow stage. It is of supreme importance, to a Soviet leader, to remain in the Moscow limelight. This fact of politics seemed obvious to Stalin, apparently, but perhaps less obvious to the over-confident Khrushchev. Judging by his behavior in the first year and a half after Khrushchev's fade-out, his serious-minded successor did not intend to forget it.

At the March plenum Suslov, though overshadowed by Brezhnev, was the only other featured speaker. His continued prominence in interpreting doctrine in relation to world political issues was indicated by a report he delivered on the "consultative conference" of Moscow-oriented communist parties, which had taken place at the beginning of March. Suslov's speech was the only other contribution by a top leader to the plenum mentioned in the published communiqué which followed it. Like the conference with which it purportedly dealt, the speech was not really reported but was merely mentioned. Such reticence seemed to prove that the Kremlin was experiencing difficult relations, not only with Chinese-oriented communist parties, but with many members of the Soviet-oriented group of parties as well. Suslov performed a similar function in reading the Twenty-third Congress' resolution denouncing United States Vietnam policy.

Brezhnev's star seemed gradually to rise throughout the first post-Khrushchev year, but essentially the new leadership was still pursuing a Soviet version of consensus politics, moderate and balanced, but, compared with Khrushchev's aspirations, also conservative. The agricultural allocation program set forth in Brezhnev's speech at the March plenum was typical. In promised state inputs into agriculture for the next five years it was considerably more generous than the ones Khrushchev had demanded. Also, the new leaders promised the peasants stable pricing and other attractive policies, and if they could redeem their pledges perhaps the peasants — more likely the party and government executives charged with supervising them — might be grateful. An editorial on the March plenum agricultural program significantly referred to the alleged "nervousness and irresponsibility" created by "subjectivism," frequent reorganizations, and other shortcomings of the (as usual unidentified) previous administration.[12]

Another significant post-Khrushchev change brought an end to the deposed leader's practice of inviting many industrial and agricultural administrators and middle-level party leaders who were not central committee members to actively participate in central committee plenums. Judging by its behavior during its first few months in office, the leadership appeared determined to temporarily cut back on Khrushchev's plan to widen some kinds of participation in political decisions, and especially to inform the Soivet public increasingly about policy formation.[13]

[12] *Pravda*, March 28, 1965.

[13] The main featured front-page items in *Pravda* for Aug. 11, Oct. 2, and Oct. 3, 1964 reflected dissension in the party presidium between Khrushchev and "some comrades" over what Khrushchev called a return to the "Leninist style of work," involving the advance publicity given by Khrushchev to items on the agenda of the party plenary session scheduled for November. As Robert Slusser was perhaps the first Sovietologist to emphasize, representation at party congresses was altered for the Twenty-second Congress, at which each delegate represented only 2,000 party members, in contrast to 5,000 at the Twentieth, and 6,000 at the Twenty-first. See his article, "Die Sonderstellung Belorusslands," *Osteuropa*, No. 11, Nov., 1964, p. 851.

Khrushchev's successors seemed to want, more than anything else, efficient, carefully planned and executed administration.[14] Although that kind of approach might impede the widening participation by previously excluded groups begun under Khrushchev, it might make it possible to transform the Soviet polity, one day, into a more carefully regulated, more efficient, and probably less tension-ridden bureaucratic society.[15] At its present stage of political consciousness, the citizenry probably would appreciate more a stable and efficient administration than it did Khrushchev's kind of ceremonial access to the political process. It is even possible that a kind of administrative constitutionalism might grow on a foundation built by some years of improved administration. In any case, post-Khrushchev political articles made one feel an urgent need for administrative competence, order, and stable expectations. If these could be provided, perhaps the developments that Khrushchev initiated could actually be carried further and improved upon by his successors. Still, all such trends toward stability might be slowed or even nullified by a new flare-up of domestic political strife or by international pressures.

Most Western experts were surprised that the Brezhnev-Kosygin leadership held together as well as it did for its first year and a half and succeeded so well, outwardly at least, in rationally dividing labor among its members. From the public record it appears that there was a studied effort to distribute work and honors so as to attain both harmony and efficiency and to avoid like the plague any appearance of strife. Outside observers were reminded how difficult it is to predict how such well-hidden statesmen as those at the Soviet helm will behave. Some observers surmised that a time of relative tranquility had begun in Soviet elite politics.

Some interesting evidence, however, made it seem likely that

[14] See in *Kommunist*, No. 1, Jan., 1965, the reply to a question on how rural local administration should be organized, and the criticism, on pp. 18–21 of the same issue, of the scheduling or conduct of meetings and other "mass measures" in such a manner as to "inflict harm upon production." Similarly, *Kommunist's* first editorial of 1965 demanded that before any decision was made all the "pros and cons" be most carefully weighed.

[15] Determination to safeguard the limited lower-level political participation provided by the formal rules of the party, and the difficulty of so doing, were indicated in the editorial in *Partiinaya zhizn*, No. 1, Jan., 1965, by criticism of the apparently still widespread practice of rural area party organizations, which force collective farms in their territories to elect as chairmen persons brought in from outside, even, in some cases, individuals who have been failures in their previous assignments.

the struggle for power at the top would produce new political landslides, though not necessarily removing Brezhnev or Kosygin, Podgorny or Suslov or Shelepin, and undoubtedly not a purge of the Stalin variety. After all, even Malenkov had held power roughly equal to that of a Brezhnev for well over a year and Khrushchev's sway had lasted seven years, or more, depending on how one defines his period of leadership.

Alert Kremlinologists pointed to numerous demands for "purity in party ranks" and to such signals of tension as the denunciation of "mistakes and deficiencies" in the work of the very important Kharkov party organization.[16] A significant indicator of hesitancy as to how to meet the challenge of the times, or perhaps of hidden differences over policy, was the failure to begin preparing in early fall, 1965 for the party congress which, according to the statutes adopted four years earlier, should have been held in 1965, but was postponed until March and April, 1966. In 1961, preparations for the congress began in early summer, although of course the 1961 congress faced the exceptionally weighty business of ratifying a new party program.

Every day that passed without political repressions, arrests, or violent political competition, increased the likelihood of continued evolution toward a bureaucratic, oligarchic order, rather than a relapse into Stalinist ways. Shortly after Khrushchev's fall, Zbigniew Brzezinski characterized the phase of Soviet politics which that event ushered in as one of "bureaucratic politics." The phrase applies to a time when there are no towering, commanding leaders such as Stalin or even Molotov, Malenkov, or Khrushchev, and in which the lesser men who share power realize that their survival depends upon a consensus and upon a tacit agreement not to use the more extreme weapons of Stalin-era political struggle. In the years since Stalin's death, except for the purges of Beria and his henchmen, the victors have shown more restraint toward their defeated opponents than students of Soviet affairs would have dared to predict in 1952 or 1953. Stalin will probably loom in Soviet history as a unique phenomenon, and Khrushchev as a truly transitional figure who, half intentionally, half fumblingly, paved the way for a time of oligarchic, bureaucratic, quasi-legal politics. Legality would increase in value in such an order, at any rate among politicians and administrators. It would lead

16 *Pravda*, Aug. 11, 1965.

to stability and to restraint in the use of force, not eliminating conspiracy or anarchy, but avoiding the wild and terrible caprice of Stalinist politics.

In the order which seemed to be foreshadowed by the words and actions of the gray post-Khrushchev collective leadership, Leninism would remain the legitimating creed, and it would serve as a symbolic link with the past. Here too, however, style and emphasis would shift. The emerging forms of Leninist doctrine, it seemed likely, would be blended with increasing doses of empirical, pragmatic, and objective thinking. Adapting and revitalizing Leninism might save it from obsolescence, but it would also rob it of its emotional force, and render it less potent as a barrier to Soviet-non-Soviet intellectual communication.

As for possible disruptive inputs from the "international arena," the prognosis here is complex, but again abstaining from major violence over a period of years could well prove decisive for the future. The parallel, if not collaborative, attitudes of Russia and America toward the crucial issue of joint survival on a planet where, as John F. Kennedy pointed out in his inaugural address in 1961, man has achieved both the power to end poverty and the power to end life, might lead to joint efforts to solve the stubborn issues dividing the two superpowers.

If the post-Khrushchev leadership's approach to political, administrative, and probably cultural, controls seemed more "conservative" than Khrushchev's, it appeared to be somewhat more "liberal" in providing economic incentives to industrial management and establishing a salutary intellectual climate for natural scientists and other highly trained professionals. Even more than the Khrushchev regime the new leaders were engineers and practical administrators. Also, they apparently lacked the anti-intellectualism which was one concomitant of the rude Khrushchevian "populism." We might expect that such a group would be less enthusiastic about freedom of artistic expression than about making life easier for army officers, administrators, engineers, and natural scientists, but information coming out of Moscow during the new regime's first few months indicated that the Soviet intelligentsia as a whole, including writers and artists, were pleased with it, or at least were not openly, actively, or intensely discontented.

The Soviet record to date leads us to expect gradual though erratic evolution toward a society in which functional, specialized elites, such as military leaders, industrial managers, scientists, writers, and other communicators will gain enough autonomy to modify, if not the political system's basic structure, then perhaps the many peripheral, subordinate structures, arrangements, and modes of operation. We may be justified in being cautiously optimistic regarding gradual progress toward empirical rationality in making decisions and toward a relatively permissive, decreasingly terroristic style of rule application and rule adjudication. The regime must permit managers, bureaucrats, natural and social scientists, and communicators to obtain the training and enjoy the conditions that they need to effectively perform their functions. Such performance, in turn, is required if Soviet domestic and foreign policy objectives are to be achieved. As interest groups composed of professionals grow in number and in proportion to the whole society, their influence too will increase. New, albeit party-controlled associations will satisfy the rising demands of specialists for recognition and for opportunities to articulate their aspirations and professional values. This hypothesis is supported by significant characteristics of the contemporary international configuration. Nuclear competition puts a premium on skills which indirectly support the scientific ethos. At the same time, survival in the nuclear age demands that large-scale violence be used with extreme caution as an instrument of national policy. In recent years, especially since the fall of Khrushchev, even the Soviet consumer has been discussed in numerous articles and editorials. The word "consumer" *(pokupatel)*, formerly ignored, is now frequently and positively used, and there is even talk of whether or not advertising should be employed to better satisfy his wants.

Such trends as we perceive probably strengthen the hand of the Soviet managerial, scientific, and artistic elites rather than the power of the party functionaries, particularly the professional theoreticians, propagandists, and agitators. The official ideology, deriving strength from fear of an "imperialist threat," may lose influence as the uneasy contemporary international "peace" continues. But at the same time the probability that military and scientific preparedness will be maintained, both in Moscow and in Washington, assures that the scientists and others whose efforts are required, will continue to gain influence.

Other trends strengthen the supposition that the zealots, agitators, and jailers will lose influence and that the locus of power will continue to swing toward the managerial, technical, and creative intelligentsia. Paradoxically, the party's success in defeating the "class enemy" may in time render superfluous or modify some of the party's functions. In 1956 the dramatist Pogodin had one of his characters say: "we no longer have hostile classes," and then, logically enough, the character asked: "Who is there to hate?" If, some day, the full logical consequences of that line of reasoning come to be, Soviet writers and other intellectuals will be able to bargain more effectively with the party apparatus. Party control over the intelligentsia has rested on the conviction that all forms of communication must serve as weapons in the life and death struggle against the political enemy.

In line with what we have been saying, the increasing representation in the policy-making bodies of the CPSU and the Soviet government of outstanding natural scientists and scientifically trained persons is noteworthy. One thinks of the aerodynamicist Mstislav Keldysh, who in 1961 became both president of the USSR Academy of Sciences and a member of the CPSU central committee, but also of such figures as Vladimir Kirillin, a physicist, whom the October, 1965 session of the Supreme Soviet elevated to the post of deputy chairman of the USSR Council of Ministers. Kirillin's career does indicate that he is perhaps as much a party functionary as a scientist, but his years of teaching at the Moscow Power Engineering Institute may qualify him to act as a bridge between the party command and the scientific and engineering communities. Such developments not only increase the direct participation of scientific leaders in the making of national policy but indirectly enhance the scientific community's influence by facilitating its access to the policy making process.

Another important related trend is the increasingly wide dissemination to the Soviet public of the somewhat unorthodox views of distinguished Soviet scientists. Thus, in 1965 and 1966 Peter Kapitsa, a leading nuclear physicist and head of the Academy of Sciences' Institute of Physical Problems, criticized the organization of Soviet scientific research and urged experiment in his country with relevant American techniques. Kapitsa and a leading Soviet computer science specialist, Anatoli Dorodnitsyn, frankly admitted in articles read by millions of Soviet citizens that in some key fields of science and technology Russia lagged behind

Western levels of achievement. Such nonchauvinist statements
may indirectly push Soviet public opinion generally toward rationality. They help to undermine authoritarian attitudes and to
foster critical scrutiny of the performance of men and methods.
Ultimately, these attitudes may bring about increased intellectual
freedom.

It is interesting that the institute headed by Kapitsa held an
exhibition of what Peter Grose described as "semi-abstract and
other nonrealistic paintings." [17] This event symbolizes what appears to be a quiet partnership between the Soviet scientific community's elite and the liberal, experimental segments of the artistic and literary communities. The scientists, though they do not
and perhaps do not wish to challenge party supremacy in shaping
overall national policy, do feel deeply the need to champion
creative autonomy in their own field, and in other spheres as well.
They are becoming, in a sense, the custodians of liberal values, as
understood in the Russian tradition.

The post-Stalin "return to Leninism," strengthening the CPSU
in all social activities, is probably leading, in the long run, toward
increased participation by more elements of Soviet society in significant parts of community life. In other words, the party's revival and expansion may ultimately bring what Harold Lasswell
describes as a "wider shaping and sharing of values." If the party
is to be a collection of all "advanced" elements in society, it
cannot fail to be influenced by society — and society is becoming
more variegated and less monolithic as the Soviet Union becomes
more industrialized, urbanized, and technically and scientifically
sophisticated.

The Soviet family, having survived, facilitates the intelligentsia's
resistance to or modification of the revolutionary, chiliastic sides
of Marxist-Leninist ideology; it is a major agency of socialization,
and also influences elite recruitment. The family at all levels of
society exerts negative influences on revolutionary goals, though
in many ways it also helps to preserve the system. One consequence of the family's survival is widespread nepotism and other
distorting influences on elite recruitment. Especially when these
occur flagrantly among non-Russians, they are likely to be sharply
condemned, but there appears to be no effective, systematic effort
to eradicate them. Following a well-established, apparently spread-

17 *The New York Times,* Feb. 25, 1966.

ing trend, high party officials' children, after graduating from the "best" institutions of higher education, receive posts in important research institutions that influence policy, or in other bureaucratic agencies. This practice may contribute to pluralism in Soviet politics by increasing government agencies' access to and influence upon party policy-making echelons. It may not be entirely idle to speculate that this influence "mellows" the perspectives brought to bear on foreign policy decisions, since the sons of the Gromykos and the Mikoyans have grown up expecting security and in relative affluence, conditions less conducive to a "hard" outlook than the environment and ideological climate which tempered their fathers. And if this generation of "golden youth" are permitted to pass on their privileges to their children, these tendencies may well be further reinforced.

We do not suggest that the American kind of affluence, liberalism, or democracy are on the horizon in Soviet Russia, but that the Soviet polity could become increasingly receptive to demands generated within Soviet society for personal and group rights, and to the world community's norms. The trends we envisage are constructive. They could make of Soviet communism a more effective competitor for the Western model of political development in the emerging nations, but they could also make it a less disturbing foe. In a word, such trends, if they developed strongly and were properly welcomed and reciprocated by the West, could give wholesome reality to "peaceful coexistence." They might also win greater, more willing support from the Russian citizenry than the political system has ever enjoyed. But, eventually, these changes might also point the way to Russia's joining a genuinely cooperative society of the world's nations. That process, if it does occur, will seem frustratingly slow, since to reach fruition it must revise tenacious official traditions that are greatly useful to deeply entrenched rulers in Russia and elsewhere — its success must, however, be desired by those who want peaceful and orderly political development.

There are, of course, less hopeful views of the Soviet future. It may seem unlikely, but a new terroristic, Stalin-like dictatorship always remains a possibility. One cannot exclude also the possibility of a military dictatorship, or, more likely perhaps, a regime nominally "civilian," but dominated by military elements. Bolshevik tradition is extraordinarily sensitive to the dangers of "Bonapartism," and a preference for civilian supremacy is at least as powerful in Soviet Russia as in the United States. Still, if the party fails to perform competently in dealing with domestic and foreign problems, its support both among the elite of production executives, scientists, and other creative elements, and among the citizenry as a whole, could falter. Military leaders might become the core, or at least the façade, of a kind of post-party "coalition government." Developments of recent years give some credence to such a line of speculation. Certainly during the V-E day celebrations in 1965 and 1966 there was an enormous effort to appropriately honor the armed forces; at the same time, however, the KGB's services to the party have received high praise. Semichastny's long article in *Pravda's* extensive coverage of the twentieth anniversary of the defeat of Hitler, in 1965, expressed pride in Soviet wartime intelligence and counterintelligence, singling out Richard Sorge and Rudolf Abel for special praise, but promising that at an appropriate time the names of other intelligence officers who had rendered great services to the foreign policy of communist Russia would be disclosed. Semichastny strove to create an impression of close army-KGB harmony by stressing the services which police formations, such as the border guards, had performed for the Red Army during particularly perilous days in World War II.

We should not flinch from the less attractive alternative futures for Russia, including the increasingly unlikely relapse into Stalin-style terror; we should do all that we can to increase the likelihood of humanly favorable solutions. It is possible that internal needs for more flexible and sophisticated responses to economic and social demands and increasing Kremlin realization that the USSR and the West face a common danger from the less responsible and more violent nationalist and revolutionary movements may eventually bring into being a Soviet-Western relationship not only sufficiently nonantagonistic to stave off nuclear catastrophe but able to begin, in due time, to lay the foundations for increasingly fruitful and positive intersystem cooperation. It seems certain that stable Soviet-Western relations would favor a gradually mellowing internal Russian political climate, though Western hopes for early relief from international burdens because of either favorable evolution (or revolution) in the USSR could be both illusory and dangerous if they distracted the noncommunist world from its responsibility for preserving democratic values. Clearly, there are no panaceas for exporting the civic culture. Full and accurate information, good will tempered by realism and, when necessary, by determined resistance to subversion and aggression, and a readiness to explore possible avenues for constructive negotiation and meaningful communication, clearly should be parts of a Western policy seeking to mould a future in which human dignity may flourish.

If we accept the favorable international prospects envisaged earlier, it is not fanciful to forecast a constructive political development for the USSR. This development may be slow and tortuous. It may even be interrupted by relapses or periods of regression. The diehards in the CPSU will not hesitate to use forceful measures to maintain the established order. They have in their favor not only police power but much in Russian and Soviet tradition, including the chauvinistic, anti-intellectual attitudes of many workers and peasants, who can easily be mobilized, in the name of patriotism, against innovators likely to be portrayed in the official press as disloyal to the socialist fatherland. It seems likely, however, that the Soviet peoples will some day fashion political institutions that will respond to and represent the varied interests of an increasingly differentiated and sophisticated society. Such a polity could claim a place of honor in a world community, which it would seek to improve rather than, as in the past, to dismantle. That Moscow already has partially accepted the international *status quo* may be a harbinger of further and greater future contributions to an international setting which, in turn, will facilitate the internal mellowing of Soviet political life long ago predicted by George F. Kennan.

Postscript

CONGRESSES OF THE Communist Party of the Soviet Union mirror Soviet politics in two ways: they sum up and justify the leaders' past actions and, by their (frequently Delphic) pronouncements, they chart the party's path to the future. In seeking to unearth clues to that future, we must bear in mind that this centralized, secretive system is capable of sudden change.

We conclude, then, by briefly analyzing the Twenty-third CPSU Congress, whose five thousand delegates began deliberating at 10:00 A.M. on March 29, 1966 and finished their work in the evening of April 8.

The proceedings were disturbing to those who hoped that the Soviet political system would respond more actively to the creative elements in Russian society who demand autonomy of action and freedom of expression. Only in the highly significant field of economic policy did reform keep its momentum, under the leadership of Premier Kosygin, probably the most popular and most widely respected member of the top party command. The congress registered defeats for liberals and innovators and victories for conservative, even reactionary forces; its style and decisions were counter-reformist. For the first time since Stalin's death, rules for admission to the party were tightened. This ominous change followed statements by some party leaders, comparing the party to a "fortress," which brought to mind the Stalin era. Before the congress, many had demanded that party members who recommend persons for recruitment into the party be held strictly accountable for the behavior of those recommended. Together with the more stringent rules, these demands might presage intensified "vigilance" in the party and, possibly, a purge.

On the whole, though, the congress seemed less than disastrous for those who have struggled in recent years for a welfare rather than a war economy, and for less restrictive control over art, science, and scholarship. Distinctly neo-Stalinist statements made during 1965 and early 1966 by some influential party leaders (including Leonid Brezhnev himself) had foretold more unpleasant results. Most alarming of these statements was that of Georgian leader D. G. Sturua, early in March, 1966, praising Stalin and his works. Neither Brezhnev nor other speakers ventured to openly praise Stalin, perhaps heeding the alarm felt by distinguished Soviet scientists, writers, and artists who feared that Stalin might be openly rehabilitated and also that there might be adverse reactions abroad. The increasingly prominent and ideologically orthodox Moscow party secretary, N. G. Egorychev, though he rejected the "blackening" of the party's "heroic past," also assured the delegates that there would be no return to the cult of personality or the violation of socialist legality. Moreover, the party leaders whom the experts feel to be most conservative, such as M. A. Suslov and A. N. Shelepin, either did not speak at all or did not express their views on ideological matters. Suslov, for instance, presented a bristling denunciation of United States policy in Vietnam. In spite of ambiguities and silences symbolizing sharp differences of opinion in leadership circles, the consensus shaped by Brezhnev, Kosygin, and other members of the ruling oligarchy was the most conservative any congress had come up with since Stalin's death.

In appraising the work of the congress we must bear in mind that a certain slowing down and cautious stocktaking was inevitable after the hectic years of Khrushchevian improvisation. Moreover, the problems facing a Kremlin again undergoing the trials of political succession were indeed difficult and were not susceptible to solution by crash programs. These factors seem peculiarly related to the exceptional reticence of this congress in the ideological sphere. It appeared that there had not yet crystallized a new line regarding such problems as the functions of the Soviet state in the present phase of transition to communism; more generally, the stage of historical development to which the congress was itself a contribution could not be adequately characterized. On these and other important theoretical problems the documents either were silent or resorted to timeworn clichés. The new leaders probably were preoccupied with economic problems and too uncertain about the shape of things to come in the international arena to commit themselves to explicit and firm ideological positions. They chose, rather, to play the part of sober, practical executives.

It would be ironic if it were to appear, later, that this congress marked a major stage in that "de-ideologization" of the Soviet Union which, before the congress began, had been denounced by authoritative propagandists as a "bourgeois" objective designed to enfeeble communism's will to victory. But the relative barrenness of ideology did not signify any lack of interest in the continued "Leninist" indoctrination of the citizenry. On such practical matters as the organization and techniques of agitation and propaganda a great deal was said.

The leadership clearly seemed determined to put an end to the attempts that some intellectuals in recent years had devoted to pushing to its logical conclusion the examination of the party's past that Khrushchev had encouraged, or at least permitted. Egorychev and other speakers charged that inept, "subjective" criticism had caused skepticism and "nihilism" among some susceptible youths. Dogmatically, Egorychev expressed hope that Soviet historians and others concerned with interpreting the past would correct their mistakes, above all because all the conditions necessary for fruitful, creative work now existed. Such statements, following so closely the trial of the writers Andrei Sinyavski and Yuli Daniel, must have deeply distressed many intellectuals. No one at the congress came to their defense, even indirectly, and novelist Mikhail Sholokov, who had been awarded a Nobel prize in 1965, viciously attacked them, though without naming them. Minister of Culture Ekaterina Furtseva and Moldavian party leader I. Bodyul indicated in their speeches that cultural imports from the West were likely henceforth to be screened more carefully than they had been in recent years. A number of speakers complained of the unhealthy state of mind of some Soviet young people, revealing anxiety over the relative ineffectiveness of the vast political socialization program described in this book. Several other party leaders did indicate, however, that political indoctrination once again was being overhauled and, presumably, was being rendered more effective. That morale was causing worry was shown in the resolution adopted by the congress, in which several points dealt with political education, the mass media, and the ideological functions of the arts.

In the selecting and recruitment of leaders, the congress and its advance preparations, which as usual dominated the communications media for months, furnished few surprises. Only one republic party organization head, Ya. N. Zarobyan of Armenia, lost his position, being replaced by A. E. Kochinyan. D. A. Kunaev, whom Khrushchev had removed as head of the party in Kazakhstan, already had been restored shortly after Khrushchev's fall from power. There was, though, a large turnover at the level just below the republic first secretaries in elections held in the months before the congress, and oblast party committees were substantially changed.

For the time being, Brezhnev clearly had consolidated his position as party leader. It seemed that the duumvirate of Brezhnev as top political leader and Kosygin as head of state and economic administration was reasonably well established. Assignments were made evident by the speeches of Brezhnev, Shelest (head of the Ukrainian party organization), Tolstikov (top Leningrad party secretary), Egorychev, and other party apparatchiki on the one hand, and those of Kosygin, N. V. Podgorny, and others primarily concerned with governmental and economic administration, on the other. The former group echoed, with interesting nuances, Brezhnev's proposal that the top party policy-making body be renamed "politburo," and that the office of general secretary be re-established. These proposals were of course adopted, and Brezhnev became the first general secretary since Stalin. Observers speculated as to whether his new office would increase Brezhnev's power or perhaps force him to tread warily, lest he arouse fears that he wanted to be a Stalin in more than his fear-inspiring title.

These changes, on the whole, probably were regressive. Both the politburo and the general secretaryship were established under Lenin; though the former was abolished by Stalin in 1952, both carry Stalinist rather than Leninist connotations. Incidentally, these evidences of devotion to Leninism characterized the gathering, and Khrushchev's ebullient, optimistic neo-Leninism or "populism" was replaced by a blend of elitism, realism, and pessimism — neo-Stalinism masqueraded as Leninism.

Governmental and economic leaders generally did not discuss high politics in their speeches. Podgorny, Kiselev (the Belorussian government chief), and others seconded Kosygin's economic reform proposals, which were adopted. It is difficult to determine to what extent this division of labor reflected divergent interests and policy positions among the nation's political leaders and the economic and administrative leaders. Perhaps it is prudent to assume that there is reasonably effective cooperation between the two groups, with the political leaders dominant in their special areas of jurisdiction (such as ultimate control over selecting personnel at all executive levels, interpreting the official ideology, etc.). In the year before the congress, however, Brezhnev and Kosygin had differed widely enough in outlook on such matters as allocation of resources as to arouse skepticism regarding the stability, even the durability of the duumvirate. Even in the months before the congress, the press had revealed differences between the party ideologists and the economic administrators and planners on how much economic policy should rely on "material," as opposed to "moral" incentives — the ideologists opposed and the production men favored priority for money as a spur to productivity. There are other problems in the party's relationship to the state and economic machines; e.g., just how standing in the party should reflect production skills and achievements. The congress confirmed the post-Khrushchev trend to return to primacy of the party apparatus, but to reserve a very important, semiautonomous role for the "businessman."

Khrushchev's attempt to create a "functional" party dedicated to production, in which party cadres would directly engage in management, was abandoned. The Brezhnev-Kosygin team seemed determined to avoid the confusion and irritation that Khrushchev's ventures in this direction had caused. A return to "normalcy" in this vital sphere may or may not permit the leadership to sufficiently adapt Soviet administration to the challenges posed by the continuing technological revolution. Judging from Kosygin's congress speech and the watering down at the September, 1965 plenum of proposals advocated by Liberman and other reformers, economic progress would be gradual and slow. Kosygin asserted at the congress that, by 1967, a third of Soviet factories would be converted to the administrative and incentive system adopted at the September, 1965 party plenum. This seems little enough progress, if we realize how cautious and limited were the concessions granted at the September plenum. It becomes clear upon carefully reading the Soviet press that even the limited concessions already accorded managerial autonomy and the profit motive already have aroused deep misgivings among some conservative party leaders and ideologists.

In the crucial agricultural sector of the economy, the congress seems to have left unchanged the cautious line initiated by Brezhnev at the April, 1965 plenum. Brezhnev did make two fairly bold, potentially constructive agricultural proposals. He recommended that collective farmers, now compensated for their labor on the land belonging to the collective farms only in shares of the farms' produce, be paid a modest, guaranteed money wage. If it could be carried out, this plan would go far toward providing the collective farm peasantry with economic security comparable to that enjoyed by wage earners in industrial establishments and state farms. Brezhnev's second proposal was that the desirability of creating a hierarchy of elected cooperative unions of collective farms be studied; such unions would enhance "democracy." Both proposals were included in the congress' resolutions; the one on collective farm unions was so worded as to reflect concession to conservative objections. Though Khrushchev had supported the same idea, he was unable to get it adopted, since many party workers seemed to fear that it would threaten tight control over the peasantry by encouraging cohesiveness among the peasants. The difficulty of realizing the guaranteed wage proposal is shown by the Ukraine's experience in 1965. Despite a good harvest, only a third of that republic's collective farms paid a guaranteed monthly wage.

Although these proposals might not reach fulfilment, they proved that the spirit of reform was not dead. If they were achieved, the welfare they might bring could create a more liberal and permissive climate within a society still confronted by problems so difficult that its policy makers may feel they cannot afford to grant the citizenry freedom that might distract it from the goals to which the Kremlin gives highest priority.

If the Twenty-third Congress revealed a certain poverty of imagination in the economic field, it was even more lacking in most other fields, including cultural policy and also state and law. Alone among the top leaders, N. V. Podgorny spoke out in favor of strict legality in public administration and demanded that party organizations cease to interfere in the work of government agencies. For a communist party in power for almost fifty years, it was ironic that the resolution included a section which began with the demand that the Soviet state be further strengthened!

Proceedings at the congress showed that the impulse toward fundamental legal reform, which had flourished in the late 1950's, for the time being was in abeyance. Not a word was said, apparently, about constitutional reform, on which subject Khrushchev had made glowing promises, as he had on many others. It was interesting that, since December, 1964, Brezhnev had been chairman of the commission set up by Khrushchev in 1962 to draft a new Soviet constitution (Khrushchev of course formerly had been chairman). There was also no indication at the congress that Khrushchev's policy of mobilizing the "public" to assist the state authorities in law enforcement would not continue to be toned down. Depending on what one thinks of Khrushchev's "populism," one may regard the new leadership's more conventional approach as beneficial or as regressive. The philosopher P. N. Fedoseev, authoritative interpreter of the official doctrine, shortly before the congress published an article in *Pravda* in which he argued that the "all-people's state" (one of Khrushchev's favorite ideological innovations) had grown directly out of the dictatorship of the proletariat, instead of being a distinctly new and different kind of state (the accepted doctrine under Khrushchev). Thus, he subtly suggested that the relationship between state and citizen was likely to become more conventional, authoritarian, and perhaps coercive when the congress was over.

Not only were Khrushchev's doctrine and policies replaced by more conservative and possibly more practical ones — they were the target of crude and plentiful innuendo. Not once was Khrushchev named (in the published reports, at least), but he served as scapegoat for failures and mistakes in many fields. As expected, he was not re-elected to the central committee. His companion, and the one who may have inspired him in de-Stalinization, Anastas Mikoyan, lost his top party leadership post but did not share with Khrushchev the ignominy of being excluded from the central committee.

In foreign relations, the congress came up with no surprises, except for the forbearance shown toward Communist China, which did not participate. The leaders, it appeared, were anxious not to add fuel to the fires of controversy in international communism or to furnish ammunition to their "bourgeois" adversaries. Toward the West, policies remained unchanged: blackening the image of the United States, at least so long it was bogged down in Vietnam, and driving wedges among the Western powers by seductive trade offers were typical aims. Many of the important speeches stressed the need for increasing economic and military strength.

According to Western liberal values, then, the congress was a somber, discouraging affair, though reactionary trends were contained and a generally "centrist" position was taken on most issues. It was typical of this moderate conservatism that although liberal intellectuals such as Tvardovski were not delegates (he also failed to gain re-election as an alternate member of the party's central committee), the extremely conservative writer Kochetov, who was a delegate, lost his position on the party's central auditing commission. Liberal Soviet intellectuals may have found a crumb of comfort in the re-election to the central committee of the relatively enlightened ideologist A. M. Rumyantsev, whose articles in *Pravda* in February and September, 1965 set forth rather reasonable ground rules for the control of intellectual life.

The congress left many fundamental issues unresolved: centralization versus decentralization in economic policy, the relative importance of material versus moral incentives, evasive secrecy versus either rehabilitation of or full disclosure regarding Stalin, and ideological dogma versus free expression in the arts. Its inconclusiveness and furtiveness obscured major problems, but it did seem certain that these problems, if not attacked with skill and vigor, would grow more difficult. The question remained whether the leadership would choose creative adaptiveness or suppressive orthodoxy in dealing with its problems and in governing its citizens. But future power alignments and policy configurations would be shaped by differences of opinion favoring permissiveness and innovation on the one hand, or coercion and distortion, on the other. And the policies of foreign powers, more than any those of the United States, would both depend on, and help to determine, the direction these forces took.

Chart 1 Integration of Communist Party (CPSU) and Soviet Government (April, 1954)

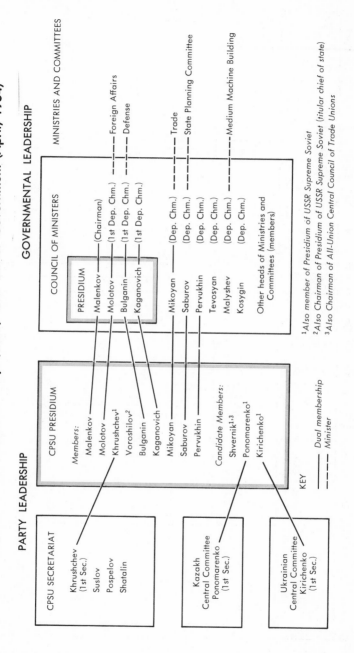

Chart 2 Interlocking Directorate — USSR Party and Government (May 1, 1962)

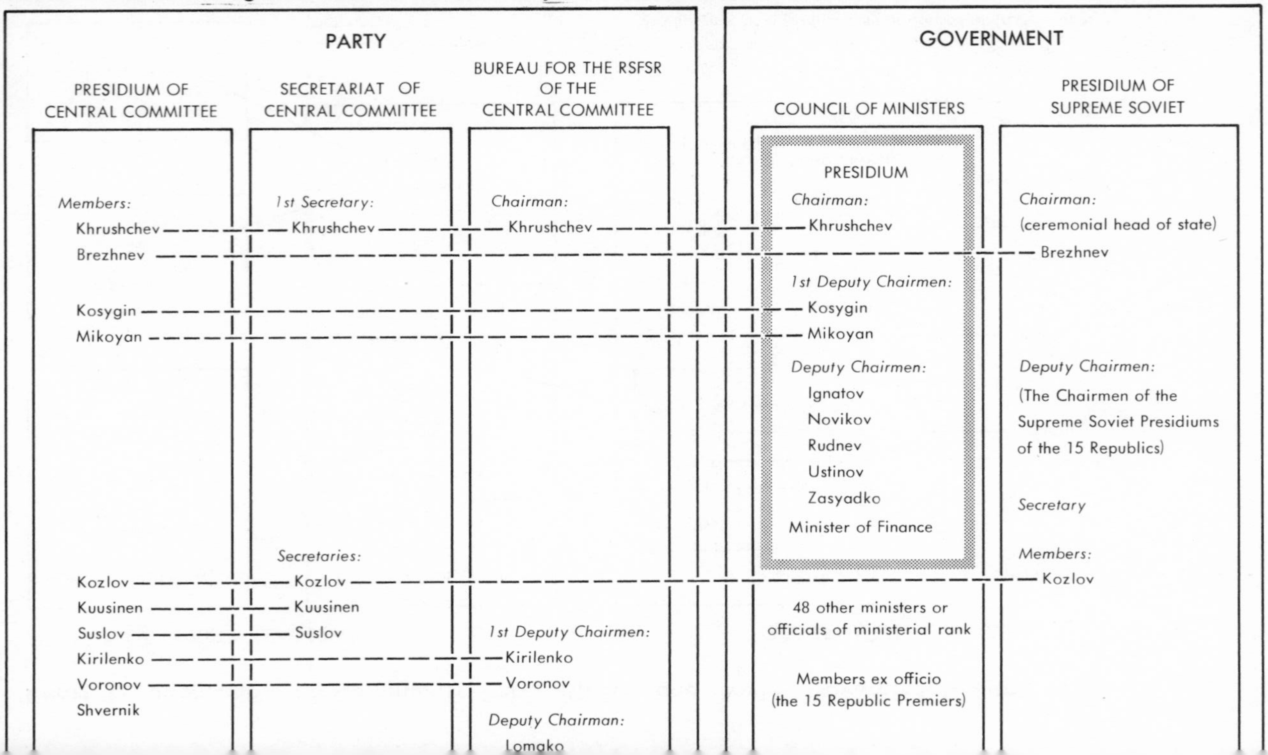

PARTY

PRESIDIUM OF CENTRAL COMMITTEE	SECRETARIAT OF CENTRAL COMMITTEE	BUREAU FOR THE RSFSR OF THE CENTRAL COMMITTEE
Members: Khrushchev	*1st Secretary:* Khrushchev	*Chairman:* Khrushchev
Brezhnev		
Kosygin		
Mikoyan		
	Secretaries: Kozlov	
Kozlov	Kuusinen	*1st Deputy Chairmen:* Kirilenko
Kuusinen	Suslov	Voronov
Suslov		
Kirilenko		*Deputy Chairman:* Lomako
Voronov		
Shvernik		

GOVERNMENT

COUNCIL OF MINISTERS	PRESIDIUM OF SUPREME SOVIET
PRESIDIUM	*Chairman:* (ceremonial head of state) Brezhnev
Chairman: Khrushchev	
1st Deputy Chairmen: Kosygin	
Mikoyan	*Deputy Chairmen:* (The Chairmen of the Supreme Soviet Presidiums of the 15 Republics)
Deputy Chairmen: Ignatov	
Novikov	
Rudnev	*Secretary*
Ustinov	
Zasyadko	*Members:* Kozlov
Minister of Finance	
48 other ministers or officials of ministerial rank	
Members ex officio (the 15 Republic Premiers)	

398

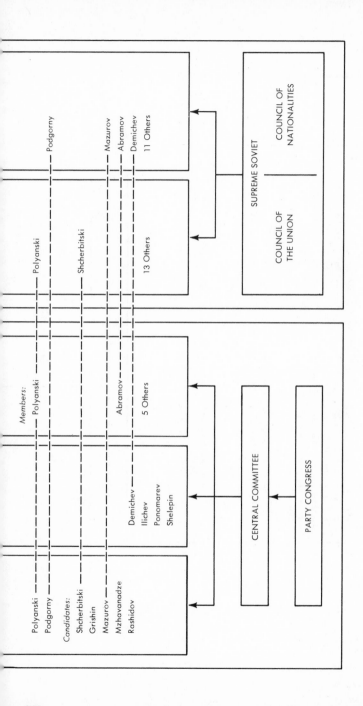

Chart 3 CPSU Central Committee Apparatus (April 9, 1966)

POLITBURO*

MEMBERS

L. I. Brezhnev (Gen. Sec., CC CPSU; Member, Presidium, USSR Supreme Soviet)

A. N. Kosygin (Chm., USSR Council of Ministers)

N. V. Podgorny (Chm., Presidium, USSR Supreme Soviet)

M. A. Suslov (Sec., CC CPSU)

G. I. Voronov (Chm., RSFSR Council of Ministers)

A. P. Kirilenko (Sec., CC CPSU)

A. N. Shelepin (Sec., CC CPSU)

K. T. Mazurov (1st Dep. Chm., USSR Council of Ministers)

D. S. Polyanski (1st Dep. Chm., USSR Council of Ministers)

P. E. Shelest (1st Sec., CC Ukrainian CP)

A. Ya. Pelshe[1] (Chm., CC CPSU Party Control Committee)

CANDIDATE MEMBERS

P. N. Demichev (Sec., CC CPSU; Member, Presidium USSR Supreme Soviet)

V. V. Grishin (Chm., A-U Central Council of Trade Unions)

V. P. Mzhavanadze (1st Sec., CC Georgian CP)

Sh. R. Rashidov (1st Sec., CC Uzbek CP)

D. F. Ustinov (Sec., CC CPSU)

V. V. Shcherbitski (Chm., UkSSR Council of Ministers)

P. M. Masherov[1] (1st Sec., CC Belorussian CP)

D. A. Kunayev[1] (1st Sec., CC Kazakh CP)

SECRETARIAT*

Gen. Sec., L. I. Brezhnev

M. A. Suslov	Yu. V. Andropov[2]
A. N. Shelepin	B. N. Ponomarev
A. P. Kirilenko[1]	I. V. Kapitonov[2]
P. N. Demichev	F. D. Kulakov[2]
D. F. Ustinov	A. P. Rudakov[2]

PARTY CONTROL COMMITTEE

Chm., A. Ya. Pelshe[1]

SECTIONS OF CENTRAL COMMITTEE

MAIN POLITICAL ADMINISTRATION
OF SOVIET ARMY AND NAVY
Chm. A. A. Epishev

CULTURE
Chm. V. F. Shauro[2]

PROPAGANDA AND AGITATION
Chm. V. I. Stepakov

SCIENCE AND EDUCATION
S. P. Trapeznikov

CADRES ABROAD
Chm. A. S. Panyushkin

ECON. REL. WITH
SOCIALIST COUNTRIES
Chm.?

INTERNATIONAL AFFAIRS
Chm. L. D. Shevlyagin?

RELATIONS WITH BLOC
PARTIES
Chm. Yu. V. Andropov[3]

AGRICULTURE FOR UNION
REPUBLICS
Chm. F. D. Kulakov

CHEMICAL INDUSTRY
Chm. V. M. Bushuyev

CONSTRUCTION
Chm. A. E. Biryukov

DEFENSE INDUSTRY
Chm. I. D. Serbin

HEAVY INDUSTRY
Chm. A. P. Rudakov

LIGHT AND FOOD
INDUSTRIES
Chm. P. K. Sizov

MACHINE BUILDING
Chm. V. S. Frolov

TRADE AND DOMESTIC
SERVICES
Chm. Ya. I. Kabkov[1]

TRANSPORT AND
COMMUNICATIONS
Chm. K. S. Simonov

ADMINISTRATIVE ORGANS
Chm.?

ADMINISTRATION OF
AFFAIRS
Chm. G. S. Pavlov

GENERAL
Chm. K. V. Chernenko[1]

ORGANIZATIONAL-PARTY WORK
Chm. I. V. Kapitonov

Unidentified Sections

[1]New incumbent
[2]Also heads of other agencies
[3]Tenure in doubt

* Listings as in Brezhnev's April 8 closing speech
to the Twenty-third Party Congress.

Chart 4 USSR Administrative-Territorial Structure Before and After Central Committee Plenum (November, 1962)

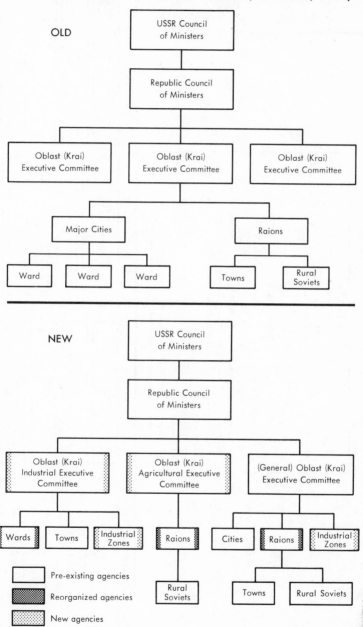

Chart 5 Organization of USSR Council of Ministers (January, 1963)

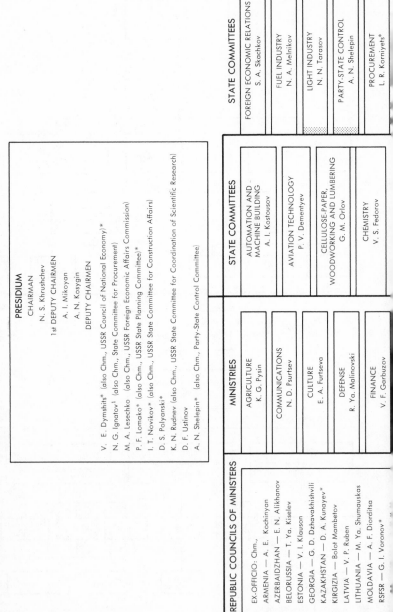

PRESIDIUM

CHAIRMAN
N. S. Khrushchev
1st DEPUTY CHAIRMEN
A. I. Mikoyan
A. N. Kosygin
DEPUTY CHAIRMEN

V. E. Dymshits* (also Chm., USSR Council of National Economy)*
N. G. Ignatov[1] (also Chm., State Committee for Procurement)
M. A. Lesechko (also Chm., USSR Foreign Economic Affairs Commission)
P. F. Lomako* (also Chm., USSR State Planning Committee)*
I. T. Novikov* (also Chm., USSR State Committee for Construction Affairs)
D. S. Polyanski*
K. N. Rudnev (also Chm., USSR State Committee for Coordination of Scientific Research)
D. F. Ustinov
A. N. Shelepin* (also Chm., Party-State Control Committee)

REPUBLIC COUNCILS OF MINISTERS	MINISTRIES	STATE COMMITTEES	STATE COMMITTEES
EX-OFFICIO: Chm.,	AGRICULTURE K. G. Pysin	AUTOMATION AND MACHINE BUILDING A. I. Kostousov	FOREIGN ECONOMIC RELATIONS S. A. Skachkov
ARMENIA — A. E. Kochinyan			
AZERBAIDZHAN — E. N. Alikhanov	COMMUNICATIONS N. D. Psurtsev	AVIATION TECHNOLOGY P. V. Dementyev	FUEL INDUSTRY N. A. Melnikov
BELORUSSIA — T. Ya. Kiselev			
ESTONIA — V. I. Klauson			
GEORGIA — G. D. Dzhavakhishvili	CULTURE E. A. Furtseva	CELLULOSE-PAPER, WOODWORKING AND LUMBERING G. M. Orlov	LIGHT INDUSTRY N. N. Tarasov
KAZAKHSTAN — D. A. Kunayev*			
KIRGIZIA — Bolot Mambetov	DEFENSE R. Ya. Malinovski		PARTY-STATE CONTROL A. N. Shelepin
LATVIA — V. P. Ruben			
LITHUANIA — M. Ya. Shumauskas		CHEMISTRY V. S. Fedorov	
MOLDAVIA — A. F. Diorditsa	FINANCE V. F. Garbuzov		PROCUREMENT L. R. Korniyets*
RSFSR — G. I. Voronov*			

UKRAINE — V. V. Shcherbitskii
UZBEKISTAN — R. Kubanov

SPECIALIZED AGENCIES

USSR COUNCIL OF NAT'L ECON.
Chm., V. E. Dymshits*
1st Dep. Chm., A. A. Etmekdzhiyan
1st Dep. Chm., V. M. Ryabikov
Dep. Chm., N. I. Strokin
Dep. Chm., V. P. Zotov

STATE PLANNING COMMITTEE
Chm., P. F. Lomako*
1st Dep. Chm., A. A. Goreglyad
Dep. Chm., N. A. Tikhonov

FOREIGN ECONOMIC AFFAIRS COMMISSION
Chm., M. A. Lesechko

STATE BANK
Chm., A. K. Koroyushkin

CONSTRUCTION BANK
Chm., G. A. Karavayev

MAIN ADMINISTRATION OF GAS INDUSTRY
Chm., A. K. Kortunov

ALL-UNION ASSOCIATION FOR AGRICULTURAL EQUIPMENT
Chm., A. A. Ezhevski*

CENTRAL STATISTICAL ADMINISTRATION
Chm., V. N. Starovski

FOREIGN AFFAIRS
A. A. Gromyko

FOREIGN TRADE
N. S. Patolichev

GEOLOGY AND PROTECTION OF NATURAL RESOURCES
A. V. Sidorenko

HEALTH
S. V. Kurashov

HIGHER AND SPECIALIZED EDUCATION
V. P. Elyutin

MARITIME FLEET
V. G. Bakayev

MEDIUM MACHINE BUILDING
E. P. Slavski

POWER INDUSTRY AND ELECTRIFICATION
P. T. Neporozhny

RAILWAY TRANSPORT
V. P. Beshchev

TRANSPORT CONSTRUCTION
E. V. Kozhevnikov

V. N. Novikov*
(without portfolio)*

COORDINATION OF SCIENTIFIC RESEARCH
K. N. Rudnev

CULTURAL RELATIONS WITH FOREIGN COUNTRIES
S. K. Romanovski

CONSTRUCTION AFFAIRS
I. T. Novikov*

DEFENSE TECHNOLOGY
L. V. Smirnov

ELECTRICAL INDUSTRY
N. Obolenski

ELECTRONIC TECHNOLOGY
A. I. Shokin

FERROUS AND NON-FERROUS METALLURGY
V. E. Boyko

FISHING INDUSTRY
A. A. Ishkov

FOOD INDUSTRY
P. V. Naumenko

PROFESSIONAL-TECHNICAL EDUCATION
G. I. Zelenko

QUESTIONS OF LABOR AND WAGES
A. P. Volkov

RADIO BROADCASTING AND TELEVISION
M. A. Kharlamov

RADIO ELECTRONICS
V. D. Kalmykov

SHIPBUILDING
B. E. Butoma

STATE CONTROL
G. B. Enyutin

STATE SECURITY
V. E. Semichastny

TRADE
A. I. Struyev

UTILIZATION OF ATOMIC ENERGY
A. M. Petrosyants

Legend:

Abolished agency

All-Union ministries

*New incumbent ¹Replaced

Pre-existing agencies

Reorganized agencies

New agencies

Chart 6   Organization of the Moscow City Council

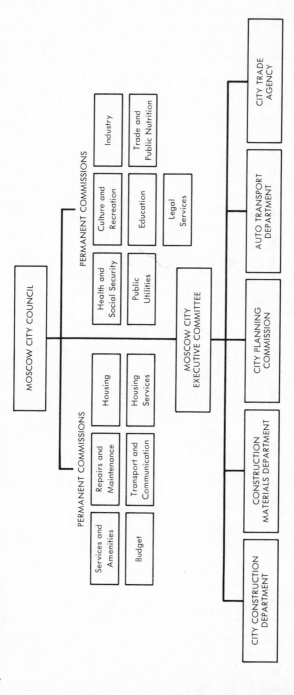

Chart 7 Reorganization of USSR Council of Ministers (December 12, 1965)

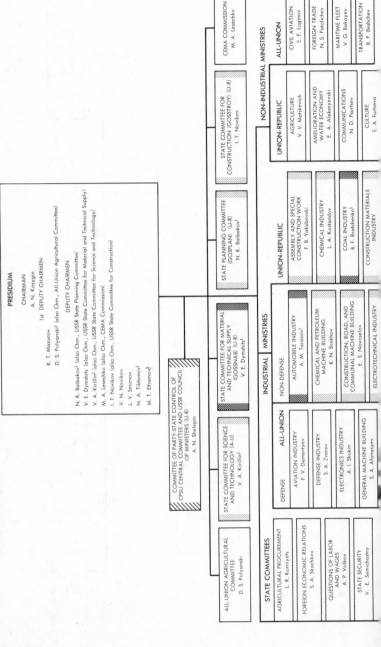

PRESIDIUM

CHAIRMAN
A. N. Kosygin
1st DEPUTY CHAIRMEN

K. T. Mazurov
D. S. Polyanski[1] (also Chm., All-Union Agricultural Committee)

DEPUTY CHAIRMEN

N. K. Baibakov[1] (also Chm., USSR State Planning Committee)
V. E. Dymshits (also Chm., USSR State Committee for Material and Technical Supply)
V. A. Kirillin[1] (also Chm., USSR State Committee for Science and Technology)
M. A. Lesechko (also Chm., CEMA Commission)
I. T. Novikov (also Chm., USSR State Committee for Construction)
V. N. Novikov
L. V. Smirnov
N. A. Tikhonov[1]
M. T. Efremov[2]

COMMITTEE OF PARTY-STATE CONTROL OF CPSU CENTRAL COMMITTEE AND USSR COUNCIL OF MINISTERS
A. N. Shelepin

STATE COMMITTEE FOR SCIENCE AND TECHNOLOGY (A-U)
V. A. Kirillin[1]

STATE COMMITTEE FOR MATERIAL AND TECHNICAL SUPPLY (GOSSNAB) (U-R)
V. E. Dymshits[1]

STATE PLANNING COMMITTEE (GOSPLAN) (U-R)
N. K. Baibakov[1]

STATE COMMITTEE FOR CONSTRUCTION (GOSSTROY) (U-R)
I. T. Novikov

CEMA COMMISSION
M. A. Lesechko

STATE COMMITTEES

ALL-UNION AGRICULTURAL COMMITTEE
D. S. Polyanski

AGRICULTURAL PROCUREMENT
L. R. Korniyets

FOREIGN ECONOMIC RELATIONS
S. A. Skachkov

QUESTIONS OF LABOR AND WAGES
A. P. Volkov

STATE SECURITY
V. E. Semichastny

INDUSTRIAL MINISTRIES

DEFENSE — ALL-UNION

AVIATION INDUSTRY
P. V. Dementyev

DEFENSE INDUSTRY
S. A. Zverev

ELECTRONICS INDUSTRY
A. I. Shokin

GENERAL MACHINE BUILDING
S. A. Afanasyev

NON-DEFENSE

AUTOMOBILE INDUSTRY
A. M. Tarasov[1]

CHEMICAL AND PETROLEUM MACHINE BUILDING
K. N. Brekhov

CONSTRUCTION, ROAD, AND COMMUNAL MACHINE BUILDING
E. S. Novoselov

ELECTROTECHNICAL INDUSTRY

UNION-REPUBLIC

ASSEMBLY AND SPECIAL CONSTRUCTION WORK
F. B. Yakubovski

CHEMICAL INDUSTRY
L. A. Kostandov

COAL INDUSTRY
B. F. Bratchenko[1]

CONSTRUCTION MATERIALS INDUSTRY

NON-INDUSTRIAL MINISTRIES

UNION-REPUBLIC

AGRICULTURE
V. V. Matskevich

AMELIORATION AND WATER ECONOMY
E. A. Alekseyevski

COMMUNICATIONS
N. D. Psurtsev

CULTURE
E. A. Furtseva

ALL-UNION

CIVIL AVIATION
E. F. Loginov

FOREIGN TRADE
N. S. Patolichev

MARITIME FLEET
V. G. Bakayev

TRANSPORTATION
B. P. Beshchev

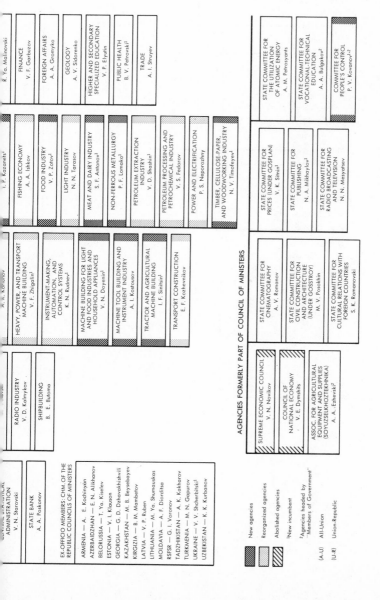

CENTRAL STATISTICAL ADMINISTRATION V. N. Starovski

STATE BANK A. A. Poskonov

EX-OFFICIO MEMBERS: CHM. OF THE REPUBLIC COUNCILS OF MINISTERS

ARMENIA — A. E. Kochinyan
AZERBAIDZHAN — E. N. Alikhanov
BELORUSSIA — T. Ya. Kiselev
ESTONIA — V. I. Klauson
GEORGIA — G. D. Dzhavakhishvili
KAZAKHSTAN — M. B. Beysebayev
KIRGIZIA — B. M. Mambetov
LATVIA — V. P. Ruben
LITHUANIA — M. Yu. Shumauskas
MOLDAVIA — A. F. Diorditsa
RSFSR — G. I. Voronov
TADZHIKISTAN — A. K. Kakharov
TURKMENIA — M. N. Gapurov
UKRAINE — V. V. Shcherbitski[1]
UZBEKISTAN — K. K. Kurbanov

RADIO INDUSTRY V. D. Kalmykov
SHIPBUILDING B. E. Butoma

A. K. Kortunov
HEAVY, POWER, AND TRANSPORT MACHINE BUILDING V. F. Zhigalin[1]
INSTRUMENT-MAKING, AUTOMATION, AND CONTROL SYSTEMS K. N. Rudnev[1]
MACHINE BUILDING FOR LIGHT AND FOOD INDUSTRIES AND HOUSEHOLD APPLIANCES V. N. Doynin[1]
MACHINE TOOL BUILDING AND INSTRUMENT INDUSTRY A. I. Kostousov
TRACTOR AND AGRICULTURAL MACHINE BUILDING I. F. Sinitsin[1]
TRANSPORT CONSTRUCTION E. F. Kozhevnikov

I. P. Kazanets[1]
FISHING ECONOMY A. A. Ishkov
FOOD INDUSTRY V. P. Zotov[1]
LIGHT INDUSTRY N. N. Tarasov
MEAT AND DAIRY INDUSTRY S. F. Antonov[1]
NON-FERROUS METALLURGY P. F. Lomako[1]
PETROLEUM EXTRACTION INDUSTRY V. D. Shashin[1]
PETROLEUM PROCESSING AND PETROCHEMICAL INDUSTRY V. S. Fedorov
POWER AND ELECTRIFICATION P. S. Neporozhny
TIMBER, CELLULOSE-PAPER, AND WOODWORKING INDUSTRY N. V. Timofeyev[1]

R. Ya. Malinovski
FINANCE V. F. Garbuzov
FOREIGN AFFAIRS A. A. Gromyko
GEOLOGY A. V. Sidorenko
HIGHER AND SECONDARY SPECIALIZED EDUCATION V. P. Elyutin
PUBLIC HEALTH B. V. Petrovski[1]
TRADE A. I. Struyev

AGENCIES FORMERLY PART OF COUNCIL OF MINISTERS

SUPREME ECONOMIC COUNCIL V. N. Novikov
COUNCIL OF NATIONAL ECONOMY V. E. Dymshits
ASSOC. FOR AGRICULTURAL EQUIPMENT AND SUPPLIES (SOYUZSELKHOZTEKHNIKA) A. A. Ezhevski[2]

STATE COMMITTEE FOR CINEMATOGRAPHY A. V. Romanov
STATE COMMITTEE FOR CIVIL CONSTRUCTION AND ARCHITECTURE (UNDER GOSSTROY) M. V. Posokhin
STATE COMMITTEE FOR CULTURAL RELATIONS WITH FOREIGN COUNTRIES S. K. Romanovski

STATE COMMITTEE FOR PRICES (UNDER GOSPLAN) V. K. Sitnin[1]
STATE COMMITTEE FOR PUBLISHING N. A. Mikhaylov[1]
STATE COMMITTEE FOR RADIO BROADCASTING AND TELEVISION N. N. Mesyatev

STATE COMMITTEE FOR THE UTILIZATION OF ATOMIC ENERGY A. M. Petrosyants
STATE COMMITTEE FOR VOCATIONAL-TECHNICAL EDUCATION A. A. Bulgakov[2]
COMMITTEE FOR PEOPLE'S CONTROL P. V. Kovanov[1,2]

New agencies
Reorganized agencies
Abolished agencies
[1]New incumbent
[2]Agencies headed by "Members of Government"
(A-U) All-Union
(U-R) Union-Republic

Chart 8 The CPSU Immediately After the Twenty-third Party Congress (April, 1966)

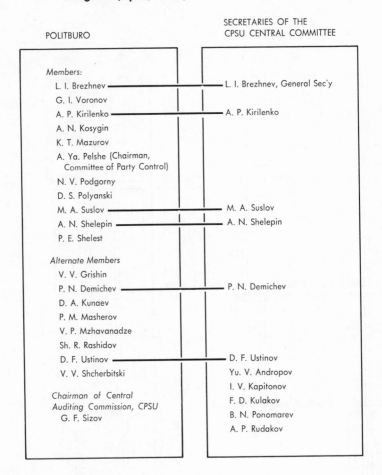

POLITBURO

SECRETARIES OF THE
CPSU CENTRAL COMMITTEE

Members:
  L. I. Brezhnev ———————————— L. I. Brezhnev, General Sec'y
  G. I. Voronov
  A. P. Kirilenko ———————————— A. P. Kirilenko
  A. N. Kosygin
  K. T. Mazurov
  A. Ya. Pelshe (Chairman,
    Committee of Party Control)
  N. V. Podgorny
  D. S. Polyanski
  M. A. Suslov ———————————— M. A. Suslov
  A. N. Shelepin ———————————— A. N. Shelepin
  P. E. Shelest

Alternate Members
  V. V. Grishin
  P. N. Demichev ———————————— P. N. Demichev
  D. A. Kunaev
  P. M. Masherov
  V. P. Mzhavanadze
  Sh. R. Rashidov
  D. F. Ustinov ———————————— D. F. Ustinov
  V. V. Shcherbitski   Yu. V. Andropov
                                            I. V. Kapitonov
Chairman of Central   F. D. Kulakov
Auditing Commission, CPSU   B. N. Ponomarev
  G. F. Sizov   A. P. Rudakov

Index